This Hollow Land

Aspects of

Norfolk Folklore

Peter Tolhurst

BLACK DOG
BOOKS

for
George Ewart Evans
In Memoriam

ACKNOWLEDGEMENTS

I would like to thank the following for their help and advice:

Clare Agate and staff (Norfolk Heritage Centre), Lindsey Bavin (True's Yard Fisherfolk Museum), Mike Burgess (Hidden East Anglia), Brian Chandler, Hugh Cobble (Ralph Vaughan Williams Charitable Trust), Sylvia Cooke (Castle Rising History Group), Megan Dennis (Gressenhall Farm and Workhouse), Clare Everitt (Picture Norfolk), Sue Gattuso (Swaffham Museum), Anna Goddard (Carnegie Publishing), Stephen Heywood and Alison Yardy (Norfolk Historic Environment Service), Brian Hoggard (folk magic researcher), Chris Holderness (Norfolk Music History Project), Katie Howson (East Anglian Traditional Music Trust), Peter Irwin (Red Cat Hotel), Joseph Mason (historical geographer), Barbara and Des Miller (Norfolk Music History Project), Gerard Stamp (artist), Edy Walker, Sue Walker White (Illustrator), Charlotte Woodley (Museum of Cambridge), Alex Wright (Bellarmine Museum). Special thanks to Caroline Davison for comments on the initial draft.

All opinions and any inaccuracies are mine entirely
Peter Tolhurst

CONTENTS

PICTURE CREDITS

Illustrations on each page are numbered clockwise from the left

Sue Walker White frontispiece/rear cover, 15d, 48a, 61a, 81a, 83, 103b, 163a, 234, 235a, 253a & b; *Norfolk Archaeology* 1, 13, 48b, 51, 102, 109a & c, 118a, 151a, 152a, 216a & b; Museum of Cambridge 6, 159; Julian Earwaker 8; Brian Chandler 9b; British Museum 11a & b,12a, 13a, 14b, 15a-c, 28b, 72a & b, 73b, 80a & b, 112a; John Davies 12b; Norfolk County Council 18, 47, 50, 52, 57b, 75, 95a, 128, 132, 175b, 211a; Richard Tilbrook estate/Picture Norfolk 21a, 152c; Picture Norfolk 25, 27a, 61b, 63, 65, 68c, 99, 148, 150, 153, 154a, 168, 173, 174a, 176, 178a, 181, 190, 199, 209, 232, 239, 243, 257b; Norfolk Museums Service 32b, 35, 64, 73a, 74b, 111, 112b, 130b, 160, 163b, 240, 241a, 242; Alex Wright 36a, 145a, 157, 158a & b; *Norfolk Archaeology* /Sue Walker White 14a & c, 15d, 16a-c-d, 29a, 37, 107, 108, 110, 116b, 151b; Stephen Heywood 53a; Folger Shakespeare Library, Washington DC 53b; Norfolk Wildlife Trust 70, 147a; Swaffham Museum 85b, 86b; Archant/EDP 91, 258a; Gerard Stamp 92; Christopher Dalton estate 105; David Gentleman 147b, 268a; Museum of London 152b; Peter Irwin 161; Clifford Harper 187; Bert Tolhurst 195a; National Trust 195b, 208; Ely Standard 222a; Castle Rising History Group 226a; Peter Sager 226b; Dragon Hall 228a; Julia Hedgecoe 235b, 237; Edwin Smith estate 241b; Vaughan Williams Charitable Trust 247b; True's Yard Fisherfolk Museum 249, 250; Mike Yates 256a; Margaret Hudson/Rig-a-jig-jig 259; Rig-a-jig-jig 261, 262

First published in England 2018
Black Dog Books,
104 Trinity Street, Norwich, Norfolk, NR2 2BJ,
www.blackdogbooks.co.uk

A CIP record of this book is available from the British Library.
ISBN 978-0-9954792-5-8

Managed by Biddles, King's Lynn
Printed by Short Run Press, Exeter,

WANDERINGS IN THE HALF LIGHT

While working on this book some of the material that came to light reminded me of incidents in my own life that, in a previous age, might have become the stuff of legend and fireside tale. Brought up in rural Kent in the 1950s the old folk ways appear now to have lost much of their potency. Half the village street had already been taken out by German bombers on their way home from a raid on Canterbury, the seasonal rhythm of village life suffered from years of post-war austerity and people on the new council estate spoke with the soft lilt of the Welsh valleys and the flat vowels of South Yorkshire. They had arrived to work in the local pit during the Depression, one of four collieries to have arisen incongruously among the cherry orchards in this corner of the Garden of England. Village life for me, at least until my voice broke, revolved around the parish church and the C of E primary school. Friday evening choir practice was a highlight of the week when we little cherubs would play tag among the tombstones, a faint echo perhaps of the circling ritual used to raise the Devil (p87). While I have no recollection of Beating the Bounds, each year on Rogation Sunday we would file out of church behind the vicar, passed the great tithe barn – venue for the village fête when wet – passed the oast houses and over the railway line to bless the crops. At Harvest Festival the church was decked out with God's bounty – enormous marrows, cottage flowers and jars of hedgerow jelly – all sold off to raise money for a missionary outpost somewhere in Africa. At school classrooms rang to the sound of recorder practice, tables learnt by rote and squeals of horror when the fish tank full of mysterious pond life came crashing to the floor during a session of country dancing. The opportunities for organised chaos provided by the curriculum were interrupted on solemn occasions by the vicar, come to announce the death of the king or some other event of national importance that we failed to appreciate. The coronation did however provide an excuse to parade through the village in vaguely historical costumes that for me included an oversize *papier-mâché* helmet lovingly fashioned by my mother, the whole convoy enveloped in diesel fumes from the tractor pulling our own carnival queen.

All this changed when I failed the 11 plus – fear of the local secondary modern with rumours of initiation rights and bullying was a significant, but ultimately ineffectual, spur to academic achievement. It transpired, however, I was a borderline case and the prospect of an interview at the grammar school in Canterbury offered me a lifeline. I came from what sociologists called a 'respectable' working class family, one with modest ambitions – we were buying our own house, we listened to the Home Service and a career in banking beckoned. When the time came I should have been prepared for the inevitable question 'And what is your favourate radio programme Peter?' Instead of some carefully rehearsed lie – the 'Brain's Trust' or 'Any Questions' – designed to impress the headmaster, I blurted out the 'Goon Show'. Shortly after I received a letter offering me a place at the Simon

Langton school – in the B stream – and I remain convinced that it was the Goons wat won it, a life-changing experience predicated on a single moment of madness. Once there I became mildly rebellious, adopted silly voices – the Goons again – and invented stories on the school bus. One, about the Sturry Treacle Mines, was dredged up from the thick orange sludge of gravel pits that scarred the Stour valley. Years later, to my amazement, someone I met admitted to having heard the story – was it really still current and had I really been responsible for its inception? It was only when consulting the *Dictionary of English Folklore* that I discovered treacle mines to be some kind of rural myth, emblems of local wit and local identity, that had sprung up quite independently in villages across the country, including Norfolk (Corpusty and Fring) and Kent, but not, until now, in Sturry.

During my time as conservation officer with Breckland Council in the 1980s and '90s the work took me all over the district and occasionally into situations which, a century earlier, would have elicited a very different response. This was illustrated quite dramatically on a visit to a woman in Great Cressingham – I forget exactly what for – but it was summer and I recall a dreary Victorian house set well back from the village street. As we sat talking she suddenly began to choke, having swallowed a wasp in her drink and, allergic to the sting, her throat had begun to swell up alarmingly. A mercy dash to her GP surgery in Swaffham and an antihistamine jab averted what could have been a life-threatening incident. A century earlier, in the absence of the kind of medical advances we take for granted today, country people often resorted to extreme measures. I was reminded of this when reading a report of one traditional remedy used in the 1850s when a mother from a nearby village took her daughter, suffering from a swollen neck, to have it rubbed with the hand of a recently deceased man in Great Cressingham (p218). As a result the swelling soon died away, a reaction attributed to the shock brought on by the experience.

When reading the chapter on ghost stories in W G Clarke's *In Breckland Wilds* I was startled to discover that, years earlier, I had unwittingly meddled in the local legend attached to one of several monastic ruins in Thetford. The Place, an early 17th century house among the remains of St George's Nunnery, was said to be haunted by the ghost of young Lord Dacre (pp 173-4). It was originally approached through a brick archway that, at some later date, had been partially blocked by a chalk rubble wall. By the 1980s the listed structure, now stranded on a roadside verge, was in need of attention and I persuaded the council to fund a scheme of repairs which included removing the rubble wall that had become a jumping off point for local youths. According to Clarke the wall had been built up and knocked down seven times by a coach and four driven by Sir Richard Fulmerston who had acquired the Nunnery at the Dissolution and was implicated in the death of Lord Dacre. The phantom coach has not been seen or heard for many years but, while the entrance arch remains unimpeded, the housing estate between the archway and the Nunnery is likely to present a more substantial obstacle should the restless spirit ever return.

On another occasion I was called out to see a woman worried about a boundary tree close to her house, one that she was convinced was threatened by the neighbouring farmer. She lived in a remote clay lump cottage on the edge of the Brecks, approached up a long bumpy track. The place seemed deserted but as I negotiated a heap of empty cat food tins the door was opened by a small, dishevelled woman of uncertain age who ushered me into a room, its surfaces piled high with old newspapers. As I listened to the woman's increasingly desperate plea for help the frail cries of an elderly relative in the next room only added to my sense of unease. When, to my great relief, I eventually drove away I recalled that, not so long ago, reclusive and eccentric women like this were still accused of witchcraft and would have been 'swum' in one of the Breckland meres (p141). The experience, unsettling at the time, took on renewed life when, years later, I tried to locate the place again. Although my memory of the exact circumstances may have begun to fade, it was as though the cottage had vanished off the face of the earth.

A range of measures were used to counter the effects of witchcraft (p157); shoes, dead cats and metal objects hidden at points in the house, often the threshold and hearth, vulnerable to evil spirits. The most common deterrent, the Bellarmine jar, was also employed as a form of retaliation. A sample of urine, hair and nail parings from the bewitched victim, together with a quantity of nails and pins, were secured in the bottle and then placed beside the fire. As the contents, especially the metal objects, heated up the jar would often explode causing intense pain to the witch and forcing her to break the spell. I was reminded forcefully of this practice when admitted to hospital last year with bladder cancer. My mother had died from it and, although she was 88 at the time, I was naturally apprehensive. At one point the urinary tract became blocked and I was in excruciating pain, but it was not until, back home and researching this book, that I began to fully appreciate the folkloric implications of my complaint. To be most effective the round-bellied jars were often inverted to represent the witch's bladder before being buried in the hearth and, as a result, according to Blagrave's *The Astrological Practice of Physick* (1671), witches 'will be grievously tormented, making their water with great difficulty, if at all'.

I have always derived much pleasure from the simple process of walking and it is often, while following the old paths, that I have experienced some of life's epiphanic moments. Some years ago while on the South West Coast Path I had set out from Lyme Regis on the last leg of my journey. The weather was fine and I was in good spirits as I ascended Golden Cap before dropping down to the pub at Seatown, quite unprepared for the tragic events that were to unfold along this most dramatic stretch of coast. It was another haul up to Thorncombe Beacon and then on to West Bay but the prospect of spending a night in this depressing arrangement of chrome and concrete, one made famous by the TV drama *Broadchurch*, persuaded me to push on to the pretty village of Burton Bradstock. Having found somewhere to stay I set out in the early evening to explore the place and found the church still open beside a stream that was the river Bride. A few moments after stepping inside I heard the door close and became aware that I was not alone.

At this juncture my story might easily have become a tale of the supernatural but the noise was, instead, the reassuring presence of the vicar who had come to lock up. He readily pointed out the salient features of St Mary's before I discovered he too was a walker or, more precisely, a committed pilgrim, and had undertaken several long journeys on foot to Canterbury and Lindisfarne. He talked enthusiastically about his plans to row along the coast to his childhood home, the Cornish fishing village of Portscatho, visiting remote coves along the way where the Celtic saints had first made landfall. We talked for just a short while in the fading light but as we shook hands and said farewell I felt glad to have met not just a fellow traveller but a generous spirit. Outside we went our separate ways – the Three Horseshoes for me and a PCC meeting for the vicar.

It was some months later, early April 2014, when, back home in Norwich, I was sitting in the cathedral refectory idly thumbing through the *Telegraph* (the choice of reading material rather limited) when I was jerked out of my reverie by the headline 'Vicar drowned on return from Celtic pilgrimage' and I knew immediately who it was and now I knew his name – the Rev'd Bob Thorn. Having spent Lent in a wooden hut on Pendower Beach living off the sea and the land this remarkable Dorset man was on his way back when his boat, empty but for a copy of the bible, was washed ashore at Seatown. The following day his body was found at East Ebb Cove, he was so nearly home. When questioned about the wisdom of such a venture at that time of year he had replied that 'the Celtic Christian saints were ascetic to a reckless degree' and 'Do you think I am mad? Answers please on the back of a piece of seaweed.'

That same year I was walking along the Northumbrian coast with a friend and, in the great tradition of pilgrimage, we set out barefoot across the three mile stretch of sand that separates the mainland from the Holy Island of Lindisfarne at low tide. As we splashed through the receding waters we heard, borne on a southerly breeze, a strange noise that seemed to come from a large colony of seals on a distant mudbank. I thought then how this same eerily beautiful sound would have greeted St Cuthbert centuries before and, more recently, the holy minstrel of Burton Bradstock who, even now, sings with creatures of the deep.

This string of events, memorable as they are, put me in mind of other, seemingly random experiences while walking. One occurred some years ago with a group of friends along a stretch of the Nar valley in west Norfolk. We had chosen Castle Acre as our base and, having eaten well at the Ostrich, with the evening air still warm and smelling fresh after rain, we set off to explore the priory ruins. Like naughty children in an Enid Blyton adventure we clambered over the locked gates and roamed about among jagged pillars of flint that cast long shadows on the grass. No-one seriously believed in ghosts but, as bats flitted above our heads and an owl hooted nearby, it was surely only a matter of time before a hooded figure disappeared through the cloisters. Or perhaps, despite the absence of ivy-clad masonry – English Heritage has seen to that – the place and the occasion now appear rather more Gothic than they did at the time.

What we did see proved to be no less remarkable – an open fire in the upper floor of a house across the river that I hadn't noted before. Continuing to stare through the gathering gloom it became apparent from the sparks rising into the air that the place was on fire. One of our company, given to sudden operatic outbursts, began hallooing, another was about to run for help – there were no mobile phones then – when the truth suddenly dawned. This was no domestic conflagration but a burning tree, one struck by lightning in the day's storm. The following morning we went to investigate and, crossing the river by the ford, we found the smoldering embers of an ancient boundary tree – ash to ashes – its charred stump still visible to this day.

Witnessed in a secular age from within the ruins of a once great religious foundation the perfectly rational explanation for this unlikely occurrence has echoes of the Burning Bush. In the Book of Exodus the Angel of the Lord appears to Moses in the desert from a blazing bush, one that may also have been fired by lightning, but never consumed by the flames. For a medieval monk on pilgrimage along the holy valley of the Nar such an event is more likely to have been received not as some freak act of nature but as a vision in the form of the Holy Spirit, a sign of God's displeasure or a warning of imminent disaster – the Dissolution of the monasteries.

Some years later we were retracing our steps beside the Nar when, faint at first but getting louder all the while, came the sound of singing – 'He who would valiant be' – from a procession of modern day pilgrims. It was Easter and they were following the old track down from Batholomew Hills, site of an important medieval fair, on their way to Walsingham. Passing close by the ash tree's blackened trunk they had taken the opportunity to bathe aching feet in the river, the large wooden cross propped up against the precinct wall a reminder of their calling, before an uphill trek into Castle Acre and a welcome rest.

My most recent excursion in the realms of folkloric fantasy and healthy exercise took on a decidedly literary flavour. On this occasion the walk was along the coast in Yorkshire and, having left Staithes that morning, we strode into Whitby and found our accommodation. No 7 East Crescent is an attractive but unremarkable early 19th century terrace with views across to the gaunt shell of Whitby Abbey perched on the top of East Cliff like some huge bird of prey. The town, once home to a sizeable whaling fleet, is today best known for the excellence of its fish 'n chips and a thriving tourist industry based on its association with *Dracula*. This explained the shiny black hearse parked in a layby that greeted us on arrival with a skeleton draped over the coffin and an invitation to partake of the Dracula Experience. In the evening after the obligatory fish supper we wandered the cobbled back streets of the old town mingling with the Undead in search of nothing more blood curdling than ghoulish car stickers and a choice of postcards of the Dying To See You variety – Welcome to Goth City. At breakfast the following morning we discovered we had, quite literally, walked into one of the nation's great horror stories. Digesting the implications of this revelation the devilled kidneys and black pudding on offer suddenly seemed far less appetising.

In Bram Stoker's Gothic tale a Russian ship, the *Demeter*, runs aground in Whitby harbour during a sudden storm, with no sign of its crew but for the captain's corpse lashed to the helm. Below deck are the fifty boxes of freshly dug soil sent by Dracula from Transylvania, enabling the Count to replenish his strength during the day and satisfy his lust for fresh blood after dark. The cargo is to be delivered to Samuel Billington, a local solicitor, at 7 The Crescent, Whitby, in transit to London and the Count's recently acquired estate. The precise address in Whitby may have changed slightly over the years but the stucco fronted terrace with its wrought iron balcony and steps up to the front door remains recognisably the same. The unsettling conjunction of fact and fiction does not end here. As the *Demeter* is grounded a huge black dog leaps ashore and runs up the steep flight of steps to St Mary's churchyard on the edge of the cliff. The beast is not seen again but is said to roam the moors behind the town.

Readers may have noticed that *This Hollow Land* is published by Black Dog Books and its derivation is not entirely coincidental. I was living in Bungay when deciding to self-publish my first book, *East Anglia: A Literary Pilgrimage* (1995). The town has long been known for its black dog legend (p192) and the name for this new venture seemed obvious, if not very original. The legend is much like that of Norfolk's most celebrated bogey beast, Black Shuck (p187), who haunts the cliff-top paths and, in one version, runs ashore from a wrecked ship. *Dracula* gave fresh impetus to tales of this kind once common along the east coast, tales that Stoker may have heard while on holiday in the town in 1870 – he is believed to have taken the title for his novel from a travel book on Moldavia in the local library. Undersea bells (p268) and black dogs were the subject of popular tales that migrated with the fishing fleets and washed up in places like Sheringham and Cromer. While on a golfing holiday in the town tales of Shuck are said to have given Conan Doyle his idea for that other great Victorian horror story, *The Hound of the Baskervilles*.

What, if at all, is the significance of these memories, gleaned from a lifetime's experience? Is there any common thread which binds them together, some pattern of awareness brought about by the peculiar atmospheres of place or some psychic echo of past lives? Perhaps, for the more sceptical, they resemble nothing more than a selection of curious, but otherwise unconnected, incidents. None of the experiences recalled here are overtly supernatural and I have yet to feel the wet flannel of fear on the back of *my* neck. In response to the inevitable question 'Do you believe in ghosts?' my reply is always 'Not yet' but there remains a nagging suspicion that the veil some believe separates this world from the next is at times thin enough for us to glimpse what may lie beyond. Those fortunate enough to possess Phillip Pullman's 'subtle knife' may, of course, pass at will between these two realms. I am reminded of the occasion when a young George Orwell saw the figure of a man dressed in brown vanish among the ruins of Walberswick church one summer evening. Not a person one readily associates with the paranormal, he was convinced he had seen a ghost. How, just as easily, might any one of us, alone in an abandoned farmhouse or remote churchyard on a stormy night, mistake the shadows cast by clouds before the moon for some wraithlike figure in the half light?

At times like these the barking of a fox or the death throes of a rabbit caught in a trap transport us back to the wildwood of fairy tale. Sin eating (p219) and the frog's bone ritual (p146) may have gone out of fashion but this book is a wide ranging exploration of traditional lore and a celebration of the Norfolk people who kept it alive. I remain unimpressed by all those spirit healers, ghost hunters and ley liners blessed with arcane knowledge but, when the north wind sobs and whimpers in the kitchen and the hag stone given me by a friend rattles the door I know that Black Shuck is never far away.

Peter Tolhurst
Norwich 2018

THE FOLKLORISTS

Fersfield Rectory, home of Francis Blomefield

The term 'Folk-Lore' was first used by W J Thoms to describe 'popular antiquities' in an article which appeared in the *Athenaeum* on August 22nd 1846. This new discipline had its roots in the much older study of antiquities established as a legitimate field of enquiry by Camden's *Britannia* in 1586. It was, however, his successor, John Aubrey, who 'emphasised the oral and marvellous element of antiquarian studies.'[1] By the late 17th century he was already lamenting the passing of traditional customs like that of sin eating in Herefordshire. Referring to 'old wives fables' he concluded 'I do prefer to regard them as the most considerable pieces of Antiquity I collect.'[2] The Society of Antiquities, founded in 1718, acted as a further stimulus to investigating the past – Roman ruins, earthworks and archaeological relics – by men of letters with private means and private libraries at their disposal.

Young graduates came down from Cambridge filled with curiosity about both the natural world and our distant ancestors. Armed with notepads and sketch books they roamed the countryside collecting specimens and local tales gleaned on their travels. Back home a lively correspondence ensued with like-minded enthusiasts working away in book-lined rectories elsewhere in the country. Among this new breed of amateur antiquarians was the rector of Elveden who, on discovering cremation urns from an Early Saxon cemetery at Rushford on the Norfolk-Suffolk border, wrote to the eminent Wiltshire archaeologist, the Rev'd Stukeley, in 1754; 'I shall be extremely glad if I can procure you any further from this fragment of *arabia deserta* and that it will raise your opinion of our barren lands as a nursery of antiquity if not fertility.'[3] At the same time the arboriculturalist and naturalist, Robert Marsham of Stratton Strawless Hall, was keeping an invaluable record of the 'Indications of Spring' and was in regular contact with Gilbert White whose *Natural History and Antiquities of Selborne* was published in 1789.

William Dugdale's *The Antiquities of Warwickshire* (1656) was regarded by many as the model county history and would have been familiar to a young Fersfield lad, Francis Blomefield, who, while still at school in Thetford, had begun to make a record of monumental inscriptions and the genealogy of local families. On graduating from Cauis, Cambridge, he returned as rector of his native parish and set to work on the great *History of Norfolk* that bears his name, a task that occupied him until his death from smallpox in 1752. The final two volumes, completed by his friend Charles Parkin, vicar of Oxborough, were not published until 1776. Blomefield was able to draw on the enormous archive assembled by Peter Le Neve (d.1729) and the results of a questionnaire sent to fellow incumbents throughout Norfolk. As a result the first three volumes are more comprehensive and volume one, printed at Fersfield rectory in 1739 on a press acquired for the purpose, contains the first references to local beliefs and customs. Covering south Norfolk, that part of the county with which Blomefield was most familiar, it mentions the annual procession to Tann's Well from Fersfield church, the legend of the Oxfootstone in Lopham and the account of the Good Sword of Winfarthing that had first appeared in the *Reliquaries of Rome* (1563). Blomefield's *Norfolk* also inclues the earliest version of The Pedlar of Swaffham and the quasi-historical figure of Lothbrok the Dane, in the life of St Edmund.

Francis Blomefield
1705-52

It was almost exactly a century after the publication of Blomefield's *Norfolk* (vol.1) that the first book devoted entirely to an aspect of regional folklore was distributed to subscribers. *The Vocabulary of East Anglia* (1830) by another Norfolk parson, the Rev'd Robert Forby of Fincham, is subtitled 'An attempt to record the vulgar tongue of the twin counties, Norfolk and Suffolk, as it existed in the last twenty years of the eighteenth century, and still exists.' Born in Stoke Ferry, Forby also went to Cauis College and on his return eventually settled in nearby Fincham in 1801 where he remained until his death in 1825, unable to see the final draft of his greatest achievement. His first love had been botany – he became a Fellow of the Linnean Society – and architectural antiquities, but with failing eyesight he turned his attention increasingly to collecting specimens of what he called 'the Doric dialect of his parishioners.' With 'large and valuable' contributions from the Rev'd George Turner of Kettleburgh in Suffolk, the result was a dialect dictionary of some 2500 words compiled from old books, pamphlets and by listening to his 'rustic neighbours.' Of more direct interest to students of folklore, however, is the Appendix, a collection of popular superstitions, weather lore, customs and proverbs noted down by Forby in his commonplace book, aspects of folklore that appeared in print for the first time.

Robert Forby
1759-1825

In 1849 an article by the Rev'd Gunn of Irstead was placed in volume two of *Norfolk Archaeology*, journal of the newly formed Norfolk and Norwich Archaeological Society. While acknowledging the importance of Forby's pioneering work at a regional level, Gunn wished to present material of a similar nature not just from a single parish but from the memory of a single individual. The person in question was an 80 year old Irstead washerwoman called Mrs Lubbock, one of the few named sources to emerge from the work of early folklore collectors. Her many sayings, learnt as a child from her father, were taken down by Gunn 'just as they fell from her mouth as nearly as possible in her own racy language.'[4] He was of the opinion that much of the weather lore, the omens, and the prophesies of Mother Shipton that had been reworked to include local places, as well as those spectral shapes – Jack O'Lantern and Black Shuck – peculiar to Norfolk, probably circulated well beyond the confines of Irstead. Aware that Mrs Lubbock's pronouncements on the weather exposed her to accusations of witchcraft, Gunn was quick to defend her sayings: 'Frivolous and superstitious as they may appear, they in reality exhibit phases of the human mind which are as much within the province of philosophical inquiry as the deductions of exact science.'[5]

The late 19th century saw the emergence of several regional magazines, especially *East Anglian Notes and Queries* that ran for just over fifity years from 1858 to 1910. It provided a forum for those with an interest in history, archaeology and the young discipline of folklore and led to the birth of a companion magazine. Between 1865 and 1870 the *East Anglian* carried a series of six articles by George Rayson of Pulham Market on what were to become standard topics of the region's folklore – weather proverbs, omens, charms, divination, bewilderment and popular superstitions. They were followed soon after by John Glyde's *Norfolk Garland* (1872), the first book devoted specifically to the folklore and customs of the county. Drawing heavily on existing material and references to the folklore of the northern counties, the author endeavoured to 'present in a collected form a mass of those traditions that have from time immemorial been floating among the peasantry of this county.'[6] This holds true for the first part of the book, arranged thematically much like Rayson's articles, but the second part, after a detailed account of Norwich pageants and calendar customs, veers off into the realms of local history with gleanings from old newspapers and anecdotes of Norfolk worthies.

Scattered throughout C J Palmer's three volume *The Perlustration of Great Yarmouth* (1872-5) are some intriguing references to the town's folklore; to kitwitches, shell grottoes and seaside mock mayors. Also active at this time was the Norfolk solicitor and antiquarian, Walter Rye, whose 'Norfolk Superstitions' in *Eastern Counties Collectanea* (1872-3) was followed by folklore articles in *The Norfolk Antiquarian Miscellany* (1877-87), a journal that Rye also edited. As a writer Rye's considerable output ranged from scholarly tracts on Norfolk heraldry and local history to more popular works like his *Tourist's Guide to the County of Norfolk* (1879). As the rail network opened up much of the county, especially the coast and the Broads, to an influx of tourists, so the demand grew for literature devoted to the history, topography and wildlife of the county. Essential to guide books of this kind was a section on folklore which, with its array of phantom coaches, spectral beasts and headless smugglers, was often rendered in lurid detail by obliging rustics for the entertainment of a public hungry for sensation. Writers like E R Suffling, with his *History and Legends of the Broad District* (1891), and William Dutt, author of *The Norfolk Broads*, 1903), were quick to oblige.

Walter Rye
1843-1929

Prompted by the publication of Lady Gurdon's *County Folk-Lore: Suffolk* in 1893, her daughter-in-law, Lady Cranworth of Letton Hall, wrote three articles on East Anglian folklore in the *Eastern Counties Magazine* (1900-01). Despite the regional title of the articles the material – ghostly coaches with lights blazing, a huge black dog called Skeff, a witch known as Mother Staselton, lantern men and even a headless donkey – was all gleaned from elderly residents in and around Letton. Among them was the old village nurse 'sitting by the deep chimney-corner in her cosy little room ... just the sort of person who clearly loves a gossip. Her picturesque old husband sat opposite...'.[7] People like this, living in tied cottages on the Letton estate were only too willing to entertain the lady of the manor with an array of those stock folklore characters she wanted to hear. As such the style is romantic, conversational and patronising.

While travel writers were content to recycle traditional tales like the Pump Hill Ghost, the legend of Callow Pit and the Hickling Skater, the rector of Scarning, Augustus Jessopp, produced two ghost stories in his book *Frivola* (1896) quite new to the reading public. The first, 'An Antiquary's Ghost Story', which had already appeared in the *Athenaeum* in 1880, recalls the author's own experience while on a visit to Mannington Hall (p168). The second, 'The Phantom Coach', played on a theme widespread in Norfolk folklore, and may have been prompted by the spectral coach associated with Longham Hall, a tale Jessopp learnt from his Bradenham Hall neighbour, the father of Rider Haggard. Jessopp chose to set his own version, the tale of the poacher George Mace, some distance south of Scarning at Breckles Hall. This ancient Elizabethan pile was, he concluded, one of those houses 'if it has not been a haunted house ... it ought to have been'.[8] To give it authenticity 'this fine specimen of the learned but somewhat eccentric country parson'[9] claimed to have heard the tale from 'Old Biddy', one of his parishioners, who in turn had it from an aunt who had been dairymaid at the hall. It was soon picked up by Dutt in his *Highways and Byways in East Anglia* (1901) and even repeated by Enid Porter in *The Folklore of East Anglia* (1974). More recently Westwood and Simpson (2005) have argued 'It is suspect, however, as a folk tradition'[10] and unlikely that a petty criminal would have been carried off in a phantom coach, a fate reserved for the gentry. As *Frivola*, the title of his collection, suggests, Jessopp was writing to entertain the leisured classes in an attempt to emulate his friend from Cambridge, the celebrated writer of ghost stories, M R James. Of far greater interest to students of folklore is an essay in Jessopp's collection *Random Roaming* (1893) entitled 'Hill Digging and Magic'. Although he failed to declare his sources Jessopp reproduced what appears to be a verbatim account of an inquiry

Augustus Jessopp
1823-1914

held at Long Stratton in 1485 into a case of barrow digging in the parish of Forncett. The two men in question had invoked a diabolical spirit and sacrificed a fowl in return for information as to the whereabouts of buried treasure. The essay also describes the hill digging attempts by a monk at St Benet's Abbey.

The origins of a much older place legend are discussed at length in the Rev'd Charles Kent's *The Land of the 'Babes in the Wood'* (1910) in which the rector of Merton equates the ballad story with historical events in the vicinity of Wayland Wood. Subtitled 'The Breckland of Norfolk' this rambling account of the region is based largely on copious notes left by his predecessor, the Rev'd George Crabbe and what he learnt from his parishioners about those wizards, witches and planet readers operating locally. W G Clarke's altogether more scholarly account of natural history and archaeology in his *In Breckland Wilds* has a short but informative chapter on 'Traditions, Customs and Ghost Tales'. Having dismissed The Swaffham Pedlar and Babes in the Wood as 'too well known to need repetition' the author concerns himself with tales of earthworks – Thetford's Castle Hill and the barrow known as Tutt's Hill – with the legend of Lord Dacre and the ghostly cortege at Quidenham. The Great War delayed publication until 1925 but the first draft had been prepared between 1909 and 1913 from a series of newspaper articles. Charles Kent acknowledged Clarke's help when writing his *Land of the 'Babes in the Wood'* and it seems likely that other folklore elements peculiar to Breckland – the white rabbit and Hummy dancing – were the result of Clarke's contribution.

Although short-lived, *Norfolk and Norwich Notes and Queries* (1896-1905) invited contributions on a wide range of subjects. Modelled on the long running *East Anglian Notes and Queries* it carried recollections on topics as diverse as the Horkey and Largesse, bough houses, limp corpses, written charms and the nefarious deeds of Sir Barney Brograve of Waxham Hall (p127). Most correspondents preferred to remain anonymous or write under a pseudonym but among those happy to sign off their work were Walter Rye, James Hooper and W B Gerish. Together with William Dutt, Hooper had written the folklore chapter in *The Norfolk Broads* and Gerish was already the author of *Hertfordshire Folklore* (1905) before his move back to Norfolk. Retiring to Caister-on-Sea he assumed the *nom de plume* William de Castre and began to amass material for a comprehensive guide to the county's folklore. Now in the Norfolk Record Office the results of his research, 'Norfolk Folklore Collections' (1915-18), are contained in six maroon bound ledgers, the entries a mixture of newspaper cuttings and neat handwritten extracts copied from local periodicals. Although his book never materialised – Gerish died in 1921 – his work remains the most extensive source for those investigating the folklore of Norfolk. All the while the demand for stories of the paranormal, especially tales of Shuck, continued to be met by popular travel books well into the 1920s with a series of chilling 'first hand' encounters with the supernatural in the style of Jessopp's own experiences. There is the mysterious appearance of a diabolical Italian in Morley Adams' *In the Footsteps of Borrow and Fitzgerald* (1916), the author's pursuit by Shuck on the Stiffkey marshes in Christopher

Marlowe's *People and Places in Marshland* (1927) and the Black Dog of Blickling retold by F J Meyrick in *Round About Norfolk and Suffolk* (1926).

The journal *Folklore* continued to be the main outlet for more serious articles on the subject including Mark Taylor's 'Norfolk Folklore' read to the Folklore Society in May 1929. Despite the title it was concerned largely with folk medicine and witchcraft – Taylor was a medical practitioner and appears to have gathered much of his material from fellow GPs in the county. Thwarted in his ambition to have the work published in book form by a move away from Norfolk and by publishers unwilling to risk their money, Taylor was obliged, like Gerish, to lodge his manuscript notes in what is now the Norfolk Record Office. Ten years later, in March 1939, another article on the county's folklore, this time on West Norfolk, was included in the Collectanea section of *Folklore*. Many of the pieces on witchcraft, horse magic and wife selling were taken down by the writer, E G Bales, from a Mr Crawford, long time resident of Wiggenhall St Germans on the banks of the Great Ouse. The work, begun for the Eastern Counties Folklore Society, ranged across the Norfolk Fens to Wisbech and Upwell on the Cambridgeshire border as well as the area around Crawford's native village. Of particular interest are the few tales recalled by him (p269) that Bales was able to equate with the relevant types in Aarne and Thompson's classification of folk tales. At the end of the war a series of articles by L F Newman on the folk life, folklore, folk medicine and witchcraft of the eastern counties appeared in *Folklore* (1944-46). By casting the net wide the references to Norfolk are inevitably reduced and the subject matter is not always original but, having first surfaced in the Cambridge Public Library Record, they, together with Bales' findings, helped prepare the ground for the pioneering work of Enid Porter.

Enid Porter, who was curator of the Cambridge and County Folklife Museum from 1947 until 1976, was well placed to chronicle the folklore of the Fens. Her mother's family had lived in the Cambridge area for centuries, and she grew up with tales of Tom Hickathrift, the marshland giant. During her time as curator she met many old people with tales to tell, either those visiting the museum or while on her travels talking to Women's Institutes and other village groups. She soon learnt that the best way to gather material was to be patient and gain the trust of informants, even if this meant several return trips. As a method of recording conversations she had misgivings about the tape recorder, preferring notepad and pencil and writing up her findings back in the museum. It was here in 1959 that she met Alan Bloom whose book *The Skaters of the Fens* had just been released. Much of his information had come from W H Barrett who was then living near Norwich. This chance meeting led to a long and hugely productive friendship between Porter and Barrett who had been stone deaf since the war and was bedridden in Framingham Pigot. He was, as Porter soon discovered, 'a remarkable man with a remarkable memory', a memory sharpened both by his deafness and his exile from the Fens.

Enid Porter
1909-1984

Born in 1891 in the remote hamlet of Brandon Creek on the Norfolk-Cambridgeshire border, Jack Barrett came from a long line of fen dwellers, people who lived in a strange, isolated world of drainage dykes, dirt tracks and big skies. Much of what he knew of this life had either been learnt at his mother's knee or from old fen tigers like Chafer Legge and Ratty Porter who gathered at the Ship Inn beside the Great Ouse to swap tales. This oral tradition stretched back in an unbroken line to the 18th century and beyond, and the customs recalled by Barrett – the love tokens, the courtship practice of 'bundling', the rough music known as 'tinging', the gruesome rituals of 'snatching the pillow' and sin eating – were fragments of a rich folklife peculiar to that flat landscape. They found their way into several articles written by Porter in *Folklore* in the late '50s and early '60s, elements woven together in what has become a classic of its kind, *Cambridgeshire Customs and Folklore* (1969), in which the Fenland material is attributed to Barrett.

Jack Barrett
1891-1974

The Ship Inn, Brandon Creek

The stories too are macabre and bawdy, laced with a humour as black as the peat soil from which they had grown. Some have their roots in historical fact but others, drawn from an area extending to Ely and Littleport, are place legends like 'The Southery Wolf-hound' (p196), 'Methwold Severals', 'The Witch of Brandon Creek' and 'The Magic Stone of Southery' (p39), from that part of the Norfolk Fens with which Barrett was most familiar. As folk tales they are difficult to categorise but as Porter concluded 'In so far as they were transmitted orally they *are* folk tales [although] there are no myths or sagas among them.' She preferred to call them traditional tales, knew they were utterly unique and, acting as editor, persuaded Routledge and Kegan Paul to publish them in two volumes as *Tales From The Fens* (1963 and '64). In a long and distinguished career Porter's final contribution was *The Folklore of East Anglia* (1974) in the incomplete *Folklore of the British Isles* series edited by Venetia Newell for Batsford, but as Porter concluded, much had been omitted and both Norfolk and Suffolk 'might well each have a volume devoted to itself.'[11]

Porter's exact contemporary in the field of folk life studies in East Anglia was the writer George Ewart Evans whose friendship with elderly residents in the remote Suffolk hamlet of Blaxhall in the 1950s laid the foundations of what has become known as Oral History. Those born at the end of the last century were the survivors of what Evans called a 'prior culture', a traditional rural society stretching back in an unbroken line to at least the middle ages that was in terminal decline. By employing the field techniques of social anthropologists, and helped by a natural affinity with working class people from his boyhood in the mining villages of South Wales, he won the trust of his informants by living and working in the community where his wife was the local school mistress. Here, among people who spoke a strange poetic language, he stumbled upon a rich vein of folk culture and, with the aid of a tape recorder, he embarked on a remarkable salvage operation to chronicle this rural culture across East Anglia before it disappeared. Evan's greatest achievement was to give the farm labourer a permanent voice in a series of books over the next thirty years. Among the many remarkable folk beliefs unearthed in the first of these, *Ask the Fellows Who Cut The Hay* (1956), is that of the Blaxhall Stone (p37) a glacial boulder that 'whoolly grew'.

The home of George Ewart Evans in Brooke

From his conversations with old horsemen in the Gipping valley Evans discovered a wealth of folklore associated with the heavy horse, powerhouse of the rural economy before mechanisation, that became the subject of *The Horse in the Furrow* (1960). Crucial to this was the secret society of elite horsemen who guarded the knowledge and passed it on through the frog's bone ritual. Evan's finest book, *The Pattern Under the Plough* (1966), explores the pagan origins of horse cults and, by gathering together the many fragments of pre-Christian beliefs relating to the farm and home, he examines the range of protective magic used against evil spirits. Among the most potent amulets was the hagstone or All-Seeing Eye hung on the cottage porch or stable door to ward off the nightmare. Much of the material recorded by Evans in Suffolk has a wider relevance to farming communities throughout East Anglia so that when, in 1968, he and his wife moved to a cottage in Brooke he was able to extend his field work across south Norfolk. In *Where Beards Wag All* (1970) he charts the seasonal migration of farm labourers to Burton-on-Trent from the Waveney valley, the hay trade and the herring industry, before returning to his main preoccupation in *Horse Power and Magic* (1979) and the most revealing verbatim account of the frog's bone ritual recorded from Albert Love of Wortwell (p147).

George Ewart Evans
1909-88

The last thirty years or so has seen the publication of works that have added considerably to our knowledge of Norfolk folklore. One of the few pieces of original research, using questionnaires sent to all branches of the WI, was conducted by the American Daniel Rabuzzi. His findings, 'In Pursuit of Norfolk's Hyter Sprites', published in *Folklore* (1984), examined this little known nursery bogey. It was followed in 1988 by Christopher Reeve's *Straunge and Terrible Wunder* which explores the origins of the Black Dog legend in Bungay. Local author Carol Twinch's quest to track down Norfolk's own folk hero-cum-fertility god in the first of three books on the subject, *In Search of St Walstan* (1995), was enlarged by Robert Halliday's article in *Norfolk Archaeology* (2003), 'St Walstan of Bawburgh'. By a process of topographical interpretation and church dedication Joseph Mason has produced a persuasive reassessment of East Anglia's martyred king in *St Edmund's Norfolk* (2010).

In 1989 a slim volume by Jennifer Westwood appeared in the county based Gothic series. *Gothick Norfolk*, the first survey of folklore sites in the county, also mapped out the territory for the Norfolk section of Westwood and Simpson's monumental *The Lore of the Land: A Guide to England's Legends* (2005). By virtue of being a Norfolk 'gal' and an eminent folklorist Westwood was well qualified for the task ahead. Born in Norton Subcourse on the edge of the Yare marshes in 1940 she went off to university (Oxford and Cambridge) and travelled widely but the village where she continued to live until her death in 2008 'remained central to her physical, intellectual and folkloric world.'[12] What she had learnt from her grandparents, together with childhood memories of riding home on dark winter evenings, pedalling furiously and singing hymns to keep Shuck at bay, helped prepare the ground for a series of acclaimed books on folklore culminating in *The Lore of the Land* and *The Fabled Coast* with Sophia Kingshill, published posthumously in 2012.

Jennifer Westwood
1940-2008

Drawing on a lifetime's work on the region's folklore, Mike Burgess created the 'Hidden East Anglia' website (*www.hiddenea.com*) in 2005. It consists of a parish-based gazetteer of sites, a section on landscape features and topics such as the quests for Tom Hickathrift and St Edmund. The black dog 'sitings' listed in the Shuckland section were mostly compiled from responses to requests for information posted in local papers in the 1970s and '80s (a similar excercise in the 1990s produced nothing). The website, which is regularly updated, is an invaluable source for anyone interested in Norfolk folklore. The most recent publication to shed new light on the subject is

Medieval Graffiti: The Lost Voices of England's Churches by the Fakenham-based archaeologist Matthew Champion. The author's ground-breaking work, which began in north Norfolk, illuminates a completely new area of protective magic. The geometric symbols (hexfoils), the ship graffiti, the charms and curses scratched on the surface of ancient churches shed new light on the workings of the medieval mind.

Champion's book is just the most recent contribution to folklore studies in a long history of research and collecting that stretches back over three hundred years. The days of Jack Barrett and Albert Love may have gone but, even as you read this, someone, somewhere, in a dusty archive or a muddy field, is unearthing new material; material that may enrich our knowledge of the county's folklore still further.

THE OLD GODS

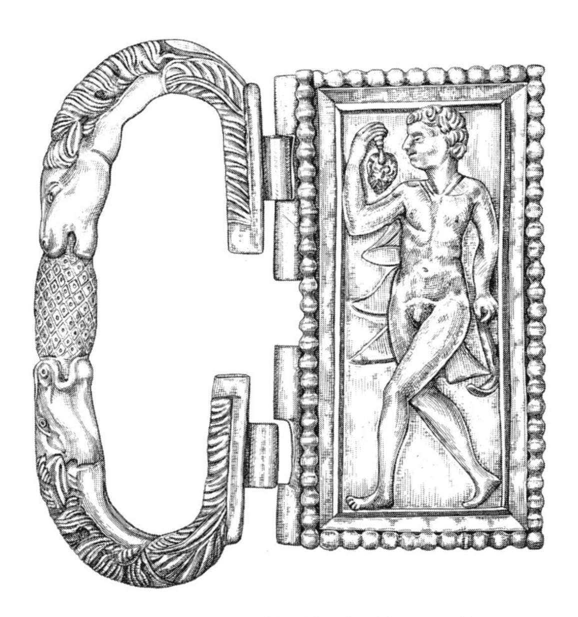

Gold buckle, Thetford Roman Treasure

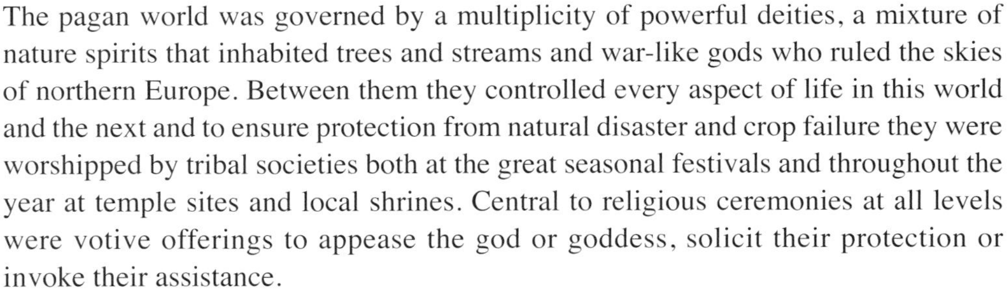

The pagan world was governed by a multiplicity of powerful deities, a mixture of nature spirits that inhabited trees and streams and war-like gods who ruled the skies of northern Europe. Between them they controlled every aspect of life in this world and the next and to ensure protection from natural disaster and crop failure they were worshipped by tribal societies both at the great seasonal festivals and throughout the year at temple sites and local shrines. Central to religious ceremonies at all levels were votive offerings to appease the god or goddess, solicit their protection or invoke their assistance.

Chalk figurine, Grimes Graves

The earliest 'evidence' for this practice in the county came to light in 1949 with a press notice in *Norfolk Archaeology* announcing the discovery of 'what appears to have been the centre of a phallic worship cult in one barren shaft' of the Neolithic flint mines at Grimes Graves. A few years earlier A L Armstrong had found a female figurine crudely carved from a lump of chalk and set on a pedestal of flat chalk slabs. Nearby was a chalk phallus and three flint nodules arranged in the form of a second phallus. Such a uniquely potent assemblage soon attracted its own folklore. Was this a shrine to a pregnant chalk goddess to ensure a good crop of the most treasured black floorstone flint at the end of a worked out seam or, as some suggested at the time, an elaborate hoax? A question mark will continue to hang over this extraordinary find until similar objects come to light elsewhere. In the meantime it is no longer on display in the British Museum.

Among the most spectacular prehistoric objects to have been recovered from across Norfolk are a number of metal weapons that appear to have been made not for use in conflict but for ceremonial purposes. Rather than accidentally lost it would seem they were ritually deposited in pools or streams to one or more water deities. During his farewell speech as director of the British Museum Neil MacGregor, referring to objects that staff could only describe as 'probably votive', joked that 'eventually I realised that "votive" means something very precious that was found in a bog in Norfolk.' Several Bronze Age swords have been recovered from the Wensum and the banks of the Wissey at Stoke Ferry but one that MacGregor probably had in mind was the unusually large bronze dirk recovered from a layer of peat at Oxborough in 1988. This superbly crafted reminder of Breckland's sacred past on the edge of the Fens had never been sharpened, had no handle and had been laid in water as an offering to some local wetland god. Remarkably a second ritual dirk, similar in size and quality, was discovered at East Rudham in 2002 but, significantly, the blade has been deliberately bent. The beautifully crafted late Bronze Age shield found at Sutton may have suffered a similar fate. Intricately decorated, it is unlikely to have been intended for use in battle and has been punctured with a hole through the centre. Both this and the Rudham dagger appear to have been 'ritually killed', a form of sacrifice to ensure their journey from the physical to the spiritual world that occurred throughout pre-Christian societies.

Bronze Age dirk, Oxborough

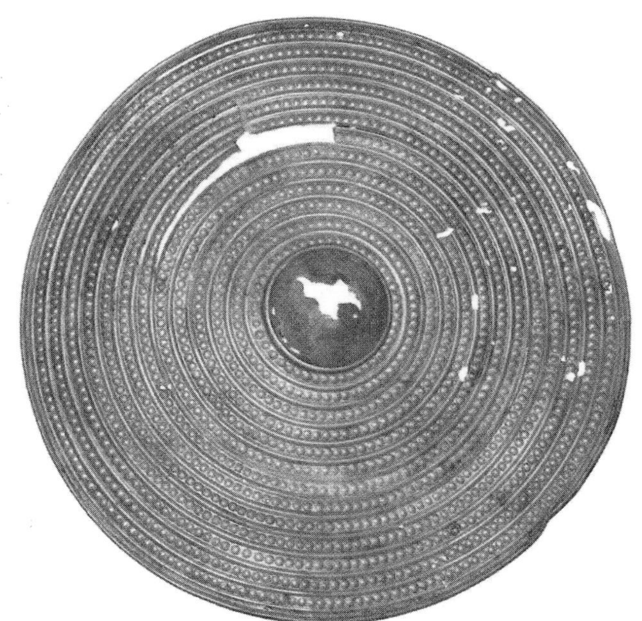

Late Bronze Age shield, Sutton

The recent discovery of a flat Romano British *mortarium* at Caistor St Edmund with a hole punched centrally through the bottom may well be another example of ritual killing. It was unearthed from one of the three perimeter ditches that defined the military fort and may have been part of a termination ritual when the ditches were filled in and the walled town laid out – Terminus was the Roman god of boundaries. The Snettisham Treasure of Iron Age torcs was originally thought to have been buried by a metalsmith for safekeeping but more recent excavation, in 1990, revealed that the 'nests' of torcs had been carefully layered according to metal type for some unknown ritual purpose. There was never any intention to recover the hoard of beautiful Roman silver drinking cups buried at Hockwold on the shore of a vast watery expanse of fenland. The bases and handles had been removed and the cups, elaborately crafted with Bacchic motifs of the highest quality, had been crushed – ritually destroyed – prior to burial near to a temple site.

Roman silver cups following restoration, Hockwold

Ritual deposits were made not only to Celtic water deities but to gods of the underworld as the discovery of a well shaft at Ashill in the 1870s revealed. Situated in a square enclosure constructed in the mid 1st century AD, the shaft was oak lined and forty feet deep. The top half had been filled with rubble but below this the nature of the deposits changed significantly. Eleven sets of near perfect urns had been carefully laid on beds of hazel leaves and nuts, a plant venerated by the Celts and traditionally associated with sacred wells. The nuts, thought to have supernatural powers, were found to be more mature in the upper layers as the deposits were built up throughout the season. This summer shrine of the Iceni was, as Daphne Nash Briggs argues, in contrast to the tribe's ceremonial centre in the winter months.

Iceni coin,
ale deity with ears of corn

Rebuilt at about the time the Ashill shaft was sunk the monumental shrine on Gallows Hill north of Thetford consisted of a huge rectangular space enclosed by nine parallel rows of large oak posts. The round timber structures within the enclosure showed no sign of domestic use and were probably part of a funerary complex with the grain store used for votive purposes. With the wind blowing through this grove of leafless trees the shrine would have been an eerie place; a shrine to the dead, but what kind of deity was worshipped at this isolated spot? Some of the earlier Iceni coins carry the head of a female deity, possibly of Andrasta, invoked by Boudica to avenge the crimes inflicted on her daughters and her people by the Roman legions (p107). Later coins more often have the head of a male deity with ears of corn or the figure of a boar sprouting corn, images paired on the reverse with that of a horse, totem animal of the Iceni tribe. The horse is female, a mare also depicted with wheat or barley sprouting from its mane; a symbolic union with the male grain god to secure the fertility of both crops and livestock throughout the coming year?

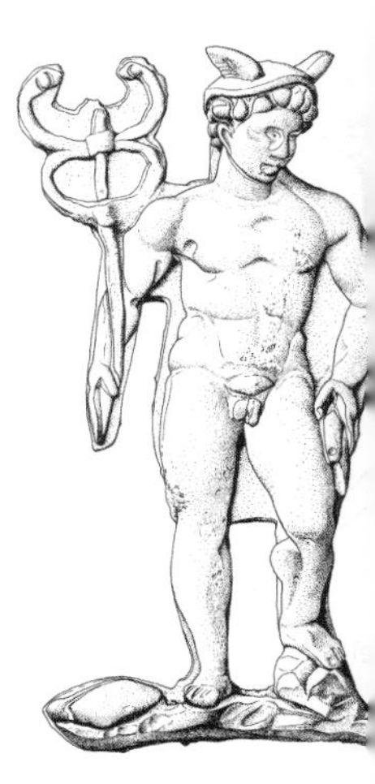

Figurine of Mercur
Hockwold

Following the rout of Boudica's army the tribal shrine on Gallows Hill was not destroyed by the Romans in an act of revenge but carefully dismantled as they set about colonising the Iceni. From the large number of metal objects retrieved across Norfolk it would seem that many of the Celtic nature spirits were replaced, at least at an official level, by the pantheon of gods imported from Imperial Rome. The territory of the Iceni was never heavily militarised, unlike much of Roman Britain, and there is little evidence for the cult of Mars, god of war, in Norfolk. A *defixio* or curse tablet invoking the sea god Neptune has been discovered at Caistor St Edmund from a time when the Tas valley was a tidal arm of the Great Estuary, and the hoard of metal objects from Kilverstone – plough coulter, adze and pewter vessels – were probably a ritual offering to Vulcan, the god of fire. It is, however, clear from the figurines of Mercury recovered from religious sites at Hockwold and elsewhere, that the winged messenger was a far more popular deity in Romano British society. At Great Walsingham the statuettes of Mercury, the votive figurines of goat and cockerel, both associated with lechery and the god, together with a bust of Minerva and a three-horned phallic deity, all suggest a sacred site of more than local importance, one possibly built on the site of an earlier Iron Age religious centre.

Jupiter figurine,
Felmingham Roman ho

Every piece of 'decorative art' had a religious significance in the daily life of the native population. It has been suggested that zoomorphic brooches may have been a substitute for the sacrifice of real animals sacred to a particular god, which would explain the hare brooches worn by followers of Venus. The large number of 'horse and rider' brooches from the Roman temple site at Hockwold, a type widely distributed across the Fens, may represent Epona, Romano British goddess of horses, but the most revealing example of religious assimilation comes from the late 4th century Thetford Treasure discovered a short distance from the Iceni shrine on Gallows Hill.

The treasure is remarkable for the number of silver spoons inscribed DEI FAUNI ('To the god Faunus'), the first evidence for the cult of this pastoral Roman deity in Britain. The pair of woodpeckers on a finger ring are a clear reference to Pictus, the woodpecker god and father of Faunus while the words SILVIO VIVAS ('Long Life to you, Silviola') appear on another spoon. Silvio or 'Little lady of the woods' is probably the name of a female cult follower; all of which points to the cult of this most

Roman goat's head mo
Kenninghall

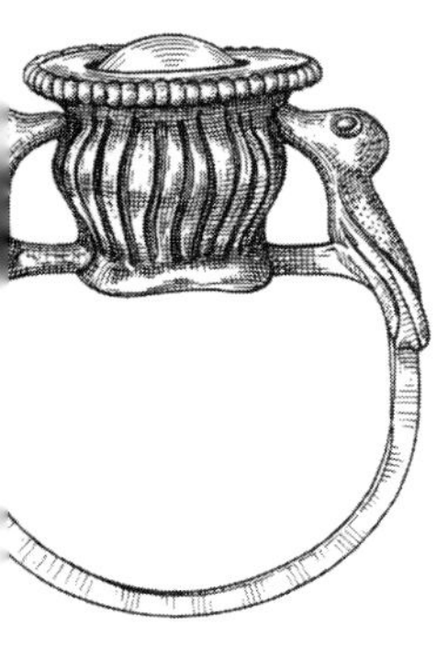

Woodpecker ring,
tford Roman Treasure

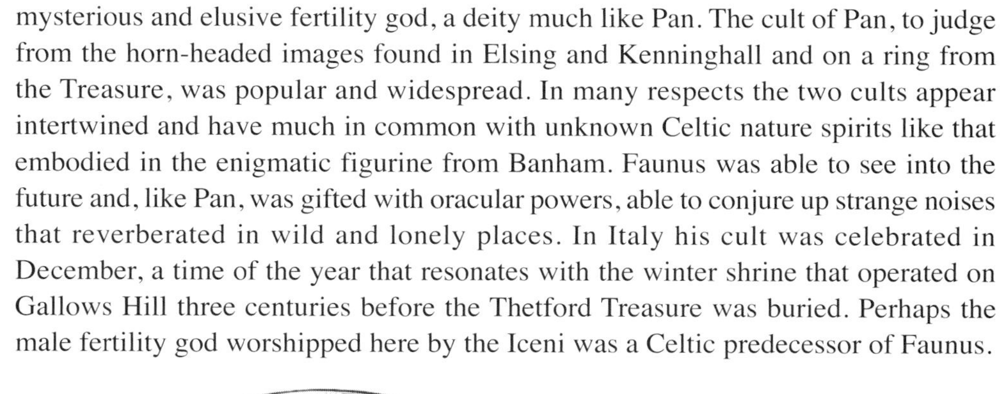

mysterious and elusive fertility god, a deity much like Pan. The cult of Pan, to judge from the horn-headed images found in Elsing and Kenninghall and on a ring from the Treasure, was popular and widespread. In many respects the two cults appear intertwined and have much in common with unknown Celtic nature spirits like that embodied in the enigmatic figurine from Banham. Faunus was able to see into the future and, like Pan, was gifted with oracular powers, able to conjure up strange noises that reverberated in wild and lonely places. In Italy his cult was celebrated in December, a time of the year that resonates with the winter shrine that operated on Gallows Hill three centuries before the Thetford Treasure was buried. Perhaps the male fertility god worshipped here by the Iceni was a Celtic predecessor of Faunus.

Panther silver spoon
inscribed to the god Faunus,
Thetford Roman Treasure

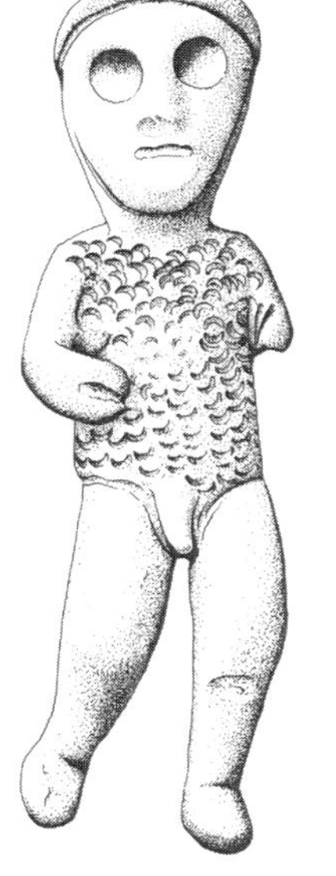

omano British figurine,
Banham

Compared with the growing evidence for religious practice among the Romano British population in Norfolk, there is rather less to suggest the nature of pagan worship among those Germanic tribes arriving from northern Europe. We know from *Beowulf* and the Sutton Hoo ship burial (p72) that they came from a land of war-like gods and dragon-slaying heroes but in Norfolk the archaeological evidence for religious structures is insubstantial. Among the many Early Saxon cremation urns unearthed from cemeteries across the county a single urn from Caistor St Edmund is decorated with images from Norse mythology. A crudely incised image of a hound, identified as the wolf Fenrir, confronts a stylised boat with thirteen oars, the ship Naglfar made with dead men's nails that appears at Ragnarok, the Fate of the Gods.

Another example of Scandinavian cultural influence can be seen from a small but important group of Early Saxon gold bracteates – circular pendants – that have come to light in north Norfolk. Of these a distinct cluster of four bracteates from Binham were probably buried together as a votive offering. The god invoked is likely to have been Tiw, an early Germanic god of war depicted here as a helmeted figure engaged in combat with a beak-headed monster in a scene almost identical to one on a Danish bracteate. A labyrinthine entanglement of these same beady-eyed demons writhe over the surface of another bracteate from Brinton. The arrow-shaped rune associated with Tiw inscribed on a cremation urn from Spong Hill, North Elmham, and on a number of Anglo Saxon swords suggest his cult was then widespread in Norfolk. Tiw was later absorbed into the great warrior gods of Norse myth, Woden and Odin, the supreme gods of the northern skies depicted on a number of mounts and pendants as bearded figures with horned helmets terminating in birds' heads. These have been

a the huntress pendant,
etford Roman Treasure

interpreted variously as the twin ravens of Woden, Hugin ('mind') and Munin ('memory') or, because the beaks are curved, as birds of prey – Woden/Odin is said to have turned himself into an eagle. An intriguing box mount recovered from the banks of the Wensum at Bylaugh depicts a Valkyrie welcoming a warrior to Odin's kingdom of Valhalla, a find illuminated by two local place names. The meaning of Bylaugh is obscure but one suggestion is 'funeral pyre enclosure' while Bawdeswell, from Old English, is 'Baldhere's spring'. Perhaps it is the spring, or well, of Balder that provides entry into his father Odin's underworld.

Early Saxon gold bracteate depicting Tiw, Binham (left), and beak-headed monsters, Brinton (above)

The wrath of an angry god has long been associated with one of nature's most terrifying phenomena – the thunderstorm. Since prehistory small weapons like flint arrowheads have been worn as protection against lightning strikes and the long cylindrical belemnite fossils – known in East Anglia as thunderbolts – were thought to have been formed when lightning struck the ground. On the principle that lightning never strikes twice these small flint objects were either placed in cottage windows or were carried about by those working out in the fields as a precautionary measure. One of the most recognisable amulets to emerge from the archaeological record is Thor's hammer. Worn by Viking settlers as a pendant round the neck or hanging from the belt it was a sign of the Norse god's protection. Fierce and vengeful, Thor bestrode the northern heavens with his hammer – Mjolliner or 'Crusher' – a missile hurled through the sky to slay giants. Viking amulets fashioned in the shape of Thor's magical weapon have been unearthed across Norfolk – a Late Saxon silver pendant decorated with gold filigree from Great Witchingham and another in gold alloy from South Lopham are among the best examples.

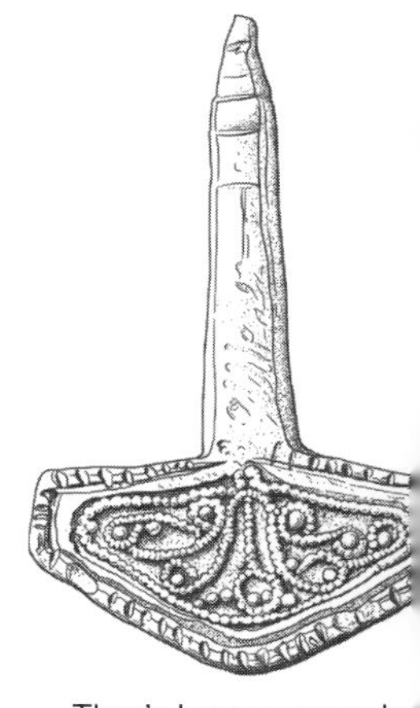

Thor's hammer penda
Great Witchingham

Viking box mount, Bylaugh

SACRED SPRINGS

Sources of water, so essential to life, have been sought after and fought over since humans first roamed the earth. In Norfolk the fluctuating meres of Breckland, a unique feature of this otherwise parched landscape, were highly prized by nomadic groups moving their livestock across country. Sheep tracks and ancient drove roads converge on these water holes, notably on Ringmere at East Wretham Heath where no less than seven parish boundaries met in order to claim valuable water rights. Much of the rest of Norfolk is well drained by a network of rivers and settlers arriving up these same riverine routes found water in plentiful supply. The first homesteads were constructed on drier ground away from the immediate threat of flooding, their exact location often determined by the presence of a spring. This is borne out by widespread references to springs or wells (the two are synonymous in this context) in Norfolk place-names; Bale from Old English 'warm springs', Beachamwell ('the spring at Bicca's homestead'), Wellingham ('homestead of the people by the spring') and Welborne ('spring stream'), among others.

Spring water rises to the surface most readily at the junction of porous rock with an impervious layer below it. In the limestone districts of northern England streams that disappear suddenly down fissures in the rock gather force underground to reappear at the base of an outcrop as fully formed rivers. There is no natural feature quite so dramatic in Norfolk where water often seeps through boggy meadows swelling rivulets as they flow downstream to feed the main watercourses. In the west of the county a regular line of settlements has evolved running south from Hunstanton to East Walton along the spring line at the foot of the chalk where it meets the underlying gault clay. This linear pattern of Saxon villages coincides with an earlier, equally distinctive, line of Roman villa sites. At least ten have been identified so far, most with their own hypocausts, attracted by the same water sources that eventually find their way to the Wash via a number of short, west flowing rivers.

Victorian wellhead, Appleton

At Appleton this sequence can be traced across the parish. The Romans built a villa at the head of a shallow valley where the Denbeck rises, and half a mile downstream this Babingley tributary is swelled by another spring that emerges on a hillside below the ruins of St Mary's church. The village it served was gradually abandoned throughout the medieval period but re-used Roman tile from either the Denbeck villa or one of several others nearby, is still visible in the fabric of the church. The spring is marked by an ash tree, its roots wrapped around a 19th century wellhead constructed, with no little irony, using blocks of stone recovered from the church. A similar picture has emerged further south in the parish of Gayton where another villa site has been identified near a source of the Gaywood river. A little downstream, earthworks of the Domesday village of Wella are proof that a constant supply of water was no guarantee of prosperity. The pattern is repeated nearby at Gayton Thorpe where St Mary's round towered church stands on a mound and where, across the green, another Gaywood stream rises in a farmyard before flowing away past the best known villa site in the county.

MERMAIDS

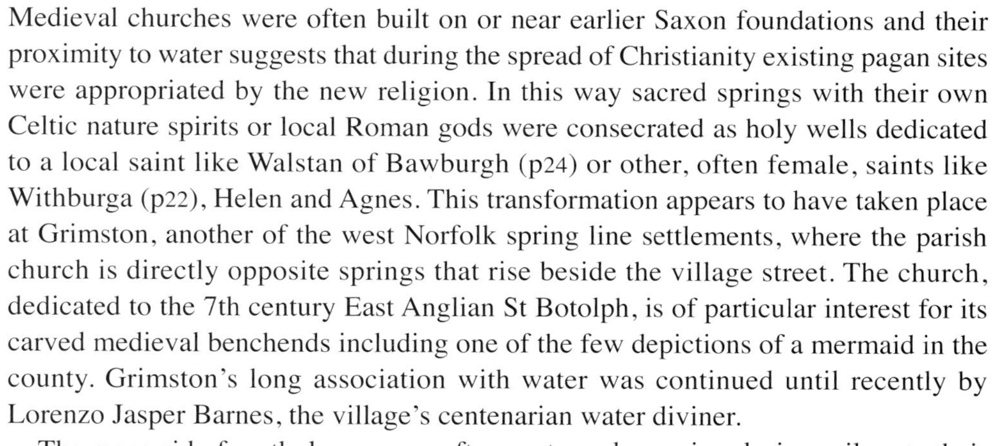

Medieval churches were often built on or near earlier Saxon foundations and their proximity to water suggests that during the spread of Christianity existing pagan sites were appropriated by the new religion. In this way sacred springs with their own Celtic nature spirits or local Roman gods were consecrated as holy wells dedicated to a local saint like Walstan of Bawburgh (p24) or other, often female, saints like Withburga (p22), Helen and Agnes. This transformation appears to have taken place at Grimston, another of the west Norfolk spring line settlements, where the parish church is directly opposite springs that rise beside the village street. The church, dedicated to the 7th century East Anglian St Botolph, is of particular interest for its carved medieval benchends including one of the few depictions of a mermaid in the county. Grimston's long association with water was continued until recently by Lorenzo Jasper Barnes, the village's centenarian water diviner.

Mermaid benchend, Grimston

The mermaid of mythology, more often portrayed as a siren luring sailors to their deaths –'I'll drown more sailors than the mermaids shall' (Shakespeare's *Richard III*) – was also said to frequent inland ponds waiting to drown passers-by, especially children. Here she 'probably represent[s] native tradition rather than [the] learned lore' of medieval bestiaries – the *mer* of mermaid is Old English for mere or pool. Writing in 1864 the Cambridgeshire poet J R Withers gave this warning:

> Play not, my dear boys, near the pond in the meadows,
> The mermaid is waiting to pull you beneath;
> Climb not for a bird's nest, the bough it may sliver,
> And the mermaid will drag you to darkness and death.

Hockham Mere was still a feature of the Breckland landscape in the 15th century when the benchends in Holy Trinity church were carved, and the mermaid here may have been intended as a reminder to village children not to venture too near this mysteriously fluctuating body of water. The legendary figure appears once more in the church at Upper Sheringham which, although in sight of the sea, is a mile inland on rising ground. The fish-tailed creature, like her Grimston sister, may be a demonised version of some pagan water spirit that once inhabited the nearby spring. Here, complete with comb and mirror, she is portrayed as Vanity and an object of sexual desire. Perhaps, like Narcissus, she first caught sight of her face reflected in the pool and fell in love with it; the mirror she acquired in later religious iconography is absent from images of the mermaid in classical art. Just beyond the churchyard wall the spring at Upper Sheringham was transformed into a handsome conduit in 1814 to provide clean water for the village. The structure was a gift from local benefactor Abbot Upcher and twenty years later his widow, Charlotte, appalled by the number of local men drowned at sea, provided Sheringham with its first lifeboat. Although the 'Augusta' plucked many from the waves, the headstones in Holy Trinity churchyard are a stark reminder that many continued to perish at the hands of the mermaid. Not surprisingly the local fishing community was notoriously

Mermaid misericord, Norwich cathedral

superstitious, inhabiting a treacherous world full of ominous sounds and phantom beasts, when noise like the cry of a drowning man beneath a boat foretold an approaching storm. The 'shrieking woman' was another portent of disaster like the black dog 'Shock' known to run out of the sea and up onto the hills (p189).

Conduit, 1814, Upper Sheringham

HOLY WELLS

Clear, mineral-rich water bubbling up from the earth is one of the most powerful expressions of the life force. Once blessed, water drawn from holy wells became an essential element in the rituals of the medieval church. People would make the sign of the cross with holy water from a stone basin, or stoup, beside the door before entering in an act of spiritual cleansing. At the font infants are admitted into the Christian family through the sacramental rite of baptism while in the chancel another stone receptacle, the piscina, was used by the priest to wash the chalice and paten after mass. In the eyes of the church the purity of spring water became synonymous with the state of virginity and holy wells were often dedicated to female saints, notably to the Virgin Mother and most famously Our Lady of Walsingham. As a result springs elsewhere in Norfolk became revered as Lady Wells. Monks from the Carmelite Friary at Burnham Norton, founded in 1241, would drink from the Lady Well near the precinct boundary; there is both a Lady Well and a glacial boulder west of the church at Sedgeford, itself dedicated to St Mary, and the Appleton spring is called 'Ladyes Well' on an early 17th century estate map. St Helen, her name probably a version of the Celtic goddess Elen, was popular in eastern England and just below the round barrow known as Blood Hill on the Santon-Thetford boundary is St Helen's Well. This isolated spot near the river Thet is said to be haunted by a farm labourer who, one hot day, came and drank from the cool water until he died. Nearby, until the Dissolution, stood a Late Saxon chapel or oratory, also dedicated to St Helen. At Spring Farm in the west of Gressenhall parish is a well dedicated to the virgin martyr, St Agnes. Her cult is said to have been ancient and widespread and her name is again probably derived from that of a Celtic goddess, Annis. The well is believed to have been used by pilgrims on their way to Walsingham.

Holy water stoup, Hackford

Victorian wellhead, Wereham

The custom of well-dressing, still widespread in the limestone district of Derbyshire, evolved in the early 19th century from the practice of decorating wells with ribbons and garlands of flowers, often to celebrate the saint's day dedication of the local church. No such tradition survives in Norfolk but there is evidence that the custom was observed in some villages before the Reformation. In Wereham the village pond is fed by a spring through the base of a stone obelisk. The well, like the church opposite, is dedicated to St Margaret, one of fifty or more dedications to the patroness of childbirth in Norfolk. According to the Norfolk historian John Chambers, writing in 1829, 'In times of popery the people diverted themselves on that Saint's day [July 20th] with cakes and ale, music and dancing; alms and offerings were brought and vows made: all this was called well worship.' A century earlier the Rev'd Francis Blomefield referred to a spring in his own parish of Fersfield just north of the church called Tann's Well, a corruption of St Anne's Well. It rose at the foot of a 'hill' and there were processions to it from the church which had a side chapel dedicated to Anne, mother of the Virgin Mary.

ST WITHBURGA

The wellhead still visible in the churchyard at Dereham is the only tangible link with the legend of St Withburga, a tale of miracles, monastic rivalry and body snatching that has become the foundation myth of this mid Norfolk market town. Withburga was certainly an historical figure, a royal princess and one of four daughters of the East Anglian King Anna who was killed in battle by his pagan adversary King Penda at Blythburgh in 654. Following the death of her father, Withburga travelled inland from Holkham on the Norfolk coast to Dereham where she founded a nunnery. It is not clear whether a settlement was already in existence or whether it grew up beside the nunnery but the miracles attributed to her were not written down until the early 12th century by William of Malmesbury. According to the chronicler, the Virgin Mary appeared to Withburga during a time of famine and told her to go down to a nearby stream where two deer would appear each day to be milked while the famine lasted. By this miracle the nunnery and local inhabitants were saved from starvation and the place acquired the name Dereham ('deer enclosure'). In another version Withburga's fame incurred the wrath of a jealous village reeve. Riding out with hounds to kill the deer he was confronted by the nun and, thrown from his horse, died from a broken neck.

St Withburga, Victorian reredos, Dereham

Following her own death some years later Withburga was buried in the grounds of the nunnery but, according to the *Anglo Saxon Chronicle*, when her body was translated to a chapel beside the parish church in 798 it was found to be 'whole and uncorrupted'. At the same time 'a spring issued forth of purest water, gifted with many healing virtues' from her original grave in the churchyard. Complete with holy relics and a sacred well, Withburga's shrine attracted pilgrims from far and wide and it survived the Danish raid that destroyed the nunnery in 870. Withburga's sister Etheldreda had founded an abbey in Ely and in 974 Brithnoth, the bishop of Ely, devised an audacious plan to redirect the funds generated by Withburga's shrine. King Edgar had already conveyed the manor of Dereham to Ely and, on the pretext that Withburga would have wanted to be buried beside her sisters – Sexburga and Etheldreda were also laid to rest in Ely – Brithnoth obtained a licence from the king to remove Withburga's remains. Foreseeing that the people of Dereham would be incensed by such a plan he arranged to travel with 'some of the most active and prudent monks' to celebrate his recent possession of Dereham manor by means of a great feast in the guildhall. While the townsfolk were sleeping off the effects of overindulgence the monks loaded Withburga's coffin onto a cart and got as far as Brandon. According to tradition, it was then covered in arum lilies, the flower of innocence, by nuns from Thetford before the people of Dereham discovered the empty shrine. By the time they reached Brandon the raiding party was already sailing away across the Fens. Lilies which fell into the river soon took root, covering the banks all the way to Ely and were said to glow in the dark.

St Withburga's well, Dereham churchyard

By way of divine consolation the healing powers of St Withburga's well and the chapel built to house it continued to prove a lucrative attraction throughout the medieval period. The Norman church of St Nicholas was largely rebuilt as a handsome cruciform structure and the town prospered from the number of pilgrims seeking cures, especially for sores and eye complaints, by drinking the holy water. In a more secular age the chapel was rebuilt as a bath house for public use, but as a commercial venture it was not a success and in the 1880s the Rev'd Armstrong had the 'hideous building of brick and plaster' removed. Despite this the spring continues to flow; in the 1930s the antiquarian M R James noted that 'the waters still have some reputation for healing'.[1] Today the wellhead in St Nicholas' churchyard is more like a grotto behind railings but still 'substantially a part subterranean c14 structure'[2] according to Pevsner.

Beyond the fact that Withburga was of royal lineage little of real substance is known about her life. The main problem is that while the medieval chronicles locate her nunnery in Dereham it is not clear whether this is East or West Dereham. The removal of Withburga's remains would have been a more plausible undertaking from West Dereham on the edge of the Fens via the river Wissey. A pattern of remote minor religious houses, especially nunneries, can be traced along these watery margins; at Catsholme upstream on the Wissey, at Marham near the Nar and at Crabhouse on the Great Ouse. The abbey founded at West Dereham in 1188 may have replaced an earlier religious house, quite possibly Withburga's nunnery. In East Dereham there is, as yet, no evidence for a monastic cell of any kind although it could lie beneath the medieval church, and when the Saxons did arrive it was probably the spring that became St Withburga's well that persuaded them to settle here on the banks of a Wensum stream.

Dereham town sign

Continued support for the Withburga legend is displayed for all to see above the High Street where it enters the Market Place. Here the town sign, which commemorates the 1300th anniversary of the founding of the nunnery, depicts Withburga defying the huntsman in pursuit of the two deer, the kind of local dignitary who would today be a member of the Rotary Club that presented the sign in 1954. In response to the mayor's campaign to persuade Ely Cathedral to return the saint's remains in 1985, the well was reported to be running more vigorously than it had for many years, testimony perhaps to some lingering belief in its supernatural powers. In 1948, as if by divine intervention, the church tower at Oxborough collapsed and its late medieval screen, with panels depicting Saints Withburga and her sister Etheldreda – the village with its moated hall was close to West Dereham – was brought to East Dereham and placed in the north transept of St Nicholas' church. Here in 1975 it was joined by the St Withburga window, 'a bright and somewhat bizarre composition' [3] in which the legendary deer are puce coloured and one of the nuns sports a speckled orange dress.

ST WALSTAN

The name of Norfolk's own patron saint of farmworkers will not be found in any liturgical calendar and, unlike Withburga, it is by no means certain that he even existed. The life of St Walstan, a heady mix of hagiographic and folkloric motifs, does contain elements common to the legend of St Withburga – the royal lineage, the

Village sign depicting St Walstan,

miracles, the coffin-laden cart, the healing well and the holy shrine – traits garnered from two *Lives* of St Walstan. The first is a Latin prose *Life* included by Wynkyn de Worde (a *nom de plume* perhaps) in his *Nova Legenda Anglia* (1516), a revised encyclopaedia of the lives of saints based on earlier medieval sources. The second is an English verse *Life* copied in 1658 from a tryptych on display in Bawburgh church where Walstan was buried. Placed there for the benefit of pilgrims but destroyed at the Reformation, it appears in both style and content to have been late 15th century.

According to the verse *Life*, Walstan was born at Blythburgh in Suffolk, although nothing is known of his father King Benet. The choice of Blythburgh may have been a word play on his mother Blide's name, a woman reputedly buried at Martham, and an attempt to infuse Walstan with royal blood for dramatic effect – the East Anglian King Anna is said to have been buried in the Benedictine Priory at Blythburgh (see St Withburga) which may also explain the name of Walstan's father. By renouncing his regal inheritance while still a youth for the nobility of manual labour Walstan's sacrifice is all the more impressive. Travelling on foot he eventually arrives at Taverham just west of Norwich where he finds work on a farm and where, for the next thirty years he lives a life of piety and toil, distributing his earnings to the poor and giving his shoes, a present from his employer, to a passing beggar. This last act of kindness enrages the farmer's wife who orders Walstan barefoot into the woods to gather fuel but, rather than scratch his feet, the thorny undergrowth becomes soft to his touch, giving off a sweet perfume.

Ford and footbridge over the Wensum at Costessey, early c20

The incident of the thorns, with its biblical overtones, prepares Walstan for a vision of his imminent death that sets him on the path to sainthood. Received while mowing in the fields, a fellow labourer is witness to the vision by treading on the blade of Walstan's scythe. As foretold Walstan dies on May 30th 1016 but the priest administering the last rites discovers there is no water to wash the body until Walstan causes a spring to flow, the first of three wells associated with the saint's death. The farm had so prospered during Walstan's time that the childless couple wish to adopt him but, sensing his death, Walstan had asked for a cow that gave birth to 'twaine bullock'. When grown and ready for their ordained task Walstan arranges for his body to be laid on a cart drawn by the two beasts of burden, declaring that he should be buried where they finally come to rest. In the prose *Life* Bawburgh, not Blythburgh, is mentioned as Walstan's birthplace and the few miles from Taverham become a journey home through a landscape full of magic and wonder. Crossing over the Wensum, marks left by the cartwheels on the surface of the water were said to be visible years later. Further on first one bull, then the other, stops to 'stale' (urinate) and from each spot a spring arose; one on top of a wooded hill, thereby emphasising the spring's miraculous origin and the other, marked as St Walstan's Well on the first edition of the O S map, on a ridge south of the river Tud. There is no trace of either today, unlike the spring that welled up in a farmyard below Bawburgh church. It marks the spot where the cortege is said to have come to a halt before passing through a hole that appeared miraculously in the north wall of the nave.

St Walstan with scythe a
oxen, Great Melton

Before his death Walstan had asked God to grant him the power to heal not just the poor who prayed to him but their sick animals too and the chapel, built against the church to house the saint's remains, soon became a place of pilgrimage. As John Bale, a protestant convert, wrote in 1551:

> He ... became after the maner of Priapus the God of their Feldes in Northfolke, and Gyde of their Harvestes, all Mowers and Sythe folowers sekynge hym once in the Yeare ... yt both Men and Beastes which had lost their Prevy Partes, had newe Members again restored to them by this Walstane.

It is clear from the eleven miracles listed in the verse *Life*, including cures for epilepsy, lameness and other debilitating illnesses, that those seeking help were drawn largely from nearby villages. Although it extended into north Suffolk the cult of St Walstan appears to have been locally based and to have flourished in the century before the Reformation. His image, regally attired and with a scythe as his emblem, is depicted on eight rood screens, mostly dating from the 15th century. They are to be found within a 20 mile radius of Bawburgh including the screen at Barnham Broom where, uniquely, he appears alongside Withburga, Norfolk's other saint. The bequests and endowments generated by his shrine helped finance fabric improvements to the church at Bawburgh, dedicated jointly to Saints Mary and Walstan – to the chancel in 1309, to the refurbishment of his chapel in 1460 and for a 'new chancel' in 1492.

St Walstan's well, Bawbu

The cult of saints was the main target of the Reformation and, along with many others, the shrine and relics of St Walstan were destroyed. Unusually though, his status as a local saint enjoyed something of a revival in the 17th century due to efforts of the staunchly Catholic Jerningham family who had helped secure the succession of Bloody Mary. For their loyalty they had been rewarded with manors in Costessey and Bawburgh. In 1633 Bawburgh church and Walstan's shrine were restored and the following year Bawburgh Hall rose on the opposite bank of the river Yare. The hall has gone but two early 17th century garden houses survive, both incorporating pieces of carved medieval stone that may have come from the Walstan chapel when it was rebuilt. One, known as the Slipper Chapel, is traditionally where pilgrims are said to have left their shoes before walking the last few yards barefoot to Bawburgh church. This would have involved crossing the bridge over the Yare with its hermit's chapel from which the second garden structure takes its name (Hermit's House). In the 19th century Walstan's shrine was thought to have been close to the hall by the river although this may have reflected the mistaken identity of the Jacobean buildings as religious structures.

c17 'Slipper Chapel', Bawburgh

Bawburgh church

In 1763 the local press reported a surge of interest in St Walstan's Well with some of the more unscrupulous visitors selling bottles of the water with 'extraordinary healing powers' on Norwich Market. This revival of interest continued throughout the 19th century, not least following the publication of the *Life of St Walstan* (1859) by Father Husenbeth, chaplain to the Jerningham family. Moss from the well was applied successfully to sores and other skin diseases and in the 20th century the sick mare of a Bawburgh farmer and churchwarden was cured after being washed in well water. Walstan's image has appeared in several other Norfolk churches and more recently an annual pilgrimage to Bawburgh on 30th May to commemorate Walstan's death is attended by both Anglicans and Catholics.

Setting aside the spurious case for Walstan's royal lineage, his miraculous folklife appears to have been shaped by some older belief in a local fertility god 'after the maner of Priapus'. As a humble labourer he transformed the fortunes of the farm where he worked, he exerted control over plants and animals, he died in springtime and, perhaps most significantly among the miracles attributed to him after his death, was his ability to reverse the effects of castration. His rustic cortege moves through a landscape made fertile by its progression – it crosses three rivers and three springs burst from the ground along the way and the spot where the ox cart comes to rest. Walstan's life has been compared to the cult of other peasant saints; to Isodore the Castilian peasant and to Notburga, a Tyrolean kitchen maid. The circumstances of her burial – the corpse-laden ox cart and the choice of her final resting place – are strikingly similar to Walstan's funeral, and to that of many Celtic saints brought to the grave in the same way including St Cuthbert whose body was taken to Durham by a dun cow. In the late middle ages Walstan's life of selfless toil and personal hardship was designed to appeal to country people in this most agricultural of counties. Its success, while largely confined to mid Norfolk, seems to have stemmed from its ability to absorb elements of a pagan fertility cult, remnants of which still survived among the rural poor.

St Walstan, c15 screen
Sparham

WALSINGHAM

Not long after Walstan's death an event occurred in north Norfolk that was to transform the village of Little Walsingham into a centre of pilgrimage second only to Becket's shrine at Canterbury. In 1061 Lady Richelde, devout widow and lady of the manor, was visited by Our Lady who commanded her to build a replica of the Holy House of Nazareth, scene of the Annunciation. The Saxon village had grown up on the banks of the river Stiffkey and it was here that Richelde chose to build the chapel although she couldn't decide which of two springs for the exact spot. Her dilemma was compounded by the carpenter's inability to 'joyne together their own proper werke'. After another night of prayer she found that her *Santa Casa* had been moved beside one of the wells and had been miraculously rebuilt, a beautifully finished structure to house an image of the seated Virgin.

Richelde's son Geoffrey travelled to the Holy Land in 1095 on the First Crusade and with an eye to the economic potential of his mother's chapel, gave land beside it for an Augustinian priory on his return. The priory grew rich as princes and commoners all flocked to the Shrine of Our Lady. Henry III and Edward I each paid several visits and the fame of Walsingham spread throughout the Christian world. Pilgrim routes across Norfolk converged on the little town that grew up outside the walls of the priory and even the Milky Way, said to point to England's Nazareth, was renamed the Walsingham Way. By the later middle ages the streets were teeming with religious tourists, the infirm and unscrupulous traders hawking souvenirs and bogus cures. Most popular were the lead badges made in the town, secondary relics that offered protection and confirmed the wearer's status as a pilgrim. On sale at the entrance to the shrine were small lead vessels or *ampullae* containing holy water or 'Mary's milk' as it was called, a cloudy mixture of spring water and chalk powder. Once inside,

Walsingham pilgrim bad
depicting the Virgin and C

pilgrims were invited to marvel at a selection of spurious relics and the bejewelled image of the Madonna. Following his visit in 1511 Erasmus, who had chosen to leave the Augustinian order, described the gaudy spectacle that greeted him in *A Pilgrimage for Religion's Sake*:

> ... It glitters on all sides with jewels, gold and silver ... as well as the statue of the Virgin there is also a finger of St Peter, the milk of the Holy Virgin encased in crystal, a piece of wood upon which the Virgin once rested and even the 'secret parts of the Virgin in the shape of a toad-stone, for she alone hath overcome all earthly passions and trodden them underfoot'.

Walsingham pilgrim badge, depicting the Holy House of Nazareth, late medieval

East window arch, Walsingham Priory, late c18

Henry VIII's pilgrimage to the shrine was to have far reaching implications for Walsingham and English monasticism. He had walked barefoot from East Barsham Manor to give thanks for the birth of his son but his mood darkened soon after, on the death of Prince Henry and the Pope's refusal to grant him a divorce. In 1536 with the jewel-encrusted image of the Virgin still fresh in his mind and with the royal coffers in need of replenishment the king ordered the Dissolution of the monasteries. Two years later the statue of Our Lady was taken to London and burnt at Smithfield, along with sister images from Ipswich, Doncaster and Worcester, while Archbishop Latimer declared 'she hath been the devil's instrument and hath, I fear, brought many to eternal fire.'

Stripped of its treasures and the lead from its roof the priory was, over the years, reduced to rubble while the springs continued to flow pure and clear. According to the Rev'd Forby writing in 1830: 'Amongst the slender remains of this once celebrated seat of superstitious devotion, are two small basins of stone ... The water of these wells had at that time, a miraculous efficacy in curing disorders of the head and stomach.'[4] In Forby's time the holy waters, although reduced to the role of wishing wells, still retained the last vestige of an ancient ritual. Participants were required to kneel on a stone placed between the two wells, immerse each hand in the waters, offer up a wish, withdraw the hands and drink from each well in turn. To be effective the procedure had to be strictly followed and the wish should remain unspoken.

Early c16 conduit, Comm Place, Little Walsingha

Slipper Chapel, Houghton St Giles

Following the penitential path trodden by a series of Plantagenet kings, medieval pilgrims traditionally walked barefoot the last mile to Walsingham along the banks of the Stiffkey having left their footware in the 14th century Slipper Chapel at Houghton St Giles. It was here in 1934 that Catholic pilgrimage was revived following the chapel's restoration by Charlotte Boyd, a recent convert. A few years earlier the Rev'd Hope Patten had knelt down in Walsingham High Street and prayed for a sign. Undeterred by the lack of response he decided to commission his own version of the House of Nazareth just north of the priory precinct 'looking for all its ambition like a minor suburban church.'[5] Despite any evidence the new Anglican shrine is said to stand on the site of Richelde's *Santa Casa*. Of more immediate importance the site chosen incorporated an old well which, since its consecration, has enabled pilgrims to receive God's blessing and to drink a little holy water from a long silver spoon. The remainder is then poured over the afflicted part of the body. With the main Christian denominations all active in Walsingham the streets are once again alive with the devout and those seeking cures as though the Reformation had never happened. The stone conduit in Common Place, built around the time of the Dissolution, is however a reminder that for ordinary townsfolk a regular supply of clean drinking water was more efficacious than a bottle of Walsingham Water.

HOLY RELICS

The cult of holy r elics, always more popular on the continent, became a key element in the spread of Christianity throughout Europe and the success of monasticism in particular. An increasing number of relics, mostly of dubious provenance, were brought back from the Holy Land to be displayed in richly decorated reliquaries. Miracle cures at the shrine of a local saint could transform a remote place of worship into a lucrative pilgrim centre and in late medieval Norfolk there was a surprising number of often quite obscure saints from which to choose. In some cases provision was made for individuals to go on extended pilgrimage and pray for souls of the diseased. Alice Cooke of Horstead left little to chance: 'I will have a man to go these pilgrimages: to our Lady at Refham; to Seynt Spryite [Elsing]; to St Parnell of Stratton; to St Wandred of Byskeley [St Wandregeselius of Bixley]; to our Lady of Pity Horstead; to St John's Head at Trimingham, and to the Holy Rood at Crostwyte.' By her will Agnes Parker of Keswick, d.1507, 'owed a pilgrimage to St Tebbald of Hobbies [St Theobald of Hautbois], and another to St Albert of Cringleford.'

ohn's head, rood screen, Trimingham

Many parochial ventures were relatively short-lived including the church, now ruinous, in the meadows at Great Hautbois that was said to house relics of its patron saint Theobald, a young Frenchman who, like St Walstan, had renounced his noble birth and embraced a life of poverty and self denial. At Trimingham the church is dedicated, uniquely in Norfolk, to St John the Baptist's Head. According to the *Norfolk Directory* of 1854 'pilgrims in ancient times came to see the head ... which the wily priests pretended they had got'. If true such a highly prized relic would have transformed this small coastal community into a pilgrimage centre of international renown to rival Walsingham. A more plausible explanation is that the church probably had in its possession one of the many alabaster replicas made in the midlands. In the church at Winfarthing a modern stained glass window commemorates both the celebrated Bible Oak (p69) and the village's other ancient curiosity, the 'Good Swerde of Winfarthing' that once resided in the south aisle chapel. According to the legend, recalled in *The Norfolk Garland* (1872), the sword attracted local women 'when the yoke of matrimony galled' or, more darkly, when a woman wished to be rid of her husband she had but to cause a light to burn continuously before the sword for a whole year'. It remains unclear how or why the sword, allegedly left by a robber who had sought sanctuary in St Mary's, acquired the status of a 'relic' but it would appear that successive priests were willing to ignore its decidedly unchristian reputation in the hope that the sword would attract pilgrims to this otherwise unremarkable parish.

St Mary's Priory, The
Basire, 1779
J S Cotman, 1818 (a

From the great religious houses in France a network of monastic outposts was established across the English countryside in the wake of the Norman invasion for whom the possession of holy relics often proved crucial to their success. Thetford Priory, a Cluniac house founded in 1104 by Roger Bigod, friend of William the Conqueror, was moved soon after to a more spacious site north of the Little Ouse river. Early in the 13th century a large Lady Chapel was added to the priory church following events recorded a century later in the chronicle of the monk John Brame. According to Brame the Virgin Mary had appeared three times to a Thetford craftsman telling him he would be cured of an affliction if he instructed the prior to build a chapel in Her honour on the north side of the church. The prior agreed but ignored the word of the craftsman who said it was Our Lady's wish the chapel should be of stone. A local woman had a similar vision; she too was ignored and her arm became paralysed, but on a monk's advice, she made offerings and was cured. By now the prior was convinced and built the Lady Chapel, its high altar adorned with an image of the Virgin from the old cathedral. The head of the statue was found to contain fragments of Christ's purple robe and stones from His tomb as well as relics from several saints. Before long pilgrims began flocking to Thetford and among the cures recorded by Brame was that of the son of William Heddrich, a young carpenter from Great Hockham killed by a harvest waggon. His parents prayed to Our Lady and the boy revived. By the late 13th century the priory had become sufficiently wealthy for the east end of the church to be rebuilt on a more elaborate scale. The town too prospered from the influx of pilgrims with several other monastic foundations, a number of hospitals and as many as 22 medieval churches in existence before Thetford's importance as a religious centre was upstaged by that of Bury St Edmunds.

It would appear that some sort of hierarchy of relics was in operation throughout the middle ages. Those directly attributable either to Christ or Our Lady were more venerated than the body parts of minor saints, with bottles of 'Mary's Milk' on sale in Walsingham and a phial of Christ's blood in the possession of the cathedral priory in Norwich. This most sacred of relics had been brought from the great Benedictine monastery in Fécamp in the late 12th century where Henry de Losinga, first abbot of

South transept remains Bromholm Priory,

Norwich Cathedral, had been abbot a century earlier. More treasured than even these holy relics was a piece of the Holy Cross on which Christ was crucified, a piece – and there were many in circulation – once in the hands of Bromholm Priory which transformed this remote Cluniac foundation into one of the great European pilgrimage centres. Originally a cell of the monastery at Castle Acre it was 'very poor and altogether destitute of buildings' on the edge of the North Sea when a wandering monk arrived with a cross made of wood from the True Cross. This cleric, according to Roger of Wendover's *Flowers of History* (1223), had been English chaplain to

Baldwin, Emperor of Constantinople. On Baldwin's death, he had returned to this country with an assortment of relics, going first to the abbey at St Albans where he managed to sell a jewelled cross and two of St Margaret's fingers but where the monks, who already had the remains of their patron saint, were less impressed by his version of the True Cross. When the cleric came eventually to Bromholm he and his two children were received into the community in return for what the monks accepted was one of the most potent relics in all Christendom. Once on display it was soon followed by the all important Witnessing of Miracles; the lame recovered the power to walk and the blind to see, the dead were restored to life and lepers were made clean. As word spread the roads to Bromholm became full of pilgrims and donations swelled the priory coffers. Following a visit from Henry III and his nobles in 1234, the right to hold a weekly market and annual fair on the festival of the Exultation of the Holy Cross were granted by the monarch, ensuring the priory's continued prosperity. This powerhouse of monasticism became renowned throughout the land; Chaucer's reeve swore 'by the Holy Cross of Bromholm' and a similar oath, 'by the rood of Bromholm bring me out of dette,' is to be found in *Piers Plowman*.

CHALYBEATE SPRINGS

Although holy wells were deprived of their religious significance at the Reformation a belief in the curative properties of chalybeate springs persisted. Water welling up from the chalk was often rich in minerals and there were a number of short-lived ventures to promote the benefits of 'taking the waters.' In 1728 the Bungay apothecary, John King, built a cold bath house over a spring in Earsham at the foot of what became known as Bath Hills in an attempt to attract the local gentry and Bungay residents. Blomefield (1739) refers to a 'petrifying spring' beneath 'a huge linden tree' in the parish of Deopham and in his *History of Lynn* (1812) William Richards mentions several springs in East Winch noted for their iron-rich properties and ability to cure rheumatism – there is a Mineral Plantation north west of the village. Following the discovery of springs in a meadow beside the Little Ouse Dr Accum published his *Guide to the Mineral Springs of Thetford* in 1819. A pump room had been built the year before and a bath house followed in 1833 but the whole enterprise, including the sale of bottled water, failed to promote Thetford as a spa town – the more discerning public had already discovered the benefits of a dip in the ocean. A few miles further east the name Shadwell has long been thought a corruption of St Chad's well near the river Thet although etymologically it is from Old English *scead wylla* or boundary well – the boundary between Guiltcross and Shropham Hundreds ran along the river. In the early 19th century the well was transformed, not for its medicinal qualities, but into a rustic curiousity, a dome-shaped flint grotto with seats and niches for statues in the park to Shadwell Court.

The most celebrated chalybeate spring was to be found in Reffley Wood, a popular destination for Lynn residents in the 18th century since the formation of the Reffley Brethren. This quasi-religious club had evolved from the Sons of Reffley, a Royalist dining club that met secretly in defiance of the Cromwellian edict that forbade the assembly of more than thirty people. The spring, on land owned by the Catholic Folkes family, became central to the activities of the Brethren. A central obelisk and stone basin were constructed to collect water used in the preperation of a punch drunk by each member at the Brethren's annual dinner. There was even a Reffley Spring

Reffley Temple, William Oldmeadow (1818)

Cantata composed by Thomas Arne which, in performance, was more like a pageant with the tenor soloist acting the part of high priest wreathed in ivy and myrtle who officiated in the preparation of the punch and the toast to Venus and Bacchus, deities of Reffley. This was followed by the smoking of a secret blend of tobacco in clay pipes. The ceremony took place in an octagonal brick temple erected for the purpose beside the spring in the late 18th century, its entrance guarded by a pair of sphinxes. There are references to Whit Sunday skipping here, a custom that may have survived from some more ancient ritual associated with the spring – evidence of Roman and Saxon activity has been unearthed nearby. The curse, 'whosoever shall remove this [the temple] or bid its removal, let him die the last of his race' failed to deter the vandals or the council who arranged for the demolition of the obelisk in the 1990s. The sphinxes were removed for safe keeping and today the site is overgrown and surrounded by the housing estates of South Wootton but the punch bowl remains safe in the hands of the Brethren who, although much reduced in numbers, continue to meet in secret each year and, no doubt, toast the the gods of Reffley Spring.

Clean drinking water was always important in the 19th century and a waterworks built over the springs at Spout Hills provided Holt with pure water while at Shouldham a drinking fountain was erected over a chalybeate spring south of the village in 1859. The water spout in the shape of a lion's head remained in the hands of a local farmer, at least until quite recently. A second spring nearby was known less for its therapeutic properties but as the Silver Well from the colour of the scum that formed on the surface, This phenomenum, the result perhaps of sunlight reflected on natural mineral particles rising to the surface, was held traditionally to be the effect of either silver stolen from the manor house which had been thrown down the well, or a chest of silver coins. According to the story, which has echoes of the Callow Pit legend from Southwood (p74), the treasure was discovered by workmen cleaning the well one day but just as they were raising it to the surface the rope snapped and the chest sank to the bottom once more where it remains to this day.

Reffley spring, base of the obelisk

The tale of Shouldham's silver well also has echoes of the silver chalice legend from Lyng. In the early 19th century the parish clerk, so often a source of local lore, recalled the time when two watermen fished a silver chalice from the channel which was said to run from St Edmund's Nunnery to the river Wensum. The argument over who should keep the chalice became so heated that one of the men uttered a terrible oath 'where upon the chalice leaped out of the boat and sunk beneath the water'. The channel, now a narrow ditch, survives as a loop which forms the parish boundary. This large meander marks the original course of the river before it was cut adrift when this section of the Wensum was straightened. The story may have arisen from the medieval censer found on the site in 1841. In another story, one with widespread variations, the nunnery bells were thrown in the river when this Benedictine outpost was transferred to Thetford in 1176 and can still be heard ringing. In folklore, while gold was believed to lie buried in the ground, silver objects were more often associated with water, with holy wells dedicated to female saints and with female religious houses like the nunneries at Lyng or Marham where the holy well was referred to rather lewdly as Maid's Hole.

Remains of St Edmun
Nunnery, Lyng

MAGIC STONES

The Cowel Stone, Beachamwell

THE GREAT STONES

The large rounded boulders ploughed up over the years are not originally from Norfolk which, despite the narrow band of carstone in the west of the county, has no indigenous rock of real substance. These wandering stones, known as erratics because of their random distribution, were plucked from their bedrock deposit by huge ice flows moving south east some 450,000 years ago from what is now Yorkshire and Lincolnshire. As the climate warmed these sizeable stones were dumped by the retreating ice in a thick mantle of glacial till that covers much of East Anglia. For people who knew nothing of natural processes or geological timescale these alien lumps of rock were things of wonder that generated their own creation legends. Some, like the Southery Stone, were thought to have been the result of a fireball or meteorite strike during a great tempest. In East Suffolk people had their own unique explanation for the Blaxhall Stone, a large smooth boulder of Spilsby Sandstone, much like the Cowel Stone near Swaffham and the Hockham Stone. Among the hours of recorded interviews made of Blaxhall residents in the 1950s by George Ewart Evans is the remarkable claim made by farm labourer Lewis Poacher:

My father-in-law ploughed it out, so he told me, in his time, ploughed it out and brought it up there and placed it down there in the farmyard in Stone Farm. And its still there now. He brought it up and he reckoned it weighed about half a hundred weight ... It weighs about five tons now ... that stone has been there for years. And that whoolly grew. I haven't seen it lately but they tell me it's a huge size. That stone ha'grew, you see. They say that stones don't grow. They do![1]

As Evans points out there is a curious logic to this story. Flints were always coming to the surface to the despair of farmers and despite the efforts of stone picking gangs, 'the land bred them' and so the Blaxhall Stone could only have become that size by continuing to grow once it had been moved. It gave this isolated community some claim to fame and so filled a need; it made the place seem more important by being identified with its 'growing stone'.

The Oxfootstone, South Lopham

According to Francis Blomefield, writing in 1739 from his Fersfield rectory, there were three natural wonders to be seen in the adjoining parish of South Lopham. The first, known as the Self-Grown Stile 'served a common footpath' and was a local curiosity that drew people from some distance, much like the nearby Winfarthing Oak (p69). The second was Lopham Ford, a low causeway that separates the Waveney on one side from the Little Ouse on the other and in so doing prevents Norfolk from becoming an island. The third wonder is the large sandstone boulder known as the Oxfootstone. Unlike the Southery Stone (see below), the legend it inspired does not seek to explain the stone's origin but its name. This is derived from a shallow, hoof-shaped impression in the surface, possibly made by a bivalve fossil, but as Blomefield reminds us, nobody knows when, but in a time of great Dearth (drought):

there came a Cow constantly to that Place, which suffered herself to be milked (as long as the Dearth lasted) by the poor People, but when that decreased she struck her Foot against that Stone, which made the impression, and immediately disappeared.

The story appears to be a local variant of a folktale that resurfaces elsewhere in England, notably to explain the Mitchell's Fold stone circle in Shropshire. Here there was always enough milk until the arrival of the witch Mitchell who milked the cow into a sieve until the cow ran dry and was never seen again. In punishment the witch was turned to stone and fenced in by a ring of stones to prevent her escape. In Lopham the stone, having come to rest in a field known, in the early 19th century, as Oxfoot Piece, appears to have continued its peripatetic life (the time span less geological) with each new owner. It was repositioned at the roadside entrance to a 16th century farmhouse, renamed Oxfootstone Farm; before becoming embedded in the floor of a new farmhouse conservatory. It has since been liberated and now forms the central feature of a small fern garden.

At the turn of the last century the village of Southery ('South island') on the edge of the Fens was an isolated community where superstitious beliefs were still rife and where folktales circulated in remote riverside pubs like the Ferry Boat Inn and The Ship at Brandon Creek. One such tale, the Magic Stone of Southery, was collected by Enid Porter in the late 1950s from Jack Barrett, the last of the great Fenland storytellers. This place legend neatly explains the origins of several local landmarks in the village. The tale begins in 1642, at a time when plans were being drawn up to drain the Fens, plans that were to have a devastating effect on the local population. It is Hallow'en, there is thunder in the air and a sense of foreboding as village folk cower in their beds. A violent crack sets the church bell tolling and sends the vicar mad. Surveying the damage next day, All Saints' Day, the villagers discover a large hole in the church roof made by a fireball and another in the ground near the mill that was still smoking, smoke with a sulphurous smell. As time went by the depression filled with water and became the village pond, known as the Way in Pond because it was once the way to Hell from which demons emerged on Hallow'en.

Ruined church, Southery

Years later when the pond dried up the chained skeleton of the vicar was discovered in the mud at the bottom together with 'a huge block of blue stone' that was removed to the village pound. Here it became a resting place for parishioners; it was used to sharpen knives, foretell the weather – it would sweat before rain – and good luck would befall those who spat on it. In this way it acquired its reputation as the Magic Stone of Southery until a new parson, 'a very clever chap' and probably fresh out of one of the Cambridge colleges, said the stone was a meteorite straight from Heaven. This made it all the more special in the eyes of the village but when an old man claimed that his ability to still father children was due to the rainwater he drank from a hollow in the rock, the parson decided to act. He had the stone turned about and used to buttress a wall at a bend in the main road through the village. The wall in question was the garden wall to Hill House, demolished in the late 1950s. The huge blue stone, most likely some kind of metamorphic rock, would have been geologically similar to some of the other erratic boulders scattered about Norfolk; at Bluestone Farm, South Creake, and several around Cawston, at Bluestone Plantation and the entrance to Church Farm. Like the village pond, filled in during the 1940s, the Southery Stone too has vanished. The only landmark to feature in Jack Barrett's story that still remains is the ruined medieval church in the middle of the village. Complete when Ladbroke drew it in 1823 St Mary's was replaced in 1858 by a new church just down the road, complete with the 15th century cross base removed from St. Mary's churchyard.

The Great Stone of Lyng

First called the Great Stone c1750 by the Thetford antiquarian Tom Martin, the supernatural powers attributed to the Great Stone of Lyng demonstrate the ability of local folklore to interpret unusual natural phenomena. The stone, originally on open, sloping ground, now stands beside a wooded track. This ancient hollow way runs downhill from what was Collen's Green and may once have marked the boundary between Lyng and the separate hamlet of Lyng Easthaugh. According to tradition birds no longer sing nearby, attempts to move the stone and reveal the treasure buried beneath have failed and, if pricked, the stone is said to bleed. At this point the lore of the stone becomes entangled with that of the medieval nunnery (p117), remains of which are still visible in a field at the bottom of Easthaugh Hill. People claimed the stone to be the Druids' Stone in a grove visited by phantom nuns and the blood to be that of sacrificial victims. According to another version the blood was shed in battle between the Danes and St Edmund – the nunnery was dedicated to the Saxon king and martyr – and the wood containing the stone is called King's Grove. With headless horsemen and ghostly soldiers at large in the area the stone is in danger of being engulfed by a surfeit of traditional motifs.

Despite its size the Merton Stone has generated rather less in the way of folklore. Weighing in at an estimated twenty tons this massive boulder, swept down from an outcrop of calcareous gritstone in Yorkshire during the last Ice Age, lies partly buried in a marl pit beside the parish boundary with Threxton. An attempt by the landowner, the 5th Lord Walsingham, to have the stone moved by a gang of estate workers and a team of horses in the late 19th century ended in failure but the occasion is remembered for its 'erotic debauch' and the love-children that followed. Another attempt to move it between the wars using a huge rotary plough fared no better, to the relief of elderly residents who foresaw a calamity of biblical proportions. If the stone were moved 'the waters would rise and cover the whole earth'.[2]

The Hockham Stone

There are no such ominous predictions and, as yet, no folklore of any kind associated with the Hockham Stone. The people of Great Hockham had rather more success than their Merton neighbours when they managed to liberate their stone from a pit and reposition it in pride of place on the village green for Queen Victoria's Golden

Jubilee in 1887. According to the writer and local resident Michael Home it soon became the focal point of children's games, May Day celebrations and the recently revived Horn Fair (p234) as well as a platform for political candidates seeking election. The tradition of turning the stone established at the Jubilee celebrations has been continued on all special occasions since. Tucked away in a corner of the grounds of Oxburgh Hall is an unusual boulder dragged up from the river Wissey in the 1960s. The large quantity of compacted oyster shells contained within have enabled it to be traced to an outcrop of Middle Jurassic rock in Lincolnshire near Sleaford. Before its identification it was known as the Roman Oyster Stone. The name seemed perfectly logical; oysters were a Roman delicacy brought upstream from the Wash and, from the large amounts of pottery and dress fittings recovered from the parish over the years, at least two probable villa sites have been identified. Now, thanks to a geologist from Ipswich Museum the Roman Stone has become the Roamin' Stone.

The village parliament, Winterton

Smaller boulders were often used to protect vulnerable buildings on street corners. Once chosen and placed in position however it was considered unlucky to move them again, as though by so doing they would lose the power invested in them. A photo taken c1930 shows a group of old fishermen beside the Winterton Stone, a black boulder at the junction of The Lane with Black Street. It includes the standing figure of Sam Larner along with Will 'Peg Leg' Bowgin and 'Blind Harry' Powles resting on the stone which had long been where the 'village parliament' met. Originally used to safeguard the corner house it was deemed an obstacle to motor coaches and removed by the council a year later, but the people of Winterton who earnt a precarious living from the sea were a notoriously superstitious crew. The reason for the poor catch that year, the worst in living memory, was clear – the stone had gone. There in the centre of the village it had come to symbolise the strength of people beset by disaster as the

The Winterton Stone

headstones in the churchyard testify. By some strange osmosis the stone had, over the years, absorbed the collective memory of a whole community. Such was the level of feeling that the council felt obliged to return the stone the following year but, as a compromise, to a spot just round the corner in The Lane. By then the damage was done, the stone never regained its power and it was several years before the fishing improved.

PLACE NAME STONES

In much the same way that people were ignorant of glaciation or the geology of large boulders, so they were unaware of place name etymology. A small group of Saxon and Viking place names incorporate both a personal name and the element *tun* (enclosure or settlement), hence Gooderstone ('Guthhere's enclosure') and Garvestone ('Gaerwulf's settlement'). But in the presence of large unexplained stones place names have taken on new phonetic meaning so that Geldeston is, according to tradition, derived from the Geld Stone that once stood at The Clumps where several tracks converge. Here locals are said to have paid their Danegeld, a tax levied to appease Viking raiders in eastern England. In around 1900 the stone was moved to the garden of Geldeston Lodge, some say from the rear of the village pub, the Wherry Inn, where all good stories begin. Today, although the stone has vanished, the tale persists and the name Geldeston has been cut into a new block of stone placed in the centre of the village.

The Millennial Geld Stone

Further up the Waveney at Harleston the name ('Herewulf's enclosure') has become the subject of ever more ingenious interpretation in an attempt to establish the town's ancient lineage. The block of granite just off the Thoroughfare in Stone Court is known variously as Herolf's Stone, named after a Danish chiefton (Herewulf was probably a Saxon thane), or the Harold Stone. This East Anglian earl is said to have used it to mount his horse, having stopped here overnight on a rather circuitous route from the battle of Stamford Bridge to Hastings. Among other semantic variations is the Herald Stone from where the imminent arrival of an enemy force was proclaimed, and Halestone has its own internal logic having fallen to earth during a violent storm.

The history of Gorleston contains several references to the Gull Stones (none as yet to gallstones), the earliest by the Suffolk historian Alfred Suckling, writing in 1846, who describes a circle 'full ten feet high' in a field called Stone-Close. Here at this easterly point in the country, according to tradition, Druids gathered at midsummer to worship the sun as it rose over the sea. The stones remained standing until 1768 when they were allegedly broken up and removed by 'vandalistic bands'. While at the same time repeating the Gull Stones legend C J Palmer, writing in his *Perlustration of Great Yarmouth* (1875), infers that the whole thing may have been invented by a certain W E Randell, 'a known forger of antiquarian documentation'[3] and editor of the *Gorleston and Southdown Magazine* (1831). Whether true or not the story is far more entertaining than the brief entry for Gorleston in the *Oxford Dictionary of English Place Names* which states rather dryly 'The first el[ement] may be related to the word *girl*.'

BOUNDARY STONES

In places like Merton and Lyng glacial boulders have come to acquire legendary status and elsewhere across the open heaths of Breckland where the soil is light and easily eroded they have assumed meaning in the landscape as marker stones, manoeuvred into position where ancient tracks and Saxon territories converged. Lengths of the Icknield Way, the great prehistoric route used to move flint from the mines at Grimes Graves down into Wessex had, by the 10th century, been adopted as boundaries between adjoining parishes. There are still markers along the route; a boulder in the park at Croxton just north of Thetford and west of Swaffham where the Way is crossed by a Roman road heading west towards the Fen Causeway. Here the Cowel Stone, a large block of Spilsby Sandstone brought down by the ice from Lincolnshire, denotes the point where no less than four parishes and the hundreds of Clackclose and South

The Stockton Stone

Greenhoe meet – Cowel may be derived from the Saxon word 'doule' for boundary marker. A similar picture has emerged at the southern end of Hempnall parish where, on Bryant's 1826 map of Norfolk, the Baron's Duel Stone was placed to identify the junction of three Saxon hundreds – Earsham, Depwade and Loddon. The stone has since been cleared away and, unlike the stone plinth erected to commemorate a duel fought on Cawston Heath in 1698, there is no record of such an encounter here. Again the word 'duel' may be a corruption of the Old English 'doule' and the boundary road between Hempnall and Topcroft parishes is still called Barondole Lane. In some places, by cutting steps into the stone, boundary markers were converted into mounting blocks. This appears to have happened to the stone that once stood beside the Norwich to Watton road in Kimberley at the junction of several cross country routes. The spot, Skipping Block Corner, is only a few yards south of the parish boundary with Barnham Broom and the stone may have been relocated and reused when the road was turnpiked in 1770. The intriguing name, however, may refer back to the custom of children dancing round the stone at Rogationtide as part of the annual Beating the Bounds ceremony.

In the parish of Stockton beside the Norwich to Beccles road is a boundary stone of such importance – payment was made in the 17th century according to the parish records for 'putting stones (posts) to Stockton Stone' – that it was known to be cursed. The prophesy that anyone moving the stone would suffer some dreadful misfortune came true in the 1930s when a workman collapsed and died while the road was being realigned. Any taboo against removing the Hingham Stone beside Mr Houchin's pork butcher's shop, where for centuries it had been used as a mounting block, was lifted in 1911. To celebrate the 275th anniversary of the founding of Hingham, Massachusetts, by Puritans from the Norfolk market town, including a forefather of Abe Lincoln, the occasion was marked by an exchange of boulders with all the civic pomp the two towns could muster. The glacial erratic became the centrepiece of a new memorial tower at a ceremony attended by the British Ambassador and two years later a large granite boulder arrived on the green in Hingham to great acclaim as the band played, the bunting fluttered and the church bells rang out over the roof tops.

'he Hingham Stone

ROLLING STONES

Reports from elsewhere suggest the sound of bells once played a more supernatural role in the movement of stones. At Oxborough a stone was said to run (perhaps roll) across the road when the bells of Caldecote church struck midnight, a belief that must go back centuries because St Mary's had become disused by the early 15th century and profaned in 1603. There is nothing visible today. In 1948 an elderly resident in the adjoining parish of Cockley Cley recalled, when young, 'how frightened we children were of a certain milestone on the Gooderstone road which turned round ... when the Swaffham church bells chimed.'[4] At Sheringham two stones placed outside a barn were believed to run across the road when the cock crowed, and somewhere on the 'Isle' of Flegg a dole stone, or boundary marker, would go down at midnight to drink from a nearby stream. A more elaborate version in Lowestoft involved a heap of stones, once part of an Elizabethan beacon that, unless bathed in fire, rushed down for a dip in the sea while the town hall clock struck midnight.

In such cases the progression of stones is often in response to the sound of bells, not a celebratory daytime peal but the chimes at midnight, an auspicious time when supernatural forces were abroad, when inanimate objects acquired the power of movement. These scraps of local lore may refer back to a time when Christianity triumphed over the old religion, when natural objects worshipped by pagan gods were obliged to dance to a new tune. There is, after all, a tradition that Caldecote church was raised on the site of a temple to the goddess Diana, a tradition strengthened by the amount of Roman activity identified nearby, including the sites of at least two villas.

The Druid's Stone, St Mary's, Bungay

DRUID STONES

Just over the county boundary in the churchyard of St Mary's, Bungay, is a granite boulder known variously as the Druid's Stone, the Devil's Stone and the Giant's Grave to suit a range of beliefs as to its origin and purpose. One belief is that if young women, having danced round or knocked on the stone twelve times, then put their ears to it, their wishes will be answered. In another variant children would dance seven times round the stone on a certain day (date and time unspecified) and wait for the Devil to appear. It is not clear how, if at all, this legendry stone is related to the well known tale of Black Shuck associated with St Mary's (p192).

There are also reports of stones built into the foundations of medieval churches that raise the possibility of earlier pagan worship. A large boulder underpinning a corner of the Saxo-Norman church at Newton-by-Castle Acre and another at the base of the south aisle, were exposed during repair work in the 1970s, and conglomerates or pudding stones are said to lie beneath the tower of St Michael's, Ingoldisthorpe. In each case it may simply have been expedient for masons to use large stones that lay nearby. Alternatively boulders weighing several tons were not just unusual but may have been sacred or ritual objects before the arrival of Christianity. What better way to heed Pope Gregory's advice to St Augustine that heathen temples should not be destroyed but ritually cleansed and adapted for worship, than to incorporate these altars of the old religion in the very foundations of the new church. But why was the stone, discovered in 1855 at St Mary's, Holme-next-the Sea, removed to the churchyard? Was it to demonstrate the triumph of Good over Evil in response to rumours of a Druids' Stone and pagan sacrifice among members of the congregation who still clung to the old ways? Something of this kind may also explain the large sandstone boulder outside the porch of St Andrew's, Wellingham, or perhaps it was placed there *because* of its protective powers.

acial boulder outside, lingham church porch

Foundation stone, Newton-by-Castle Acre

WAYSIDE CROSSES

For most country people glacial boulders remained objects of wonder in a world governed by supernatural forces that sat uneasily alongside emblems of the new religion in what Nicola Whyte has called 'a palimpsest of references'.[5] Like boundary stones roadside crosses were often used as parish markers, or as preaching stations for pilgrims on their way to the great monastic centres. Placed symbolically at crossroads, on hilltops or at river crossings they became part of a network of religious sites – shrines, holy wells and chapels – leading the sick and the penitent to Walsingham, to Binham and to Bromholm. These new structures, fashioned from the same Jurassic rock from which many of the erratic boulders originated, were cut from Barnack stone quarried near Peterborough and transported along the waterways to build the great Marshland churches. Glinting in the sun when new these slender cream columns of stone soon weathered to a dull grey and required frequent coats of limewash to remain conspicuous; many were called Whitecross for this reason. Over tracts of open land like the Breckland heaths crosses erected on low hills were visible for miles around – in 1720 Tom Martin noted the remains of one on a hill between Weeting and Methwold and another survives on Cross Hill in Feltwell. In a landscape dotted with Bronze Age burials these low hills were often round barrows. In this way their use 'evokes a powerful Christian metaphor, the Hill of Golgotha', where one 'place of the skull' replaces another more ancient repository.

The earliest structures, like the circular head of a rare Saxon cross found in Whissonsett churchyard in 1902, were often the initial focal points for outdoor worship. In remote outposts like Terrington St John this practice continued until 1423 when Peykes Cross was eventually replaced by a chapel of ease. The dedication of churches like Holy Cross at Caston may refer to a similar process. Crosses not only helped to define the parish as an ecclesiastical unit but the structure that gave its name to Barnham Cross Common marked the boundary between the liberties of the abbey at Bury St Edmunds and the Thetford diocese. Detached portions of land held by the great monastic houses were identified by crosses in parishes like Great Witchingham where Bennet Cross (corrupted to Ben's Cross by the 19th century) denoted land held by St Benet's Abbey. In the same way the manor in Edgefield owned by Binham Priory was commemorated on Cross Green.

Saxon cross, Whissonsett

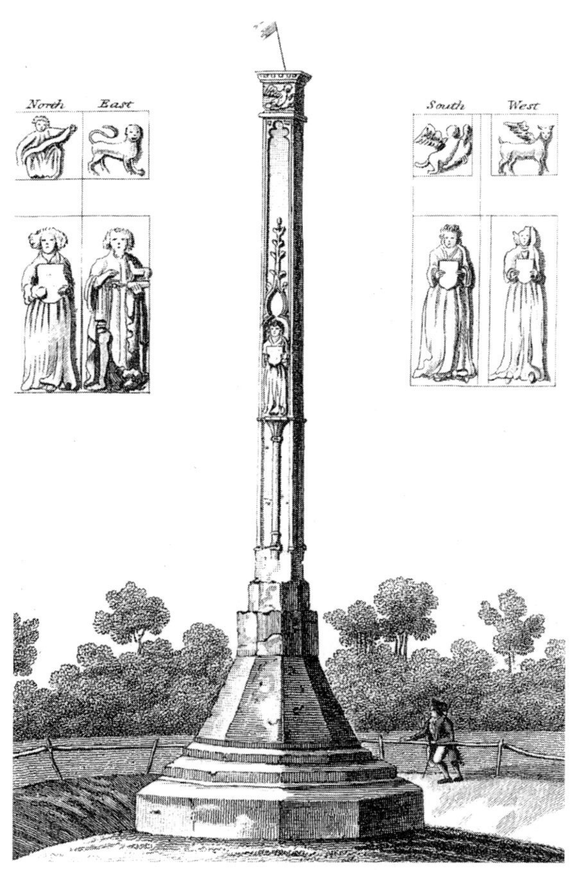

c15 market cross in the park to Langley Hall

Medieval market cross, Feltwell

Wayside crosses may have deepened the religious experience, sanctifying the paths taken by those in search of miracles, but for the majority who put their trust in a mixture of herbal remedies and sympathetic magic these markers were expressions of a faith they only dimly recognised. A religion that offered only a remote prospect of salvation imposed a more immediate burden on the working poor in the form of tithes, fines and other obligations. In the aftermath of the Reformation the whole edifice of Catholic doctrine was systematically dismantled; churches stripped of idolatrous effigies, monasteries pillaged for their stone and left to rot and chapels abandoned or used as barns. Torn down, defaced and devoid of religious significance, the remaining stump crosses became little more than topographic references in a landscape of secular ownership and territorial disputes.

Crosses on the green – those at Binham and Castle Rising are impressive survivals – remained the centrepieces of village life around which the weekly market and seasonal festivities were held. These commonplace structures have seldom become the subject of local lore except for the 15th century Langley Cross which originally stood on the green just outside the abbey precinct and, like the one at Binham, had been erected by the abbey to raise revenue from market tolls. Following the Dissolution, tales began to circulate concerning the misuse of monastic property. In the 1630s the antiquarian and Catholic apologist, Sir Henry Spelman, was quick to draw attention to the many tragedies that had befallen those Norfolk families who had profited from the redistribution of monastic land. In 1801, incensed by the decision of Lady Beauchamp Proctor to reposition the cross in the grounds of Langley Hall, there were those in the village who prophesied its removal would result in a fire at the hall. What amounted to a thinly veiled threat came true when smoke was seen billowing from one of the corner towers. As Simpson and Westwood have argued, by the time the gentry decided to 'safeguard' the cross – it now stands remote and inaccessible in the park marking the spot where four parishes meet – the villagers were simply adapting old beliefs to meet a new threat to what had, over the years, become a cherished landmark.

Parish boundary stor
Beachamwell

The stub cross at some lonely crossroads is the kind of liminal place where at dusk one might expect to encounter a headless monk or Black Shuck or Old Nick himself but the written records and the oral evidence are curiously silent on the matter. Unlike more substantial remnants of the Catholic faith – monastic remains and abandoned churches – wayside crosses do not feature prominently in the folklore of religious sites. The remains of two crosses at Tilney All Saints, known as Hickathrift's Candlesticks, have become part of the Fenland giant's story (p121) in the churchyard where he is traditionally buried but, broken up and overgrown, many others were soon forgotten. Even at Aylmerton it is not the cross but the passage said to run beneath it (p83) that is the subject of long held belief.

THE GREENWOOD TREE

Green man misericord,
Norwich cathedral

SACRED TREES

Those elements of the natural world associated with the old gods were once worshipped by tribal societies throughout western Europe and it was the oak, above all other trees, that became revered for its strength and longevity. Ancient bog oaks dredged from the Norfolk Fens, some up to 5000 years old, and the Bronze Age monument known as Seahenge, discovered on the north Norfolk coast in 1998, are witness to the tree's durability. The inverted bole of the 'henge', set within a circle of split oak posts, would appear to have been either a funerary enclosure or perhaps a monument to the tree itself. The oak was also sacred to the Druids and central to their religious rites, especially those rare specimens that bore the mistletoe, symbol of eternal life and renowned for its healing qualities. It was in an oak grove that Boudica offered up sacrifices to her goddess Andrasta (Victory) before leading the Iceni into battle against the might of the Roman empire. A set of Early Saxon 'druid's beads' was found in an oak tree at Old Buckenham when it was taken down in the early 19th century. A drawing of the find exists in the British Museum but the exact nature and location of this discovery are uncertain. It is rather more clear from place name evidence that trees, either as isolated specimens or in woodland clearances, were of great symbolic importance to early settlers both as points of reference in the landscape and as sacred places of assembly. In Norfolk trees large and small were recognised in this way, from more unusual shrubs like box in a grove at Bixley and the blackthorn clearing at Sloley to 'the meeting place under the ash tree' (Matlaske) and the oak grove clearly visible to Saxon adventurers approaching across the Great Estuary to settle at Acle. Although the tree has gone the church of St Martin-at-Oak in Oak Street, Norwich, is, like St Michael-at-Thorn (p63), testament to the ability of Christianity to absorb elements of the old religion.

Seahenge, Holme-next-the Sea

The ash grove at Ashill and the ash stream at Ashwellthorpe are reminders that, while the oak was also sacred to the Norse god Thor, it was the great ash tree Yggdrasill that became central to the Viking world. Beneath its roots flowed the spring of Minir, the source of wisdom, and from its branches Odin, pierced with a spear, hanged himself for nine days and nights to obtain the secret of the runes. This image of the suffering pagan deity is not unlike that of the crucifixion or the martyrdom of East Anglia's St Edmund (p113), tied to a tree and shot through with arrows by his Danish persecutors. In medieval manuscripts Christ is usually portrayed on a cross made from planks or lopped branches but in the psalter of Robert de Lindsey, early 13th century Abbot of Peterborough, the cross is in full leaf and covered with red and white flowers. Here the cross is both the instrument of sacrifice and a symbol of renewal, the Tree of Life itself. The foliate cross had become a popular motif on coffin lids by the late middle ages but one of the earliest and most elaborate is the 13th century grave slab in Fordham church on the edge of the Fens. The stem, with leafy sprigs, ends in the jaws of a twin-bodied dragon, a motif rare on crosses of this design that may be both a symbol of evil and a visual pun on John of Wormegay. He was vicar here in 1278 and this may be his grave slab. By the 15th century the trilobed leaf design was typical of processional crosses like the rare survival discovered in a house near the Suffolk border in 2009 that may have been hidden during the Reformation.

c13 grave slab with foliate cross, Fordham

In East Anglia and elsewhere there was a belief among country people that the True Cross was made not from one of the forest trees but from the elder. Because of this it would never be struck by lightning and was often grown near cottages as protection against both thunderbolts and witchcraft. In some places though, despite the medicinal properties of elderflower tea and elderberry wine, the plant was considered to be evil and, like its hedgerow companion the hawthorn, it was unlucky to bring the flower indoors or burn the wood in the hearth where it would often spit. The reason for this may also have had a basis, however unlikely, in the belief that Judas hanged himself from an elder tree. Most woodland trees, while sacred to the gods, seldom feature in traditional folk remedies, although a form of imitative magic associated with the ash was widely held to be a cure for hernia among young children. The wood splits cleanly and once a young tree had been cleft and wedged open the ill child was passed through the space. The sapling was then bound up tightly and as it healed so the hernia would disappear, providing the tree was not cut down while the child lived. Details of the ritual vary from one district to another so that in the Pulhams the child was to be naked and the practice carried out three times with its head towards the rising sun.

Elder,
Sambucus nigra

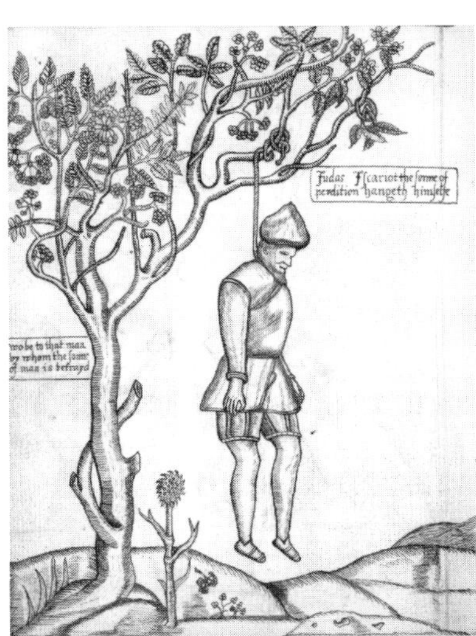

Judas hanged from an elder tree,
Booke of diverse devices and sortes of pictures,
Thomas Fella, c1585-1622

THE GREEN MAN

From remote churches to cathedral cloisters the face that peers out from behind a mask of vegetation is among the most haunting and enigmatic expressions of medieval craftsmanship. Following the publication of *The Golden Bough* in 1922, Sir James Frazer's seminal work on religion and mythology, this figure became the embodiment of pagan nature worship, a symbol of fertility and renewal inhabiting the very fabric of the Christian church. This attempt to interpret evidence in terms of the distant past was part of a more general interest in aspects of folk culture fashionable at the time that saw the appearance of an article in the journal *Folklore* by Lady Raglan in May 1939. In it she coined the phrase 'Green Man' for the first time and it caught the popular imagination – the term 'Foliate Head' favoured by art historians never had the same resonance. Lady Raglan took the name from the number of Green Man inns around the country, especially in East Anglia, although the name did not appear on inn signs until the 17th century. She also used in evidence the figure popular in English pageantry known variously as the Green Man, Jack-in-the-Green and Robin Hood, but in giving birth to the Green Man she appears to have relied more on inspiration than persuasive argument.

Green man, sedilia, Weston Longeville

Green man, sedilia, Thompson

The figure has its origins in classical antiquity; in deities like Pan, Bacchus and the Roman sea god Oceanus depicted on the great Roman silver dish from Mildenhall with seaweed trailing from his beard, but the image we know from 10th century illuminated manuscripts reached these shores from the sculptural forms of Romanesque France. Baptism is the first great rite of passage in the Christian church and on the font the image is both a symbol of rebirth and a protective figure ensuring the safe journey of the unbaptised child. In Norfolk the Green Man first appears on an important group of Norman fonts; in the remote little church at Shernborne in the north west of the county where each face of the bowl is richly decorated round a central, barbaric mask, and at Breccles on the edge of Breckland. Here the 12th century font is adorned with a matching pair of stylised faces and big leaf foliage. While far less common than in other parts of the country like Devon and the Midlands that were once more heavily forested, the foliate head does appear elsewhere in Norfolk, especially in those naturalistic forms associated with Gothic architecture. Most evident are the little faces on the Decorated chancel sedilias at Weston Longville and Thompson. At Weston leaves sprout from one mouth, an impish tongue from another with leaves like horns, while the third image is a man in tunic and tights holding a spray of vine leaves in one hand and oak in the other. In this single composition the Green Man is transformed from nature spirit into May Day reveller or Rogationtide celebrant.

Green men, c12 font, Breccles

en man, c15 south porch, Great Moulton

Elsewhere the image of the Green Man is only occasionally visible; embracing the porch at Great Moulton and the rood screen panels at Wilton on the edge of the Fens. At Scottow he looks down from a roof boss in the porch of All Saints' church, a rare example of its kind in the Norfolk countryside but one for which Norwich Cathedral is justly famous. As both a structural and stylistic innovation in the 14th century ribbed vaulting provided the stone mason with numerous possibilities in the shape of the roof boss, the keystone that hold the ribs together. The thousand or more bosses in the cathedral represent one of the great achievements in medieval art, a series of stories in stone, both biblical and allegorical, in which the Green Man appears, not visibly in the main body of the cathedral, but always round the edges like the marginalia of illuminated manuscripts. He is there on the Ethelbert Gate and in the cloisters where some of the finest examples are to be found along the east range. Here the earliest are foliage bosses – oak, ivy and field maple – and the haunting image of a human face behind a mask of gilded hawthorn leaves, one of several alongside saints and scenes from the Apocalypse. Inside the cathedral and hidden away, the misericord seats in the choir enabled medieval craftsman to indulge his preference for the bawdy and the grotesque. The Green Men here display both aspects of this equivocal image; the one a beautiful young face luxuriantly wreathed in leaves in the spirit of springtime; the other, crudely finished with crossed eyes and leaves curling from either side of bared teeth, is a more disturbing embodiment of evil.

Green man & foliate roof boss,
Norwich cathedral cloisters

Among the array of choir stall creatures are several club-wielding Wild Men or Wodewose, subduing a lion in one tableau and fighting together in another. Deep-rooted in medieval iconography these Herculean figures, crowned and belted with leaves and covered in hair, became the epitome of brute force. By the 15th century they had begun to appear elsewhere in church architecture; above the west door at Cawston in combat with a dragon, astride the parapet of Pulham St Mary's sumptuous south porch, and part of a protective alliance with benign looking lions around the base of fonts in places like Acle, Happisburgh, Ludham and Salthouse. As a symbol of strength they became a popular heraldic device, prominent supporters on the arms of one of Norfolk's oldest families, the Wodehouses, – motto 'Frappe fort' or 'Beat down the fort' – on display in Kimberley church and in plaster above the fire-place at Lodge Farm, Bawburgh, a 17th dower house for Grizell Wodehouse. By

Wildman and dragon,
Cawston south transept

the late 16th century guests in Wild Men costumes had begun to appear in courtly masques and as whifflers at civic pageants like the annual St George's guild procession through Norwich (p229) where it was their responsibility to clear a way for the main event. At this stage the two traditions of Wild Man and Green Man were almost indistinguishable but for one thing. The role of the Wild Man was more that of sober doorman, exemplified by the well known statues – originally 17c – guarding the entrance to the Samson and Hercules House in Tombland, Norwich. The Green Man – 'pleasantly stupefied, whereas the Wild Man was merely stupid'[1]– was by now the warm-up act, a Bacchanalian figure entertaining the crowds. Not surprisingly he was adopted by ale houses and distilleries as their logo. Many of the Green Man inns that Lady Raglan noticed in East Anglia have disappeared; in Norfolk there is still a Green Man Lane in Kirstead but the tavern marked on Faden's Map (1797) is long gone. More recently the Briston Green Man has been rebranded the Explorer Bar but the traditional name survives for pubs in Little Snoring, Rackheath and Methwold Hythe.

Wild Man, c17 illustration

Rococo plaster frieze, Gateley Hall

With the Reformation and an abrupt halt to church building, images of the Green Man, already less fashionable by the 16th century, reappear briefly as a neo-classical motif in secular buildings like Gateley Hall. Here it assumes centre stage as a striking leaf mask on the Rococo plaster frieze. A renewed interest in the medieval world brought about by the Gothic Revival saw the re-emergence of the Green Man in some of the many churches restored in late 19th century Norfolk, including St Mary's, Redenhall, where huge Green Men gaze down over the congregation from the High Victorian organ case installed in 1897 for the Jubilee. By then the image had lost much of its potency but, whether pagan deity, May Day reveller or emblem of today's Green movement, the Green Man has been reinterpreted down the years to suit the needs of the time. The true meaning, if one exists, will forever remain a mystery.

THE DARK WOOD

Etched against the evening sky the Trysting Pine on Barnham Cross Common was both a place of secret assignations beneath its twisted branches and a welcome sight for weary travellers approaching Thetford across miles of barren heath. But for those remnants of ancient woodland that still covered parts of Norfolk the response to the natural world was far more ambiguous. Woodland formed an integral part of the local economy and was a valuable source of timber, alive to the sound of the axe and the hurdle maker's mallet, but at dusk, beyond the dying brushwood embers, the place would become eerily silent. Inhabited by thieves and creatures of the night, both real and imagined, the wood assumed a darker purpose lodged deep in the collective folk memory. Here the wildwood of fairy tale has always been a frightening prospect, a place of sacrifice and retribution.

In an attempt to transform St Benet's Abbey into a pilgrimage centre to rival Walsingham and Bromholm the monks invented the cult of St Margaret of Holm who, according to the medieval chronicler, was strangled nearby in the Little Wood at Hoveton St John in 1170. This barbarous act recalled to mind the crucifixion of the boy saint William of Norwich within living memory in 1144, whose body had been dumped in Thorpe Wood. In more recent times, when the death of a religious leader was no longer considered to be an act of martyrdom, the vicar of Starston – the Rev'd Whitear – died of his wounds in 1826 after he, with others from the village, had gone armed to confront poachers in Gawdyhall Big Wood. Far more macabre were the circumstances surrounding the death of Richard Nobbs in 1785. A few days before his son's skeleton had been discovered in a ditch at Tasburgh and displayed in the church, suspicion fell on the father who was later found hanging from a tree in Pope's Wood, Hempnall. The coroner's verdict was one of 'self-murder' and, like most suicides, he was buried on the parish boundary at the crossroads still known as Nobbs' Corner.

Until 1828 suicide was a sin in the eyes of the law and those poor souls driven to self-murder were required by law to be buried in the roadway, in unhallowed ground, as an example to others. Banished to the outskirts of the parish a stake was often used to prevent the outcast's restless spirit from rising up to haunt the place, a drastic measure that often proved counterproductive. Some years earlier another disturbing case from south Norfolk was reported in the local press. It concerned the suicide of Mary Turrel in 1813, buried in a lonely grave between Harleston and Redenhall near Gawdyhall Big Wood. Here a stake was driven through her body by the local policeman, the whole macabre ritual witnessed by onlookers and supervised by the Rev'd Oldershaw. The exact spot chosen for Turrel's final resting place was Lush's Bush, named after a previous suicide. The bush is said to have grown from the stake used to secure Lush's body. In a similar case Thomas Harvey, a Thetford joiner who had hanged himself, was buried at a crossroads south of the town in 1786, but the sorry tale soon passed into local folklore and became associated with a certain Chunk Harvey, known variously as a pirate (less likely as Thetford is well inland), or a highwayman. His grave beside the road to Euston was supposedly marked by a tree grown from the stake through his body. In one sense at least the stake through a criminal like Chunk Harvey is not so unlike the True Cross; from each sprouted the green shoots of life renewed.

It is perhaps surprising that the bloody deeds for so long associated with ancient woodland are not more widely reflected in the folklore of the county, but at Foxley ('woodland clearing frequented by foxes') the ragged staff emblem of the Grey family carved above the south porch of the church it helped finance is linked in local legend to an incident in Foxley Wood. The motif is reputedly the badge of a strong man who rescued the king from a wild beast while out hunting in the wood by slaying the animal with a branch ripped from a nearby tree. The story, which might just be rooted in truth, is more likely to have arisen by way of explaining the armorial bearings of the Grey family, lords of the manor here throughout the 15th century. Listed in *Domesday Book* when the wood was far more extensive, it remains, at 123ha, the largest fragment of wildwood in Norfolk with a long history of coppicing and an exceptionally rich ground flora.

pped branch emblem, south porch, Foxley

Babes in the Wood and the Two Villains, c17 woodcut

Victorian illustration, *Babes in the Wood*

The most famous tale to emerge from the undergrowth and one of the few to be set specifically in Norfolk is 'Babes in the Wood', although elements of the tale – the wicked uncle, children abandoned in a wood and heartless ruffians – have their origins in the European folk tradition, in tales like 'Hansel and Gretel'. But in 1595, with the publication of the broadside ballad 'The Two Children in the Wood' by Norwich printer Thomas Millington, the story is transformed from classic fairytale to local legend. Retold in chapbooks, plays and children's books the tragedy became associated with Wayland Wood near Watton which, like Foxley Wood, is a remnant of the wildwood. The name 'Waneland', recorded in *Domesday Book*, is derived in part from the Viking *lundre* or 'sacred grove' and, long before Millington's ballad, the place had already acquired a sinister reputation. Corrupted to 'Wailing Wood' it soon echoed to the mournful cries of children left to die by one of the two villains employed to murder them. Having killed his accomplice the remaining villain goes in search of food, never to return, swallowed up perhaps by the wood. And so:

These pretty babes, with hand in hand
Went wandering up and down,
But never more could see the man
Approaching from the town.
Their pretty lips with blackberries
Were all besmear'd and dyed
And when they saw the darksome night
They sat them down and cried.

Thus wandered these poor innocents
Till death did end their grief
In one another's arms they died
As wanting due relief
No burial this pretty pair
Of any man receives
Till Robin Redbreast piously
Did cover them with leaves.

Merton Hall and gatehouse, home of the de Greys, early c19 engraving

The story has also become associated with a scandal involving the Catholic de Grey family whose ancestral seat, Merton Hall, lies just a mile south of Wayland Wood. Here in 1562, following the death of his father, young Thomas de Grey was made a ward of court but died soon after on a visit to his stepmother at the tender age of eleven. Rumours spread rapidly among the locally Protestant population that the boy had been murdered and suspicion fell on Thomas' uncle, Robert de Grey, who stood to inherit his nephew's property. The uncle, a Popish recusant, died at Merton in 1601 having served time in a debtor's prison for failing to pay the fines incurred by refusing to attend Church of England services. Griston Old Hall had been purchased by the de Greys in 1541 and, together with its position on the edge of Wayland Wood, has traditionally been home to the wicked uncle who, according to the ballad, also died in penury, deserted by his sons, his property destroyed:

Babes in the Wood,
marble sculpture, John Bell, c1842

Griston Old Hall, early c20

His barns were fired, his goods consum'd
His lands were barren made,
His cattle died within the field,
And nothing with him staid.

In the late 19th century elderly locals could still remember seeing, when young, a carved overmantel in Griston Old Hall depicting scenes from the story that may have been installed when the place was substantially rebuilt by its new owner Thomas May. According to the date plaque above the door this was in 1597, just after the publication of 'The Two Children in the Wood'. A final postscript to this 'Lamentable Tragedy' occurred in 1879 when the massive oak in Wayland Wood with a girth of 36 feet, beneath which the children were said to have perished, was itself destroyed by a lightning strike. Folk came 'from far and wide' to witness the shattered remains and claim a piece of their heritage. In the 1950s Lord Walsingham (the barony was created in 1780) might have been forgiven for thinking that his Merton estate, like that of his 'wicked uncle', was cursed. Several thousand acres had been requisitioned by the Ministry of Defence on a broken promise that the land would be returned after the war. What remained included some of the most impoverished soil in the Brecks and, if that wasn't sufficient retribution for the sins of the family, the Elizabethan Hall was destroyed by fire in 1956.

Babes in the Wood, town sign

Unlike the tale of Hansel and Gretel there is no happy ending for Norfolk's babes in the wood. These innocent victims, abandoned to their fate, were destined to wander through the undergrowth until, lost and exhausted, they laid down to die. There is no redemption, the wood exacts its revenge against a backdrop of religious intolerance, superstition and peasant unrest ('his barns were fired'). For years after the two ruffians were said to haunt the wood and were likely to come for any child who misbehaved. Even today when the wind howls through the tree tops you may still hear the anguished cry of young children deep in the heart of 'Wailing Wood'.

THE HAWTHORN

The hawthorn (*Crataegus monogyna*), or whitethorn, has acquired more local names and supernatural attributes than almost any tree in the English countryside. In Norfolk it was known variously as the May-bush and among children as the May bread-and-cheese tree because of its edible young leaves. Throughout western Europe the hawthorn was a magical tree but why should this scrub-like bush, hardly a tree at all, have become so iconic? The mass of white blossom – 'the risen cream of all the milkiness of May'[2] – and its stale, sweet scent, together with its blood red berries of the autumn hedgerows; and the belief, long held from classical literature, that Christ's crown was made from hawthorn, have given this most common plant an almost cult-like status. Small shrub-like trees – rowan, elderberry, whitethorn and holly among them – had been quick to colonise open ground in the immediate aftermath of woodland clearance and became familiar features in the emerging agricultural landscape of prehistoric Britain. These bushes, heavy with white blossom, heralded the onset of spring and the berries, blood red and dark purple by turn, were an expression both of nature's bounty and of harvest safely gathered in. Little wonder they became symbols of the farming year.

Hawthorn, (Mattioli, 1562)

The most widespread belief associated with the plant, both in Norfolk and elsewhere, was that it was unlucky to bring the blossom indoors on account of its 'decadently sweet odours'[3] – and that to do so would bring illness and even death to the family. At all other times the 'death-stench of the hawthorn'[4] as Sylvia Plath has it, was banished from the home. This 'sweet enchanting smell of death'[5] comes from the trimethylamine in the flower, a chemical also given off during the decay of human flesh. As a result it was thought to carry the stench of the plague and the smell would have been familiar in the days when corpses were laid out at home before burial. For some the fishy scent has also about it the smell of sex and may help explain why it was 'a plant kept outdoors, associated with unregulated love in the fields rather than conjugal love in the bed'.[6] For country people hawthorn blossom carried with it the smell both of procreation *and* of putrefaction, of birth and death, and was heavy with symbolism.

With its tangle of thorns and rampant growth the plant produced an effective stock-proof barrier and was a key element in parliamentary enclosures of the 18th and 19th centuries. A new pattern of rectangular fields bounded by straight quickthorn hedges became synonymous with the great improving estates like Holkham and Houghton in north Norfolk, birthplace of the agricultural revolution. At the same time it became a symbol of oppression for the dispossessed who saw their homes destroyed and their common rights extinguished. Until then the whitethorn was just one species among many in the old pre-enclosure hedgerows or a focal point on open ground where it might serve as a meeting point or boundary marker.

t Michael-at-Thorn, Norwich

This could explain the origin of the church in Ber Street, Norwich, and its unusual dedication. Here on a windswept hillside overlooking the Yare valley a lone whitethorn tree, perhaps where the old gods were worshipped, would have been a prominent landmark to early Christian settlers arriving upstream. Anxious to supplant the old religion a new church took shape nearby dedicated to the dragon-slaying saint, St Michael-at-Thorn. James Grigor in 1841 recorded a thorn tree in the churchyard 'which bears the mark of great antiquity' but a German bomb in WWII destroyed both the church and the tree. South of the city the Thickthorn service station owes its name to the moated site of Alan de Thickthorn's 13th century manor but travel further south and there at the end of a narrow country lane in the parish of Bracon Ash stands the isolated church of All Saints', Hethel. The village has gone, visible only as crop marks in the adjoining field. This in itself is not unusual, there are many deserted villages in Norfolk 'By reason of pestilences and mortalities, barrenness of lands, ruin of buildings, the malice of times,' but what makes Hethel so special is not the church, originally Norman like its tower, but a rather arthritic thorn bush in the middle of a nearby meadow which has claim to be the oldest in East Anglia.

There is no longer a 'heather covered hill' (Old English *haeth* + *hyll*) in this flat clayland from which the Saxon name Hethel is derived, it more likely refers to a pre-historic burial mound, levelled by the plough over the centuries. Elsewhere in Norfolk round barrows were often used by the local Saxon elders as meeting places when the Hundred Court or moot hall was held out of doors. Hethel Old Thorn is on a slight rise and may have taken root or been deliberately planted on an artificial mound where it became venerated over the years. Hethel was part of an important Saxon estate and the thorn may have featured as a boundary marker – it was already described as 'old thorn' in an early 13th century charter. According to tradition it was a place where local peasants gathered during their revolt against King John. Today a combination of farm tracks and footpaths – at least six – converge here linking early moated halls to this pagan site and its Christian successor built nearby.

By the mid 18th century the Hethel Thorn had already achieved celebrity status among arboriculturalists when the Norfolk naturalist and correspondent of Gilbert White, Robert Marsham, measured its girth in excess of nine feet. A century later and it had increased to fourteen feet according to James Grigor who described the bush covered in lichen and crowned with mistletoe as 'one of our vegetable patriarchs' in his *Remarkable Trees* (1841). The etching, one of several by Norwich School artist Henry Ninham which illustrates the book, shows its branches propped up on oak supports. In 1856 the *Gentleman's Magazine* reported that in a neighbourhood rich in old thorns the trunk of the Hethel Thorn had been 'reduced to a mere shell'. Soon after it split into several pieces but continued growing. Older residents could still remember children gathering boughs of blossom and who, after dancing round the maypole on May Day, would then run to the thorn and count the number of props. With its mass of tangled branches outstretched like so many long bony fingers, the bush has long been known as the Witch of Hethel. As a macabre postscript one of the field paths leading to the thorn runs through the woods from Potash Farm, home of the notorious murderer James Rush who in 1841, shot his landlord in nearby Stanfield Hall. Despite this the Hethel Thorn remains a symbol of regeneration and a thing of wonder, now at least a thousand years old and, since 1961, Norfolk Wildlife Trust's smallest nature reserve.

The Hethel Thorn, Henry Ninham etching, 1841

VENERABLE OAKS

Despite its majestic size and great age only a few remnants of folklore still cling to the oak tree in Norfolk. The 19th century arboriculturalist James Grigor refers to one such tree, a shattered landmark on Crostwick Common near the church which had been 'struck no less than three times by a *thunderbolt*'.[7] The claim that under its branches a 'Queen of England' once held court may have been prompted by Elizabeth I's progression through Norfolk in 1578 although she never ventured north of Norwich. By the 1920s this same tree had become the subject of an equally strange royal prophecy.

According to the travel writer Christopher Marlowe 'a miller with three thumbs shall hold three kings' horses [here] during the progress of a great battle' in the course of which 'nearly every man in the county shall be killed.'[8]

Ashwellthorpe Hall

The most intriguing piece of folklore is contained in the Ballad of Ashwell-thorpe and refers not to the original ash from which the place takes its name but a magical oak tree. First recorded in Blomefield's *History of Norfolk* (1739) the tale is much older, set in the moated hall during the time of its Elizabethan owner, Sir Thomas Knyvet, a man renowned for his hospitality. Here, on Christmas Eve, while the lord of the manor is entertaining guests in the great hall the feast is interrupted by the arrival of a stranger from London. He asks not for sustenance but offers to perform a trick in front of the assembled company. From his pocket he produces a magic acorn which he places on the floor. From it springs a mighty tree and, filling the hall, it sheds acorns both black and brown. Having expressed his amazement at the oak's miraculous growth Sir Thomas requests it be removed but the stranger appears unable to reverse the trick. Two workmen eventually manage to fell the tree but have not the strength to carry it out and, to their shame, the stranger summons two goslings 'young and green' to complete the task leaving no trace of the magic tree. Although the hall was largely rebuilt in the 19th century it still contains fragments of Sir Thomas' brick mansion and, it is said, geese still swim in the moat. While the story has echoes of fairytale and, at least initially, of *Sir Gawain and the Green Knight*, the Ballad of Ash-well-thorpe is a tale briefly told in which older folklore motifs appear to have been grafted on to the visit of a travelling illusionist to the home of a man recently knighted by his queen.

Until well into the 20th century the festival on May 29th, known as Oak Apple Day, was regarded as a public holiday to celebrate the restoration of the monarchy in 1660. Central to the event in Aylsham, which extended over two days, was the parade of

Friendly Societies through the town while oak boughs were hung in cottage porches and from church towers. Oak sprigs were worn as a sign of loyalty to the crown and as an emblem of the Boscobel Oak in which Charles II took refuge from Cromwell's troops after the Battle of Worcester in 1651. Those who chose not to wear a sprig risked being pinched, kicked or whipped with nettles. As the fame of the Boscobel Oak spread so ancient oaks elsewhere became associated with the monarch's flight and throughout the land inns and taverns adopted the name of the Royal Oak, including those in Norfolk at Bintree (Old English Bynna's tree) and Poringland, made famous by John Crome's *Poringland Oak* (1822). While there are no King Charles oaks in the county there is a oak in the park to Heydon Hall where Cromwell, without his New Model Army, is said to have sought refuge from an angry bull while visiting his lawyer, Erasmus Earle. The tale, intended to portray the great Protector in a poor light, may well have been spread abroad by local Royalist sympathisers.

Kett's Oak, Hethersett

Arguably the best known tree in Norfolk and one that boasts a more plausible pedigree is decidedly unimpressive; the tree in question is Kett's Oak beside the old London turnpike in Hethersett where Robert Kett is said to have addressed his followers before their march on Norwich in 1549. Incensed by the enclosure of common land and their loss of precious grazing rights a group of local protesters had approached Kett, a Wymondham landowner, who became sympathetic to their cause. With their numbers swelled to some 12,000 disaffected rebels, Kett set up camp on Mousehold Heath and planned his attack on the city from beneath another landmark tree known as the Oak of Reformation. Although the rebellion was eventually quashed by the Earl of Warwick at Dussindale just outside the city and its leader hanged from the castle walls, Kett's reputation had, by the 19th century, been transformed from 'reviled symbol of rustic violence' to champion of the common people in a county renowned for its radicalism. Burdened by association, filled with concrete and propped up on crutches the arthritic specimen known as Kett's Oak is, at best, a replacement for the tree that stood here in Kett's day, one possibly grown from an acorn of the original tree. Ironically another tree, also known as Kett's Oak, which survives in the park to Ryston Hall, appears old enough. When Grigor visited in 1841 it was 'highly grotesque in its outline, and we have seldom seen a tree with so much of the fearful in its character'.[9] Despite this and the tradition that six of the rebels were hanged from its outstretched limbs, there appears to be no evidence that Kett or his men were ever active in west Norfolk.

Robert Kett beneath the Oak of Reformation, Mousehold Heath, 1549

Before the advent of Ordnance Survey maps trees played an important role in the definition of parish boundaries and were often marked out, quite literally, during the annual ceremony of Beating the Bounds. A perambulation of Alburgh parish in 1794 records how the assembled company went 'into the meadows up to the Great Oak' and then 'turned left across the field to a pollard Elm in the hedge'. A length of Peddars Way lined by oak trees which forms the boundary between Swaffham and Sporle parishes is still called Procession Way and elsewhere the Gospel Oak often marked the spot where the priest would read a passage from the bible.

By the late 18th century trees that might once have been the centrepiece of pagan ritual or local folktales were increasingly revered just for their size and majestic appearance. Like ivy-clad ruins these shattered relics of the natural world became objects of fascination, at least among those antiquarians in search of the picturesque. John Evelyn in his *Sylva* (1664) drew attention to the 'extraordinarily large and stately' linden (lime) tree in the parish of Deopham, felled in 1705, and the spring at its foot which, according to Blomefield, 'petrifies sticks, leaves etc'. Gnarled forest trees and veterans of medieval deer parks became things of wonder in the landscaped grounds of Norfolk's oldest estates. Great parkland specimens in places like Merton, Kimberley,

Procession Way-Peddars Way, Swaffham-Sporle parish boundary

Bayfield and Felbrigg were much admired by the curious while arboriculturalists like Grigor took measurements and made notes. His *Eastern Arboretum, a Register of Remarkable Trees, Seats, Gardens etc* (1847). became essential reading among the gentry. In Gunton Park the oak known as the King of Thorpe (70 feet tall and with a girth of 21.5 feet) was not only a source of pride to Lord Suffield but 'an object of veneration and awe' to local people, while the most celebrated tree in north Norfolk was the Bale Oak which stood on the green beside the church. Dead by the mid 19th century, its hollow trunk measured an enormous 36 feet in the round and was 'capable

Village sign, Bale

Ancient oak, Tharston

of containing with ease 20 men standing upright'. According to Blomefield 'a cobbler had his shop and lodge there of late and it is or was used for a swinestry' – the cobbler is commemorated on the village sign carved, appropriately, in oak. Planted as a replacement the grove of twelve holm oaks in front of the church is now one of the National Trust's smallest properties.

The Winfarthing Oak, 1841

Unlike the hedgerow oaks, said to have been planted in the 18th century to provide timber for Nelson's ships, these ancient pollards were often at least 500 years old. Several in south Norfolk were highlighted by contributors to *Norfolk and Norwich Notes and Queries* in 1898; a mighty oak chained together for support near the Chequers Inn at Tharston and Thwaite's Oak, an equally fine specimen and 'the pride of Tivetshall' visible from the London train. Soon after it was felled, the meadow ploughed and the tree carted away by a firm of church furnishers. Greater still, and a tree famous well beyond the county, was the Winfarthing Oak. It measured a massive 40 feet in circumference and was already hollow in 1836 when described in Taylor's *Arboretum et Fruticetum Britannicum* as 'a mere shell, a mighty ruin, blasted to a snowy white but ... magnificent in its decay.' It had the distinction of being the only tree identified on Faden's 1797 map of the county and, together with the Companion Oak in the adjoining field, was a remnant of Lord Arundel's medieval deer park and may well have been up to 800 years old. In the 19th century it became known as the Bible Oak, not for any lingering religious association but because it attracted so many visitors that a collecting box for the British and Foreign Bible Society was nailed to the tree. An inscription on the box read:

Ye who this venerable oak survey,
Which still survives through many a stormy day,
Deposit here your mite with willing hands,
To spread in foreign climes, through foreign lands,
The Sacred Volume, so divinely given,
Whose pages teach the narrow way to heaven.

A door cut in the trunk enabled the space inside to be used on one occasion for a meeting of the Parish Council. The shell survived until the 1950s when it finally collapsed, but the Winfarthing Oak lives on in nearby Diss in the shape of a sizeable specimen grown from an acorn together with enough saplings to plant an avenue in Toronto near the cathedral.

Venerable oak, Thursford

FIELDS OF GOLD

GIANTS AND DRAGONS

The Celtic realms of Arthurian legend have their stronghold among the wild, rocky outcrops of Cornwall, Wales and northern Britain; a world of giants, dragons and shape shifting demons who terrorised the land but who have seldom set foot in Norfolk. There *was* a real life giant in the shape of Robert Hale, born at West Somerton in 1820, who grew to a height of 7 feet 6 inches and earned a living in Victorian freak shows, and Norfolk's own folk hero from the Fens, Tom Hickathrift (p118). Renowned for his great strength Tom defeated a club-wielding giant who dwelt in a cave and attacked those foolish enough to try and cross the expanse of marshland known as The Smeeth. Elsewhere the place name evidence, so often a clue to local folklore, is reduced to a single reference that raises more questions than it answers. The water filled moat stranded in a field outside Reepham was once the home of the powerful Kerdiston family. The medieval hall has long gone and the earthworks are no larger or more complex than many others dotted about the Norfolk countryside, but for some reason the moat was called Giant's Moat on the O S map, the legacy perhaps of an imaginative child or a story, since forgotten, passed down through the family. The county does have its own dragon tale, from Ludham (p104), few churches are without an image of one of the dragon-slaying saints popular in the middle ages, and in Snap, the dragon on display in Norwich Castle, the city has the last in a series of effigies used in the St George's Day procession. This is where the trail of the dragon goes cold apart from the record of a round barrow, once visible on the Sandringham estate which, according to the deeds, was called 'Drakenhowe' or Dragon's Mount. It was once widely believed that treasure lay buried beneath prominent earthworks but here the name has added resonance with echoes of the Saxon poem *Beowulf*.

This 8th century epic poem, written in Anglo Saxon England but set in the semi-mythical world of Scandinavia, contains a famous account of buried treasure in which the hero does battle with a fearsome dragon that has been terrorising the land. The beast is asleep in his lair – a barrow – guarding the hoard of treasure that lies within. Beowulf, determined to win the gold by his courage, eventually overcomes the dragon after a prolonged struggle, only to die of his wounds and enter the legendary world of his people. In the introduction to his 1999 translation of the poem Seamus Heaney stresses the importance of gold in the tribal land of the Geats:

> Gold is a constant element, gleaming solidly in the underground vaults, on the breasts of queens or the arms and regalia of warriors on the mead benches. It is loaded into boats as spoil, handed out in bent bars as hall-gifts, buried in earth as treasure, persisting underground as an affirmation of a people's glorious past and an elegy for it. It pervades the ethos of the poem and adds lustre to its diction.[1]

Purse, gold with cloisonne garnets, bird and animal motifs, Sutton Hoo Treasure

Silver interlace animals, maplewood bottle decoration, Sutton Hoo Treasure

According to his last wish, following his cremation on a funerary pyre, Beowulf's remains are buried in a mound on a headland along with his weapons and treasure hoard ready for his journey to the afterworld. In a memorable instance of life (or perhaps death) imitating art, the discovery of the Sutton Hoo ship burial overlooking the Deben estuary near Woodbridge in 1939 revealed a spectacular array of grave goods.

dragon, Roman parade helmet, Worthing

The burial, dating from the early 7th century, a hundred or more years before *Beowulf*, is probably the grave of Raedwold, King of East Anglia. In addition to his helmet and sword are fabulous decorative pieces – clasps, buckles, a purse containing 40 gold coins – and lavish preparation for a great feast in the after-life. Among the many exquisitely worked items of metalwork is a stylised dragon from the shield with four pairs of wings and jaws crammed with sharp teeth to protect the wearer in battle, much like the sea-dragon emblazoned on a Roman parade helmet dragged out of the Wensum at Worthing in 1947. As the legend of Beowulf and his exploits filtered down from the great Saxon mead halls so, over the years, it became embedded in the folk tradition of East Anglia. Despite growing evidence to the contrary burial mounds like the Drakenhowe barrow were believed to contain dragon hoards and across the land coin hoards lay just below the surface.

Roman jeweller's hoard, Snettisham

The allure of gold hidden in rocks deep underground – its purity, rarity and malleability – has made it the most desirable of precious metals, a symbol of wealth and status among successive cultures – Celts, Romans and Saxons – that have settled in Norfolk, bringing their treasure and metal-working skills with them. There was, at least until the late 19th century, a widespread belief that gold lay underfoot, not just the proverbial pot of gold said to be buried somewhere along the length of Peddars Way but tales of gold worked into shapes both fanciful and functional. The belief that the golden wheel of a chariot lay below an Aylsham field may have its roots in Iceni occupation while the golden plough that, according to the archaeologist Rainbird Clarke, lay beneath Bell Hill near Yarmouth has echoes of the folk tale 'The Ploughman and the Fairies' (p266).

Another lesson for those who find treasure is to remain silent about their good fortune. To do otherwise is to invite some form of supernatural retribution as both Joe Hobble, the main character in 'The Ploughman and the Fairies', and two 'adventurous men' in Southwood discovered to their cost. According to tradition an iron chest filled with gold lay at the bottom of Callow Pit, a water filled depression on the boundary between the parishes of Southwood and Moulton St Mary. The legend sheds no light on how and when the chest ended up in the pit but one year when the water was unusually low two local men managed to haul it out by passing an iron hook through the 'ringle' (ring) on the lid. Flushed with success and tempting fate, one of them shouted out 'We've got it safe and the Devil himself can't get it from us.' In an instance the surface of the pit was enveloped in a 'roke' (mist) and a strong smell of sulphur when a black hand broke the surface and grabbed the chest. After a desperate struggle the ringle was torn from the lid and the chest sank back down to the bottom, never to be seen again. As a reminder perhaps of their greed the two men fixed the ring to the door of Southwood church and there it remained until, later in the 19th century St Edmund's fell into disrepair and was abandoned. The ring was saved and is now the door handle to St Botolph's in the neighbouring parish of Limpenhoe, rebuilt in 1881-2. There are similarities between this tale and the legend of both the Shouldham Treasure (p36) and, closer to home, the Hell Hole legend and the fate of Tunstall's church bells (p97).

Door handle,
St Botolph's, Limpenh

EARTHWORKS

The burial mounds where treasure was believed to lie hidden were once a common sight across much of Norfolk. These, after all, were the resting places of tribal elders and warrior chiefs like Queen Boudica, buried with their finest possessions – jewellery, weapons and gold ornaments – to ensure safe passage to the afterlife. It was the prospect of finding wealth on this scale – wealth that would transform lives – that drove medieval hill diggers like John Cans and Robert Hikkes of Forncett to practice the dark arts (p81). By the 18th century, while dreams of gold among the rural poor were just as great, barrow digging had become something of a field sport among the local gentry which led them to plunder the graves of their ancestors in pursuit of 'antique relics'. The most exciting find, made at Little Cressingham in 1849, was from one of a group of Bronze Age barrows near the Icknield Way. Beside the crouched skeleton of a man with an amber bead necklace were a ribbed gold breast plate and three small gold boxes, the most spectacular discovery of 'Wessex Culture' grave goods in the region. The Bronze Age gold torc from Foulsham ploughed up in 1846 is now thought to have come from a barrow visible only from the air as a ring ditch. It is impossible to know what other valuables were destroyed or went unrecorded but the result of excavating a barrow on Harpley Common a few years earlier (1843) seems typical. Despite a local tradition that it contained treasure the burial mound revealed nothing more than some pottery and fragments of cremated bones.

Gold breast plate,
Bronze Age barrow,
Little Cressingham

In a landscape with few striking natural features those artificial structures, from Neolithic barrows to Saxon dykes, became part of an increasingly complex belief system but today much of what Trevor Ashwin has called 'the topographical drama of the landscape'[2] has been lost. Steep sided mounds and ditches thrown up by our ancestors have either been deliberately levelled, flattened by centuries of cultivation or degraded by the natural processes of wind and rain. Much of the destruction took place in the 19th century, especially on the larger, more progressive estates but often the names persist and with them a body of associated folk memory. The Iron Age fort at Bloodgate Hill overlooking the Burn valley in South Creake, circular in appearance like Warham Camp, was levelled in 1827, but as the name suggests, it was believed to have been the site of 'a dismal slaughter'. Despite the lack of archaeological evidence it is one of several places in the county where the local Saxon population is said to have clashed with Danish invaders. The explanation may, however, lie elsewhere; in the herb dwarf elder, known as danewort which has purple centred flowers and which, according to Camden, grew locally where Danes' blood had been spilt. The purging quality of the plant also produced the 'danes' or diarrhoea.

Danewort,
Mattioli, 1562

Bronze Age barrows, Harpley Common

As Thomas Browne observed 'man is a Noble Animal, splendid in ashes, and pompous in the grave'[3] and, until the arrival of Christianity, the preferred type of burial for warriors and the ruling elite remained the round barrow. In isolation or more often in large groups the barrow was an integral part of a complex mortuary landscape across much of Norfolk. Many of those beside the ancient tracks that traversed large areas of Breckland heath or were once clearly visible on top of the Cromer Ridge are now only discernible from the air as ring ditches on the face of the land. The most prominent of these sacred sites were often chosen as places of assembly where the courts of Saxon Hundreds met in the open air. The barrow known as Smithdon (Smoothdown) Hill, one of a group on Great Bircham Common, appears to have been chosen for its strategic position beside Peddars Way where the Hundreds of Smithdon, Docking and Freebridge met. The last remaining barrow north of the green at Gayton Thorpe called the Hill of Peace may also have been used as a moot convenient to the parishes which made up Freebridge Hundred. In South Norfolk the court of Forehoe Hundred met at 'Four Howes', or hills, in Carleton Forehoe while in Breckland the Hundred court of Grimshoe takes its name from the barrow known as Grim's Hoe just east of Grimes Graves; and Greenhoe (Greenhill) Hundred may also have convened at an important barrow cemetery.

Barrows occasionally assumed a more macabre reputation as places of execution, their steep sided profile providing an effective drop and their position at crossroads remote from settlements. Here the body, left to rot on the gibbet, would be a chilling reminder of the fate that awaited those who transgressed the law. The dramatic discovery in 1987 of the decapitated bodies of a large number of Saxon criminals dumped in the shallow ditch around one of a group of barrows at South Acre is a graphic illustration of vengeful justice meted out by the Hundred courts – the site was close to the boundary of South Greenhoe Hundred. This was the fate of places like Gallows Green in Forncett (p82), Dead Man Hill beside the Icknield Way at Bodney and Gallows Hill above Thetford. South of the town on a ridge formed by a loop of the Little Ouse stands Tutt's Hill. Now hidden among the shelter belts of Nunnery Stud this Bronze Age barrow was once a landmark on an expanse of windswept heath overlooking an important Saxon town ravaged by the Danes on several occasions in the 10th and 11th centuries. According to tradition the town's fortifications were only breached when a local shepherd called Tutt agreed to lead the invaders over marshy ground and across the river to a weak point in the town's defences. In return the shepherd, who had been promised his reward would be 'beyond his expectations', was strung up on the burial mound that bears his name. This tale, which first appeared in W G Clarke's *In Breckland Wilds* (1925), is a local variant on the theme of traitorous monks who led the Normans into Ely and Tutt's counterpart, the monk of St Benet's Abbey (p102).

Hangour Hill barrow, Beachamwell

Medieval graffito, St Mary's, Beachamwell

Although it may be a dialect version of Anchor Hill, the name Hangour Hill for one of several barrows in the large Breckland parish of Beachamwell suggests it may too have been a place of retribution. Standing beside the Roman road which heads west into the Fens the barrow is of particular interest to folklorists as one of the few features in Norfolk attributed to the Devil. There is, in the west of the county, a sequence of linear earthworks running north-south between rivers that date from the 6-7th century AD. Their purpose, as yet unclear, was either defensive, to guard against incursions from out of the Fens, or definitive between large Saxon estates. Long after their original purpose had been forgotten, earthworks on this scale were explained away as the Devil's work. There is a four mile stretch between the Thet and Little Ouse called Devil's Ditch and a ten mile length between the Nar and the Wissey called Devil's Dyke where, having accomplished his task, Satan is said to have created Hangour Hill by scraping the earth from his spade. Buried deep within the barrow is a pair of silver gates, one of several pairs said to have been hidden below ground in Norfolk (p82), that gave access to the underworld. The medieval graffito in Beachamwell church depicting a horned devil holding either a flail or an antler pick suggests that the memory of his exploits were lodged deep in the community.

The attribution of landscape features, natural or otherwise, to the devil was not uncommon in the absence of any rational explanation. In 1836, on the first edition of the O S map, the horseshoe enclosure north of Wayford Bridge in Stalham was identified as another Devil's Ditch, as a Roman camp on a later edition and more recently as a natural feature destroyed by gravel pits. The smallest of Breckland's mysteriously fluctuating meres is the perfectly round and steep-sided expanse of water known as the Devil's Punchbowl just south of the old drove road 'over which on dank autumn evenings' a pall of mist known as the Devil's Nightcap may form. In central Norfolk

Castle Hill, Thetford, early 20c

on the boundary between Corpusty and Itteringham stands Mossey Mere Wood and here, on its boggy southern edge is a depression where human remains are said to have been found in 1717 and reburied *in situ* rather than in the churchyard. This apparently incurred God's displeasure and later that year, on 23rd July, several oak trees were seen to sink into the ground 'with water bubbling up around'. There is no sign of either the trees or the water today but this is how the Devil's Dish was formed.

An earthwork as impressive as Castle Hill in Thetford which, at eighty feet high, is the largest of its kind in East Anglia, was one that 18th century travellers could only marvel at, one that has inevitably given rise to much speculation, both historical and wildly speculative, as to its origins. The Devil has been busy here too, having dragged his boot along the ground between the Wissey and Little Ouse to form a second linear earthwork – the Fossditch – he swirled round on one foot to create Castle Hill. Its construction has otherwise been variously assigned to every successive invasion from the Celts and Romans to the Danes, the Normans and even Oliver

Norwich Castle

Cromwell. It was not until the 1960s that excavations identified two separate periods – a Norman motte-and-bailey castle set within the oval ramparts of an earlier Iron Age fort (p110). Another tale mentions the royal castle of some long forgotten king who, following an attack, is said to have ordered that both the castle and its hoard of treasure be buried beneath the huge mound of earth visible today; but the most generally held belief links the hill to the town's other great archaeological site, the Cluniac priory. At the Dissolution six silver bells from the priory church were thought to have been buried for safekeeping beneath Castle Hill, a story associated with several other ruined churches in the county.

ROYAL TREASURE

In Norwich a fanciful foundation myth has been fashioned for the city's great civic landmark. Despite its obvious architectural credentials Norwich castle mound was, according to Blomefield's *History of Norfolk* (1745), said to have been raised by the mythical King Gurgunt and the walls built by Julius Caesar. The role of Gurgunt, a Celtic leader invented by the medieval chronicler Geoffrey of Monmouth, may well have been revived for the visit of Queen Elizabeth I in 1578. Among the assembled dignitaries ready to welcome his Queen was King Gurgunt with a speech but 'by reason of a showre of raine which came, hir Majestie hasted away, the speech not uttered'. Although not mentioned by name, Gurgunt had, by the mid 19th century, been transformed into the 'sleeping hero', an Arthurian figure waiting to defend his realm. Referring to the castle motte in *Lavengro* (1851) George Borrow describes 'an old heathen king, who sits deep within it, his sword in his hand and his gold and silver treasures about him.'

The only treasure, lost rather than buried, that has any claim on real events lies deep in the mud of the Fens somewhere west of Sutton Bridge. According to the chronicles it was here in 1216, the year after King John had signed Magna Carta, that his baggage train of royal gold and silver overturned and sank as it tried to skirt round the edge of the Wash. Now covered in a deep layer of silt its exact whereabouts remains one of history's great unsolved mysteries and led to any number of tales recounted in isolated Fenland pubs well into the last century. One locates the treasure at King John's Hole in Walpole St Andrew just south of the main Lynn to Long Sutton road but the great Fenland storyteller Jack Barrett has a more entertaining version in 'The Legend of Gold Hill'. This slight mound is in Welney on the border with Cambridgeshire near the suspension bridge over the Hundred Foot River. According to Barrett the treasure was stolen by a serving wench while the King was enjoying himself at Wisbech Fair and ended up in the hands of a group of Fenmen who lived in huts on the mound. It was here they buried the jewels they couldn't spend and centuries later as bits of the hoard were turned up by the plough the place became Gold Hill and is marked as such on the O S map. The story is one of several in which, long before the Fens were drained, wiley old Fen tigers triumphed over authority whether it be the loathsome monks of Ely, Norman invaders or the king himself.

HILL DIGGING

From the first appearance of precious metals in the Bronze Age – bronze itself for tools and weaponry and gold for personal adornment – wealth in the form of jewellery and ceremonial objects was placed in the ground either as a votive offering to the gods, grave goods to accompany the dead or for safekeeping in time of trouble. The belief, long held by people of every class, from landowners to farm labourers, that treasure of one sort or another lay just below the surface, has been substantiated by some of the most exciting finds in British archaeology. In the wake of the Mildenhall

Treasure – a magnificent hoard of Roman silverware ploughed up during WWII just over the border in Suffolk – a series of remarkable discoveries have been made along the edge of the Fens. Among these are the lavish gold torcs of a kind worn by Queen Boudica herself unearthed at Snettisham in 1948 by a tractor driver who thought them bits of a brass bedstead; the hoard of six Saxon disc brooches beautifully worked in silver dug up in 1977 by the village sexton in Pentney churchyard and the Thetford Treasure recovered from Gallows Hill two years later. This fabulous hoard of silver spoons, gold rings set with precious stones and a superb gold buckle are among the finest pieces to have been found anywhere in the Roman Empire. In recent years the hoard of six Anglo Saxon pendants or bracteates unearthed in a field at Binham is one of the most remarkable collections of gold objects from the 6th century AD to have been discovered anywhere in England.

Snettisham Treasure of Ir[illegible] Age gold torcs (far lef[illegible] Middle Saxon silver brooc[illegible] Pentney (abov[illegible]

These trophies from a rich and powerful elite, brought to light in part by deep ploughing and the use of metal detectors, are rare and exceptional finds. Far more numerous were the small decorative items and coin hoards that have been turning up across Norfolk for centuries but which have gone unrecorded. Much has no doubt been lost, discarded or melted down and reused, but in the early 19th century the increase in cultivated land, some of it recently enclosed commons, coincided with a new antiquarian interest in the distant past and the number of known finds began to grow. The small hoard of Roman coins found in a silver vase in 1801 was the first of several from Fincham, and elsewhere throughout the 19th century Roman silver *denarii* and gold *solidi* coins, silver pennies from the Late Saxon and early medieval period continued to be unearthed, culminating in the largest haul of Roman coins yet found in the county, upwards of 10,000 in a huge earthenware vessel ploughed up near Baconsthorpe Castle in 1878. News of each new hoard would have spread quickly, its size and the circumstances of its discovery embellished with each retelling in alehouse and market place along the way. This, the very stuff of folklore, fired the imagination and kept alive hopes of wealth (had they been able to spend it) people could only dream of.

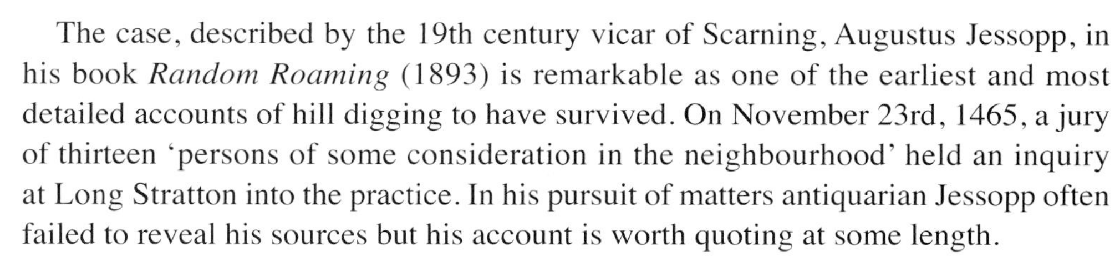

The case, described by the 19th century vicar of Scarning, Augustus Jessopp, in his book *Random Roaming* (1893) is remarkable as one of the earliest and most detailed accounts of hill digging to have survived. On November 23rd, 1465, a jury of thirteen 'persons of some consideration in the neighbourhood' held an inquiry at Long Stratton into the practice. In his pursuit of matters antiquarian Jessopp often failed to reveal his sources but his account is worth quoting at some length.

oman gold *solidus* coin, Deopham

John Cans, late of Bunwell and Robert Hikkes, late of Forncett, worsted-weaver, *during divers years past* on divers occasions and in various places in the county had been wont to avail themselves of the arts of magic and darkness and invocations of disembodied spirits of the damned, and had most wickedly been in the habit of making sacrifices and offerings to the same spirits. By means of which arts and sacrifices they had incited many persons unknown to idolatry and to the practice of *hill-digging* and other disturbances...

Especially too, they had made assemblies of such persons at night-time again and again for the finding of treasures concealed in the said hills. Moreover, having assembled to themselves many persons unknown on the night of Sunday before the Feast of Bartholomew (1465) they did cause to appear before the same disorderly persons, practising the same unlawful arts, a certain accursed disembodied spirit (*spiritum aerialem*) at Bunwell aforesaid, and did promise and covenant that they would sacrifice, give and make a burnt offering to the self-same spirit, of the (dead) body of a Christian man, if so be that the aforesaid spirit there and then would show and make known to them in some place within the county aforesaid, so that a treasure therein lying might come to the hands of them.

Whereupon the said spirit, under promise of a sacrifice to be made, did show to them *by the help of a certain crystal* a vast treasure hidden in a certain hill (*in quodam monte*) at Forncett called Nonmete Hill. Upon the which discovery the same John Cans and Robert Hikkes in return for the aforesaid treasure so found and to be applied to their own use, did then seize upon a certain fowl called a cock at Bunwell aforesaid, and there and then in the presence of their fathers and mothers, baptise the said cock in holy water, and gave to the said cock a Christian name, and slew the same cock so named, and did offer it as a whole burnt offering as a Christian carcass to the accursed spirit, according to covenant. Which being done, the said John Cans and Robert Hikkes and the other unknown person did proceed to Forncett along with the said accursed spirit and did dig in the hill called Nonmete Hill and made an entry into the said hill, insomuch that there and then they found to the value of more than a hundred shillings in coined money in the said hill. For all of which they shall make an answer to our Lord the King, inasmuch as the said treasure they did appropriate to their own use and do still retain.

Benchend, St Peter's, Forncett

Jessopp thought the silver coins had been placed in the ground by the two accomplices to convince others of their skill in the black arts, but more likely the coins were part of a Romano British hoard buried during a time of strife. So where exactly was Nonmete? John Balls, the elderly parish clerk in Forncett interviewed by Jessopp in 1886, recalled a hill-digging story associated with a mound called 'Old Groggrams', that Jessopp took to be the name of the 'accursed spirit', on the edge of a common that Balls and others used to slide down as lads and that had been levelled some time later. The parish of Forncett was situated in the centre of Depwade Hundred and Jessopp concluded the mound was probably adopted as the place where the Hundred court once met. This appeared to be the end of the story until, a century later, local historian Marilyn Tolhurst discovered the name 'Old Groggrams' on the Tacolneston tithe map beside the parish boundary with Forncett. One of the lanes that meet at this point had long been known as Galgrym Way, a name the Norfolk historian Blomefield considered to be a corruption of Gallows Green. If true the earthwork had served as both a meeting place, a place of execution and the source of buried treasure.

From here the story moves to Forncett St Peter church and its set of replacement benchends, originally late 15th century and from the same period as the hill-digging episode but, according to Pevsner, 'apparently skilful work of 1857'. This gallery of local Victorian worthies, probably crafted from real life, includes a painter with palette and brushes and, more particularly, a man holding a box brimful with coins. Is this the infamous Robert Hikkes and is the devil below him with hand outstretched the 'accursed disembodied spirit', Old Groggrams, who, 400 years after the event, was commemorated both in the parish church and in the minds of elderly residents like John Balls? Old Groggrams was, however, not an isolated incident. Cans and Hikkes were clearly experienced hill-diggers well versed in the dark arts and Jessopp was of the opinion that treasure hunting had been 'endemic in the neighbourhood for several years past'. He cites the case of another local, John Youngeman, who with others had unearthed treasure worth £100 at Carleton Rode some years before the Nonmete episode.

Jessopp also refers to the case of William Stapleton, an indolent monk at St Benet's Abbey who, in 1520, wrote to Cardinal Wolsey requesting permission to become a secular priest. To raise money for his dispensation Stapleton turned to treasure hunting with the help of esoteric books 'a little ring, a plate, a circle and also a sword for the art of digging'[4] obtained for him from the vicar of Watton. He then set out with two men who had a licence to hunt for treasure trove, visiting those places where parish priests 'had awful dealings with familiar spirits ... most notable of these friends were Oberon, Incubus and Andrew Malchus'[5] and one known as a 'shower' called Anthony Fulcar who would locate the spoils. They went in turn to Syderstone, Felmingham and North Creake Abbey, abandoned after an outbreak of the 'sweating sickness' in 1506, which had led to rumours of treasure left there. Unlike his Forncett predecessors Stapleton's efforts were singularly unsuccessful. He found nothing at Creake or at Bell Hill in the parish of Fritton, where a golden plough was said to be buried, despite help from the vicar of Gorleston.

GOLDEN GATES

The idea that golden gates have been lost at sites of some historic importance like *Venta Icenorum* is almost as popular as the secret tunnel in the folklore of the county. The Roman town, known as Caistor Castle in the early 18th century when the perimeter walls were more substantial, would have been a place of wonder about which locals and antiquarians could only speculate. The grand entrance to this defensive stronghold, the headquarters of some powerful noble perhaps, would have been fitted with a pair of finely wrought gates, gates of shining gold that were lost when the place was eventually overrun. A century later and the gates had been recast in the oral tradition – they were made of brass, stronger but less magical. By a similar logic the golden gates to Hautbois Castle, Sir Robert Barnard's fortified manor house (licence to crenellate 1312), were believed to have been removed by the owner during a period of unrest and dropped into a bottomless pit nearby. Today an atmosphere of romantic decay hovers about this place in the meadows beside the Bure; the ruins of St Theobold's church, the dense undergrowth where the castle once stood and Golden Gate Pond near the lane.

North wall, Caistor St Edmund

Stranded in a field and approached along a footpath at North Green, Pulham St Mary, is an oval earthwork about which almost nothing is known. It may be the site of a medieval hall – Broughton Manor Farm is close by – and it is known as Golden Cradle Moat. Does it simply refer to the shape of the moat or is it the remnant of a locally recurring folk tale? At East Harling another golden cradle is said to lie at the bottom of a deep pit, since filled, in Pilgrim's Meadow, while another, the memory of its whereabouts increasingly vague, is buried in or near Sculthorpe.

Gold in one form or another – plough, wheel, gates or cradle – has come to be associated most often with medieval ruins, notably at Gresham where a tunnel was believed to run several miles north from the castle, another fortified manor like Hautbois Castle, to the Augustinian Priory at Beeston Regis. At some point in the story gold is reshaped in the image of a golden calf lost somewhere in the tunnel that ran beneath Aylmerton cross. This wayside cross on the boundary with Gresham parish where several lanes converge is thought to have marked the way for pilgrims en route to Walsingham. In the early 18th century an old lady who lived nearby was convinced that the tunnel ran beneath her cottage and engaged a 'cunning man' to try and locate it. A pit was dug in her parlour without success and the search came to an abrupt halt when the work began to undermine the adjoining cottage. The linking of two religious sites may be the local story of a pagan deity, unscrupulous monks or idolatrous Catholics or it may refer back to the Golden Calf of the Old Testament, a reminder that gold, in whatever form, is a false god. By pure chance workmen digging a soak-away in Gresham in 2004 unearthed nine gold Bronze Age rings threaded together.

Boundary cross, Aylmerton

THE SWAFFHAM PEDLAR

Another migratory tale is one, like 'Babes in the Wood', that has been transposed from a universal story into a local legend – 'The Pedlar of Swaffham'. As 'The Treasure at Home' it was popular throughout much of central and eastern Europe in collections like 'The Arabian Nights' and in Britain there are versions in Yorkshire, Scotland and Wales. The town of Swaffham still retains an air of faded elegance, its domed butter cross (1781) a handsome centrepiece to the market place, a large triangular space lined with fine Georgian buildings. The greatest single expression of its medieval prosperity is the 15th century parish church tucked away up an alley, financed by a number of wealthy benefactors. Among them was John Botewright who rebuilt the chancel while churchwarden John Chapman's generosity paid for the north aisle in 1462 and contributed towards the cost of the tower. In the middle ages surnames were often derived from family occupations – Botewright was a maker of boats and Chapman was a pedlar or merchant, the latter commemorated in a north aisle window and in the chancel. Here two early 16th century benchends that once adorned the family box pew have been incorporated in Victorian choir stalls. One, depicting Chapman with his pedlar's pack and his dog, the other his wife in a shop window with her counting beads, are reminders of his philanthropy and of the legend the carvings have inspired since its first appearance in the mid 17th century.

Swaffham town sign

'The Pedlar of Swaffham' performed by the Swaffham Players, 1906

Made popular a century later in chapbooks and subsequently in Victorian children's books the tale of the Swaffham pedlar is essentially one of good fortune. Chapman dreams that if he travels to the capital and stands on London Bridge he will hear joyful news. And so, bidding his wife farewell, he sets out with his dog and, on arrival, waits for three days on the bridge. A local shopkeeper (there were shops on London Bridge in those days) who asks the pedlar what he is doing, laughs at his foolishness, adding that he too had dreamed that he was in Swaffham, 'a place I don't know, and thought I'd find a vast treasure under an oak tree in an orchard behind a pedlar's house. But I'm not such a fool as to make a long journey because of a silly dream. Be like me, good fellow – go home and see to your business'. The pedlar did just that and right quick, digging under his tree until he found a 'prodigious great treasure', a pot of gold coins and on it a Latin inscription which, sometime later, a passing stranger identified and which read 'Where this stood is another as good.' John Chapman took his spade and dug again under the oak (some versions say a hawthorn) and unearthed a second larger pot of coins. In gratitude the pedlar, now a rich man, paid to 're-edify the church most sumptuously' and for a statue to be cut in stone of himself with his pack and his dog.

Today the pedlar adorns the town sign in a corner of the market place but the statue of Ceres, Roman corn Goddess, on top of the market cross and the wheat sheaf emblazoned on the former corn exchange are potent reminders of the real source of Swaffham's prosperity – the fields of golden corn that stretch away from the town in all directions. Since the town received its market charter in the mid 13th century farmers have haggled with corn merchants each year at harvest time, men like John Chapman who let the golden grain slip through their fingers, much like his legendry self tipped the pot of gold coins out on his kitchen table.

Benchend, Swaffham church

Swaffham's golden reputation was enhanced still further in the early years of last century by the exploits of Howard Carter who, as a boy, spent long periods with his aunts in the town. While there, a visit to nearby Didlington Hall and Lord Amherst's magnificent collection of Egyptian antiquities instilled in the young Carter a passion for Middle Eastern archaeology. Already a promising draughtsman, by 1915 he had begun working for Lord Carnarvon in Egypt in the Valley of the Kings when on November 26th 1922, he made the most sensational archaeological discovery the world has ever seen – the great treasure house of Tutankhamun's tomb. Although the Egyptian ambassador travelled to Swaffham in 1989 to open an exhibition about the excavation the fabulous artefacts that accompanied the pharaoh on his journey into the next world remain in Cairo. But in Swaffham Howard Carter had already become something of a folk hero to rival John Chapman – they both had the Midas touch.

Early 20c book cover

CHURCH LORE

CIRCLING

The practice of circling round an ancient site – a mound, a stone or, more often in Norfolk, a church – as a way of releasing supernatural forces, was one of the most widespread of local traditions. There were many variations but to be sure of success it was important to perform the ritual at some auspicious time; at midnight or midsummer, when the moon was full or on New Year's Eve, and it had to be carried out in time honoured fashion. It was necessary to run round the site several times – the numbers three and seven are most often specified – without pausing for breath. This was intended to disorientate and exhaust the participant, inducing an altered state of perception necessary to raise the Devil or conjure up a ghost. Crucial to the ritual's success was the direction of movement. Rightward progression followed the course of the sun and was deemed to be beneficial but circling anticlockwise or 'widdershins' (a Scottish dialect word) would unscrew the lid on the otherworld.

Practised on St Mark's Eve (24th April) as a form of divination circling was once a commonplace ritual. By running round a church and waiting in the porch a future spouse or those who were to die later that year would be revealed (p217). At Thorseway in Lincolnshire on St Mark's Eve a witch would circle the church three times backward and then look through the keyhole. She would do this each year while reciting certain words in order to renew her powers. At Swanton Morley those children brave enough to run round All Saints' church as the clock struck midnight and then whistle through the keyhole of the main door would see the Devil – whistling was a recognised way to raise spirits. According to another local resident, children would peer into a grille which lit the old crypt. In late Victorian Yarmouth to run three times round St George's church and shout 'Bloody Queen Mary' would conjure up the monarch's face in a nearby window. The legend is of no great age – the Wren-style church was built between 1714 and 1716 – and was probably contrived as a piece of anti-Catholic propaganda. Until at least the 1940s in Hilgay on the edge of the Fens a ghost could still be summoned up by first sticking a pin in the church door and then running round the building three times. Here the pin, rather like a key, was both a means to contact the otherworld and afforded a measure of protection against the spirits unleashed. In other parts of Britain knives, needles or other metal objects were used in the same way much like horseshoes were hung above cottage doors to ward off evil spirits. Do the circling traditions from Swanton Morley and Hilgay, both involving children, originate from games of 'dare' in the churchyard or are they remnants of some older, more solemn ritual? A drunken version is known to have taken place in North Walsham in the 19th century when, at closing time, regulars from the White Swan would challenge each other to run backwards three times round the church, a difficult enough task to avoid the headstones when sober. Those who succeeded would hear the sound of the organ coming from an empty church and one participant looked through a window to see ghostly figures approach the altar; a testament, no doubt, to the strength of the local brew.

Ruins of Whitlingham church, early c19 engraving

There are suggestions of circling rituals associated with two ruined churches just east of Norwich, both now in the parish of Kirby Bedon. The tales, like the churches themselves, are fragmentary and, intriguingly, concern abandoned places of worship that are not just ruinous but round towered. At St Mary's, Kirby Bedon, a tall woman clad all in white and mounted on a white horse was said to ride slowly round the churchyard before crossing the lane to encircle the new St Andrew's church, virtually rebuilt in 1876. The tale, which has echoes of the spectral 'lady on a white horse' raised by circling the Sussex hill fort, Chanctonbury Ring, sheds no light on who the

Ruined tower, St Margaret's, Wolterton

tall woman might be or why she haunts both churches. The Kirby Bedon ruin is dedicated to the Virgin who may have been reimagined as a romantic Victorian heroine – the tale was first recorded in 1885. Circling each church in turn was perhaps a symbolic binding of the two together in a ritual that ensured the transfer of spiritual power from the old to the new place of worship. The second ruin is at Whitlingham where the remains of St Andrew's church, perched on a river cliff overlooking the Yare, was a picturesque destination for visitors in the 19th century. Before its collapse in 1940 the tower supported lifesize figures of the four evangelists, a decorative device more often used to finish off the corners of square towers. Always vulnerable in high wind they occasionally crashed to the ground or were removed for safekeeping and in this way gained a reputation for movement. At Horsford the statues were believed to come down one at a time in successive years before returning to stand guard over the church, but at Whitlingham the tower was round and at midnight on New Year's Eve the stone figures were said to walk around the parapet, shake hands and resume their sentinel positions for another year. A decidedly Gothic version of the circling tradition is contained in *Mannington and the Walpoles* (1894) as part of the White Lady legend of Wolterton Hall (p167). She was believed to be a member of the Scamler family, lords of the manor before Horatio Walpole engaged Thomas Ripley to design a grand new country seat in the early 18th century. As a result the village of Wolterton was swept away leaving the ruined tower of St Margaret's church as an eye catcher in the park. In the process the ancestral tombs of the Scamlers were thought to have been disturbed, releasing the spirit of the White Lady. To placate the apparition and atone for the desecration the Walpole hearse was driven three times around the ruin – round towered again – before heading off to Wickmere where the coffin would be laid to rest in the family vault.

Ruined tower, Kirby Bedon

Not surprisingly rituals of this kind with sexual and diabolic overtones were condemned from the pulpit much like maypole dancing on the village green. It was a short step from circling, and the belief that stone circles were girls petrified for dancing on the Sabbath, to dancing in a churchyard. There are suggestions of these traditions in the strange tale of two maidens who gave land to the parish in Carbrooke and who then danced themselves to death. It would appear from the presence of Dance Meadow on a late c18 map that this incident took place not in the churchyard, where the benefactors were buried on the south side of the church, but quite possibly on the parcel of land donated, in some bizarre ritual to honour the bequest. It has been suggested that the story may have evolved from the kind of cautionary tale advanced by the church in medieval Europe to discourage making merry in churchyards on Sundays and holy festivals, but its origins may lie much closer to home. The tale, which was collected in the late 19th century by the Norfolk folklorist W B Gerish, would appear to be medieval – the land was in the parish of Great Carbrooke which was only combined with Carbrooke Parva in 1424. Just south of Carbrooke church are earthworks of the Knights Hospitallers Commandery, established in 1193 by Roger de Clare on the site of a nunnery founded by his wife Matilda a few years earlier. Could the 'Dancing to Death' tale referred to by Gerish have been part of some frenzied religious ceremony enacted by the nuns, of a kind sweeping across Europe at the time? There is both a Dance Meadow and a Nunns Hill on the 1791 map of Carbrooke.

TOWERS

The village church is often the oldest and most prominent building in any rural community and was for centuries a familiar site to the majority of parishioners who worshipped there each Sunday, whether they were true believers or, at heart, still clung to the old religion. Rising in splendid isolation from the fields or above the red pantile roofs of a Norfolk village, the church tower is often visible for miles around and any eccentricity in shape or design was both a source of local pride and an obvious subject for speculation.

The round tower, subject of several circling traditions, is the most recognisable type of church tower in Norfolk, particularly in the south east of the county which, together with north east Suffolk, has by far the highest concentration in England. This distinctive structure has been traditionally regarded as a Saxon response to the lack of good local stone for quoins despite the presence of round towers in or near the carstone belt of west Norfolk. A more likely explanation, given their distribution, is the adoption of this new stylistic feature from northern Europe in the 11th century where it was often deployed. A far more colourful belief current in the late 19th century, a mixture of biblical rhetoric and folklore, was that round towers were once antediluvian wells and that the surrounding soil had, over time, been worn away leaving them exposed. These flint structures were, as the story goes, later transformed into round towered churches by the addition of nave and chancel.

Brick well shaft exposed by cliff erosion, 1976, Covehythe, Suffolk

In Great Yarmouth the spire of St Nicholas' church was twisted out of shape by a lightning strike in 1683. It may originally have been seen, at least by the church authorities, as evidence of God's wrath visited on a sinful congregation but, at least until its replacement in 1807, any suggestion of divine intervention was soon countered in the popular imagination by a more down-to-earth 'explanation'. As with Chesterfield's famous crooked spire on the edge of the Peak District, the Yarmouth needle is said to have become distorted with the arrival of a virgin bride. This, by tradition, was such a rare occurrence that the spire bowed down to get a better look; a piece of local lore that may also have been prompted by the proverb 'when an old maid dies, the steeple nods'. The Yarmouth version was not the only outlandish tale of domestic politics emanating from St Nicholas' church. The skull from a sperm whale washed up at Caister-on-Sea in 1582 had been placed outside the church where it became known as the Devil's chair – in the bible this deep sea monster, while ultimately Jonah's saviour, was more often regarded as the mouth of Satan. The original prophesy, that misfortune would befall all those who dared to sit on the skull, was gradually replaced by the superstition current among the fishing community that the first of a newly-wed couple to sit on the chair would rule the home.

West Walton bell tower, Gerard Stamp, 2008

Deep in the Fens the Marshland parish of West Walton was for centuries vulnerable to flooding – a board in the church records several occasions in the 17th century when the country around was 'overflowed by the violence of the sea.' St Mary's detached bell tower, rising majestically at the edge of the churchyard, and one of only two in the county, was a wise precaution in this marshy terrain. Had it been raised on the body of the church it would almost certainly have led to serious structural problems but in later years a more imaginative explanation for such an unusual feature was required. According to local tradition the tower, which was built in the same Early English style of the mid 13th century, had originally been raised against the nave of St Mary's. Even the marshland giant Tom Hickathrift, who had tried to lift if for a bet, had found the tower too heavy. It was a task for the Devil himself who hated the sound of church bells. But the humans he chose to help him, while strong, were not very clever. Unable to manoeuvre the tower through the churchyard gate or over the wall they were forced to leave it where it stands to this day at a sharp bend in the road.

Bell tower, St Nicholas', Dereham

The other detached bell tower – in Dereham – is the subject of a rather more ingenious piece of folklore. Historically the bells were originally housed in the central tower of St Nicholas' church but, with the acquisition of a new peal of eight bells in the early 16th century, the structure was unable to take the additional weight. It was decided to build a much stronger tower some distance to the south and a few years after its completion in 1525 the central tower was reduced in height. This explanation failed to satisfy local opinion that the bell tower had once been attached to the church. Because the builder had used the wrong mortar the tower was said to leak and the rector ordered it to be tarred all over. While the surface was still sticky all the birds of the town – some say a flock of starlings – flew over to satisfy their curiosity and landed on the tower where they became stuck fast. The birds, great in number, flapped their wings so hard that they managed to dislodge the tower and flew a short distance with it until their feet eventually came unstuck and the tower came to rest where it stands today in a corner of the churchyard.

The most distinctive church tower in Norfolk overlooks the Waveney marshes at Burgh St Peter. Rather confusingly St Peter's church has disappeared leaving St Mary's alone at the end of a farm track, its bizarre ziggurat tower rising above the trees like a stack of diminishing red bricks. Born of eccentricity and bred in isolation it was raised in 1793 on a Tudor brick base as a mausoleum for the Boycott family who served as vicars of the parish continuously from 1764 to 1899. Perhaps surprisingly a tower so unique in appearance does not feature more prominently in the folklore of the district, although as a local landmark visible to boats on the river it was said to fold up at the end of the yachting season and reopen the following spring. A legend with more ancient credentials seeks to explain not the peculiar profile of the tower but rather the origin of the medieval church. By pledging his soul to the Devil a poor man borrowed enough money to build the parish church. When, years later, the Devil returned for the loan to be repaid he found the man had recently died and been buried in consecrated ground beyond his reach. As a result, on the anniversary of the man's death, a skeleton was said to roam the churchyard in an attempt to claim his soul.

Burgh St Peter chur

St Margaret's (ruined), and St Mary's, Antingham, Ladbroke drawing, 1823

A more widespread peculiarity of Norfolk churches is where two places of worship occupy the same churchyard. There are a dozen or more examples across the county where, at the Conquest, parishes were often divided into two or more manors, each served by a separate church but sharing the same burial ground. In places like Stiffkey, Snetterton and Blo'Norton a single church has survived depopulation and the ravages of time, but elsewhere, notably at Antingham and Great Melton, the crumbling ruins of an abandoned church still remain. At Reepham there were, uniquely, three medieval churches crammed together where the parishes of Whitwell, Reepham and Hackford converged. Inevitably the proximity of sister churches has given rise to tales of sibling rivalry; at South Walsham when, it was believed, two daughters quarrelled over their inheritance. Each decided to build a church but when it became clear which would be the more impressive the jealous sister arranged to have the other murdered. This, so the story goes, is why St Mary's is the parish church and why St Laurence's, the larger of the two, has the appearance of being 'unfinished' although, following years of neglect, its tower survived until 1971. A similar story ia associated with the two churches at Antingham where the dedications are to St Mary and St Margaret, the earlier and ruinous structure, have given rise to local speculation that they were built by and named after two rival sisters.

In some Norfolk parishes population decline in the middle ages has led to the complete disappearance of both village and church and, especially on the 'Isle' of Flegg, to a number of combined parishes. At Ashby-with-Oby the exact whereabouts of Ashby church had been forgotten until the 1976 drought when crop marks revealed the ghostly footprint of a little Norman structure complete with round tower and apsidal chancel. In the 19th century, although the outline of Oby churchyard could still be traced, the church itself had gone and was believed to have sunk beneath the ground. As such it is one of a more widespread group of sunken church legends attributed to earthquakes or coastal erosion. In Dilham near the river Thurne the church was rebuilt in 1931 but in the mid 19th century, according to the Rev'd Gunn's informant Mrs Lubbock (p3), a deep, boggy depression called 'Seagar-ma-hole' had been a 'Fairies Bay' where the earlier church had been swallowed up. Sometime later when rushes had grown over the spot a team of oxen suffered a similar fate.

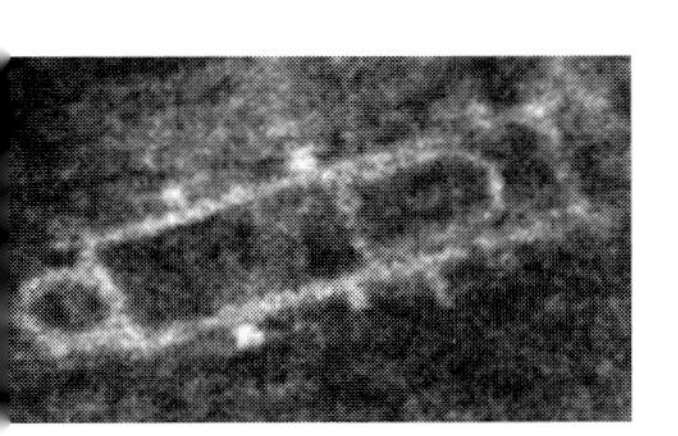

Ghostly outline of
'mesby St Peter's lost church

St Laurence and St Mary churches, South Walsham

BELL RINGING

Throughout the medieval period monastic life was regulated by the ringing of bells to denote the canonical hours and summon the community to prayer while the English countryside was alive to the sound of church bells calling the faithful, celebrating a wedding or signalling a feast day. In towns and villages the tolling of a single bell, known as the Passing Bell, announced the death of a parishioner. In some communities it would be rung daily between a death and the funeral denoting a rite of passage with the number of 'knocks' proclaiming the sex and marital status of the deceased. At Marsham near Aylsham it was three for a girl and four for a boy, five for a spinster and seven for a wife, eight for a bachelor and nine 'knocks' for a husband or widower. The position of widow (six 'knocks'?) appears to have been overlooked. In some parishes this was followed by ringing the age of the dead person. Before the advent of a clock on church tower or town hall, church bells were also rung on more secular occasions – at dawn (the Morning Bell) and at dusk (the Curfew Bell) to announce the start and finish of the working day. In Norwich the curfew bell at St Peter Mancroft was rung at 8pm followed by the day of the month. Peals were often rung on royal occasions or to celebrate a victory, however remote. In the Fens, a ringers board in the tower of St Clement's church records the 5040 changes rung by 'six of the Outwell youths' to commemorate the treaty signed between England and China in 1843 that brought to an end the Opium Wars. Closer to home the erratic jangling of bells – an alarum – might warn against invasion or was, more often, a signal that fire had broken out.

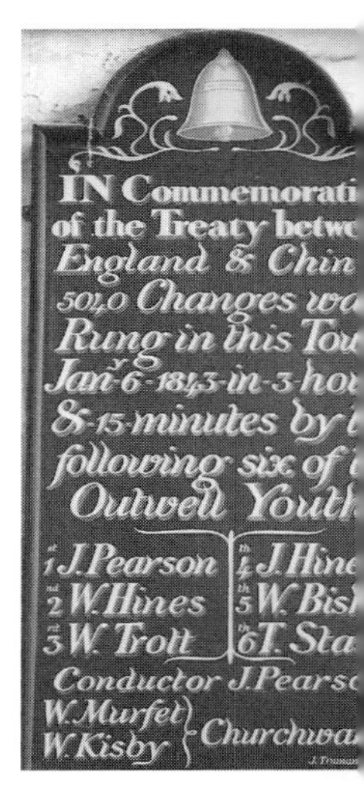

Ringers' board, Outwell

Bells played a dramatic part in daily life. For many they were the 'voice' of the church and were widely believed to possess supernatural powers. A peal of bells was said to enrage the Devil and to chase away those demons of the air that would conjure up storms. At certain times of the year they were known to ring out of their own accord – traditionally on Christmas morning in Dereham followed by a muffled peal on St Stephen's day. A more elaborate version was collected by the author of *Haunted East Anglia* in the Breckland hamlet of Didlington from the local police constable who, late one winter's evening was cycling along a lane when he heard, carried on the wind, the tolling of St Michael's bell. As he reached the churchyard gate the bell fell silent. Retrieving the door key the constable let himself in and there, caught in the beam of his torch, he saw the bell rope still swinging but with not a soul in sight. Perhaps it had been disturbed by a sudden gust of wind as the door opened but, soon after, he learnt that ten years earlier, on the very same November day in 1946, the owner of Didlington Hall had died.

'The White Lady of Worstead', an altogether more macabre tale of bell-ringing, is based on an incident which, according to E R Suffling in his *History and Legends of the Broad District* (1895), occurred in about 1830. By tradition the White Lady appeared on Christmas Eve as the church clock struck midnight. It was then customary for the sexton to ring in Christmas Day for a few minutes. On the occasion in question one of the regulars in the King's Head boasted that he would go alone and ring the bell and if he saw the White Lady he would give her a kiss. His companions gathered at the door of the inn to hear the peal but after the hour struck there was silence. A few minutes passed until, each grabbing a lantern, they hurried across to the church and climbed the tower to find their friend a jabbering wreck crouched in a corner of the ringing chamber. They managed to get him down and back to the inn where he

Pub sign, Worstea

revived enough to shout out 'I've seen her!' before lapsing into a stupor only to die later that day. Whether he was the victim of a practical joke that had gone horribly wrong, the truth never emerged and no-one was ever suspected but today the pub has a new name, the White Lady, and her wraith-like face peers down from the creaking signboard.

The world of campanology provided Dorothy L Sayers with fertile ground for her fiendishly convoluted thriller *The Nine Taylors* (1934). While there is no suggestion she was aware of the Worstead tale, the White Lady in the tower falls into a more general class of folklore that Sayers may have drawn on. The setting, Fenchurch St Paul, is based partly on her time as French tutor at Upwell Rectory on the Norfolk-Cambridge border in 1921 but in the novel it is the appalling sound of the bells rather than the appearance of a White Lady that drives the main suspect mad. Tied up in the tower he is subjected to a nine hour ordeal as the bells ring out on New Year's Eve.

Whitbread inn sign, from the Worms Bible, 1148 AD

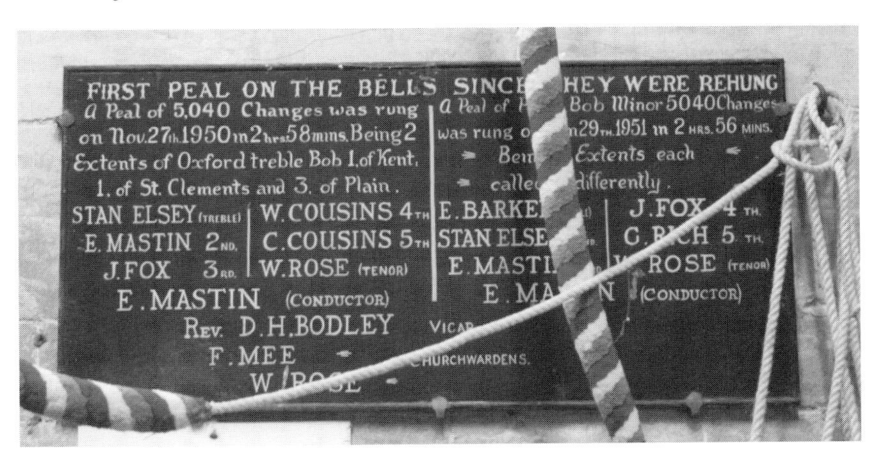

Ringers' board, 1950s, Tilney All Saints

Bells were the only means of broadcasting news quickly, especially in rural areas, and were highly prized by the community. The proceeds of land set aside for the purpose, like Bell Pightle in Attleborough, were often used to ensure that the bells were rung on all occasions. They were cast from a mixture of alloy and tin but those that feature in folklore are more often made of silver and therefore more desirable. The loss of silver, whether in the form of the Shouldham Treasure (p36) or the silver chalice from Lyng nunnery (p36), is often associated with water, a belief shared in Attlebridge where two silver bells were said to have been removed from the church tower during the Civil War and hidden in the bed of the Wensum. Was this measure taken to save them from Cromwell's troops or to ensure the troops would arrive unannounced once the bells had been silenced? Just south of Acle on the edge of the marshes Tunstall church had become ruinous in 1704 when the nave roof collapsed. According to tradition this was the result of a fire but the bells survived. While the rector and churchwardens argued over who, by rights, should take possession of them, the Devil swept them up and carried them away pursued by the rector invoking God in Latin. Confronted by the power of prayer the Devil jumped into a boggy pond called Hell Hole near the parish boundary with Acle – a nearby alder wood is still referred to as Hell Carr on the O S map – where bubbles of marsh gas, rising to the surface, were thought to have been caused by the bells still sinking in the bottomless pit.

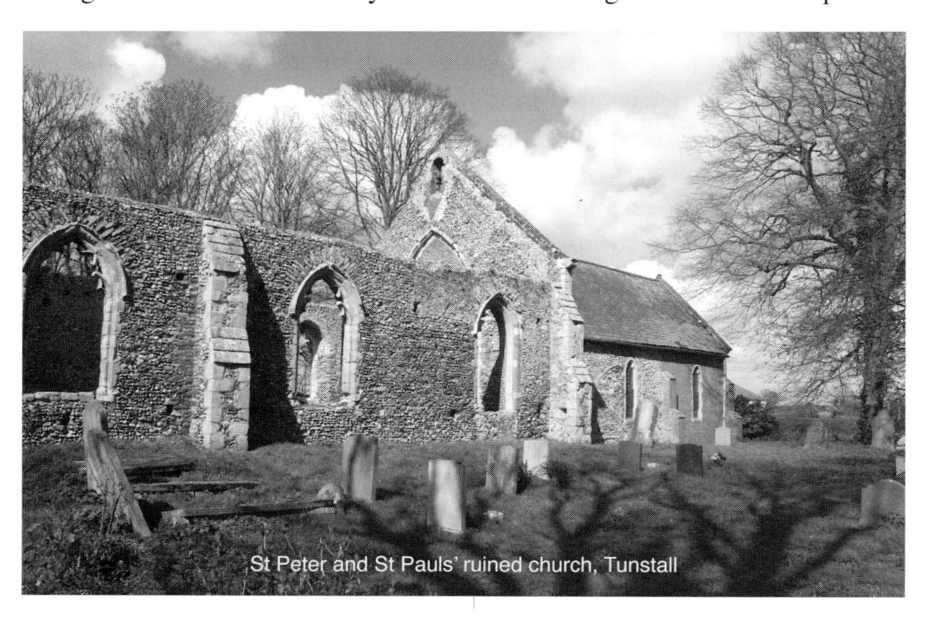

St Peter and St Pauls' ruined church, Tunstall

In May 1888 Docking parish magazine reported that the church bell was cracked and would need to be recast. It was the last of a peal of five bells that, by tradition, were thought to have been lost in the Wash, possibly buried beneath the area known to sailors as 'Docking Sands', despite the village being a good five miles inland. The report sheds no light on how or why this tradition arose but it may have been a confused version of the more widely held belief among coastal communities in the power of bells to 'dispel ... The fury of the rising gale'. The sound of bells still ringing below the waves was also said to be a portent of stormy weather. Dunwich on the Suffolk coast was one of the most prosperous medieval ports along the whole eastern seaboard until much of the town was swept away in the terrible storm of January 19th, 1328. Since then Dunwich has gradually slipped beneath the waves until early last century the ruined tower of All Saints' church finally toppled down the cliff face. There had been time enough to remove the bells here and from those other churches – eight or nine in total – that over the centuries had been lost to the sea, but the romantic legend of bells ringing out from a watery grave persists. Although Dunwich remains the most famous and well documented sunken city, the Norfolk coast has its own litany of settlements lost to the sea, notably the busy Domesday port of Shipden on the seaward side of Cromer. Despite its steadfast dedication to St Peter the church had been abandoned by the mid 14th century and today the flint faced base of the tower, known as Church Rock, can occasionally be seen at very low tide just north of Cromer pier.

From Weybourne round to Happisburgh the relentless power of the sea has continued to eat away at the crumbling cliffline at such an alarming rate that it was necessary to move Sidestrand church inland in 1881 leaving the round tower of its medieval predecessor perched on the edge. Further round where low sandy cliffs give way to a line of yet more vulnerable marram hills the sequence of destruction includes the fishing villages of Keswick, its church severely damaged in 1382; Whimpwell, seaward of Happisburgh; Eccles, claimed by the sea during the ferocious storm of 1604 and Waxham Parva. It was the custom for a sermon to be preached once a year in the ruins at Eccles, exposed on the beach until its round tower finally collapsed in 1895. Bones exposed in the cliff face together with the bodies of sailors shipwrecked on the notorious Haisbro' Sands, known locally as the Devil's Throat, and washed up on the foreshore made this a grizzly stretch of coast, one rife with tales like 'The Undersea Bells' (p268).

Tower of Eccles-next-the Sea in the dunes, Ladbroke drawing, 1823

RUINS

The prosperity of Norfolk in the middle ages is reflected in the astonishing number of churches – at least 920 – built during this period. Some 660 have survived, another 100 have disappeared, but of greater interest in this context are the 100 or so that remain, ruinous and overgrown. Add to these another 100 or so monastic sites and the Norfolk countryside should be fertile ground for students of folklore, so quite why little of substance has emerged is not immediately apparent. At Ranworth several popular motifs have been woven together in the belief that a tunnel runs from the church and under the river Bure to St Benet's. It is said to contain treasure from the abbey guarded by a huge phantom dog. Substantial ruins like those of Castle Acre priory are, in themselves, no guarantee of legendary status whereas even the scant remains of a minor religious house like Hickling or Beeston Regis priories are said to be haunted by the familiar figure of a hooded monk. At Binham it is the secret passage believed to run between the priory and Walsingham rather than the ruins themselves that has given rise to the tale of the fiddler and his dog (p185).

Apart from circling traditions and the place legend associated with Southery church (p39) surprisingly few beliefs appear to have been inspired by ruined churches. Among those that have stood the test of time is the brief reference to the Roman goddess of the hunt, Diana and her dogs, that were said to haunt the remains of All Saints', Beachamwell, at least until the last upstanding wall of the chancel collapsed in 1989. The belief may well have its origin just south of here in the neighbouring parish of Oxborough where the footprint of Caldecott church is still discernible on a low mound. With no evidence to support the claim, the church, according to local tradition, was built on the site of a Romano British temple to the goddess. At the other end of the county the overgrown ruin of St Mary's, East Somerton, has an oak tree growing in the nave. In another example of the Catholic faith triumphant, at least

Ruins of St Mary's, East Somerton

initially, over the old religion, the church was believed to have been built on top of a witch; a witch with a wooden leg that eventually grew into the tree that destroyed God's House. The tale which, like so many, defies logic, has survived despite the medieval fabric of St Mary's and the fact that the oak is only about 100 years old. The evil spirit of the witch may be released by walking round the tree three times, presumably in an anti-clockwise direction.

ST BENET'S ABBEY

The one ruin rich in folklore is St Benet's Abbey in the Broads, the earliest religious site in the county, refounded as a Benedictine monastery by Cnut around 1020 beside the river Bure. Little remains of the great abbey church and its associated buildings, once enclosed by a large D shaped precinct wall, except for its late 14th century gatehouse. This curious sight in the meadows contains the brick tower of an early 18th century windmill rising from within it. Grown rich on extensive peat workings the abbey tried, with little success, to swell its coffers when the workings became flooded by rising sea levels in the late middle ages. It did so by promoting the cult of the uncanonised St Wolfeius and the equally obscure St Margaret, the martyr of Holm,

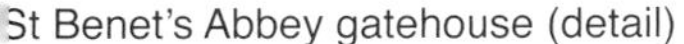

St Benet's Abbey gatehouse (detail)

St Benet's Abbey gatehouse and windmill, from an engraving by J Grieg for *Excursions Through Norfolk*, 1818

reputedly murdered in a wood at nearby Hoveton. St Benet's main claim to fame is that it was the only monastery not dissolved by Henry VIII, but the result was the same; Bishop Rugge of Norwich was made abbot but just a few years later the remaining monks had left and the buildings were plundered for their stonework. A reminder of the abbey's unique status is one of the more bizarre customs inserted in the English calender in 1939. On the first Sunday in August the Bishop of Norwich arrives in full regalia, complete with crosier, standing in the prow of a Norfolk wherry like some benign river god, to be greeted by the black robed Bretheren of St Benet's. This is followed by an open-air service on the site of the high altar marked by a large cross made of oak from the Sandringham estate. This symbolic union of Church and State on Cowholm island is a world away from the old tales of shrieking monks and devilish beasts that have circulated over the years.

The Traitorous Monk is a common enough theme in East Anglian forklore; in the legend of Hereward the Wake (p126) and more particularly in the Thetford tale of how Tutt's Hill got its name (p76). According to the historian Francis Blomefield writing in the early 18th century a troop of soldiers was sent by William the Conqueror to subdue the remote but powerful stronghold of St Benet's. They met with stiff resistance and only succeeded by bribing the monk Ethelwold to open the abbey gates under cover of darkness. Having slaughtered the abbot and his brethren the attackers granted the monk his wish to be elevated to the position of abbot. Dressed in the robes of the murdered priest he was promised a still higher reward for his treachery and was straightway strung up from 'his' Abbey gatehouse. Elaborated with each retelling, by the time of William Dutt's *Highways and Byways in East Anglia* (1901) the tale, re-counted in broad dialect, is of a Ludham marshman on his way home from his bullocks. As he draws near the gatehouse he notices something or someone emerge from the shadows that 'started screechin' like a stuck pig'.[1] Ten years later and the story, as retold by the Stalham folklorist W H Cooke, had become The Shrieking Monk that terrifies a local wherryman one foggy night – All Hallows' Eve. Rushing away to his boat moored close by the Chequers Inn he falls into the cold waters of the Bure and is drowned.

St Benet's Abbey seal

The gatehouse carvings at St Benet's hold the key to the tale of another errant monk and are part of a complex web of dragon lore that links the abbey to the nearby villages of Ludham and Horning. The iconography, although now very worn, depicts a man, possibly a wodewose, armed with spear and shield, about to engage a beast on the other side of the archway. The beast may be a lion but Blomefield refers to an early 12th century seal of the abbey which shows a knight in contemporary armour doing battle with a dragon-like creature (more like a cockatrice) that holds a young man in its beak. Blomefield is of the opinion that the seal illustrates a scene from the earliest biography of St Benedict, written in the late 6th century, in which a profligate young monk who has fled the monastery is caught by the devil in the shape of a dragon. On hearing of this the patron saint confronts the beast and returns the novice to the safety of the abbey which he vows never to leave. This cautionary tale, so graphically depicted on the gatehouse, was the first lesson in obedience to greet all those arriving at St Benet's. A better preserved example of the wodewose/dragon confrontation can be seen above the west doorway to Cawston church. The carvings here were originally early 14th century (redone in 1965), like St Ethelbert's gate to Norwich Cathedral, another Benedictine foundation where, although renewed, the same struggle between Good and Evil is re-enacted.

St Ethelbert's gate, Norwich Cathedral

Serpent benchend,
St Benedict's, Horning

Another intriguing element in this unfolding drama can be traced to Horning where the church, dedicated to St Benedict, was the parish church for the abbey. Here in the chancel the set of medieval benchends displays a preoccupation with dragons unique in Norfolk. There are carvings of dragons and other reptilian beasts crawling up the armrests of benches in places like Gateley, Great Walsingham and Cley, but at Horning the scenes – a sinner in the jaws of hell below a triumphant devil, a man wrestling a dragon, a dragon with its tail in the stocks and two serpents attacking a man – are carved across the whole flat surface of each benchend. The set may have been removed from St Benet's following its demise in the mid 16th century – one benchend carries the abbey's coat of arms.

From Horning the trail of the dragon extends a short distance to Ludham, the scene of one of the most extraordinary incidents ever recorded in Norfolk folklore. An account appeared in the *Norfolk Chronicle* for September 28th 1782 without further comment, between an article on the Yarmouth Company of Volunteers and a report on the death of a local wine merchant. This is the tale of the Ludham Worm, a 'surprising reptile':

On Monday the 16th inst. a snake of an enormous size was destroyed at Ludham, in this county, by Jasper ANDREWS, of that place. It measured five feet eight inches long, was almost three feet in circumference, and had a very long snout; what is remarkable, there were two excrescences on the fore part of the head which very much resembled horns. This creature seldom made its appearance in the day-time, but kept concealed in subterranean retreats, several of which have been discovered in the town; one near the tanning-office, another in the premises [sic] of the Rev. Mr JEFFREY, and another in the lands occupied by Mr William POPPLE, at the Hall... The skin of the above surprising reptile is now in the possession of Mr J GARRETT, a wealthy farmer in the neighborourhood.

St Michael, Ranworth church scre

Had the reporter just come across a copy of Blomefield or was he drawing on an older oral tradition? The reader might have been forgiven for thinking the whole episode was some elaborate hoax dreamt up one evening over a bottle or two of port by the local worthies named in the article. The brief reference a few years later (July 19th 1788) to 'a surprisingly large viper' that bit the person who had picked it up in the throat 'and wounded him so mortally that his life is despaired of',[2] while entirely realistic, does suggest that, in the late 18th century at least, Ludham was crawling with reptiles. By the early 20th century, in W H Cooke's embroidered version, the tale had come full circle. According to Cooke the dragon took up residence in a tunnel in the churchyard from where it terrorised the neighbourhood. Biding his time until the beast was away, one brave villager blocked the entrance to the dragon's lair with a large boulder that today rests beside the tea rooms opposite the church. On its return the dragon flew into a rage and headed off along the causeway to St Benet's, flying through the gatehouse and into a subterranean vault where it remains to this day.

While there is no single folktale that neatly weaves together the various strands of this Benedictine chronicle, the religious landscape of St Benet's was full of dragon-slaying saints in the middle ages. In addition to St Benedict defeating a dragon on the abbey seal there was, as Blomefield points out, a medieval guild to St Michael in Horning church and the benchends may refect this. At Ranworth, a place linked in folklore to St Benet's, its painted screen is adorned with images of saints – George, Margaret and Michael – the last dispatching the Book of Revelation's seven-headed serpent. Today it is merely dragonflies that haunt St Benet's and skim the surface of Ranworth Broad.

MONUMENTS

In the Hare chapel at Stow Bardolph, built by John Hare in 1624 as 'a spacious dormitory for .. himself and his family,'[3] is the largest collection of funerary monuments in Norfolk. Among them is the effigy of young Sarah Hare who died in 1744, aged eighteen, a monument unique in English parish churches. Having pricked her finger while doing some needlework she died of blood poisoning, a punishment, so the story goes, for sewing on a Sunday. She left detailed instructions that she should be buried by 'six poor men of the parish' and that her effigy should be made of wax, with her face and

Sarah Hare wax effigy
Stow Bardolph

hands cast from life, as a warning to all those who break the Sabbath. And there she is, a grim spectacle draped in a crimson silk scarf peering out from a mahogany cabinet in a corner of the chapel, according to her instructions. Her piercing glass eyes stare straight ahead to disconcert the village children who gather here for Sunday School.

At the other end of the county on the very edge of Great Yarmouth stands Bradwell church where the alabaster figure of William Vesey of Hobland Hall in the south of the parish kneels near the altar, flanked by his two wives. Below in the Jacobean style of the time are his daughters, one each side of his son reclining on an elbow and holding a skull. This striking arrangement, by convention, indicates he had died young but, according to local tradition, the tableau portrays the discovery, by his sisters, of the little boy in Bradwell Wood. It is not clear whether he was dead or simply lost but the story may have been inspired by the popularity of the Babes in the Wood tale (p59) published a little earlier, in 1595, as a broadside ballad.

The Gerbrygge monuments, Wickhampton church

Overlooking a wide expanse of grazing marsh, Wickhampton church contains the late 13th century effigies of Sir William and Lady Gerbrygge recumbent in the chancel beneath sumptuous canopies. Sir William was a rich landowner – the name Gerbrygge means 'Yare Bridge' – and he was responsible for the first bridge over the river at Haddiscoe. For the purposes of an ingenious tale known as The Wicked Brothers that probably originated in some medieval boundary dispute, the Gerbrygges are transformed into the Hampton brothers who had once fought so ferociously they had '*... torn each others hearts out...*'.[4] As a punishment they were turned to stone and placed in the church with their hearts in their hands as a monument to their wickedness – Lady

Gerbrygge's heart and hands have since been removed. One of the two parishes at the centre of this unnatural conflict became Wicked Hampton, since contracted to Wickhampton, and the other was renamed Hell-fire-gate, now Halvergate. In the nave the remains of a 14th century wall painting, 'The Three Living and the Three Dead', a popular medieval fable graphically portraying the vanity of earthly desires, is a timely reflection on the sin of Greed that provoked the Wicked Brothers into such a violent frenzy.

Late c13 effigy of Sir William Gerbrygge,
St Andrew's, Wickhampton

FOLK HEROES

QUEEN BOUDICA

Once upon a time every school child knew about Queen Boudica and her bloody revolt against the might of imperial Rome. As a woman and a symbol of resistance around whom the Iceni rebellion coalesced, her place in history is secure, but like most folk heroes she remains a shadowy figure. We know that she was married to Prasutagus, king of the Iceni tribe but even her personal name has gone unrecorded. Boudica, the spelling recently corrected from 'Boudicea', is from the Celtic *Bouda* meaning 'Victory'. What little we know comes directly from Roman historians like Dio Cassius whose description, written c200AD, has immortalised the warrior queen:

> She was very tall, and her aspect was terrifying, for her eyes flashed fiercely and her voice was harsh. A mass of red hair fell down to her hips, and around her neck was a twisted gold necklace: over a tunic of many colours she wore a thick mantle fastened with a brooch – this was her invariable attire. Now she clutched a spear to help her strike fear into all beholders, and spoke in this manner ... When she had finished, she consulted the will of the gods by

letting a hare escape from the folds of her robes: it ran in what they considered to be a lucky direction, and the crowd gave a mighty cheer. Boudica then raised her hands to heaven and said, 'I thank you, Andrasta, and call upon you as woman speaking to woman … I beg you for victory and preservation of liberty ... Mistress, be forever our leader.

Boudica was not only a formidable leader, intelligent and charismatic, but the revenge she sought for the rape of her daughters and the insults borne by her tribe were, in themselves, sufficient to explain her position at the head of the rebellion. Another possible explanation is that, as in some other Celtic tribes, succession in the Iceni royal family may have been matrilineal. Caesar mentions the hare as especially sacred to the British and its use by Boudica as a means of divination suggest the warrior queen was at one level an agent of divine retribution with access to occult powers. Her followers may have regarded her as a direct descendant of Andrasta, 'The Invincible One', and the Celtic goddess invoked by Boudica whose own name Victory may have been an hereditary religious title passed down through the female line.

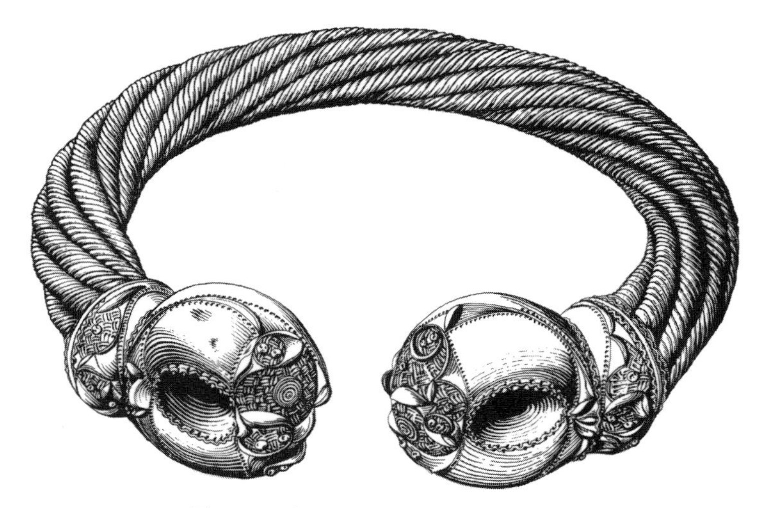

The great Iron Age torc, Snettishamp

This much is speculation but what do we know of the tribe that Boudica led into battle? Who were the Iceni and where was their tribal territory? Caesar first identifies a tribe living north of the Thames called the Cenimagni or 'the Great Iceni' and Tacitus, writing shortly after, refers to them living north of the Trinovantes, the Essex-based tribe that extended up into Suffolk. Defended from attack along the north coast by hill forts at Holkham, Warham and South Creake and by undrained fen to the west, the tribal heartland of the Iceni can be traced to north west Norfolk. The Iceni may well have been a loose knit confederation of extended family units but if there was a single nucleus it is likely to have been at Ken Hill, Snettisham, the spur of high land overlooking the Wash. The case rests on both the natural advantage of the site and the fabulous archaeological finds made at what has become known as the 'torc field'. First discovered in 1948 and at regular intervals over the next 40 years these intricately

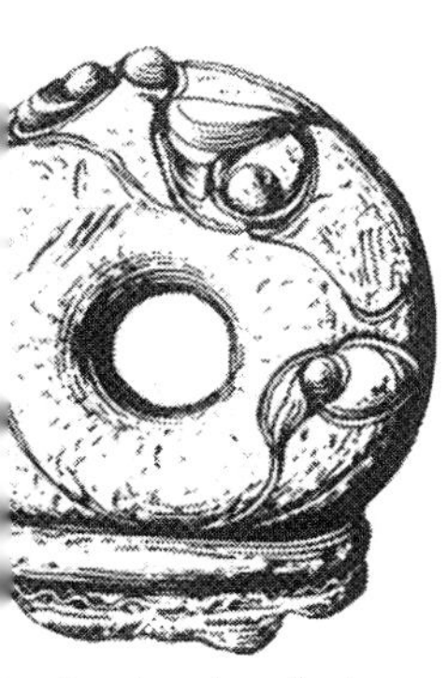
on Age torc terminal, North Creake

twisted gold necklaces were the ultimate status symbol worn by Boudica and the Iceni aristocracy. Together they represent the collective wealth of a high ranking family, buried either for safekeeping or as a votive offering to the gods. Significant too, but as yet unexplored, is the large polygonal enclosure nearby; more likely a sacred rather than defensive structure, it would emphasise the ritual importance of Ken Hill. The finds here and elsewhere in this part of Norfolk represent the greatest concentration of gold torcs in western Europe.

Since the first spectacular finds at Ken Hill much of what we know about the nature of Iceni society has continued to come from an increasing range of archaeological objects. Although the tribal structure was not highly centralised it appears from the growing number of elaborate harness fittings – enamelled terrets, strap unions and decorative bridle bits – that there was a strong local identity based on the horse. Unlike coins from other parts of the country, the horse is depicted on almost every Icenian coin and the distaste for horsemeat in Britain that persists to this day may well date from the time when the horse was a totem animal. The wolf and boar, both once widespread in Norfolk, also appear on Iceni coins, on votive figurines like the Methwold boar and the helmet crest unearthed in Ashmanhaugh. Coins are occasionally inscribed with ECE or ECEN, rulers named after the tribe, or distinguished by astrological symbols, notably the back-to-back crescent, and the triplet dot motif, all of which were used to enhance identity in the Kingdom of the Horse.

Iron Age boar figurine, Methwold

Iceni coin

The Little Ouse had long been regarded as the southern border with the Trinovantes, and the point where the river and its tributary, the Thet, were crossed by the Icknield Way became of strategic importance to the Iceni. This major overland route which enabled Iron Age tribes to trade along the chalk uplands and into Wessex, was also a line of attack. By about 500BC the Iceni had thrown up a great defensive earthwork with oval shaped ramparts and double ditches immediately north of the Thet in what became the town of Thetford. It was almost certainly here that Boudica gathered together the various Iceni groups before marching south to confront the Roman legions at Colchester.

In the opposite direction the route of the Icknield Way lay northwards, up out of the valley and over what is now Gallows Hill. It was not until 1980 that the full significance of this site on the edge of Thetford came dramatically to light. Commanding views down over large tracts of open heath it had begun life as a square ditched enclosure around a Bronze Age barrow but was transformed c40AD, probably in response to the Claudian invasion of Britain, into a huge rectangular space. Bounded by another ditch it contained five round structures, the central one a massive building and probably two storey aligned with the main eastern entrance. The whole complex was surrounded by a unique arrangement of nine parallel rows of timber palisades. When first uncovered on the edge of an industrial estate the site was thought to be that of Boudica's palace but with few signs of domestic occupation it is now considered more likely to have served some ceremonial purpose, the immense layers of perimeter fencing creating a formalised oak grove (p13). As a ritual site familiar to Boudica it would have been a focal point for the whole tribe and a potent symbol of Iceni resistance.

Reconstruction of the Iceni religious site, Gallows Hill, Thetford

The rebellion led by Boudica in 60AD was the culmination of resentment that had been simmering for years and which finally boiled over following the indignities visited on their leader and on the whole Iceni tribe. King Prasutagus had agreed to rule as a client king under Roman control, an arrangement which in practice was fraught with difficulty. Before marching on north Wales the governer Ostorius

Scapula decided to disarm 'all suspect tribes' including the Iceni who regarded themselves as allies of Rome. This open display of mistrust led directly to the rebellion of 47AD, an uprising savagely put down by superior Roman forces. Prasutagus managed to keep order for the next few years but on his death in 60AD, and contrary to the terms of his agreement, he attempted to leave half his kingdom to his two daughters. This, compounded by a demand for the repayment of loans that the Iceni had thought to be gifts, the public flogging of Boudica and the rape of her daughters, ignited the flame of rebellion. Joined by the Trinovantes, the Iceni, led by their queen, swept south, laying waste to the provincial Roman capital at Colchester before moving on to sack London and St Albans in turn. The rebellion was short-lived and Boudica's overstretched army was finally defeated somewhere in the midlands by a smaller, more disciplined Roman force, but not before a series of humiliating defeats had been inflicted on the enemy.

Crownthorpe Hoard, Roman drinking vessel

In these troubled times the native population sought to safeguard their valuables underground until some semblance of order had been established. Coin hoards from the late first century AD have been unearthed near *Venta Icenorum* (Caistor St Edmund) and around Thetford while the Crownthorpe hoard of Roman drinking vessels discovered in 1992 near Wymondham was probably buried by the owner fleeing Boudica's army as it gathered momentum. Another notable find from this period, the beautiful Roman silver cups unearthed at Hockwold on the edge of the Fens in 1962, may have been looted treasure or deposited as votive offerings during a time of unprecedented upheaval – several had been deliberately damaged before burial (p13). When Colchester was razed to the ground the life-size equestrian statue of Claudius was also destroyed, its ultimate fate a mystery until the remarkable discovery in 1907 of the emperor's bronze head in the river Alde at Rendham in Suffolk. Even more remarkable was the recovery, some 72 years later, of the bronze knee of a horse hacked off at each end, from an area of Iron Age occupation in Ashill. Both pieces are hollow-cast, have a similar alloy content and are almost certainly from the same statue. Most likely brought back as trophies by Boudican veterans they were each deposited in a river and may have been offered to the gods for their safe return.

Head of Claudius, Rendham

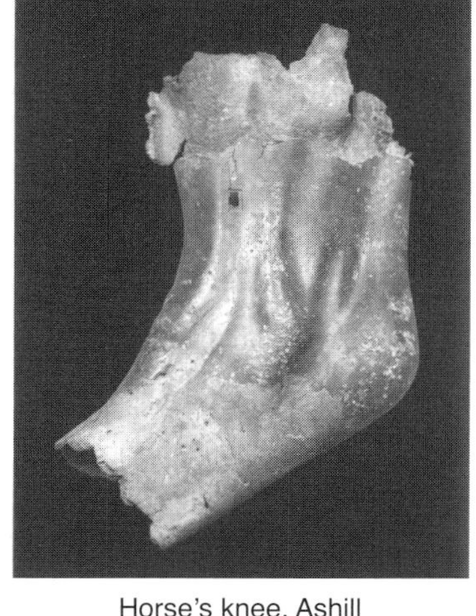

Horse's knee, Ashill

Although she escaped the final battle the fate of Boudica is uncertain. According to Tacitus she took poison rather than face the ignominy of capture but Dio Cassius records her death from disease and her burial with great ceremony. Most probably her body was brought back to Norfolk for a final resting place near her Thetford headquarters but the ceremonial enclosure on Gallows Hill had been destroyed soon after the rebellion. The cluster of sites that claim to be Boudica's grave lie some eight miles to the east on the edge of Breckland, claims that may owe much to parochial rivalry. Just north of the main road to Diss is Garboldisham Heath, long since ploughed up except for one large barrow known, at least since the mid 19th century, as both Soldier's Hill and Boudica's Grave. A few miles north at Quidenham the Iceni queen

Village sign, Quidenham

in her war chariot bestrides the village sign and is believed to be buried opposite the church 'along with all her jewels' beneath what, in truth, is a small, overgrown Norman motte still referred to as Viking's Mound on the O S map. A large quantity of bones unearthed in the churchyard in the 18th century has also led to the belief that the mound was the site of a battle.

'Boudica's grave', Garboldisham

One explanation for the number of royal burial sites believed to exist in this part of Norfolk may be found in the adjoining parish of Kenninghall at Candle Yards, where according to the local historian Walter Rye, 'Boudicca is said to have held court'. This double moat, the site of Easthall Manor, was replaced by a much grander brick house, Kenninghall Place (palace) in the early 16th century for the Duke of Norfolk. The antiquarian John Leyland who visited the new house in 1525, said of the old manor that 'there lay a Queen or sum grete lady, and there dyed'. Not long after, in 1578, Elizabeth I stayed with the Duke on her progress through the county and her visit, together with the far older Boudican tradition, appear to have become conflated in the minds of local people. Kenninghall, a royal manor at the Conquest, became a place of royal lineage, the Hundred court of Guiltcross met in the parish and the manor included land in those nearby parishes with their own rival burial mounds – Garboldisham and Quidenham.

ST EDMUND

As the last Saxon king of East Anglia more is known about the circumstances of St Edmund's death than his life. According to a brief entry in the *Anglo Saxon Chronicle*, compiled some twenty years after his death in 870AD 'In this year the raiding army rode across Mercia into East Anglia, and took up winter quarters at Thetford. And that winter King Edmund fought against them, and the Danes had the victory and killed the king and conquered all the land.' There is no suggestion here that Edmund was martyred and neither is it clear that he was killed in battle. It is another century or more before the story of his transformation from warrior king to Christian saint is told in the earliest 'Life' of Edmund, *Regis et Martyris*, written c985 by the monk Abbo of Fleury while resident in the Fens at Ramsey Abbey.

By way of verification the story, in which Edmund was captured *in palatio* by the pagan Hunguar at a place called *Haegilisdun*, is said to have come from the mouth of Edmund's armour-bearer. Edmund's life was to be spared if he agreed to rule the region as a 'puppet' king under Danish control. His refusal to submit to such terms results in his execution; he is tied to a tree and shot through with arrows much like Saint Sebastian, his death a form of ritual sacrifice to the Scandinavian god Odin. Edmund's severed head is then thrown into the undergrowth of Haegilisdun Wood where it remains, guarded by an enormous wolf, until the Danish withdrawl and some semblance of peace is restored. At this point Edmund's followers emerge and go in search of his head, hoping to reunite it with his body so that they can give their much-loved leader a proper Christian burial. In response to their cries of 'Where are you?' Abbo has the severed head reply 'Here, here, here!' and it is found between the front paws of the wolf. Edmund's body is buried in a humble chapel where it remains until news of the miracles attendant at his grave lead to the translation of the royal corpse to the place that becomes Bury St Edmunds. Here, before Edmund's body is enshrined in the church built for the purpose, it is found to be uncorrupt and to bear the scar that makes plain his beheading.

Wolf benchend with St Edmund's hea[d] Walpole St Peter

Martyrdom of St Edmund, c13 glass, Saxlingham Nethergate

In this way the cult of East Anglia's saint was established; 'Edmund the political symbol had been absorbed into Edmund the monastic patron.'[1] By the 12th century, as pilgrims flocked to pay homage at his magnificently gilded casket in the abbey church, St Edmund acquired a past life that sought to provide the young heir apparent with a Norfolk background. This is set out in the *De infantia sancti Edmundi* compiled c1155 by the Thetford monk Geoffrey of Wells in which Edmund's childless predecessor, King Offa, nominates the boy as his successor. Returning from Saxony Edmund lands on the north Norfolk coast at Hunstanton and travels inland to Attleborough where he spends a year studying in preparation for his coronation on the Suffolk/Essex border at Bures and his allotted role as King of East Anglia. While much of Geoffrey's 'Life' of Edmund has been dismissed as 'fictional, folkloric or legendary'[2] it may well have reflected stories circulating in Norfolk at the time.

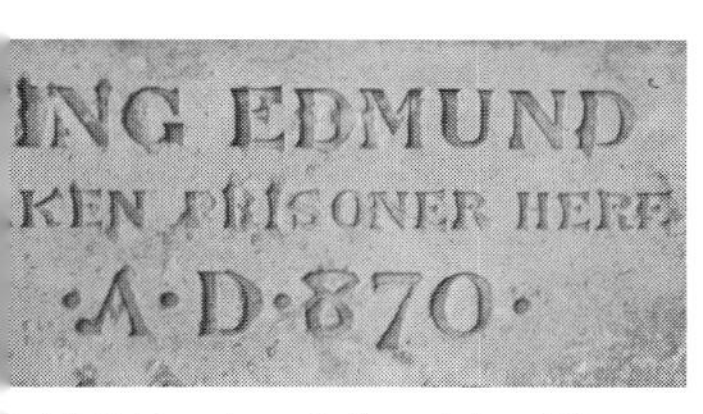

Gold Bridge inscription, late c19, Hoxne, Suffolk

Bloods Dale, Hellesdon/Drayton

ument marking the spot in Hoxne where Edmund's oak stood

The cult of St Edmund became so closely identified with the notion of East Anglia as an ancient kingdom that the exact whereabouts of his martyrdom has inevitably become the subject of rival claims, claims based on the etymological interpretation of *Haegelisdun*. From the late 18th century the village of Hoxne, just south of the Waveney in Suffolk, has become associated with Edmund's death. Gold Bridge just south of the village over Gold Brook is where he is said to have hidden from the Danes only to be betrayed by a newly married couple who saw the king's spurs glinting in the moonlight. As a result Edmund cursed all couples passing over the bridge on their way to be married, and for years after wedding groups would make a wide detour to avoid it. In a field, east of the road towards Cross Street, St Edmund's monument marks the site of an ancient oak that finally collapsed in August 1843. Stretching credulity just a little, it was said to be the tree where, almost exactly a thousand years earlier, Edmund had been shot through with arrows. This belief was given fresh impetus by the discovery of 'a piece of curved iron, possibly an arrowhead' in the tree when it split open, and by locals removing pieces of wood as souvenirs.

A more plausible site was identified in the 1970s on the basis of place name evidence a few miles south east of Bury St Edmunds in the parish of Bradfield St Clare; from a field name 'Hellesden' and Kingshall Street in the adjoining parish of Rougham. But what of Hellesdon in the Wensum valley just west of Norwich? According to the *Oxford Dictionary of English Place Names* it 'was the place where St Edmund suffered martyrdom. *Haegelisdun* has been identified with Hoxne and with Hollesley (both in Suffolk) but is obviously Hellesdon.' The argument in favour of Hellesdon is supported by the presence of a field sloping down to the Wensum called Bloods Dale that is traditionally the site of a battle between Saxons and Danes. Although the field is just in the adjoining parish of Drayton, in the time of Edmund's death parish boundaries were not then fixed and the site could well have been either wholly in Hellesdon or have straddled the two parishes.

The importance of Hellesdon and the Wensum valley should be seen in a wider geographic context and in particular in relation to the distribution of churches dedicated to the martyred king. The cult of St Edmund had, after all, evolved in response to Danish incursions and in Abbo's 'Life' the Danes arrived in Norfolk by sea, raiding down the east coast from Northumbria, not overland from Mercia. From the Wash they moved up the Great Ouse and its tributaries, burning churches as they went, churches which, in places like Emneth, Lynn, Downham Market and Foulden, were rebuilt and dedicated to the Saxons' heroic resistance leader. Approached up the Little Ouse the strategically placed town of Thetford, sacked by the Danes who overwintered there, re-emerged with two more religious houses dedicated to St Edmund.

Martyrdom of St Edmund, mural, Pickering, North Yorkshire

Martyrdom of St Edmund, c15 pilgrim badge, Quidenham

The Danish fleet, continuing round the Norfolk coast, sailed into the Great Estuary – there are St Edmund churches around the shoreline at Thurne, Acle, West Caister and Fritton – before moving inland up the Yare. Under their leaders, Ivor the Boneless (Abbo's 'Hunguar'), the Danes slaughtered those Saxons still living in and around the abandoned Roman town of *Venta Icenorum* before setting up winter quarters there. The place is not refered to by name in Abbo's 'Life' but the reference to a *civitas* or administrative centre is unmistakably the settlement that came to be known as Caistor St Edmund, its church dedicated to the saint in a corner of the walled town and another

c15 remains of
dmund's Nunnery, Lyng

rtyrdom of St Edmund,
ood screen, Wellingham

at Markshall on the opposite side of the Tas valley. Meanwhile Edmund and his men have occupied a strategic position on the banks of the Wensum at Hellesdon where they can control land and river routes, thereby thwarting any attempt to attack the Saxon bishopric upstream at North Elmham, the most important religious foundation in Norfolk at the time. Having learnt of Edmund's whereabouts and his refusal to accept terms, Ivor's army fall upon the Saxon force. The ensuing conflict is more like a massacre – Abbo does not even mention a battle but merely observes that 'few Christians remained alive'. Instead of pushing on inland to plunder the cathedral at North Elmham, Ivor returns to Caistor; Edmund dead is no use to the Danish leader and without a client king to rule East Anglia on his behalf he sails back down the Yare to pursue his bloody campaign elsewhere. Ivor's sudden departure after his military success at Hellesdon appears to Edmund's followers as little short of miraculous, testament to the ultimate strength of their martyred king who, even in death, has driven the heathen army from his kingdom.

Edmund's body, taken upstream passed the smouldering remains of churches at Costessey and Taverham, both later rebuilt and dedicated to him, is entrusted to the nunnery at Lyng on the banks of the Wensum. It is here in this minor religious house that his body would have been prepared for burial. We know from Abbo that it was first attended by a woman called Olwen who cut Edmund's hair and nails that had continued to grow. The nunnery had, according to another tradition, been founded to pray for the souls of those killed in a nearby battle between Saxons and Danes and it was here that the martyr's body was laid to rest until its translation to Bury c900AD. Today there is evidence of Mid/Late Saxon activity near the site of the nunnery in the shape of pottery sherds, fasteners and a rare prick spur while the wooded valley slope overlooking the site was still known as King's Grove in the 19th century. The scant remains that survive are however of a later Benedictine chapel transferred in 1176 to its mother foundation, St George's Nunnery in Thetford.

The suggestion that the Danish army used the Great Estuary as a base from which to carry out raids deep into East Anglia is supported by the legend of Lothbrock, associated with Reedham. This tale of treachery and revenge, first set down by Roger of Wendover in his early 13th century *Flowers of History*, was retold by Blomefield in his *History of Norfolk* (1775). In Blomefield's version Ragnor Lothbrock ('Hairy Breeks') is a shadowy historical figure 'said to be a Danish King' who:

> while hawking among certain little islands, in a boat, was by a sudden tempest carried out to sea, and drove ashore here [Reedham], and brought to *Edmund*, king of the *East Angles* then residing at *Castor* in *Flegg*, who being pleased with his behaviour, fortune and great skill in hunting, *Bern*, the king's falconer, envying him, murdered him privately in a wood. *Lothbrock's* dog was observed in a day or two, to come to the King's house, half famished, and as soon as fed to be gone again, and being on the King's command watched, brought them to the body of his dead master.
>
> *Bern* being found guilty of this murder, was condemned to be put into the boat that *Lothbrock* arrived in, and committed to the mercy of the sea, without provision or tackle. This boat being

providentially driven on the same place it came from, and known, *Bern* was seised, and to save himself, declared that *Lothbrock*, on his arrival into *England* had been killed by order of King *Edmund*.

Hingar [Ivor], and Hubba, the 2 sons of *Lothbrock*, swearing revenge, invaded with 20,000 men, *Edmund's* kingdom of the *East-Angles*, attended by *Bern* the traitor, and by them *Edmund* was barbarously murdered, in the year 870.

Medieval tile depictir a falconer, Reedhar

While there is no evidence to identify Reedham as the location for what the *Anglo Saxon Chronicle* called 'the great heathen army' invasion, the village was then on the shoreline of the Great Estuary and the Lothbrock legend provides a colourful explanation for both why and where the Danes made landfall in Norfolk. It also explains Ivor's part in the death of Edmund, although the exact nature of his martyrdom, beyond its barbarity, is left unclear. The detail of Lothbrock's dog guarding his master's body may have been inserted to draw comparison with that of the wolf keeping watch over Edmund's severed head. The medieval floor tile discovered in Reedham church depicting a falconer on horseback is probably coincidental – hunting scenes were popular in medieval art and literature – but could have been a reference to the Lothbrock legend then current among the people along this tidal shoreline.

St Edmund, rood screen, Ludhan

Following the translation of Edmund's body to Bury, healing miracles at his shrine and in places like the nunnery at Lyng, began to appear in the records as the cult of St Edmund spread throughout East Anglia. To judge by the number of medieval churches and chapels once dedicated to his name in Norfolk – 25 – the county has far greater claim to have been the centre of his cult than Suffolk, with a mere half dozen dedications. Throughout the medieval period St Edmund was venerated across the county, his martyrdom graphically depicted in many forms from the 12th century mural in the apse of Fritton church near Yarmouth, 'like an episode from the Bayeax Tapestry'[3] to the beautiful mid 13th century glass roundels in the chancel at Saxlingham Nethergate, the roof bosses in the cloisters of Norwich Cathedral, and the 15th century choirstall carving of the wolf guarding the saint's crowned head at Walpole St Peter in the Fens. He is most often depicted on late medieval rood screens, including Wellingham and the great Broadland screens at Ludham and Barton Turf, where he is regally arrayed in ermine in the company of those other royal saints, Edward the Confessor and Henry VI, with the emblem of his martyrdom, an arrow, in one hand and a sceptre in the other.

TOM HICKATHRIFT

Deep in the heart of the Norfolk Fens lies the parish of Marshland St James, the dedication taken from the medieval chapel swept away years before in one of several catastrophic floods. As an administrative unit the parish is however relatively new, created in 1923 to amalgamate detached parcels of land belonging to the 'Seven Towns of Marshland' (Clenchwarton, Emneth, Terrington, Tilney, Walpole, Walsoken and West Walton). They stretch in a great arc to the north and west of an expanse of flat marsh known as the Smeeth (from Old English 'smooth') which had been grazed communally since the middle ages. United by their struggle to maintain the sea wall and drain the land, the rich grazing marsh was divided up by the surrounding parishes. This complex pattern of land management inevitably led to numerous disputes and it was from one of these that the giant Tom Hickathrift first emerged 'in the reign before William the Conqueror' as a most unlikely folk hero.

The deeds of Tom Hickathrift, c17 woodcut

Brought up by his hardworking mother, Tom, like most giants, is lazy, dull and endowed with great strength. One day, having eventually found work with a Lynn brewer, he is on his way to Wisbech across the Smeeth when he comes across a group of angry tenants in hot dispute with their landlord over grazing rights on the common. In the earliest account of this confrontation, in John Weever's *Ancient Funeral Monuments* (1631), Tom arms himself with an axle-tree and wheel from his cart that become his trademark weapons, and sets about the landlord and his men. Cast in the role of champion of the poor he urges his village neighbours to defend their liberties over the common. Weever's account was accepted by most later antiquarians including Spelman and Blomefield, but from the late 17th century a more colourful folkloric version began to appear under the title 'The History of Tom Hickathrift' in chapbooks circulating in the area. Drawing on other themes popular at the time, the evil landlord is recast as a fearsome ogre and Tom as the hero of Marshland. The ogre, so much bigger and more terrifying than Tom, lives in a cave on the Smeeth. To avoid him, local people are forced to make a wide detour, but one day on his way to Wisbech Tom decides to cut across the marsh only to be confronted by the club-wielding giant. 'Do you not see how many heads hang upon yonder tree that have offended my law! But thy head shall hang higher than all the rest for an example'. Up spoke brave young Tom (some might say 'foolhardy young Tom' but this is a folktale) to deliver the memorable risposte: 'A turd in your teeth for your news, for you shall not find me like one of them.' After a long and bloody battle and with only his axle-tree and cart wheel to defend himself, Tom defeats the ogre and cuts off his head. On entering the cave he finds a treasure trove of gold and silver that the ogre has accumulated over the years by terrorising the district. As the people's champion he redistributes some of the land acquired by the ogre, destroys his lair and builds a fine new house on the site for himself and his mother.

Village sign depicting Tom Hickathrift

Not surprisingly, perhaps, it is this version of Tom's triumph that has proved more enduring and which has attracted other increasingly outlandish tales of the Fenland giant's strength and valour, as the local hero grew into a legendary figure. Among the earliest feats of strength described in the chapbooks is the occasion Tom lifts an enormous bundle of straw without effort, a load far greater than anyone else can attempt, even though, to test his strength still further, a number of large stones have been hidden in the bundle. On another occasion Tom dispatches four armed robbers, thieves who in the retelling become a band of robbers driven from the region. He then comes upon a sturdy tinker blocking his path. Neither man will step aside and so they set to, armed with staves, much like Robin Hood and Little John, before agreeing to put an end to their struggle. Tom invites the tinker home and they become brothers-in-arms, but who is this man that Tom fails to overcome? His name, Henry Nonsuch, suggests he is no mere mortal and perhaps his special powers are derived from his trade as an itinerant dealer in metal goods. Together they travel to Ely to put down a rebellion, a force of some 10,000 men, but when Tom's club breaks he 'seized upon a lusty, raw-boned miller' (millers had a reputation for dishonesty) and made use of him as a weapon, 'till at length he cleared the field ...' As a reward the tinker receives a pension for life and Tom is knighted by the king, a position of respectability that persuades Tom to seek a wife. After defeating a rival and his band of ruffians he marries Sarah Gedyng, a rich young widow from Cambridge. During the wedding feast a silver cup that had disappeared is discovered about the person of an old woman called Strumbolow. Ignoring calls for her to be hacked to pieces in traditional fashion, Tom decides to spare her life in favour of public humiliation but this is no morality tale; folktales were, after all, somewhat gruesome forms of entertainment:

> He bored a hole through her nose, and tied a string thereto, then tied her hands behind her back, and ordered her to be stripped naked, commanding the rest of the old women to stick a candle in her fundament, and then lead her by the nose through the streets and lanes of Cambridge, which comical sight caused a genial laughter.

The story of Tom Hickathrift culminates in a final battle of mythic proportions when he is deployed by the king to engage a cyclopean monster 'mounted on a dreadful dragon, beating upon his shoulder a club of iron' who, in the company of bears and lions, had landed in Kent and was terrifying the Isle of Thanet. The eye in the middle of his forehead '... seemed to appear like a flaming fire; his visage was grim and tawney, his back and shoulders like snakes of prodigious length, the bristles of his beard like rusty wire ...'. In the face of overwhelming odds the reader might well expect Tom to have struggled to overcome such a monstrous foe but there is no account of a long and bloody encounter. True to form Tom emerges unscathed having run the ogre through with his sword, an axle-tree no longer appropriate to this fearless knight of the realm. The dragon and assorted beasts are dispatched in similar fashion but the tinker is eventually killed by a lion. Tom returns home to the Fens where he dies soon after, grieving for his friend.

Hickathrift candlestick, Tilney All Saints

Although the various written sources shed no light on where Tom was born there is general agreement that he was buried at Tilney All Saints. The exact position of his grave and the choice of All Saints have however given rise to much confusion among antiquarians. Whereas the arrows loosed by folk heroes like Robin Hood and the Hertfordshire giant Jack of Legs determined their final resting places, for Tom it was where the stone ball landed that he had kicked from two miles distant at Tilney St Lawrence – some say it was a hammer thrown from the Smeeth, at least six miles away. The indentation made by the missile which struck All Saints' church can still be seen in the chancel wall but another version refers to a crack that can never be properly repaired. Below the point of impact is the long stone slab that is said to mark the grave of Tom Hickathrift. The problem is that several 17th century sources describe the lid of his grave 'upon which an Axell-tree and cartwheel are insculped' and yet the churchyard coffin lid is a plain granite slab. Murray's 1870 *East Anglian Handbook* suggests the original lid had recently been moved into the church whereas the most likely explanation is that there are two large and quite separate graves. Blomefield was of the opinion that the decorative finish on the lid inside the church that had been misinterpreted as Hickathrift's axle-tree and wheel was 'a cross patteé on the summit of a staff', the emblem of a Knight Templar. The worn decoration is now thought to be an omega slab and the grave of Sir Frederick de Tylney, a crusader knight killed at Acre in Syria in 1191. Of particular relevance is that he was known to be a warrior of great strength and stature; the historical figure most likely to have given rise to the legend of Tom the Marshland giant. Attention has also been drawn to the resemblance, at least superficially, between the names Frederick and Hickathrift.

Tom Hickathrift and the Wisbech giant, former Sun Inn, Saffron Walden

The de Tylney connection is intriguing but there is also a convincing explanation for the ogre's lair in the Smeeth, based on several late 19th century references to a low artificial mound near the village crossroads in Marshland St James. Known locally as the Giant's Grave it was visible in a field, since partially developed, that also contained a dry pond, Hickathrift's Hand Basin. If the earthwork had been a burial mound the hollow internal space may have given rise to the idea of the ogre's cave which in this marshy landscape would soon have become a rather waterlogged hole in the ground. Having killed the giant, Tom's discovery of a gold and silver hoard deep inside the cave is at least consistent with the widespread belief in treasure buried in ancient earthworks (p74). The mound was never excavated but the presence of a prehistoric barrow in an expanse of undrained marsh seems unlikely. The 1925 edition of *Kelly's Directory* suggests it may have been raised as a moot place where it was customary, right up until the late 18th century, for commoners from the Seven Towns of Marshland to meet at midsummer each year.

The mound was once crowned by an ancient stone cross, the base of which was discovered in the 1930s when soil was taken to fill in the pond. It now forms the base of the village sign at Marshland St James that proudly displays its hero, but several Marshland churches lay claim to the Hickathrift legend. For years the cross from the mound was believed to have been removed to the churchyard at Terrington St John where, as at Tilney All Saints, there are the shafts of preaching crosses known as Hickathrift's Candlesticks. A variation on the ball-kicking episode that determined where Tom would be buried, is the occasion when he beat the devil at a game of football in the churchyard at Walpole St Peter during which Satan kicked the ball so hard it made a hole in the wall of the church. There is also a small and very worn satyr-like figure on the north side of the church at Walpole with arms upraised that, according to Murray's *Handbook* (1892), local people believed to be an image of Hickathrift. One thing to emerge from the legend of the Marshland giant is that there is no simple narrative but an accumulation of locally associated stories, often in circulation long before they were first written down, by which each of the Seven Towns of Marshland contributed to the collective memory of their folk hero.

Grave slab of Sir Frederick de Tylney

HEREWARD THE WAKE

In the introduction to his remarkable collection *More Tales from the Fens* (1964) Jack Barrett asks why, in tales of 'wily fenmen getting the better of Ely monks',[4] there is no mention of Hereward the Wake and why the old story tellers had never heard of the Fenland hero? Barrett, himself an accomplished story teller, was of the opinion that Hereward had been dreamed up by some monk in a remote Fenland abbey, his brain stimulated by 'liberal draughts of poppy-head tea'.[5] The document Barrett had in mind was almost certainly the chronicle of Croyland Abbey, supposedly written by Hereward's contemporary Abbot Ingulf in the monastery where both Hereward and his first wife Torfrida are said to have been buried. The chronicle is now known to have been a late medieval forgery but another early account of Hereward's exploits, the *Gesta Herewardi*, is no more reliable. This mid 12th century Latin text written by an Ely monk is based on an earlier, incomplete book apparently by the hand of Hereward's priest, Leofric the Deacon, augmented by memories of Hereward's surviving outlaws and full of tales of 'giants and warriors out of old fables.'

Domesday Book first mentions a small tenant of land near Bourne on the edge of the Lincolnshire Fens, but by the 13th century Hereward emerges from the monastic chronicles as a minor folk hero with an elevated pedigree as the son of Leofric, Earl of Mercia, and Lady Godiva. At some later date the web of oral and written traditions that had given birth to Hereward the Wake became disentangled and, unlike that other Fenland hero Tom Hickathrift, his exploits were never the subject of chapbooks circulating among the rural poor in the 17th and 18th centuries. As a mythical figure Hereward remained in relative obscurity until the mid 19th century when he was rediscovered and reinvented as a romantic hero of Victorian fiction, most notably in Charles Kingsley's adventure story *Hereward the Wake* (1865). The subtitle 'Last of the English' makes clear the author's intention; to portray his subject as an Anglo Saxon resistance leader in the face of ruthless Norman oppression. While the Rev'd Kingsley's hugely popular tale was read aloud in remote outposts such as Southery rectory, the old fen tigers – Chafer Legge and Ratty Porter among them – were entertaining regulars down at the Ship Inn on Brandon Creek. The tales they told, often laced with a macabre wit, were part of an oral tradition that stretched back well into the 18th century and beyond; a tradition entirely silent on the subject of Hereward the Wake.

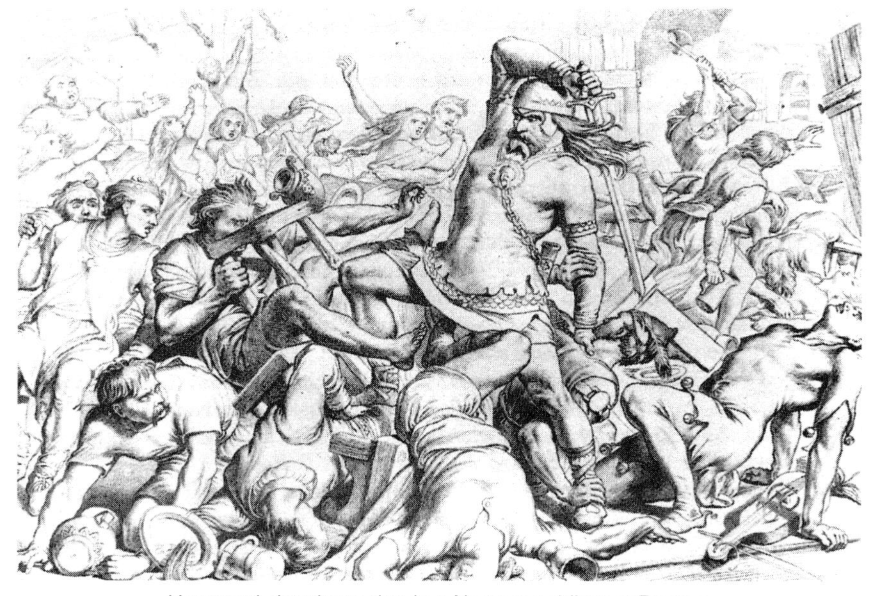

Hereward slaughters drunken Norman soldiers at Bourne

According to the *Gesta* Hereward grew up in Bourne, becoming such an unruly teenager that he was exiled c1062 by Edward the Confessor. While abroad he acquires Swallow, 'the swiftest of steeds,' his wife Torfrida and a reputation for heroic deeds, but on his return he finds the Normans have conquered England and slain his brother. Seeking revenge, and accompanied only by his friend Martin Lightfoot, Hereward heads for Bourne where he slaughters a room full of drunken knights celebrating the death of his brother in the family home, the first of many encounters with the French.

Men flock to his stronghold in Bromeswold Forest from across the Fens and beyond including one known only as 'the Robber of Drayton' and men like local heroes Leofwine the Scythe who dispatched twenty brigands and Wulric the Heron. Wulric, who had slain 'the Norman butchers' about to hang four innocent brothers on Wroke-sham (Wroxham) Bridge, was one of many dispossessed of his land who, in Kingsley's tale, lures his pursuers deeper into the Fens. Striking with deadly purpose when they flounder in the mud he then vanishes into the mist across the water with the aid of his 'leaping poles'; the kind of stilts used by fen tigers to negotiate the dykes.

Weeting Castle

Hereward the Wake may not have been familiar to a largely illiterate rural population but Kingsley, who drew heavily on the *Gesta Herewardi*, also knew the watery landscape from wildfowling trips with his father when growing up near Peterborough. Whereas Mark Twain actually stayed at the Ship Inn while recuperating in Cambridge, and exchanged stories with the locals (p183), Kingsley is unlikely to have come into such direct contact. Like many Cambridge academics he did however make excursions into the Fens and may well have picked up snippets of folklore. The incident in which Hereward splits the war arrow before it is carried into every corner of the Fens with the whisper 'the Wake is coming' is rather like the Chafer Legge story 'Grey Goose Feathers'. Here Charles I is ensured safe passage from Snowre Hall in Fordham because the men guarding the king carried the split goose feather. By this old tradition anyone in need would receive help from a true Fenman.

With his outlaw band Hereward strikes at the heart of the enemy. Travelling first into Norfolk to seek revenge for the death of his brother he attacks William de Warenne's stronghold at Castle Acre, killing de Warenne's brother Frederick before disappearing in a great cloud of sea birds. This skirmish is a prelude to the dramatic set piece siege of Ely c1070. Well defended by its natural position the cathedral city, allied to the spirit of its patron St Etheldreda, becomes the last enclave of English resistance. With the largest army he can muster William the Conqueror marches on Ely but before entering the island he must first cross an expanse of marshy terrain. A floating causeway is hurriedly constructed at Aldreth but in their rush to gain the opposite bank and plunder the cathedral treasures the bridge collapses and the flower of Norman chivalry are drowned.

Thwarted by the greed of his troops William retires to Brandune (Brandon) to consider his next move – in Kingsley's version of events he withdraws to Weeting Castle. Although this fortified house was built a century later it suited the author's purpose on the edge of the Fens, his choice prompted by the proximity of Brandune Heath. Fearing a renewed attack on Ely, Hereward, disguised as a potter, leaves the city on his horse Swallow. Spending the night in a hut on the heath he overhears two old crones foretell the time and place of William's next attack. The following day he enters the king's court and becomes involved in a kitchen brawl before escaping back to Ely.

Despite Hereward's success in destroying the French landing craft, the second assault on Ely involves a more substantial causeway, complete with high tower. This is the theatrical backdrop to the final battle. From the tower one of the Brandon hags 'howl[s] and gibber[s] [6] with filthy gestures' hurling down vile curses on the English and calling for the storm that does not come. In Kingsley's *Hereward* the heroe's wife Torfrida, having renounced the black arts and embraced the new religion, agrees to counter the witch's incantations with the power of prayer. Working herself into a religious frenzy she leads Hereward's men into battle riding 'at their head on a white charger'. As the French advance across the causeway Torfrida begins to sing 'like an angel', her voice rising above the noise of battle while pointing to where the smoke is already rising – Hereward has fired the reed beds. The flames, 'leaping and cackling, laughing and shrieking like a fiend,' [7]sweep over the causeway consuming the enemy while on the opposite bank with the tower ablaze 'the witch of Brandon throws herself desperately from the top ... falling dead upon the embers, a motionless heap of rags'[8].

So the day ends with good triumphant and William's men put to flight. Although Hereward knows he cannot hold out indefinitely, it is an act of treachery that eventually secures Ely for the French. William sends word to Abbot Thurstan that all his monastic land will be confiscated unless he surrenders. Terms are hastily drawn up and the monks agree to lead the French onto the isle. Hereward and his men escape, rowing hard for the 'wide mere by Well' near Upwell and Outwell on the Norfolk border. Harried through the Fens they take refuge deep in Bromeswold Forest where they merge into the greenwood of folklore to inspire the tales of Robin Hood. Hereward finally surrenders to William and returns home to Bourne where he is set upon by French knights. With his strength failing and without either his sword Brainbiter or his magic armour he is eventually hacked down. Torfrida sails from Croyland to claim her husband's body and lays it to rest in the abbey.

Kingsley's claim that Hereward's deeds were celebrated in song and folklore, long after his death, was made in the hope that his own story would live on. Although he managed to resurrect his hero from the obscurity of the medieval chronicles, Hereward's role as freedom fighter does not reflect his true nature. He embodies the very spirit of the Fens, a mythical will o'the wisp figure haunting the reedbeds, and it was in this guise that Hereward was ultimately defeated – not by the French but by the Dutch engineers brought over to drain the Fens in the 17th century. The complex network of dykes and levels destroyed a traditional way of life and the fierce resistance of many fenmen earned them the nickname 'Fen Tigers'. Men like Chafer Legge may not have been aware of Hereward the Wake but they inherited the same rebellious spirit that emboldened the great Fenland hero.

British Rail 'See Britain By Train' poster

SIR BARNEY BROGRAVE

Gaunt and weatherbeaten below the marram hills Waxham Hall stands at the centre of the most important group of manorial buildings in Norfolk. In the 18th century it was home to 'Owd Sir Barney Brograve', one of the most notorious landowners in the county, his reputation so fearsome that a whole cycle of macabre tales has grown up around the exploits of this real life anti-hero. In 1913, when Sir Barney's deeds were still fresh in the memory of local people, the antiquarian Walter Rye observed 'As in many other cases nearly all the local instances of extreme cunning and audacity have been fathered on him.'[9]

The low-lying coast here has always been vulnerable to flooding with numerous inundations throughout the middle ages culminating in the loss of Waxham Parva in the late 13th century. The monk John of Oxenedes, writing from his island sanctuary at St Benet's Abbey, described the devastation thus:

> In dense darkness in the month of December 1287, the sea, agitated by the violence of the wind, burst through its accustomed limits, occupying towns, fields and other places adjacent to the coast. Issuing forth about the middle of the night it suffocated or drowned men and women sleeping in their beds, with infants in their cradles, and all kinds of cattle and fresh water fishes; and it tore up houses from their foundations, with all they contained and carried them away, and threw them into the sea with irrevocable damage.

Waxham Hall

Following the Dissolution it was the ancient Wodehouse family who first grew rich from the redistribution of monastic land. By the late 16th century Sir Thomas Wodehouse had put together a sizeable estate at Waxham from land once held by Bromeholm, Ingham and Hickling priories. He built the hall, a handsome Elizabethan courtyard house, and the magnificent thatched barn. Begun just three years after the completion of the great tithe barn up the coast at Paston, the Waxham barn is a few feet longer and a testament to the rivalry between two powerful local dynasties. When Thomas Brograve arrived in east Norfolk from Essex in 1725 he had ambitions of his own, becoming heir to the Westwick estate by marrying into the Berney family. Once established he set about purchasing the manors of Waxham and Horsey, much of which, despite the presence of the largest threshing barn in Norfolk, was an expanse of marsh and reedbed. The isolated and impoverished nature of the estate may have appealed to the Brograves who came to 'epitomise the district over which they ruled; they were wild and wayward lords of a rough, untamed land.'[10]

Thomas Brograve's reputation as a ruthless individual soon became clear when, shortly after his marriage, he killed a distant relative in a duel in the year his son, Barney Brograve, was born. The son inherited not only property in Worstead and the Waxham estates on the death of his father in 1753 but a belligerent and wilful disposition. Such was his nature that he decided to dispense with a bailiff and took direct charge of his 3000 acre estate. As William Marshall discovered on a visit in 1782 while collecting material for his book *The Rural Economy of Norfolk*, Barney Brograve was no ordinary Norfolk squire:

Waxham Hall barn

The character of this man is so very extraordinary, that I cannot refrain from sketching some of its principal features. He was, I believe, bred in the army; served some time in the militia; has fought two or three duels; quarrelled with most of the gentlemen of the county; and, coming to a good paternal estate, discharged his tenants and commenced farming. His person is gross and his appearance bacchanalian – his dress that of a slovenly gentleman. – There is a politeness in his manner; and his conversation bespeaks a sensible intelligent mind; borne away, however, by a wildness and ferocity which is obvious in his countenance and discovers itself in every word and action.

The decision to undertake the day-to-day running of his estate inevitably brought 'Owd Sir Barney' into frequent contact with his employees who would be instructed to wait in the hall for their wages while he sat at a desk with the money and a loaded blunderbuss. He often fought with his farmhands but his reputation as a pugilist took a knock one day when, having decided a local sweep's fee for cleaning the hall chimneys was excessive, he challenged the man to a fight. The squire of Waxham Hall was forced to concede when he almost choked on the soot coming from the sweep's clothing. Despite the threats of violence and lawful retribution he was 'daily robbed' by a resentful workforce and local villagers who stole his livestock and shipwrecked cargo from the foreshore to which, as lord of the manor, Sir Barney was entitled. Elevated to the peerage in 1791 his coat of arms acquired the 'red hand of Ulster' but, according to local tradition, Sir Barney had been forced to wear the 'bloody hand of baronetcy' as a badge of shame having whipped a boy to death. Another version of this widely held belief resurfaced in Homersfield where the red hand is displayed on the bridge over the Waveney commissioned in 1870 by Sir 'Bobby' Shafto Adair of Flixton Hall who was said to have beaten a young ostler to death.

The Adair arms, Homersfield bridge

In the light of Sir Barney's reputation, the tale, while entirely plausible, signalled his transformation from an abusive, hard drinking landowner to legendary figure about whom increasingly sinister tales began to circulate. There were rumours he had murdered his wife, that a Brograve had cut his throat in the attic and that the hall was haunted by a succession of chivalric ancestors killed in battle over the centuries. One New Year's Eve Sir Barney invited six of these illustrious forebears to a banquet; the table was laid and toasts drunk but as midnight chimed they all vanished as mysteriously as they had arrived. After the death of his third wife in 1793 Sir Barney retreated to the new Georgian pile built for him at Worstead where he died soon after and where he lies buried in the family vault. As in life he continued to terrorise the district long after his death. Walter Rye noted that 'Everybody out Stalham way knew that "Owd Sir Barney" rode on certain nights in the year along the "carnser" [causeway] from Waxham Hall to Worstead ...'[11]. He was also said to drive the phantom coach pulled by headless horses that would ride through the gateway and into the courtyard at Waxham but the most famous Brograve legend, recounted by the Rev'd Gillett in *Bygone Norfolk* (1898) describes how Sir Barney outwitted the Devil. Unfortunately Gillett provides no source for the tale.

Monument to John Byg[...] 1818, Hickling

A certain Sir Barnabas Brograve... in a fit of reckless boasting to his mowers, said that he would mow the devil a match for his soul. Henceforward he was at the mercy of the evil one. At last he was brought to his wits' end for a device to escape the bargain, the completion of which was now insisted upon. Two acres of black stalked beans had been staked out side by side, and the fatal night drew near. Cunning Sir Barney had some small iron rods made about the size of beanstalks, these he stuck all over the devil's acre. The dread contest commenced; and while, spurred on by fear, the knight made excellent progress, His Majesty did nothing but mop his brow and stop to sharpen his scythe. As Sir Barney was running out an easy winner, his cloven-hoofed opponent shouted out – 'I say Barney bor these bunks [thistles] do cut damned hard'.

There are other problems with Gillett's version. Folklorists have either dismissed Sir Barnabas Brograve as a fictional character or have failed to recognise that he and Barney Brograve were the same historical figure. As Westwood points out the tale belongs to the international group of folktales known as 'The Mowing Contest' from the category 'Tales of the Stupid Ogre'. It has been given a local context in which the dialect word 'bunks' more likely refers either to angelica, common along the east Norfolk coast, or possibly, in view of Brograve's adversary, Devil's-bit scabious. Triumphant on this occasion the reckless squire then sells his soul to the Devil. On his death he presents himself to the Lord of the Underworld who says, in the broad Norfolk dialect of the old marshman from whom the story was collected:

Title page of *The Mowing Devil*, 1678

> I've been looking trew your account and it fare to me if I hev you in here tw'ont be a sennight afore yew'll be top dog, and I shall hev to play second fiddle, so there's your writing back, and now be off.' And Sir Barney he sayd, 'Where am I to go tew?' and the owd devil he forgot hisself, and got angry, and he say, 'Go to hell'... And they dew say there's tew devils there now.

On Sir Barney's death the sins of the father were visited on his sons as the curse of the Brograves continued down through the generations. Captain Roger Brograve shot himself in 1813 and the eldest son, Sir George, inherited mounting debts and a pack of half starved hounds kept at Waxham to guard the empty hall. On one occasion, according to the Stalham historian William Cooke, the hounds were so hungry they killed and ate their keeper. In another version it was a huntsman at Hempstead who suffered an equally gruesome fate. The death of Sir George in 1828 brought to an end one hundred years of the Brograve dynasty at Waxham but the two branches of the family are commemorated today in familiar Broads landmarks; the mill at Berney Arms on the edge of Breydon Water and Brograve drainage mill precariously balanced beside a dyke on the expanse of marsh known as Brograve Level where:

> The wind roars across sodden marshland, the sea pounds a crumbling shore and Sir Barney Brograve, gasping for breath, clumsy with fear, staggers towards the sanctuary of his mill.

Half falling into the darkness, he turns to slam the door in the devil's face. Outside the storm rages and the devil is so desperate to snatch the soul he has been promised that he kicks at the door with his cloven hoofs, and howls his sulphurous breath at the building with such diabolical power that it lurches on its waterlogged foundations.[12]

An air of desolation still hangs over Waxham and it is no small wonder that Sir Barney's domain has survived intact, although reduced in both size and status. The 15th century hall has lost a wing, and is now a farmhouse, its ivy-shrouded gatehouse on the point of collapse; the chancel of St John's church lies in ruins and its tower windows are blocked with brickwork eroded by the salt laden air. The huge thatched barn was only rescued from the ravages of time and neglect and the destructive power of the '87 hurricane by the concerted efforts of the County Council and Norfolk Historic Buildings Trust. But the dunes here are no real defence against the kind of sea surge that laid waste the coast from Happisburgh to Winterton in the '53 flood. It is only a matter of time before all trace of Sir Barney's evil outpost is swept away and his ghost, which still haunts the marshes, is consigned to a watery grave. Until then the hell hounds of Waxham may still be heard baying at the moon.

Brograve drainage mill, Waxham

THE EVIL EYE

WITCHCRAFT

The creation of the National Health Service in 1948 provided free health care to the whole population. Before the introduction of this universal welfare system, advances in medicine were largely available to those who could afford it, leaving the poorest in society, especially those in remote rural areas, to rely on their Christian faith and a mixture of folk remedies and witchcraft. People had always been at the mercy of natural disasters but most villages still had their healers, wart charmers and cunning men to alleviate the random misfortunes that continued to blight daily life; a lame horse, diseased crops or the sudden death of an infant. There had long been a distinction between these practitioners, wise women and wizards who cured minor ailments by the use of herbal remedies, and malevolent individuals who sought to do harm to others by uttering wild threats and employing occult methods.

The popular image of a witch with a tall pointed hat and black cloak astride a broomstick in mid air owes much to children's literature and European folktales but there is no evidence in this country that there were ever ritual Sabbaths or witch covens. The black witch was often old, poor and female, a marginal figure feared by many but often consulted *in extremis* who, 'at her most malevolent was an isolated individual; the creature of her own fantasies'[1]. Such was the level of witch mania in the 17th century that:

> Every old woman with a wrinkled face, a furr'd brow, a hairy lip, a gabber tooth, a squint eye, a squeaking voice or a scolding tongue, having a ragged coat on her back, a skull-cap on her head, a spindle in her hand, and a dog or a cat by her side, is not only suspected but pronounced for a witch.[2]

Most incriminating was the use of familiars or imps to do the Devil's work. They took many forms, usually small animals seen around the house or farm – cats, hares, rats and toads among the most common – and belief in them as agents of Satan lasted until well into the 19th century. An old woman living near a horse dealer in Attleborough was said to have three imps to do her bidding called Pug, Lightfoot and Bluebell. The dealer who scoffed at such nonsense showed his contempt for the witch by naming his three best horses after the imps, a foolhardy decision that would have disastrous consequences. Sure enough Bluebell was killed in an accident, Lightfoot developed a tendency to kick out dangerously and Pug went lame. Pug only recovered when his owner decided to rename him. A witch's occult knowledge and her familiars were often passed down through the generations from mother to daughter, though in this late 19th century case from Loddon, the girl was bound over to the Devil against her will:

Witches with familiars

> The night that the witch died was a terrible one; it thundered and lightened, and the wind blew afterwards like a hurricane. Just before she died she gave her daughter the box containing the imps, and bade her let them bite her breasts. She opened the box a little way, and one of the imps put its webbed wing out, but a loud clap of thunder caused the girl to shut down the lid, and the imp shrieked 'something cruel.' After telling her daughter that Satan must certainly have her as she was bound over to him, she died in a terrible fit. There was a great fire in the

room, and the girl took the box containing the imps and was going to put it on the fire; but the women who were in the room had never seen an imp, and they asked her to open the box and show them. She hesitated, but the imps screeched, and so she threw the box in the heart of the fire, and the imps crackled and howled before they were burned. Soon after, a strange man came along and made love to the girl and carried her off. Some said that it was no man at all, but Satan, to whom the girl had been bound.[3]

The violent storm brought on by the death of this witch is mirrored by the sudden tempest that accompanied the burial of a witch in Rockland St Mary in the mid 19th century. The account is from W H Dutt's *The Norfolk Broads* (1903):

as the hour for the interment approached ... [the storm] so increased in fury that at the time when the coffin was being borne to the church, and from the church to the grave, the bearers could scarcely keep their feet. So long as the witch's body was above ground the storm continued to rage; but the moment the coffin was lowered into the grave the storm ceased.[4]

Witch conjuring up a storm

Accusations of witchcraft were usually triggerd by a quarrel or long running dispute between neighbours, and victims often complained that either they or their livestock had been 'overlooked' by one with the Evil Eye. Another way for a witch to avenge herself on an enemy was by image magic. A model of the intended victim was fashioned in wax or clay and then stuck with pins in those parts of the body to be affected. Pins driven into the heart or head were meant to kill. The burning of a piece of paper with the victim's name on it was intended to inflict harm in much the same way, while burying an item of the victim's clothing would ensure a slow wasting away as the material rotted.

The most common way to bring about misfortune was to hurl abuse or by cursing the one who had caused offence and if the curse subsequently took effect the victim was said to have been 'forespoken'. The survival of cursing tablets like the lead *defixio* found at the Roman town of *Venta Icenorum* are a testament to this ancient practice. This particular tablet, dedicated to Neptune, had been tightly folded and was inscribed with a request to the god to identify the thief who had stolen a number of domestic items that were listed including a mirror, bracelets and several pewter vessels. The *defixio*, which referred to the fixing of the person cursed in their evil state, was the specialist work of a sorcerer who would also have fixed the tablet to Neptune's shrine.

Ritual cursing was used extensively by the medieval church and all sinners would feel the wrath of God. The practice became enshrined in the *Book of Common Prayer* (1549) and was read out during the Commination service: 'Curseth is he that removeth away the mark of his neighbour's land' and 'curseth is he that lieth with his neighbour's wife' etc. The pronouncement of a curse was often sufficient to bring about the desired result by means of the threat weighing heavily on the mind of the victim. Those witches with a fiercesome reputation could cause injury in this way simply through the power of suggestion, but by invoking the authority of the church the very mention of Satan could have a dramatic effect as the vicar of Helmingham discovered in 1597. 'In catechising one Estall's boy, [he] told the boy the Devil was upon his shoulders; whereat the boy ran out of the church crying and screeching to the terror of all that were present.'[5] While protective graffiti have been found extensively in Norfolk churches (p164) the survival of magical curses is far more unusual but three examples have been discovered in Norwich cathedral. The most clearly visible consists simply of the name Keynfford written backwards with an astrological symbol associated with the moon below it. Both the symbol and the inversion of the name were probably intended to 'add strength and potency to the curse' much like saying the Lord's Prayer backwards empowered those who practiced the black arts. Keynfford was the name of a prominent merchant family in late 15th century Norwich but who and what provoked the curse remains a mystery.

THE TRIALS

Throughout the middle ages a belief in the efficacy of occult powers was 'deeply entrenched in the popular imagination'.[6] Although the fear of witchcraft was endemic in society few cases were brought to court involving those accused of *maleficium* – mysteriously injuring others – before 1500. Reminders of the Devil, 'God's grand cosmic antagonist',[7] and images of eternal damnation were everywhere in the medieval church but the very religion that had conjured up the Prince of Darkness provided its flock with a protective framework against the Devil's worst temptations. Those trappings of religious magic – guardian angels, holy water, bells, candles and saints to intercede on one's behalf – that had provided immunity from witchcraft, were suddenly deprived of their power at the Reformation. While the Devil continued to loom large in the new Protestant religion the only recourse now available was prayer and the Word of God. Once the defence mechanisms of the old religion had been dismantled incidents of witchcraft increased and once witches were seen as heretical then drastic action soon followed.

One of the first instances of witchcraft to come to light in Norfolk is recorded in the parish register of Wells-next-the-Sea for 1583. The loss of all thirteen crew aboard a ship that had foundered at the western approach to the harbour was found to have been caused by 'the detestable working of an execrable witch of King's Lynn'[8] called Mother Gabley who had boiled eggs in a pail full of cold water. She managed to escape conviction in Lynn 'through the good-natured stupidity of ... our addle pated mayor'[9] who, even then, probably found the charge preposterous in the absence of witnesses prepared to testify.

The only certain way to eradicate what was perceived as a growing epidemic was to have faith in the law – witchcraft was first outlawed in 1542 and the number of trials increased throughout Elizabeth I's reign. The normal penalty for those found guilty was death by hanging but where witchcraft was thought to have resulted in the death of a spouse, most often a husband, a crime of petty-treason was deemed to have been committed and women were burnt at the stake. One of the earliest victims in Norfolk was Margaret Reed, burnt in the Tuesday Market Place at King's Lynn in 1590. Above the window of a house in one corner of the market place is a heart framed within a diamond cut into the brickwork, probably a public expression of love by the owner for his sweetheart, but not according to local folklore. It is said to mark the spot where Margaret Reed's heart landed when it burst from her body, even though the house was not built until the late 1700s. In another version popular around the turn of the last century the heart rolled out of the market place, down a lane and into the river Ouse.

18c house, Tuesday Market Place, King's Lynn

Following her trial for witchcraft in King's Lynn Mary Smith was sent to the gallows in 1626. Before her execution she confessed her sins to the Rev'd Alexander Roberts whose account of the trial appeared in his *Treatise of Witchcraft*. It was one of a number of sensational reports published in the 17th century that helped create the moral climate in which Matthew Hopkins' anti-witchcraft crusade was to flourish.

It appears that Mary Smith was a quarrelsome individual who easily took offence and her neighbours lost no time in accusing her of bewitching them at the slightest excuse. She cursed them often and when the Devil appeared to her 'sometimes as a mist, sometimes as a ball of fire ... mostly as a black man, but sometimes as a horned man' he encouraged her to continue her campaign of revenge. Unlike most witches Mary Smith was married, her husband respectably employed as a hosier, and her neighbours, too, were mainly traders and shopkeepers.

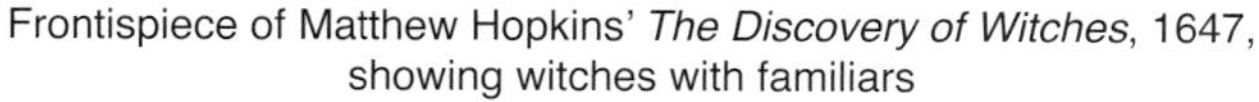
Frontispiece of Matthew Hopkins' *The Discovery of Witches*, 1647, showing witches with familiars

Matthew Hopkins, Infamous witch-finder, c17 print

John Oakton, a sailor, was Smith's first victim, after he struck her son for some minor misdemeanour. She cursed Oakton and said that his fingers would fall off. He was soon racked with terrible pains and two years later gangrene forced him to retire from the sea. Smith then accused Elizabeth Hancock of stealing her hen and told her she hoped the bones would stick in her throat. She, too, was seized with pains and fits so severe that her father consulted a local wizard who advised making a witch cake with 'all the nastiest ingredients imaginable.' When applied to the affected parts of her body the patient was 'in time' cured. On another occasion a neighbour's housemaid swept dust in Smith's direction. For her sins she was nearly suffocated by the witch's cat that sat on her chest, and Smith called her 'a fat-tailed sow' who would soon waste away. The poor girl, Cicily Bayle, told the court how she had seen Smith through the partition in league with her imp. The 'evidence' against Smith continued to grow when she flew into a rage and accused the cheesemonger, Edmund Newton, of undercutting the price of her Dutch cheese. He claimed to have been struck in the face with dirty linen and to have been visited by a person clothed in russet with a little bush beard and cloven feet together with the witch's imps, crabs and a toad. When a servant threw the toad on the fire it transpired that Smith screamed with pain as it burned. Soon after, Newton's health began to fail, he lost the use of one hand and when he tried to scratch Smith to draw blood and so break her power over him, his 'nails turned like feathers'.

Hanging a witch, c17 illustration

East Anglia became notorious for the witch hunting frenzy that gripped the region in the mid 17th century, whipped up by the infamous Matthew Hopkins. Together with his associates he toured Essex, Suffolk and Norfolk in a reign of terror between 1645 and 1647 that sent dozens of women to the scaffold. A distinctive feature of English witchcraft was the importance attached to the identification of 'unnatural' marks on the bodies of the accused. They were believed to be extra teats suckled by the witch's familiar in an unholy alliance that strengthened the bond between the devil and his earthly accomplice. For Hopkins these devil marks were incriminating evidence in themselves and he had the naked bodies of his suspects pricked with sharp, pointed instruments to identify the offending growths. In addition the methods used to secure a conviction involved starvation, sleep deprivation and the employment of watchers to keep suspects under surveillance in order to verify their imps. Confessions of a covenant with the devil and allegations of sex with the devil were confined almost exclusively to those cases investigated by Hopkins. In August 1645 the corporation in Yarmouth invited Hopkins to search for witchs in the town 'if any be here'. As a result sixteen people were brought to trial and of those five, all either spinsters or widows, were found guilty and hanged. As a result of his investigations in King's Lynn the following year another two women were sent to the gallows but by then, in the face of mounting criticism of his methods and the fees charged for his services, Hopkins retreated to Manningtree where he died of ill-health two years later. Amy Dury and Rose Cullender from Lowestoft were the last to be hanged for witch-craft in East Anglia in 1662, their conviction secured in part by Sir Thomas Browne, the Norwich physician and philosopher, who declared at their trial that the Devil could make natural illness worse.

SWIMMING WITCHES

The last witch trial in England took place in 1717 but by then there was little appetite, at least among the law makers, for official condemnation of this kind, and in 1738 the Witchcraft Act brought to an end the most shameful persecution of suspects. Cases of this kind were now dealt with as 'vulgar fraud' or on the lesser charge of public disorder. Educated opinion may have changed but popular opinion still regarded witchcraft as a fearful reality and the mob often resorted to the infamous practice of 'swimming' those suspected of witchcraft. This form of rough justice had been used in Hopkin's time and was occasionally resorted to throughout the 19th century, although by then the courts took a dim view of the matter. In April 1857 it was reported in the *Times* that a local magistrate had been asked by a farmer from Great Hockham to have a woman that he suspected of being a witch 'proved' by having her 'swum'. The magistrate concluded the interview by saying he'd heard enough of such nonsense but the Rev'd Gunn of Irstead, writing at about the same time (1849) concluded that 'the popular belief in spirits and witches is far from extinct' by quoting the case of a seaworthy fishing boat recently burnt 'stick and stem' near Northrepps because it was thought to be bewitched.

Ducking a scold, c17 engraving

There was little difference in the eyes of many between the medieval notion of the scold, an unruly and cantankerous individual, and that of a witch. The punishment too was comparable; the scold, strapped into a cucking stool, would be cooled down by being dipped in the local stream – Cucking Stool Lane in Castle Acre beside the river Nar is a reminder of this practice. The process of 'swimming' involved tying the suspect by her thumbs and toes and then pushing her out into the village pond. If she floated this was a measure of her guilt on the basis that water, the medium by which people were baptised, would reject all those who had renounced God. If the victim sank it was proof of her innocence but either way the outcome was of little comfort to the woman, especially if she had drowned.

Swimming a witch, c17 engraving

Among the reports of 'swimming' that came before magistrates in Norfolk was that of Betsy Norris accused of bewitching a farmer's livestock. 'A wonderful strong woman' called Huggins decided to take matters into her own hands and put Norris to the test. 'She put her on a faggot and shoved her off into a pond, and turned her over and over with a pitch fork, but she came up again every time and swam like a duck or a goose.'[10] On another occasion old Mrs Pointer was subjected to the same humiliating treatment: 'A long ladder was put across the river, and old Mr Loveday stood on it, pushing her under the water, but 'twas no use... then they pulled her out and began to mob her.'[11] Most districts had one or more favoured spots for this gruesome ritual. The Breckland meres were utilised by the people of Wretham, a village with a rich tradition of witchcraft, and a bend in the Waveney near Harleston, where the river is deep, was known as Witch-pool. Cruelty of this kind was not confined solely to 'swimming'. A complaint was lodged before magistrates in Cromer by a poor woman who, while carrying a letter bag along the coast, was pelted with stones by a group of boys on the pretext that only by drawing blood from her could those she had bewitched be free of her spell.

Among the range of protective magic available, the effectiveness of the witch bottle relied on the contents being heated to break the spell (p158) and the purifying effect of fire was used to destroy disease believed to have been caused by witchcraft. The rural poor often relied on a few chickens and a pig to supplement their diet and any disease could spell disaster for the whole family. To prevent disease spreading a dying animal might be suspended by its feet over a fire until reduced to ashes in the firm belief that the witch too would be consumed by sympathetic combustion, a drastic but practical measure with echoes of ritual animal sacrifice in other cultures. Young pigs are known for their erratic, often comical, behaviour and were regarded as 'rare subject for bewitchment.' There were reports of pigs walking backwards, of 'two o'the little uns a-playing see-saw on a bit o'wood across the trough upside down'[12] like a scene from the margins of an illuminated manuscript. In Wiggenhall St Germans between the wars a farmer whose young sow had got sick sought the advice of a local woman. She told him to give the sow two or three chops on the nose with a sharp knife, to wipe the blood on a piece of grey paper and burn it. This he did and sure enough the sow recovered and had ten piglets. The Rev'd Kent writing from his Merton rectory in 1910 recalled the occasion when the pigs of a local dealer fell sick:

> 'Tis an old woman, sure enough, who got wrong with us, and our pigs fared right bad, a screaming and frothing at the mouth and then a-setting on their tails a-squealing as if old Nick were inside of 'em. Howsomever I goes to a chap as knows a bit about witchery and I give him a couple of half-crowns and he say, 'Cut a bit of their tails and ears and burn 'em, that will do the old girl sure enough.' So I went wum and snipped a bit off their ears and tails and watched 'em sizzle up in the fire, and they began to mend and put on a fat and that's how the old witch was balked![13]

The ritual mutilation and slaughter of sick animals was not confined to pigs however. In 1866 a man living near Great Yarmouth who had bad luck rearing chickens, threw two of them on the fire saying 'if these chickens are bewitched I will find it out.' Afterwards his poultry thrived and the old woman under suspicion was much frightened next time they met. In Merton a notorious old woman, 'unmolested but greatly feared' was thought to have performed one last malicious act. The day before she died 'a whole brood of goslings belonging to her neighbour ran beneath the fireplace, and all were burnt to death!'[14]

BRANDON CREEK WITCHES

Shortly before her death in 1904 aged 90 Jack Barrett's grandmother told him that 'when I was a gal witches were very real and everyone believed they had the power to do harm.' This fear of witchcraft in the Fens continued through until the early 20th century and several of the stories Barrett learnt from elderly relatives and men like Johnny Blowers, who lived in Sedge Fen near Southery, appear in *More Tales from the Fens* (1964). Enid Porter was of the opinion that they were deliberately laced with humour to allay the fears of those listening around the fireside.

Along with Leah Brinkley, the gipsy, and club-footed Aggie, Spinning Jenny was typical of the eccentric old women who terrorised the district and preyed on the credulity of their neighbours. She lived alone with her cats and a tame jackdaw in a ruinous hovel at the end of a drove road and, having cursed the squire, everything he owned went to waste. There was Mother Kemp out at Burnt Fen who had been married five times and all her husbands had died suddenly, and Crazy Moll from Southery dressed always in a long black cape and an old felt hat. 'She was a terror was Moll, mad as a March hare when she was sober, and a proper hell cat when she wasn't.'[15] Mother Hensly, another Burnt Fen resident, frightened the gullible into parting with their money by placing small mounds of silt on doorsteps overnight. She would call next morning to say the house was cursed for she'd seen the Devil remove the sand from a freshly dug grave and she could remove the sand and the curse for a fee of half a crown. The following tale that Jack Barrett learnt from his grandmother concerns her husband and is typical of the witch tales circulating at the time. He was a millwright working on a remote drainage mill and was in the habit of staying overnight during the week in the loft of the abandoned mill cottage:

Evil Eye motif, rag hearth rug, True's Yard, King's Lynn

One night, after he had had his supper out of doors as usual, he climbed the ladder leading to the loft and was soon fast asleep. During the night he was awakened by noises below and, on peering through the trap door in the floor of the loft, he saw two old women preparing to light a fire on the hearth with pieces of wood he had discarded during his work. Wondering what it was all about, he lay face-downwards on the floor and, by the light of the fire as it blazed up, saw four more women open the cottage door and come into the room. One of them he recognised as coming from his own village.

Each of the old women had a rush basket containing food and drink and soon they were all squatting on the floor, eating and drinking. After their meal they sat in a circle, talking in whispers. Presently the room got warm, so they took off their long cloaks, revealing that they had little on beneath them. Round one woman's bare leg was a garter of plaited horsehair, which she proudly showed her companions, one of whom triumphantly displayed her own pair of garters, made, she declared, from a viper's skin. The third woman pointed to her breasts, which were cupped with ferret skin, while the fourth rose from the floor to show that she was dressed in a lambskin chemise.[16]

At this juncture, W H Barrett's grandfather inadvertently touched the open trap door. It fell with a loud bang startling the women, who, grabbing their cloaks, ran shrieking from the cottage. The unseen watcher found, next morning, that one of them had left behind her black cloak and rush basket, and these he delivered, the following Saturday, to the old woman from Brandon Creek, who, he knew, was considered by everyone to be a witch. 'Here you are', he said, 'these were left behind by you or your pals the other night in the millman's cottage down in Prickwillow Fen.'[17] The old woman seized the basket and cloak and then, spitting in the young man's face told him that as surely as he lived by making windmills a windmill would finish him off. This did indeed come true some years later for, as he was repairing a mill, the top collapsed and crushed him to death.

THE LAST WITCHES

The Rev'd Charles Kent, whose domain extended over several impoverished parishes on the Merton estate, felt moved to declare 'It is a remarkable fact that in past days the rustics of our villages were devoted Bible readers, and at the same time firm believers in ... planet readers, wizards and witches'.[18] By the late 19th century the mid Norfolk village of Shipdham had become something of a centre for occult practices with no less than seven witches by tradition at any one time. Among them was Master Cobel, a Methodist preacher, whose services were in great demand – 'There is a sight of folks go to Master Cobel' including the sister of a man dangerously ill with diphtheria. Cobel decided the man had been bedevilled and gave him an ounce of saltpetre to take; three weeks later he had made a full recovery. The Rev'd Armstrong of East Dereham recorded in his diary (May 15th 1860) how Miss Hales, a well placed parishioner, had lost a precious diamond ring and had sent her maidservants to consult Cobel. The 'wise' man predicted it would be found 'before Saturday' and it was duly found in a cupboard not used for storing valuables. Shipdham 'also bestowed a further blessing on the neighbourhood' in the shape of Mr Rix, a planet reader who, by consulting the stars, could tell your fortune, remedy an illness and recover lost property. In practice his methods differed only slightly from those of Master Cobel. A Tottington shepherd declared he had lost a score of lambs, having wrongly counted the tails that had been docked the previous day. He duly paid Rix's fee of one sovereign and was given a special kind of tobacco to smoke. He was told to go home and speak to no-one. Two weeks later, as reported in the *Eastern Daily Press* (Oct. 13th 1891), the shepherd counted the tails again and found the number correct – the 'lost' lambs had all returned.

In 1929 the Norwich GP, Mark Taylor, published the results of his enquiries into Norfolk folklore. Much of his information came from patients and the experience of fellow GPs elsewhere in the county. These included the doctor practising in Shipdham who told him of a woman who asked him to stop a swelling behind her ear. When he asked to see it she replied rather strangely that it wasn't there yet but it would be soon. It transpired that her children had quarrelled with those of the witch next door and to put an end to it she rather foolishly clouted one of her neighbours' children 'whereupon the witch came out and hit her behind the ear with a hazel stick. Now every spring, when the sap rises in the hazel, a lump comes up behind her ear and disappears in the autumn when the sap dies down.'[19] Some years before in a case of gender reversal, a woman in the village was overlooked by a farmer. 'Something cold went through her, and her blood curdled.' Ever after if she 'put milk in a bowl it broke, and if she put meat into an oven it came out raw.'[20] Eventually she wrote the Lord's Prayer on a piece of paper, soaked the ink off and drank the water to effect a cure, but her faith in the ritual proved insufficient to counter the belief she had been bewitched, and six months later she killed herself.

Witch bottle
from Lattice House,

Lattice House, King's Lynn

Much of what is known about witchcraft in 19th century Norfolk comes from the small band of clergymen who jotted down snippets of folklore from their parishioners. While in many ways remote from their flocks this local elite were firmly of the opinion that an undercurrent of magical practice had never really died out in rural areas. They viewed much of what they heard with a mixture of scepticism and a belief that the scientific advances of the day, together with their own unshakeable faith, would overcome the old superstitions. In the light of this the reports of witchcraft that filtered through to the rectory or appeared in the local press seemed increasingly bizarre. For half a crown a woman in Warham would cover your enemy with lice, a common sign of witchcraft, and her lice could be identified by their black and white spots. Old Mrs Wesby in North Walsham sold pills made from little balls of paper with biblical quotes written on them and elsewhere a form of divination known as bibliomancy was used to discover a thief by suspending the holy book from a piece of string. As it revolved the names of the suspect were read out until it stopped, revealing the culprit, a dubious practice and one prone to abuse. People like this, and others like Master Cobel and Mr Rix, preyed on the vulnerable and the disturbed in much the same way that disreputable traders sold 'Mary's milk' and other bogus potions to the sick who once travelled to the shrine of Our Lady at Walsingham (p28). In this respect little had changed in 500 years. The following statement from Skepper Carman of Raveningham is typical of the fulsome apologies that had begun to appear in the *Norwich Gazette*. He admitted to have:

> in a most wicked, detracting and slanderous manner abused, defamed and even taken away the reputation of Mr James Scarning of Norton Subcourse... by calling him an old wizardly rogue, and such scurrilous language....I do acknowledge what I said then (being in liquor) to be false and groundless .... This is the sincere acknowledgment and submissive recantation of your poor and humble servant, Skepper Carman.[21]

Some herbal remedies were based on sound medical practice but far more that relied on the power of faith and suggestion were entirely spurious and a form of extortion. The Rev'd Kent's last words on the fate of Master Cobel could equally well have applied to any number of witch doctors still at large in the Norfolk countryside. 'The end of Master Cobel was that he was sent to prison as a rogue and a vagabond, and afterwards died in the workhouse.'[22]

By the early 20th century cases of witchcraft, while less frequently reported, were by no means at an end as Mark Taylor's work on folk medicine illustrates only too well. The year before its publication in June 1929 a Yarmouth woman, Aquila Hewitt, was prosecuted for threatening to 'fill a neighbour's house with witchcraft', and as late as 1947 Gordon Sutton of East Dereham was hauled before the magistrates for assaulting his neighbour, Mrs Spinks, who, he was convinced, had bewitched him. 'Many a time she has tied a bunch of flowers on my front gate and I have spat on them and thrown them away [spittle was traditionally believed to have prevented evil]... I dare not tell you half the terrible things she has done to me. I have been tortured for years.'[23] By the 1960s belief in witchcraft had been reduced to a lingering suspicion in remote rural areas as George Ewart Evans discovered when interviewing an old horseman on the Norfolk-Suffolk border. The man recalled an old woman in Blo'Norton whose son was a notorious poacher and petty thief and one that the police seemed unable to confront. Whenever they came calling there was no-one at home except his mother sitting with a black cat in her arms. The cat was only ever there when her son was away but 'you never saw the two together.' According to Evans' informant 'people in the village said she was a witch ... you can make of it what you like, can't you?'[24]

TOADSMEN

The toad was the creature most readily associated with witchcraft. It was the Devil's agent and gave its mistress her power over others and, in particular, over their animals. Tilly Baldry, the Horningtoft witch, became an initiate in much the same way that male horse witches, or Toadsmen as they were known in the Fens, underwent the frog's bone ritual:

> you ketch a hopping toad and carry that in your bowsom till that's rotted right away to the backboon. Then you take and hold that over running water at midnight till the Devil he come to you and pull you over the water, and then you be a witch and you kin dew all mander of badness to people and hev power over them ....[25]

Tales of old crones causing horses to fall down in a heap in the road or tipping a cart into the ditch circulated in west Norfolk where it was not unusual to hear someone complain they had been 'tudded' or that someone had 'put the toad on him' i.e. he had been bewitched. In 1879 William Butler of Etling Green was up before Dereham magistrates for accusing his neighbour of bewitching him with a 'walking toad' (a natterjack) that she had put under a clod to charm him.

Natterjack toad

To this extent the power of the female witch impinged on the secret world of that elite band of men who worked with heavy horses and who had the 'knowledge' or the 'horseman's word'. Before the introduction of the tractor the frog's bone ritual (both toads and frogs were used) was deeply embedded in the rural culture of East Anglia according to George Ewart Evans, at a time when horse power was still the driving force in this largely arable region. From his conversations with old Suffolk horsemen in the 1960s, especially those in and around the Gipping valley, it became clear to Evans that the ritual, and the secret knowledge imparted to those who had undergone it, gave the initiate a clear advantage over other horsemen when it came to controlling an unruly colt or a difficult stallion or simply getting the best out of his team.

Despite some initial reluctance to talk openly about the ritual the essential elements were well known and had been summarised in *The Country Horse-Doctor*, published in Swaffham in 1835. In order to make a horse lay down it instructed 'Get some grey toads, hang them on a whitethorn bush until they are dead, then lay them in an ant-hill... put them in a stream.... dry them and beat them to a powder, touch a horse on the shoulder to jade him and on the rump to draw him.' Evans recorded several versions of the ritual, the most illuminating from Albert Love who worked on a farm at Wortwell in the Waveney valley and came from several generations of horsemen. A chance remark about a fellow contender in a ploughing competition produced this account of what he referred to as The Water of the Moon:

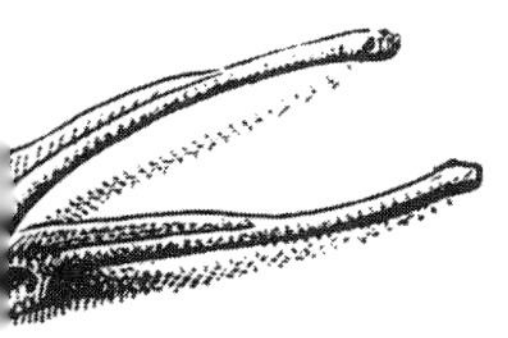

Frog's crotch bone

> He've been round 'the water and streams' – the toad's bone I'm alluding to, the walking-toad as we call it. Well, the toads that we use for this are actually in the Yarmouth area in and around Fritton. We get these toads alive and bring them home. They have a ring round their necks and are what they call walking-toads. We bring them home, kill them, and put them on a whitethorn bush. They are there for twenty-four hours till they dry. Then we bury the toad in an anthill; and it's there for a full month till the moon is at the full. Then you get it out; and it's only a skeleton. You take it down to a running stream when the moon is at full. You watch it carefully, particularly not to take your eyes off it. There's a certain bone, a little crotch bone

it is, it leaves the rest of the skeleton and floats uphill against the stream. Well, you take that out of the stream, take it home, bake it, powder it, and put it in a box; and you use oils with it the same as you do with the milch (milt). While you are watching this bone in the water you must on no consideration take your eyes off it. Do [if you do] you will lose all the power. That's where you get the power from for messing about with the horses. But once you got the bone, you take it home, bake it and break into a powder. You can mix it in a bottle with the oil, so it's always handy in your pocket if you ever have occasion to use it. You put it on your finger, wipe the horse's tongue, his nostrils, chin and chest – and he's your servant. You can do what you like with him.[26]

Horseman with plough team, Harleston area, 1960s

The frog's bone was also cured in oils, wrapped in linen and kept about the person as a charm. The bone, Albert Love's 'little crotch bone', was almost certainly the ilium or pelvic bone that, because of its V shape, had a tendency to get caught in the eddies of a stream and float against the current. It was also the same shape as the 'frog' in a horse's hoof and was therefore believed to operate on the principle of imitative magic; that like controls like and that the bones of one dead animal will immobilise another. The milt referred to by Love was used in much the same way. Known also by the dialect words *milch* and *melt* it describes the small lump of fibrous material that lies on the colt's tongue at birth and is believed to encourage the foal to suckle. It was carefully removed, mixed with oils and baked hard. It was then ground to a powder, mixed with olive oil, baked again and put in a muslin bag to be sweated under the arm.

Burdock,
Fuchs, 1542

Elecampane,
Mattioli, 1562

It becomes clear from Love's account that the powdered bone and the ground up milt are only effective when mixed with certain oils and this goes to the nub of the matter. The elite horseman's power over animals relied on the horse's highly developed sense of smell. Horse witches, like wise women, were well versed in herbal remedies to keep their horses in fine fettle and infusions of wayside plants like agrimony, burdock and elecampane were often used to cure sickness. The medicinal properties of wild plants were well known and widely used but a horseman would never divulge the secret oils wherein his power resided. There are many reports of horses that refused to leave the stable yard or who stopped suddenly in their tracks and would only move, sometimes hours later, when the old horseman decided to lift the spell. Tricks like this were often played to repay a grudge, put a less experienced farm worker in his place or simply to demonstrate a horseman's skill. One example, quoted by Enid Porter, involved tethering two cart horses to a pitch fork stuck in a dung hill. When ordered to pull, despite their strenuous efforts, they were unable to shift the fork until the horseman touched them and they were free to move.

This dramatic ability to immobilise a horse that so impressed less skilled horsemen was known as *jading* and relied on the use of a mixture of obnoxious substances. Each practitioner had his own secret recipe including one old chap out in the fields who, having observed a stoat paralyse a rabbit with its scent, went home and made up a jading mixture from the liver of each animal. To this he added what was known as dragon's blood, a red-gum resin extracted from a particular palm fruit and one of the horseman's most effective jading substances. The mixture would then be smeared on a stable door, a gate post or some other object upwind of the horse and it would stop dead, refusing to move until an antidote was applied to neutralise the smell. This consisted of a mixture of aromatic oils – origanum, rosemary, cinnamon and fennel among others – known as *drawing* oils that would attract a horse. They were sometimes baked into sweet-scented cakes and fed to the horse as titbits. A wad of cotton wool impregnated with the concoction was sometimes inserted into a split in the horseman's walking stick just above the ferule, or he might carry a bottle of the mixture with him and, as Love describes, wipe some on the horse. Love was unusual in using the frog's bone powder with oils as a drawing agent while most horsemen used the milt powder in this way and the bone dust as a jading material. His account is unusual too for its insight into the psychological effects of repeating the frog's bone ritual, an undertaking that, despite the ordeal, was necessary to renew a horseman's power, but which in his case ultimately failed:

> Once you took your eyes off the bone you were helpless. That's what they always told me. And I did prove it in the end. The third time I went I could do nothing with it. Just down there in the water at the back here, going up to Alburgh. You'd think all these farm buildings right close were falling down. You see, that noise! Rattling – well all sorts of noises you hear; you nearly bound to take your eyes off. Of course, I turned round and looked up. It was never no use. It wouldn't work! They always say that was all done, moonlight, midnight, full moon, *Chimes Hours*, and the Devil's work – the noises, the whole thing, toad's bone and everything. The first time I went to the stream I made up my mind I was going to do it; because I was horse-crazy I know. [27]

Although the jading and drawing oils had a greater practical application and the various recipes were jealously guarded, the old horsemen believed implicitly in the ritual. Loud noise of some kind was a key element here, as it often was in initiation ceremonies around the world. It impressed upon the initiate the gravity of the occasion and marked his acceptance into the group, but not all passed the test. A man on the edge of the Fens near Wiggenhall was about to throw what he called the witch bone into a stream when he dared to go no further because of the thunder and lightning – his friends had heard nothing – and on his third attempt Albert Love found the noises so distracting he was unable to go through with the ritual. Evans was of the opinion that anyone concentrating for long on the bone floating upstream in the moonlight was likely to have been in a highly suggestible state. The noises, he argues, were not real but hallucinations and a folk memory of the time when the initiation ceremony was more elaborate. The frog's bone ritual appears to have been a vestige of the ceremony which, in the 1960s, was still practiced in north east Scotland by the Society of the Horseman's Word. Held in secret it involved arcane language, a secret oath and the receipt of ancient lore and was in many respects similar to the Freemasons' initiation ceremony.

There was no such degree of organisation in East Anglia and master horsemen undertook the ritual on their own. The knowledge they acquired was often passed on from father to son or, in the case of Albert Love, because he had been selected. When a young man he was asked by a farmer in Rushall called Nobbs to go to the Yarmouth area and bring back two walking toads. From this seemingly casual beginning he learnt about both the ritual, which gave him the confidence, and the way in which the oils should be used. Together they gave him the power but they also placed him outside the rural community. In the absence of a close support group it was believed that those who dealt in the black arts would either go mad or come to a violent end.

'A Stiff Pull', P H Emerson, 1888

PROTECTIVE MAGIC

Medieval gold reliquary, Matlaske

AMULETS

Amber bead necklace, Bronze Age barrow, Little Cressingham

Amulets and charms form a distinct branch of protective magic and have been used down the centuries to combat the forces of evil, both real and imagined. In Roman Britain charms, or *lamellae*, were written on thin sheets of gold and addressed to gods seeking their protection. One of the few discovered to date, from west Norfolk, is from 'Similis, son of Marcellina' and invokes the protection of Abrasax, an eastern deity. Unlike today's jewellery, gold and precious stones obtained from distant lands were worn not just as an outward display of wealth and status but because of the magical power invested in them. The amber necklace found in the grave of a Bronze Age man at Little Cressingham, the medieval pilgrim badge bought at Walsingham or the St Christopher pendant worn today, although separated in time, have a common purpose. These ritual objects were worn for safekeeping at the start of a long and potentially hazardous journey, whether in this world or in the next, by invoking the protection of a spiritual being; a beneficent god in whom the wearer has absolute trust. In 2003 a lead plaque with runic inscription was recovered from a molehill at St Benet's abbey, the site of a Late Saxon Benedictine monastery. The plaque had been folded up to contain the magic but when deciphered the inscription appeared meaningless, 'a further example of the type of amuletic/protective use of bamboozling runic text.'[1] Amulets like these or like the holed stone, or mascots like the silver horseshoe, were essentially all forms of lucky charm worn or carried by an individual.

The traditional picture of life in the middle ages; a static, rural population tethered to its open fields and cluster of cottages gathered about the church, is undercut by the significant number who, at any one time, were on the move. The crowds of beggars and itinerant traders travelling between weekly markets was, at any one time, swelled by pilgrims on their way to Walsingham and other lesser shrines in search of a cure or as a penance. Wall paintings of St Christopher, patron saint of travellers, greeted all those who entered the parish church and ensured their safety for the rest of the day. Many images have been destroyed or remain hidden below layers of limewash but, even allowing for the incomplete pattern of those that have survived, there is evidence of a thriving cult in and around the Broads including scenes from the life of St Christopher at Hemblington. Here, as elsewhere, his gigantic figure wading across a river with the Christ Child on his shoulder, would have been a welcome sight to all those pilgrims negotiating large tracks of boggy terrain on their way to St Benet's Abbey or to be healed by the Holy Rood of Broomholm, on the coast near Bacton (p33).

Late Saxon page holder runic text, Baconsthor

St Christopher mural, Edingthorpe

Walsingham pilgrim badge depicting the Annunciation

At Bromholm, and more especially at Walsingham, pilgrims would be presented with an array of holy relics, miraculous cures and souvenirs. Among the cheapest were lead alloy badges, a popular form of lucky charm worn as a holy protector on the journey home. Once there these pilgrim badges were often dropped from bridges as a thanksgiving for a safe return – Walsingham badges have been recovered from below London Bridge. Rivers have long been liminal spaces, boundaries between worlds, and in classical mythology Charon the ferryman rowed dead souls over the river Styx that separated earth from the underworld (Hades). Throughout the middle ages prayers were offered up at crossing points to ensure safe passage and for a fee, pilgrims might receive God's blessing from a holy man in a wayside chapel like the one on the bridge over the Yare at Bawburgh that delivered pilgrims to St Walstan's shrine (p27).

Pilgrim badges, Great Ouse river, King's Lynn, 1912

The medieval stone bridge at Wiveton originally supported a chapel used by pilgrims who, having landed at one of the Glaven ports, headed off on foot to Walsingham. The Glaven estuary was then navigable inland as far as Cley and Wiveton where boats tied up below the churchyard wall. The magnificent 15th century churches here and on the coast at Blakeney and at Salthouse, are a testament to the lucrative trade with North Sea ports, and contain a wealth of graffiti; merchants' marks and a large number of crudely drawn ships. The church at Blakeney, like those at Yarmouth and Lynn, is dedicated to St Nicholas, patron saint of seamen, and most of the thirty or more ship drawings are to be found scratched in the stonework of the south aisle where the saint's chapel once stood. Each crude image represents 'a silent prayer made solid in stone'[2] for those embarking on, or returning safely from, a long voyage. These, too, are charms, rendered permanent and visible, another protective device in addition to the prayers offered up at the little chapel at Blakeney Eye. Here ships were blessed before heading out across the high seas to the Baltic or the Icelandic fishing grounds.

Ship graffiti, choir stalls, Salthouse

Ship graffiti, rood screen, Salthouse

FEAR OF DROWNING

Life at sea has always been fraught with danger and North Sea fishermen would rarely set sail without some charm to ensure their safe return. Among the most sought after was a child's caul, that part of the amniotic sac that covers the face of a new born baby. Its removal ensures the baby does not suffocate or drown in its own moisture and by the logic of sympathetic magic it became generally regarded as a charm against drowning. It was probably on his visit to Yarmouth in 1848 that Dickens became acquainted with the tradition and incorporated it in *David Copperfield*. The young hero is born with a caul and, after it fails to attract the asking price of fifteen guineas in the press, it is raffled locally. The Fenland storyteller Jack Barrett was born in 1891 with a caul which his Irish doctor quickly laid on a sheet of brown paper before smoothing it out with a cold flat iron. Several relatives then borrowed it, wrapped in oiled silk in a tin, and took it with them on long sea journeys. If sold, the power of the charm was transferred to the purchaser – as early as 1292 John atte Churchyard complained of William de Walsingham that he had sold him a false caul and he was adjudged to have the pillory for his falseness. 'Caul for sale' adverts were not uncommon in newspapers circulating in seaport towns at the turn of the last century. Once acquired a caul would save not just the owner's life but his ship from sinking, although the efficacy of this was laid bare in the following report from 1902: 'Along the coast inquests are occasionally held on the bodies of drowned seamen who are found to have been in possession of one of these charms, usually a child's caul, or a cabalistic inscription on a scrap of paper.'[3]

The headstones of sailors and fishermen in churchyards all along the Norfolk coast bear witness to the destructive power of the waves. The dangers of life on board ship were great and those who earned their living from the sea were so notoriously superstitious it is a wonder they ever set sail. A new ship was never launched on a Friday and there was a general reluctance to begin a voyage on that day. 'Friday's sail is sure to fail' was a common refrain and the taboo was probably a reference to the time when Good Friday was held sacred. Women refused to do any washing on the day their loved ones left harbour because to do so would prove fatal – they would be washing their lives away. In much the same way, women were sure not to wind wool after sunset or they would soon be making shrouds for their husbands. Instead, between mending nets, they would sit at home knitting the patterned pullovers or ganseys worn by every fisherman. The mixture of rope, flag and knot motifs peculiar to each coastal community were not just waterproof and extremely warm but enabled dead bodies washed ashore to be easily identified.

mes 'Duggie' Carter, King's Lynn, wearing his gansey

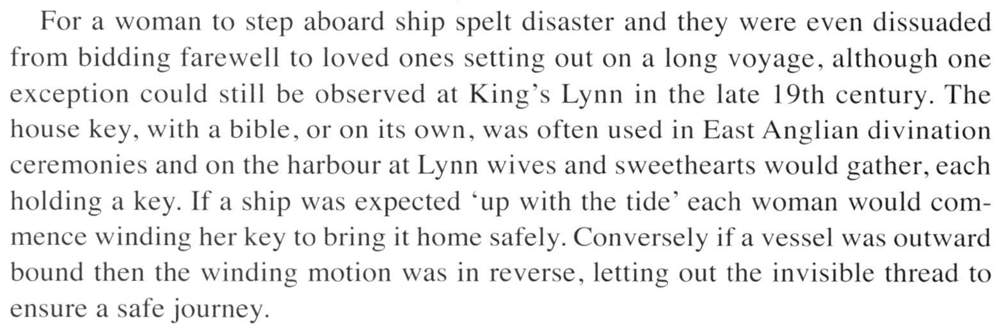

For a woman to step aboard ship spelt disaster and they were even dissuaded from bidding farewell to loved ones setting out on a long voyage, although one exception could still be observed at King's Lynn in the late 19th century. The house key, with a bible, or on its own, was often used in East Anglian divination ceremonies and on the harbour at Lynn wives and sweethearts would gather, each holding a key. If a ship was expected 'up with the tide' each woman would commence winding her key to bring it home safely. Conversely if a vessel was outward bound then the winding motion was in reverse, letting out the invisible thread to ensure a safe journey.

Animals, too, were not allowed aboard and were never mentioned once a boat had left harbour. Pigs in particular had a bad reputation for unruly behaviour, derived originally from the gospel story of the Gaderine Swine that ran into the sea and drowned. Whistling on board ship was strictly forbidden on the grounds that the shrill expulsion of air would conjure up strong wind and high seas, hence the expression to 'whistle up a storm.' The colour green, the fairy hue, was never worn and ships were seldom painted that colour; bone handled knives for eating or gutting fish were never carried at sea because of their 'corpse colour' and egg-shells were always broken to prevent witches setting sail in them to create havoc. Such were the precautions taken by mariners to avoid disaster along with the use of good luck charms. The custom of wearing a single gold ring in the left ear was said to improve sight, while fairy loaves – sea urchin fossils – and hag stones, more often associated with the farmhouse and the stable, were also carried around by fishermen or hung up in the wheelhouse. Another belief widely held in coastal communities was the way in which birth and death were governed by the tide.

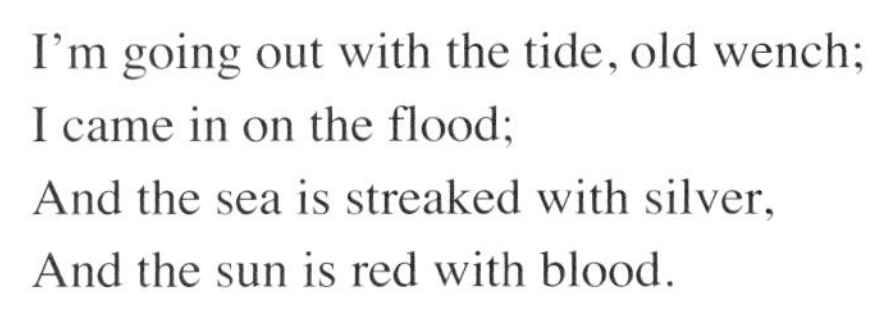

I'm going out with the tide, old wench;
I came in on the flood;
And the sea is streaked with silver,
And the sun is red with blood.

The sentiments expressed here rely on the association of birth with the breaking of the mother's waters and of death with the drying out of the corpse. A telling reference to the belief comes again from *David Copperfield* and the Barkiss deathbed scene when the old salty dog, Mr Peggotty, observes 'He's a going out with the tide ... If he lives 'till it turns, he'll hold his own 'till past the flood, and go out with the next tide.'[4]

WRITTEN CHARMS

The other main category of charm is distinguished by the use of incantations, cryptic texts and astrological or occult symbols. These written charms were an essential ingredient of folk magic employed by 'wise women' and 'cunning men' to protect livestock or bring about the healing of an otherwise incurable ailment and were deemed most effective if worn about the person.

The church of St Edmund at Acle, perched on a rise, which once overlooked a vast expanse of open water and undrained marsh, contains two rare glimpses into the workings of the medieval mind. Written in Latin on the north wall of the chancel is a stark reminder that death stalked the land. The lines refer to a visitation of the plague early in the 15th century:

> Oh lamentable death, how many dost thou cast into the pit!
> Anon the infants fade away, and of the aged death makes an end.
> Now these, now those, thou ravagest, O death on every side;
> Those that wear horns or veils, fate spareth not.
> Therefore, while in the world the brute beast plague rages hour by hour,
> With prayer and with remembrance deplore death's deadlines.

A few decades later the church reeve, Robert Reynes, was compiling his commonplace book, a curious ragbag of the mundane and the miraculous; curious by today's standards but not unusual for the late 15th century. Among Reynes' household hints are rules for bloodletting, charges to the constables and the watch, charms to make angels appear and charms to counteract all manner of danger and disease including fever and falling sickness (epilepsy). The Rev'd Linnell, writing in 1961, concluded that Reyne's book shows 'how the majority of medieval men lived according to pagan customs overlooked by Christian doctrine and theology.'[5]

Following the Reformation the array of saints that adorned the rood screens of Norfolk churches could no longer, according to the new Protestant doctrine, be called upon to cure everyday ailments like toothache (St Apollinaire) or alleviate the pain of childbirth (St Margaret). Despite this, the demand for all manner of magical charms and remedies increased throughout the 17th century along with the popularity of dried toads, pebbles and other amulets – Samuel Pepys wore a hare's foot round his neck as a cure for colic. Although their pious faces had been horribly disfigured by Puritan iconoclasts the power of saints was not so easily erased from the memory of a largely superstitious congregation. The efficacy of charms relied much on their obscurity as 'debased versions of Christian prayers or barely intelligible bits of semi-religious verse, describing supposed episodes in the life of Christ or the saints'.[6] Many were written in Latin or were inverted or otherwise encrypted and even the clergy were not immune to their perceived potency. Following his death in November 1709, the Rev'd Forbes, recently appointed to the living of Rougham in west Norfolk, was found with a small blue bag tied round his neck. Inside, written in capital letters on a piece of paper 'very yellow with sweat' was an encryption which, once decoded, read:

> When Christ saw the cross whereon he was .... to be crucified the Jews asked him 'Art thou hafraid or hast Thou an ague?' Jesus said 'I am not afraid nor have not an ague.' Whosoever w[e]ars these words shall never be troubled with ague. Amen. Amen. Sweet Jesus.[7]

The service of wizards was often sought to counter the effects of malicious magic. One of the earliest examples is the written charm used by Christopher Hill in 1654, a schoolmaster and presumed cunning man from Harpley, to counter the injury suffered by a Joan Smithbourne from a 'bad' spell. In this case it was the cunning man, not the witch, who was accused of witchcraft and sent for trial and the charm, a mixture of 'phrases and diagrams with Catholic and Kabbalistic overtones, invoking the names of saints and evangelists'[8] was produced as evidence at the trial. Hill's fate is not known. More unusual still is the charm in the form of a carving inscribed as a gift to Miles Cunstance of Corpusty by Old Mother Fyson, 'the witch of Holme Hale' in the late 18th century – Elizabeth Fyson was a white witch known for her curative powers. A belief in charms of this kind continued until at least the 19th century and among all classes of society. When arrested in 1840 a notorious Norwich thief was found to have a copy of the Lord's Prayer written backwards on a piece of paper stitched into the waistband of his trousers, a charm that failed to prevent him being apprehended.

COUNTER-WITCHCRAFT

Witch bottles were among the most common attempts to counter witchcraft and evil spirits in the home. The bottles were actually pottery jugs made in the Rhineland and imported in large numbers from the Netherlands. They were known as Greybeard or Bellarmine jugs after the bearded image applied to the neck of most stoneware vessels. It was thought to be a likeness of Cardinal Bellarmine who persecuted Protestants in the Low Counties although George Ewart Evans has a more intriguing explanation. He suggests the fiercesome mask might be a representation of the god Esus, a Gallic version of Zeus, drawing attention to the oak leaf decoration often found on the jars and the association of the oak tree with both the Gallic and Greek deities.

Cardinal Bellarmine
eware jug, King's Lynn

The bottles were used to counter illness in humans and livestock caused by witchcraft, in the belief that a magical link had been created between the witch and her victim. According to one 17th century source, having established this contagious bond, the witch who had cast a spell was then vulnerable to a counter device through the medium of urine, the reasoning being that part of the vital spirit of the witch was thought to reside in the liquid. With this in mind a sample of urine together with hair and nail parings from the victim were corked up in a bottle with a quantity of metal objects, usually iron nails or pins. The bottle was then placed near the fire until it exploded, but if the cork flew out the witch was deemed to have escaped. Buried in an inverted position the round-bellied bottle was meant to represent the witch's bladder, a form of sympathetic magic intended to cause the witch intense pain when the mixture of urine and nails was heated, compelling her to break the spell. A simpler version, but one believed to be just as effective, was the dropping of pins into holy wells. Unlike coins they were not good luck offerings to the spirit of the well but were intended to injure the person called to mind at the time, a practice similar in intent to sticking pins in a wax effigy. To be most effective the pins should be of brass because, under water, they become coated in verdigris which is poisonous.

Witch bottle with contents, Swardeston

Most of the witch bottles found so far date from the 17th century at the height of Matthew Hopkins' crusade to round up those suspected of witchcraft in East Anglia. Recipes were readily available in a number of books circulating at the time, notably Joseph Blagrave's *The Astrological Practice of Physick* (1671), which 'will endanger the witches life for … they will be grievously tormented, making their water with great difficulty, if at all.' Belief in the efficacy of these recipes survived in some rural areas until well into the 20th century. The following instruction on how to break a witch's spell was collected from a Mr Crawford of Wiggenhall St Germans in 1939:

> Take a stone bottle, make water in it, fill it with your own toe-nails and finger-nails, iron nails and anything which belongs to you. Hang the bottle over the fire and keep stirring it. The room must be in darkness; you must not speak or make a noise. The witch will come to your door and make a lot of noise and beg you to open the door and let her in. If you do not take any notice, but keep silent, the witch will burst. The strain on the mind of the person when the witch is begging to be let in is usually so great that the person often speaks and the witch is set free.[9]

The majority of Bellarmine jars have been found in East Anglia, not surprising in view of their north European origin, with at least thirty examples from across Norfolk. They range from rural cottages and isolated farmsteads to townhouses, especially in Norwich (from King Street in particular) and King's Lynn where examples have come to light in Thoresby College and from the site of the Plough Inn which contained a heart-shaped piece of cloth pierced with eight bronze pins. The most unusual find came from beneath the hearth of a cottage in the south Norfolk parish of Hellington in 1976 during renovation work. The inverted jar, which bore the arms of Amsterdam, contained eight large thorns cut from a hawthorn bush, a looped piece of string and fragments of a 16th century book in French, one of which was tightly bound with hair and stuck through with a large bronze pin. The bottle is remarkable both for the diversity of its contents and the cabalistic inscription.

Witch bottles unearthed during building work have usually been buried either beneath the hearth or below the threshold of the main entrance and occasionally above the lintel. The external doorway and the chimney were recognised weak points where evil spirits could gain access and dwellings may have been considered more vulnerable to intrusion in the 17th century following the construction of new brick chimney stacks. They replaced the old open hearths in the centre of the floor where the smoke was left to drift out through the thatch. Witch bottles hidden strategically were often used as a preventative measure instead of, or as well as, a retaliatory precaution against an individual witch. For this reason bottles were sometimes buried out of doors in ditches or at the base of hedgerows to guard against the bewitching of livestock or 'the blasting of the fertility of the land itself.'

Cambridgeshire witch bottle with coloured thread

By the 18th century Bellarmine jugs had been replaced by long slim bottles of green glass but their purpose was the same. They were more commonly found in the Fens as a protection against witchcraft and were often stuffed with coloured threads, especially red thread, the colour of blood. Blood, like urine, contained the life force that bound together the witch and her victim and the most effective way to break the link was either by means of sympathetic magic or by drawing blood directly from the suspect. An incident of this kind occurred near Wisbech in the early 19th century when a young girl ran out and scratched an old woman with a pin who had power over horses. The spell was broken and the girl was never afraid of her again.

While witch bottles have received most attention, a range of other objects has come to light that were also probably concealed in houses as protection against witchcraft. The importance of these finds has become recognised through the archaeology of counter-witchcraft, notably in Merrifield's 1987 book *The Archaeology of Ritual and Magic* and more recently through the work of people like Brian Hoggard. Although many examples will have been destroyed during building work, a growing body of evidence has been uncovered in Norfolk through the careful restoration of historic buildings. The single object most often hidden away in houses from the 17th until well into the 20th century is the shoe. At least a dozen examples from the county have been discovered to date including two children's shoes, c1850, from behind the kitchen range of a cottage in Freethorpe, two shoes in the roof of the Gardner's Cottage, Hilborough, and a woman's clog, c1700, above the fireplace of a house in Pottergate, Norwich. As late as 1934 a child observed her father place a worn out old boot in the rubble of a new kitchen floor of a house in Warham. When asked why, he refused to explain his action either through embarrassment or perhaps because to do so would negate the potency of the action.

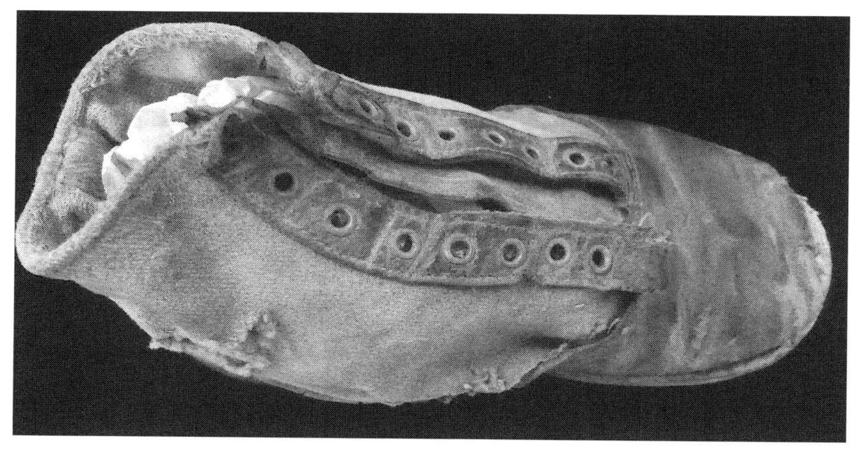

Child's boot, c1850, Freethorpe

As one possible explanation for the practice Merrifield cites the figure of Sir John Schorn (d.1313), a Buckinghamshire rector who was said to have conjured the Devil into his boot and kept him imprisoned there. Although never formally canonised he was a popular medieval saint and appears on Norfolk rood screens in Gateley, Suffield and Cawston. As a result shoes may have come to be regarded as some form of spirit trap or the legend may be the first written account of an earlier belief in folk magic. To throw light on the number of children's shoes found in houses and their role as fertility symbols Merrifield also quotes the popular nursery rhyme 'There was an old woman who lived in a shoe/She had so many children she didn't know what to do.' Most children's shoes date from the 19th century and, in view of the high mortality rate among the young, they may have been kept as good luck charms or as a spiritual link to the dead child.

More gruesome but equally significant are the remains of animals, especially cats, that have been recovered from houses in Norfolk. Examples have come to light from Thetford, Norwich and King's Lynn – the mummified cat sealed up in a house in Lynn now hangs above the bar of the Red Cat Hotel in North Wootton. At one time almost every household, especially in rural areas, had a cat to keep down vermin and, when dead, the animal may have been buried as a protection against pestilence or because it was believed to have been a witch's familiar. Once associated with the powers of darkness, in death the role of the creature was reversed and its ritual burial in a dwelling would ward off evil spirits. The remains of creatures great and small were used in this way, from the rat and vole bones placed inside two Bellarmine jars in cottages on the Heydon estate to the leg bones of a cow deposited beneath the hearth of a cottage in Gressenhall and the skeleton of a pig in front of the fireplace of a property in South Wootton. It seems unlikely, from the number and range of finds, that these were household pets buried for sentimental reasons or accidentally trapped in a void beside the chimney or in the roof space. Most likely they were carefully placed in position to safeguard the house.

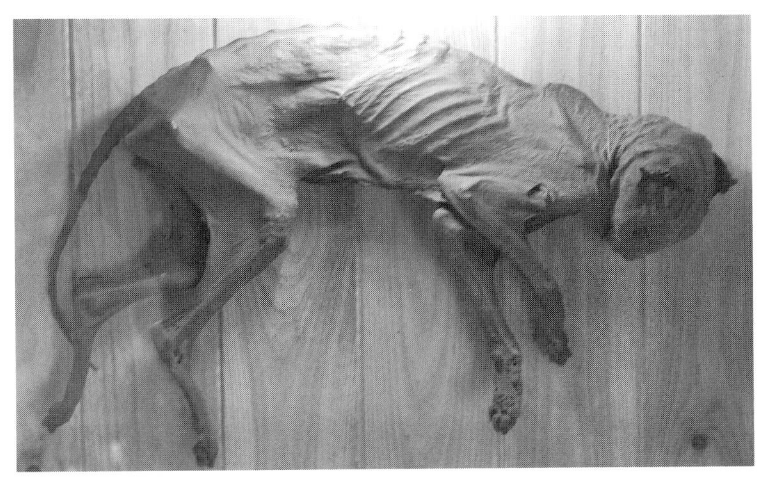

Mummified cat, Red Cat Hotel, North Wootton

The large quantity of horse skulls (about 40) discovered in 1933 beneath the ground floor of a house in Bungay may have been used for acoustic effect but the arrangement of the incision teeth, resting on a square of either oak or stone, suggests some additional ritual or esoteric purpose. The horse, both as a high status possession in time of conflict or as a beast of burden, was of great importance to Celtic, Roman and Germanic cultures. Its prominence on Iceni coins and the number of bridle pieces unearthed, suggest the horse was sacred to this Iron Age tribe based in north west Norfolk (p109). Although horse burials are rare in this country, two of the most complete are from Suffolk, near the famous ship burial at Sutton Hoo and close to the Norfolk border at Lakenheath. Here a horse in harness with a bucket of food at its head accompanied its owner into the afterlife.

Nothing quite so impressive has yet been uncovered in Norfolk although there is evidence of foundation sacrifice from the horse skull removed from the baulk of a 7th century Saxon hut excavated on the banks of the river Tas opposite Caistor Roman town. Skulls buried in the medieval village of Thuxton were arranged at the entrance to an outbuilding, possibly a granary, with the intention of safeguarding its valuable contents. The discovery of a horse skull and bridle beneath the front entrance to Mitre House, Acle, a jettied timberframe house of c1700, is a reminder that this practice extended well beyond the medieval period. The most recent and most remarkable example comes not from the archaeological record but the growing body of oral evidence and, more particulary, from the recollections of Fenland storyteller Jack Barrett.

Late c19 chapel, Black Horse Drove

In 1897 Barrett's uncle was contracted to build a new chapel at Black Horse Drove near Littleport. Barrett and his elder brother were sent off to the local knacker's yard to buy a horse's head which his uncle carefully placed in the centre of a foundation trench. The workmen gathered round while he uncorked a bottle of beer and poured the first glass over the severed head as a form of libation before passing the bottle round and then filling in the trench. It was explained to Barrett as an old heathen custom to drive away evil – it was after all a *Primitive* Methodist Chapel – but quite what the church elders thought when they heard went unrecorded. For the same reason it was not unusual in the Littleport area before WWI to mix animal blood from the butcher's shop with mortar for use in the brickwork of chimneys and fireplaces as a safeguard against witchcraft.

St Paul, alabaster figurine, Burgh Apton

In 1965 during the demolition of a derelict cottage in Burgh Apton a small alabaster figurine of St Paul was found in a niche beside the fireplace. Late 14th century, the statuette may originally have come from the parish church which is dedicated to St Peter and St Paul, hidden during the Reformation, or from Puritan iconoclasts like William Dowsing in the hope that the old religion would be restored. Another possible explanation however is that the image was placed in position during or shortly after the chimney's construction as a protective measure. What could be more effective than an image of Christ's apostle to drive away evil.

The idea that Iron Age tribes were able to overcome those still armed with bronze swords and stone axes through the magical quality of their weaponry has been dismissed by some folklorists as 'a picturesque 19th century theory' based on 'flimsy guesswork.'[10] Swords were, however, a high status possession of the elite warrior class in Celtic and Saxon societies. They often accompanied the dead into the afterlife and it would be no surprise if such weapons, especially those tested in battle, were believed to have acquired miraculous powers. There was something magical about the transformation of base metal into beautifully crafted and lethal weapons which meant that blacksmiths, like Wayland the fairy smith, were revered in Germanic folklore.The superior strength of iron weapons is not in doubt and the archaeological record suggests that a belief in the supernatural power of iron persisted well into the last century. This was especially true when the metal had been fashioned into sharp blades like the sickle found in the chimney of Church House, Aylmerton, and the unused knives retrieved from the thatch of a cottage in Dunham.

Early 19c crossed knives from the thatch of a cottage in Dunham

Naturally holed flint stones were among the most common of amulets or good luck charms. Known in East Anglia as hag stones they were often picked up by farm labourers at work in the fields and hung above the stable door to prevent horses being hag-ridden by a witch. The following account from an 18th century veterinary manual makes clear the difference between superstition and good husbandry:

I have been surprised at the Stupidity and Ignorance of the Vulgar who believe that their horses are rode in the Night by Sprites and Hobgoblins because they find the Creature all of a damp Sweat in his stall, as if he had been on a Journey ... when the Piece of Old Iron or Hollow Stone has been over his Back a week or a Fortnight on a String, and the Horse better taken care of with respect to Food and Exercise, the Filthy Bitch-daughter leaves him.

Hag stone and horses[hoe] amulets

A hollow stone was sometimes hung above the bed to drive away nightmares and, according to George Ewart Evans, it was a symbol of the All-Seeing Eye in many cultures. In the 19th century country people often complained that either they or their livestock had been 'overlooked' by a witch and it was the hole in the flint that gave the stone its power as an amulet against the Evil Eye.

Iron in the form of a horseshoe was considered to be just as effective fixed above either stable or cottage door but to contain the good luck it was necessary to nail the shoe with its horns pointing upwards. The one exception was the blacksmith. His position in rural society conferred on him the privilege of placing a horseshoe with the horns pointing downwards above his forge. More important was the power of iron to repel evil and this probably accounts for the number of tiny horseshoes found in the chimney of an East Tuddenham cottage.

In addition to objects carefully placed in houses to defend those inside from the dark forces ranged against them, are the increasing numbers of geometric shapes revealed during renovation work. These ritual protection marks were scratched onto internal surfaces for much the same reason. Most common is the daisy wheel or hexfoil, found across Norfolk, from the plasterwork of a medieval barn at Hall Farm, Hemsby in the east, to a late 18th century cottage, formerly the village forge, at Narborough in the west where there are various daisy wheel patterns on the bressumer and an external door. In the south of the county at Shelton Green a hag stone was found suspended over a daisy wheel in a barn to Sundial Farm. Whereas the main entrance of a house could always be bolted at night against the threat of evil forces, the chimney was the most vulnerable point of access at all times and it was here that counter measures were most often concentrated. A cottage at Forncett End was heavily protected, quite possibly from the time of its construction in the early 17th century, by a psychic shield to combat witchcraft. In addition to the complex of Sussex marigolds or hexes scribed on the main chimney lintel, fragments of scythe blades and small bones with holes drilled in them were recovered from the back of the fireplace, and a number of crosses within circles had also been painted on the ceiling joists.

Graffito,
south porch, Sustea[d]

These esoteric marks or apotropaic graffiti, from the Greek *apotroperios* 'to turn away evil', appear to date from the 17th century onward, although little domestic architecture survives from the medieval period. It is, however, now clear from the work of Matthew Champion on graffiti in East Anglian churches that markings of this kind are much older than previously thought. Scratched on choir stalls or the surface of stone columns and then covered in layers of post-Reformation limewash they are scarcely visible today but in churches like those at Blakeney and Litcham they would originally have been cut through a coating of red ochre paint and would therefore have been much more visible. For most of the medieval congregation these folk images were full of meaning and were intended to be seen; they are far too numerous to be dismissed as childish doodles or explained away as the work of apprentice masons. As Champion argues magic and ritual were essential to the workings of the medieval church. Catholicism provided a comprehensive belief system predicated on an all-powerful deity and the fires of hell, graphically illustrated in brightly painted images, awaited all those who ignored or transgressed the teachings of the church. Alongside these reminders were the many esoteric symbols designed to keep at bay the everyday dangers of illness, pestilence and starvation that threatened the 'faithful'.

Daisy wheel graffito

Norman font, Toftrees

It is impossible to date these symbols accurately but the daisy wheel and its many variants probably have their origins in ancient sacred patterns like the maze, the pentangle and Solomon's knot. These shapes are all devised from a single, continuous line and this is the source of their power, attracting devils that, once ensnared in these spirit traps, are doomed forever to follow the never-ending line. The most common form, in both religious and secular buildings is the daisy wheel or six-petal design with recognisable clusters in the churches at Belaugh, Brisley and Litcham, among others. The motif, along with other knot patterns, appears not as graffiti but carved in sharp relief on an important group of Norman fonts in north west Norfolk as part of the original design: at Sculthorpe, Toftrees, Bagthorpe and Warham St Mary, where the form of the daisy wheel is almost identical and suggests the work of a single craftsman. To the medieval mind this was not simply a decorative device but was deployed to provide additional protection for the unbaptised child. A century or more later and the daisy wheel had disappeared from fonts to reappear nearby as graffiti on columns in the nave where they served a similar purpose. Champion has found particular concentrations at the west end of the churches in Swannington and Bedingfield and concludes that 'while the church offered its own form of protection, via prayer, ritual and ceremony, the parish could augment and enhance that with defences of its own ... [in] a direct attempt to combat the forces of evil ...'[11]

Solomon's knot

Scratched on the stone, wood and lead surfaces of the medieval church the letters VV were the most frequently deployed graffiti in the constant struggle between good and evil. This shorthand for 'Virgo Virginium' was emblematic of the cult of the Virgin Mary and continued to be used as an apotropaic device on post Reformation domestic buildings, much like the daisy wheel. The VV symbol is often found in its inverted form as the letter M, another reference to Mary, the Mother of Christ.

Knot patterns, Norman fonts, Bagthorpe and Toftrees

RESTLESS SPIRITS

The mistletoe bride

WHITE LADIES

In the years before the Great War readers of popular guide books might have been forgiven for thinking that the Norfolk countryside resounded to the noise of phantom coaches and that every stately home possessed an ancestral ghost. Anecdotal evidence was often presented in lurid detail by an array of rural clerics, antiquarians and titled ladies with a passing interest in the supernatural. Among the latter was Lady Cranworth of Letton Hall near Dereham with 'a real white ghost, who to my joy I find belongs to my own family.'[1] Letton Hall, an elegant country house designed in the late 18th century by Sir John Soane, had replaced a moated Elizabethan manor and it was along the avenue to this ancestral pile, home to the Brampton Gurdons since the Reformation, that this restless spirit was seen to pace up and down before vanishing in the lane.

In the 19th century some of Norfolk's grandest country houses were found to be haunted by ghosts far less welcome than the apparition claimed by Lady Cranworth. At Gunton Park it was servants who first heard the cry of the White Lady, 'the family warning of death,' before Lord Suffield was 'startled by a long unearthly shriek, upon which, running to the window, he saw a pale figure, in the deep twilight, glide across the lawn; and that night Lady Suffield died.'[2] Another portentous White Lady was said to haunt Wolterton Hall, appearing whenever some disaster was about to threaten the family. She was, according to Lady Dorothy Nevill, writing in 1894, one of the Scamlers (p90) who lived at Wolterton before Horatio Walpole replaced the hall with a fine Palladian mansion early in the 18th century. The hall acquired a second ghost, that of Lady Walpole in search of her divided relatives, after her family portrait had been cut up and distributed among descendants of those depicted.

Letton Hall, 1781, seat of Thornhagh Gurdon

The ghost of Lady Dorothy, sister of Sir Robert Walpole, who had died of smallpox in 1726, was known as the Brown Lady of Raynham Hall from the portrait showing her in a dress of brown silk brocade spangled with gold. There were several reported sightings in the mid 19th century by, among others, the author Captain Marryat who lived locally at Langham. According to his daughter, the ghost, appearing with a lamp, 'grinned in a malicious and diabolical manner'[3] which so angered Marryat that he drew a pistol and fired, whereupon it vanished, at least temporarily. In December 1936 a photo appeared in *Country Life* of a ghostly figure in a long white dress on the stairs at Raynham Hall. Lady Dorothy was also known to haunt the corridors of Houghton Hall, built by her brother on the site of their family home, and was said to have appeared in the state bedroom before George IV who declared 'I will not pass another hour in this accursed house.' Among the various explanations for her presence at Raynham the most plausible seems to be disputed inheritance on her marriage to the Marquis of Townshend. Her ability to move between houses 'is characteristic of spirits attached to families such as banshees and dynastic White Ladies, both of which normally serve as death omens.'[4] The Brown Lady, who appeared shortly before the death of the Marquis of Townshend in 1863, not only changed places but colour, referred to as a White Lady by Palmer in 1875 and a Grey Lady by Walter Rye.

Mannington Hall was home to the antiquarian Earl of Orford when the writer Augustus Jessopp paid a visit in 1879. The two shared an interest in all things medieval and the hall became the setting for a ghost story that appeared in the *Athenaeum* the following year. Jessopp's friendship with the celebrated Cambridge academic and ghost story writer M R James, together with the conducive atmosphere at Mannington (licence to crenellate in 1451) may have triggered the author's susceptibility to the paranormal. Late one evening while at work in the library, the rector of Scarning was disturbed by the presence of a large man dressed in ecclesiastical garb bent over the books that he, Jessopp, had been studying. According to Enid Porter, the steward at Mannington had once revealed the 'ghost' to have been an Italian servant called Carlo. While in the habit of helping himself to a nip of brandy before retiring, Carlo had entered the room to retrieve the decanter from the desk where Jessopp sat deep in thought or half asleep. Perhaps Jessopp dreamt up the tale to entertain his host, but as a ghost story it falls short of an M R James contribution to the genre.

Mannington Hall

Brockdish Hall, its handsome brick porch with the date 1634, is one of several places in England associated with the legend of the 'Mistletoe Bride'. By the early 19th century the legend had given rise to the ballad known as 'The Mistletoe Bough' which tells the tale of the baron's beautiful daughter. Set at Christmas when the hall is decked with holly and mistletoe the company are making merry when the daughter, 'young Lovell's bride', becomes tired of dancing and begins a game of hide-and-seek. Try as they might neither her friends or her lover can find her until, years later:

> At length an oak chest that had long lain hid,
> Was found in the castle. They raised the lid
> And a skeleton form lay mouldering there,
> In the bridal wreath of the lady fair.

Female effigy, Brockdish Hall

The song became a great favourite at village concerts throughout the Victorian period and the legend has been claimed by several ancient family seats, notably Minster Lovell in Oxfordshire, Bramshill House and Marwell Old Hall, both in Hampshire. Its relationship to Brockdish Hall appears to rest entirely on the effigy that still adorns the parapet of the Georgianised south front. In 1927 it prompted a correspondent of *Word-Lore* to write:

I was taken the last autumn to Brockdish, in Norfolk, where I was told the tragedy took place. But there is no mention of the bride in the parish register, nor is her body buried in the churchyard. The effigy too, over the door of the Jacobean farmhouse looks more like that of a child than of a young woman.[5]

PHANTOM COACHES

The phantom coach at Wicklewood that, according to Lady Cranworth, starts its journey each night from a pit, appears to be an adaptation of the tale from Great Melton recalled by Walter Rye in his *Antiquarian Miscellany* (1873). Here at Blow Hill a coach carrying a bridal party left the road and toppled into a bottomless pit never to be seen again. Since then, at midnight and at noon each day a carriage with four headless ladies in white, driven by a headless coachman, 'rises silently and dripping wet from the pool'[6] to circuit the field before sinking silently back into the pond. Beside the road stood a huge beech tree and at midnight under its spreading canopy sat a mother 'rocking herself to and fro, and nursing a child, seeming in great distress.'[7] It is not clear whether she had been among the bridal party – was she the bride and was she then pregnant? – but folklore collectors appear to have taken a special interest in Blow Hill which was also frequented by hyter sprites (p198). Quite why this part of the parish was inhabited by so many spectral shapes is not immediately apparent but one clue may lie at the bottom of Blow, or Bow, Hill where it runs beside a great loop in the river Yare. In the same way that tales of black shuck were deployed along the coast to allow smugglers to carry on their illicit trade unhindered, tales of the supernatural may have been spread abroad in and around Great Melton to allow the safe transfer of contraband upstream from Norwich.

The Bigods, Norman lords who built their stronghold at Bungay in the late 12th century, are the most ancient subject of a phantom coach legend, although like most others there is no recorded sighting until the turn of the 20th century. The twin-towered gatehouse that still stands in the town dates from the 13th century by which time the power of the Bigod dynasty was in steep decline. 'Notorious for their profanity and wickedness ... part of their penance was to haunt the scenes of their crimes in a carriage and four with the horses' mouths and nostrils pouring flames and smoke.'[8] The circuit of this ghastly spectacle extended along the Waveney valley to Geldeston, past the church and down what became known as Bigod Hill. As Morley Adams wrote in 1916, it was never seen *and* heard; 'Like a silent wraith the phantom coach glides by and though the prancing hooves of the horses strike fire from the ground, no sound is heard.'[9]

Blickling Hall, the Jacobean mansion begun in 1619 for Sir Henry Hobart, replaced a moated manor owned in turn throughout the middle ages by several prominent Norfolk families including the Boleyns. Sir Thomas certainly lived here but, contrary to local opinion, there is no evidence that his ill-fated daughter Anne was born at Blickling or that she was ever more than a childhood visitor. Following Anne's execution her body was buried in the chapel at the tower of London and yet there is a persistent tradition that it was smuggled out and brought to Salle near Blickling, ancestral home of the Boleyn family. Here it was said to have been laid beneath a plain stone slab in the nave of the church but, according to the Victorian biographer Agnes Strickland, when the slab was raised sometime in the 19th century it was found to be empty. Oblivious to the lessons of history the people of Norfolk were determined to lay claim to their Queen and each year on May 29th, days after her execution, she returns to Blickling in a hearse-like carriage. Dressed all in white she sits cradling her severed head as the coach, driven by a headless coachman and drawn by four headless horses, advances slowly up the avenue. At the main entrance it vanishes leaving the spectre to glide about inside unheeded by the servants who are used to the rustling of its ghostly garments. From Blickling the coach was said to ride along the lanes and stop outside Salle church. In 1924, to test the veracity of the legend the verger, James Clements, decided to keep a vigil in the church between 10pm and 4am on May 29th, sitting in a pew opposite the family vault. As he told George Ewart Evans years later (1966), seeing nothing he stepped outside:

Boleyn tomb, Salle church

> … it was bright moonlight and you could see quite plain – and [I] looked along all the old routes, you know, where she was supposed to come... And then I saw a hare right near me ... I made a shuffle and it turned and ran by me – ran into the church! … I chased and chased, and we went round and round … And then he went round the font. I followed and tripped up … and as I was getting up he got across to the doorway … and he got by somehow and was away.[10]

Anne Boleyn, late 16c

Salle church

The appearance of the hare is a reminder of the old belief, current during her lifetime, that Anne Boleyn was a witch; a belief fostered by the presence of a sixth finger on one hand and the power she seemed to exert over her husband, Henry VIII. In folklore the hare was often regarded as either a witch's familiar or an embodiment of the witch herself. When asked whether he thought the creature was in any way connected to Anne, Clements was noncommittal, but from his next remark Evans thought he had clearly been affected by the experience. He had, he said, been born during the chime hours, the old monastic hours of prayer rung at three hourly intervals through the night until the Reformation. Those born at such times were supposed to be blessed with second sight.

Blickling Hall

The ghostly return of Anne Boleyn to Blickling Hall, retold in all its distressing detail in several late 19th century travel books, was designed to entertain country house gatherings. As one local author observed, while the servants seemed used to her presence in the corridors 'the appearance of Sir Thomas Boleyn is not to be treated with such calm indifference.'[11] With questions raised by his rapid rise to a position of wealth and status he was also implicated in the death of his daughter Anne. To atone for his sins Sir Thomas was doomed for 1000 years to drive a coach and headless horses furiously over twelve bridges in the Bure valley on the anniversary of her death (May 19th 1536) with 'his head under his arm, and flames issuing from his mouth.'[12] The circuit may represent the extent of his original domain but anyone abroad on the night in question was well advised to ignore requests for help or risk being carried off by 'the fiendish apparition.' As described, the phantom coach and its pack of hounds may represent a form of the hell-wain that spirited away souls of the damned and the best way to handle such an encounter with the supernatural was to remain silent.

Sir Thomas Boleyn

In 1849 the Rev'd John Gunn, writing from the Broadland parish of Irstead, drew attention to another local version of the hell-wain; the spectral coach drawn by four headless horses that each year pulls up in the courtyard of Caister Castle and 'carries away some unearthly passengers.'[13] It led Charles Palmer in his edition of Manship's *History of Yarmouth* (1854) to suggest a link with Sir Thomas Boleyn and the possibility of dynastic rivalry. Sir John Fastolf had returned home victorious from France to build Caister Castle in the mid 15th century while disposing of Blickling Hall to Sir Thomas' father, Geoffrey Boleyn, who 'complained of his bargain.'[14] Palmer's speculation may have been prompted by versions of the Blickling coach circulating at the time in which Sir Thomas' restless spirit ranged further afield over not twelve but forty bridges along the Bure and Yare valleys. Caister Castle was approached originally up the Pickerill Stream, a tributary of the Bure, and Sir Thomas 'occasionally extends his drive to Caister'[15] in a gesture of defiance or seeking retribution.

Caister Castle

In the middle ages Thetford was an important religious centre with at least six monastic foundations but after the Dissolution people like Sir Richard Fulmerston were well placed to benefit from the redistribution of monastic land. He purchased St George's Nunnery from the crown and turned it into a house called The Place, at the same time converting the church into 'lodgings and convenient rooms.' It was here in the long gallery that the young Lord Dacre met his death in bizarre circumstances by a fall from his rocking horse in 1569. Sir Richard had met his own death some three years before this accident but, according to the Breckland writer W G Clarke 'tradition has cast an unnecessary sully on the name of a pious man.'[16] Sir Richard was said to have tampered with the toy in a way that caused young Dacre's death and the boy was said to haunt the gallery riding on a headless rocking horse. In another version of the story his ghost became so troublesome nearby, in and around Nun's Bridges, that steps were necessary to lay the spirit. A pound of candles was thrown into the Little Ouse, presumably by the local priest, and the spirit ordered not to return until 'they were burned up completely';[17] no further sightings have been recorded. The Place was approached through an early 17th century redbrick gateway which still stands, separated from the property by a housing estate. Until the 1980s it was partially blocked by a chalk lump wall, one that had been knocked down by a phantom coach driven by an ancestor of the family on the anniversary of his death, and built up again seven times. Sir Richard is not mentioned by name but is the most likely candidate, denounced by local opinion as the 'wicked uncle' for his alleged role in Dacre's death. Although he stood to gain nothing by it he is, as Westwood and Simpson conclude, more probably victim of 'the traditional curse falling on those who acquire or damage former church property' [18] – the almshouses he bequeathed in Thetford that bear his name incorporated medieval stone from Thetford Priory.

Gateway to The Place,Thetford, early c19, (above) & today (right)

In Long Stratton it was Sir Edmund Reeve (d.1647), a judge of Common Pleas, who became the subject of another phantom coach legend, brought about by a popular mistrust of the law and the belief that he had wrongly obtained the manor and advowson. Resentment, especially among those who may have suffered at his hands, is likely to have been inflamed by the sight of his pompous effigy in the chancel of St Mary's church. Reclining on one elbow in a pose popular at the time and dressed in the robes of his profession – a scarlet gown and mortar board – Sir Edmund awaits God's judgement while most of the congregation had already made their minds up. According to the *East Anglian Handbook* for 1885 his ghost, known locally as 'old Hunch', a reference perhaps to the manner in which he dispensed justice, drove about the parish in a carriage and four. On one occasion a labourer, returning home late one night, saw the coach being driven furiously towards him. Scrambling up into a tree as it passed by he shouted, somewhat recklessly, 'Old Hunch, Old Hunch', but managed to survive with just a warning. A hideous face thrust out of the carriage and shouted back 'If I was as far behind you as I am in front, you would never call me Hunch again!'[19] In Spixworth is the equally ostentatious alabaster tomb of Sir William Peck (d.1635). A contemporary of Sir Edmund he too was condemned in the court of popular opinion to ride out at midnight to atone for some unspecified injustices handed down in his capacity as a high court judge.

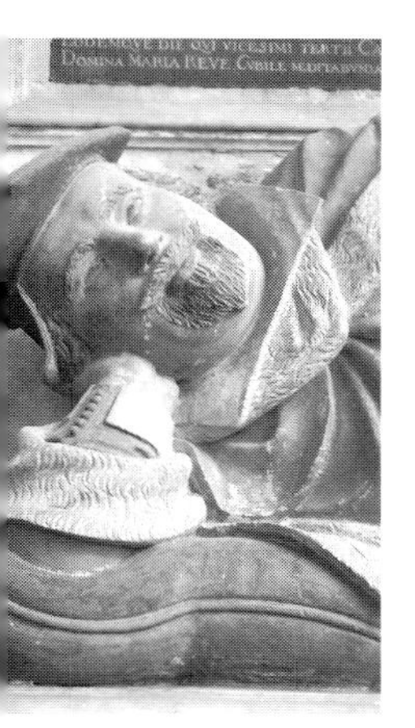

Edmund Reeve, 1647, Long Stratton

The legal profession was universally despised by the rural poor who were often in receipt of harsh sentences for the most trivial offences, but the presence of a grand effigy in the local church did not always become the subject of local lore. Narborough church has a fine collection of tombs to a succession of Spelman lawyers and antiquarians including the monumental brass to Sir John (d.1545). As Justice of the King's Bench he prepared the indictment that brought Anne Boleyn to the block. Perhaps his place in history was approved of by his Narborough tenants despite the large tract of former monastic land he recieved as his reward. The pink-veined statue of Clement Spelman (d.1673) stands on a pedestal in the chancel decked out in wig and robes. He was buried in an upright position – no one trod on the Recorder of Nottingham. So why have these upstanding barristers escaped the ridicule of popular scrutiny? Were they generous landlords to the people of Narborough or, as seems more likely, does their absence from local legend reflect the selective nature of folklore collecting in the 19th century?

Ranworth Old Hall

Colonel Thomas Sedley who lived at Ranworth Hall in the 1770s was a law unto himself; a hard drinking huntsman rather like his contemporary Sir Barney Brograve, the notorious squire of Waxham Hall (p127). In one version of the Sedley legend he was carried off one evening by the Evil One disguised as a cloaked horseman, while entertaining guests at the hall. Ever since, the squire's apparition is said to appear on the anniversary of his death riding frantically at the head of his hounds round

Ranworth Broad before disappearing into the water. W B Gerish, writing in 1898, was of the opinion that the tale was probably of 'great antiquity' possibly in origin a Norse legend adapted to suit local circumstances. In the Simpson version, written a century later, Sedley challenges a local landowner to a race but, finding himself out-paced, shoots the horse in front causing its rider to fall and break his neck. For his sins Sedley was carried off by the Master of the Wild Hunt that very night, galloping across the broad with steam hissing up whenever the hooves of his steed touch the surface of the water. The remaining wing of what had become Ranworth Old Hall was demolished in 1985 after years of neglect leaving just the red brick porch as a reminder of this once handsome Elizabethan pile; a legacy perhaps of the Sedley curse.

Breckles Hall, tucked away off the road between Watton and Thetford, is a rambling Elizabethan pile that had been partially demolished and reduced to a farmhouse in the 19th century. This warren of rooms and corridors adorned with heraldic glass and ancestral portraits had been home to suicides, 'popish seducing recusants' – it has a genuine priests' hole – and to Ursula Hewyt (d.1658) who insisted on being buried in an upright position, 'upright as in life.' The hall was, for Augustus Jessopp, a place that 'if it has not been a haunted house ... it ought to have been' [20] and he set about providing it with the kind of ghost story it so obviously deserved; the tale of George Mace and the phantom coach.

Breccles (or Breckles) Hall, early c20

In the early 19th century Breckles Hall was surrounded by a 'wild stretch of open country', the domain of smugglers. The land was poor, times were hard and the squire was forced to fell much of the valuable timber. 'Bad times had a tendency to bring out badness in half-staved men.'[21] It is against this background of poverty and lawlessness that Jessopp introduces the villainous character of George Mace, 'a very black sheep' from Watton and leader of a gang of poachers. One night just before Christmas the gang from nearby villages had arranged to meet in a plantation behind

Breckles Hall where Mace stood guard while the others went about their business. They had agreed to reconvene near the hall and '*settle* up before the moon went down' but Mace failed to return and as they waited the other gang members heard the rumble of an approaching carriage and:

> saw the coach-lamps flashing through the stained glass windows of the old mansion – *the very coats of arms were painted on the hoar-frost at their feet*. At the front door the coach stopped; they heard the carriage door open, the steps let down – the door was shut again with a slam. The next moment was utter darkness, the moon had set, and the stillness was as the stillness of the grave ... The coach had vanished.[22]

No one in the hall that night had heard a thing but the following day the body of George Mace was found at the front entrance 'not a mark upon his body; not a stain upon his garments; his eyes staring glassily, still and cold.'[23] Jessopp was writing for a middle class audience and as a cautionary tale put about to discourage rural crime it is unlikely to have been heard in the alehouses where George Mace was said to have spent most of his time playing skittles. As its name suggest Breckles lies in that part of Norfolk known as Breckland but the absence of the tale from W G Clarke's authoritative study of the region underlines the literary nature of Jessop's tale. Written just before WW1 but not published until 1925, the penultimate chapter of *In Breckland Wilds* is devoted to aspects of folklore and although Clarke's sources are not identified, it contains scraps of stories that fall readily into the phantom coach category of traditional tales.

Quidenham church

Among them are several from the parish of Quidenham including the legend of a previous 'godless and profligate' owner of the hall called Holland who directed that on his death his coffin should be carried to St Andrew's church as the clock struck midnight by twelve drunken men. When the bearers reach the bridge they all fall over the parapet with the coffin. 'To this day the villagers maintain that on certain nights the ghostly tramp of that unhallowed funerary train can still be heard, moving along with shouting, laughter and ribald songs ... then comes the loud splash as it falls headlong into the stream followed by the horrible curses and cries of the drowning men.'[24] Despite the river Whittle being no more than a shallow ditch at this point, the tale, bawdy and macabre by turn, continued to circulate in the area. The immediate vicinity of the haunted bridge proved to be something of a folklore hotspot. It stands beside a large, overgrown mound believed to be one of several places where Queen Boudica is buried (p113) and it features in a more recent tale of the fourth Earl of Albermarle (d.1849), late of Quidenham Hall. Determined to catch a gang of poachers one night he and his keepers lay in wait a short distance below the bridge when he sees a coach and horses driven by a headless coachman pass by. A spectre of this kind is usually seen as portentous but, although Lord Albermarle looked ashen on his return to the hall, he appears to have been spared any disaster.

The tale is reminiscent of another from *In Breckland Wilds* of a silent carriage drawn by four headless horses that was said to haunt the road between Threxton and

and Saham Toney. The passengers too were headless but those unfortunate enough to witness the spectacle were said to have recognised their deceased friends. Another version of the funeral procession, set further down the social scale, involved the killing of a gamekeeper by poachers near Croxton. Having thrown the body into their cart along with the night's haul of rabbits and hares they decide to dispose of it in an old chalk pit near Thetford. Unfortunately for them the gamekeeper had partially recovered and swore to haunt his assailants all their lives before he was killed outright. After that a hearse, coffin and bearers could be seen emerging from the pit and proceeding along the lane a short distance before disappearing through a field gate.

Hassett's House, Pockthorpe, 1791

The Blennerhassetts, a Cumbrian family who became lords of the manor at Frenze in the 16th century, had also benefitted from the redistribution of religious land at the Reformation. From their power base just outside Diss they extended their influence through marriage down the Waveney to Barsham on the Suffolk side of the valley. Here 'Old Blunderhazard' was said to ride out each Christmas eve in a coach pulled by headless horses even though there was always 'fire flashing from their nostrils'[25] His destination was Norwich to visit another of his properties, Hassett's Manor House, at the foot of St James' Hill in Thorpe. The house had formerly been the grange to the cathedral priory and the acquisition of church property may have led to the Blennerhassett curse. 'Old Hassett's' coach was seen crossing Bishop's Bridge over the Wensum before heading off in the direction of Pockthorpe or up onto Mousehold Heath. On occasions it appeared flying through the air over trees and rooftops 'driven by a coach and horses without heads, and when the whip was cracked, flashes of fire came from it and illuminated the whole city',[26] a pyrotechnic display which elevates this phantom coach tale into a class of its own. By the late 18th century Hassett's House, faced with demolition to make way for a cavalry barracks, was still reluctant to yield up its secrets. A dead body was seen to roll across a room and two workmen attempting to unblock doors were struck blind; tales most likely spread abroad by smugglers who would have found an abandoned house near the river a convenient place to store illicit goods.

HAUNTED CLIFFS

The whole of the Norfolk coast with its bewildering network of creeks and salt-marshes and low, crumbling cliffs provided ample opportunities for contraband to be unloaded on moonlit nights in some remote spot. The rewards of this illegal trade were considerable, so too were the risks of being caught but desperate men were prepared to take desperate measures. The unusually explicit epitaph of one unfortunate excise man killed at Old Hunstanton in 1784 is, like the clifftop lighthouse and the row of coastguard cottages, a reminder of those dangerous times:

> Here be the mangled remains of poor William Green
> An honest officer of Government who
> in the faithful discharge of his duty
> was inhumanely murdered
> by a gang of smugglers in this parish.

Nearby is the grave of William Webb, a young Dragoon drafted in to support the revenue men who was shot from his horse by the same gang of smugglers the following day. Several were caught and twice put on trial but no jury could be assembled to convict them. Further round the coast at Great Yarmouth a headstone in St Nicholas' churchyard commemorates the bravery of Daniel Bartleman, master of a brigg from North Shields, who died of wounds incurred off the Norfolk coast on 31st January 1781 while fighting off a much larger and well armed cutter with 'upward of a hundred men' commanded by a notorious English pirate who went by the name of Fall.

Between these two dramatic incidents, recorded in stone at either end of the coast in the late 18th century, a number of tales, both alarming and grisly, began to circulate among the north Norfolk fishing villages. Some were no doubt spread abroad by those with an interest in protecting the lucrative trade in bootleg brandy, silks and tobacco from the Low Countries to persuade the locals to stay indoors after dark. Among the tales was the spectre of a fiercesome black dog padding along the cliffs between Overstrand and Sheringham, and the Long Coastguardsman who haunts another stretch of the coast at midnight between Bacton and Mundesley. He revels in the wind and when a storm rages he shouts and sings at the top of his voice. During a lull he can be heard laughing but at other times his cries for help are audible some distance away. No one knows who he is or how he died except perhaps the writer Ernest Suffling who first mentioned the apparition in his book *History and Legends of the Broad District* (1891). Suffling claims to have caught sight of the ghost one night on the beach near Walcott before it disappeared. Having discovered a brace of rabbits and a hare at the base of the cliffs Suffling was of the opinion the 'ghost' was more likely a poacher. A little further along he claimed a dog appeared on the clifftop silhouetted against the night sky, all of which was good copy for a writer intent on entertaining visitors to the Broads. Suffling's book also contains the first version of the story known as the Pump Hill Ghost. More substantial than that of the Long Coastguardsman there is, however, no way to validate its authenticity as a traditional tale but it was included in subsequent collections.

The cliffs at Overstrand

The isolated coastal community of Happisburgh was once haunted by the grotesque figure of a headless and legless sailor. Wearing a dark blue coat with a pistol tucked in his belt he would make his way from Cart Gap, a mile or so down the coast, and along the village street, carrying a bundle. One night two farmers plucked up enough courage to follow the ghost until it stopped and threw the bundle down the village well before disappearing after it. The following day a villager volunteered to be lowered down the well with a lantern where he found a piece of dark blue cloth caught on a protruding stick. An iron pot hook was lowered down and a sodden sack brought to the surface that was found to contain a pair of boots containing legs hacked off at the thigh. After a few pints a second local was persuaded to retrieve what appeared to be a bundle of clothes but which turned out to be the decomposed body of the sailor, his severed head still hanging down between his shoulder blades. Days later a search party went to Cart Gap where, among the empty brandy bottles, were several coins, a pistol to match the one found on the dead body and a sizeable patch of blood, all of which pointed to a quarrel having taken place when the spoils were divided up. It is not clear why the murderer(s) decided to dump the body some distance away from the scene of the crime but years after diabolical groans that foretold an approaching storm could be heard at Well Corner in Whimpwell Street, groans which only ceased when the well was replaced with a pump. It was still there in Suffling's time, disused and overgrown, but the people of Happisburgh refused to remove it lest the groans should return.

A not dissimilar tale is mentioned briefly in C J Palmer's *The Perlustration of Great Yarmouth* (1875) which took place in the Cliff Hill area of Gorleston, known in the early 19th century as Deadman's Hill. According to Palmer a gang of sailors had killed a rich Jew at sea and buried his 'treasure chest' at the foot of the hill, returning later to share out the gold and 'rich laces'. One member of the gang was caught and transported to Australia where he was said to have written a confession in 1826 although there is no evidence the events ever took place.

Hickling Broad

WATERY GRAVES

Yarmouth, a great seaport town in the 18th century, has its own broadside ballad, 'The Yarmouth Tragedy', that was printed from about 1720 onwards. This lengthy tale – it runs to some 56 verses – takes up a maritime theme familiar in the English folk song tradition, one in which the young lovers are consigned to a watery grave by a cruel and possessive father. The father in question is a rich local merchant determined that his daughter, beautiful 'Nancy of Yarmouth', shall not marry her honest, but poor, sweetheart Jemmy. To thwart their plans he sends the lad on a long sea voyage to Barbados aboard one of his ships. On the return journey the boatswain, on the order of Nancy's father, throws Jemmy overboard. That same night Nancy hears her lover's voice at the window but only after his embrace, 'colder than the clay', does she know him for a ghost, and fulfils her vow to follow him to the grave. Three days later the couple are spotted, locked in each other's arms, floating alongside the ship. The boatswain, terrified by the spectacle, confesses to his part in the tragedy and is hung from the yardarm while the brutish father dies of a broken heart.

Just north of Yarmouth and a mile inland is the shell of St Edmund's church at West Caister. Until its removal in 1896 the tower, a landmark from out at sea, was topped off by a pyramidal roof protruding above the parapet like a neat little hat. As a result of the tale, invented by locals to explain its appearance, the tiled structure became known as the Maiden's Tomb. According to Walter White's *Eastern England* (1855) the Caister girl's sweetheart was drowned when his ship was wrecked on the coast on its return home after a long journey. The maid, before dying of grief, directed that her body should be entombed on top of the tower in a structure visible as a beacon to passing ships.

The Potter Heigham drun

Hickling Broad is the subject of another tale 'collected' by Ernest Suffling, known variously as the Hickling Skater or the Potter Heigham Drummer. It features another disapproving father who objected to the liaison between his daughter and a young soldier on leave from his regiment during the Napoleonic Wars. The couple are forced to meet secretly in a part of the marsh called Swim Coots on the Heigham side of the broad. It is February and the 'bold soldier boy' decides to skate across to his lover, but one night, at the deepest point near the Wherry Channel, the ice gives way and it is his ghost that reaches the girl on the other side. Afterwards the luckless soldier could be seen early on a February evening skating at full speed across the broad while beating a drum, but by the late 19th century when Suffling was writing, the ghost had not been seen for some years.

The Ship Inn, Brandon Creek

In one version of the tale the drum was beaten to attract the attention of the soldier's lover but in another it was to act as a warning of thin ice, a precaution that has echoes of a bizarre ritual enacted on the Little Ouse in 1892 when a Brandon woman went missing and was feared drowned. The Thetford Navigation Superintendent rowed down the river accompanied by a policeman 'mildly and slowly beating a drum.' It was believed that a distinct difference in the sound of the drum would occur if the boat came to a part of the river containing a dead body. The woman was later found safe and well but a belief in the efficacy of such a practice appears to have been widespread. Readers of *Tom Sawyer* may recall the occasion when relatives of the boy, fearing he and his companions had drowned, take soundings on the Mississippi by beating a drum in a boat. At Brandon Creek, where the Little and Great Ouse rivers meet, stands the Ship Inn, renowned as a storytelling pub in the late 19th century. It was here that Jack Barrett first heard many of the tales collected from him by Enid Porter and it was here too that, according to Porter, Mark Twain spent time while recuperating in Cambridge from a nervous breakdown. In The Ship he is said to have entertained locals with some of the many tales from his own repertoire while relishing those recounted by fenmen like Chafer Legge. Twain's visit may itself be a colourful fiction, a sly piece of wishful thinking, but if true it is tempting to think that he could have noted down the drum beating ritual on the river and put it straight into his novel. The only trouble with this suggestion is that *Tom Sawyer* was published some years before, in 1875, and it may have been Twain who had given the story to locals in The Ship and so it found its way upstream to Thetford.

Medieval undercroft, Blakeney

UNDERGROUND PASSAGES

Among the most common motifs in English folklore, and the one most frequently held up to ridicule, is the underground passage. There was a time in the 19th century when few parishes in Norfolk were without a tunnel running between one ancient landmark and another – between castle earthworks and priory remains at Horsford, but usually from church to hall in places like Besthorpe, Foulsham, Oxnead and Terrington St Clement. Reports of these mysterious structures have often been prompted by the chance discovery of a brick-lined void which, on closer inspection, proves to be a culvert or cellar or, as at Mannington Hall, a drain into the moat. Along the coast in places like Cromer, Blakeney and Wells tunnels thought to run from quay-side cellars were said to have been used to move contraband inland. From the number of medieval undercrofts that survive in Norwich, together with the remains of old chalk workings, it is little surprise that the city centre is thought to be riddled with passages connecting the principal historic buildings – castle, cathedral and guildhall.

While the origin and true purpose of these structures may be 'lost in the mists of time' their underground nature suggests a whole range of nefarious activity from the storage of illicit goods or escape routes for Royalist sympathisers, eloping lovers or disgraced priests. The secret tunnel running from Wymondham abbey to the Green Dragon Inn might have been attractive to wayward monks, but why build a tunnel the short distance between the church at Congham and the rectory next door, or between the bishop's chapel and the church across the lane at North Elmham? The logistical problems posed by those subterranean routes said to run for miles beneath rivers and marshy terrain, from South Walsham to St Benet's Abbey or from the Augustinian Priory at St Olaves to Burgh Castle, were of no concern to the rumour-mongers and story-tellers who had little grasp of time or distance beyond the reach of their daily lives. The appetite for stories and encounters with the supernatural far outweighed any practical considerations, but the tunnel as folk motif, while satisfying some psychological need to make 'historical' sense of ruins, ancient and enigmatic, stranded in the landscape, has seldom become the focus of more substantive folk tales. There are suggestions of more complex narratives in the tale of the golden calf lost somewhere along the tunnel between Gresham Castle and Beeston Regis Priory (p83), and in the secret passage from Ranworth church to St Benet's where gold from the ruined abbey is believed to be guarded by a huge phantom dog. But these embryonic, or possibly fragmentary tales, like the subject matter itself, ultimately lead nowhere.

The only story of note to emerge from Norfolk's underground network is that of the Binham Fiddler, although it closely resembles the Hertfordshire tale of the Blind Fiddler of Anstey and there are echoes of this particular place legend elsewhere in the county. At St. Olave's Priory the last person to enter the tunnel was a fiddler whose music, initially heard above ground, gradually fades away until the fiddler is never heard or seen again. At Elsing Hall a dog with a bell round its neck was sent down to explore the passage said to lead to the church but again the sound of the bell dies away, the dog never returns and the entrance is blocked up, its exact position long since forgotten. The Red Mount chapel in King's Lynn is a curious octagonal structure built in the late 15th century as a pilgrims' chapel with a tunnel-vaulted basement from which several legendary tunnels are said to radiate. The longest runs four miles north to the gatehouse at Castle Rising which, by tradition was often used by

Edward III who had his mother imprisoned in the keep. Years later it was followed by a drunken fiddler and his dog who 'were never seen again.' This too was the fate of Jimmy Griggs the fiddler and his dog Trap who volunteered to walk through the tunnel that was thought to run between the ruins of two of Norfolk's great monastic houses at Little Walsingham and Binham priory. A dialect version of the tale that first appeared in the *East Anglian Handbook* for 1892 had been collected by 'Beeston Loke' from 'an aged labourer' in the Red Lion at Wighton. People living locally thought that the line of the tunnel could be traced along a green bank and that people followed it listening to Jimmy's jigs and reels until, suddenly, his fiddle fell silent at a spot known thereafter as Fiddler's Hill. Jimmy never re-emerged but Trap ran out trembling all over and that night a great storm destroyed the entrance. Each following night 'a grate tall feller, like an old monk, and dressed in black'[27] walked the line peering about in search of something. This preoccupied spectre wore the black habit of the Benedictine order that had founded Binham priory in 1091 and, so the story goes, it was the Black Monk who spirited Jimmy Griggs away. It was the Devil who disposed of the Anstey fiddler and by casting the monk in a similar role this twist in the Binham tale may have been a Protestant attempt to discredit the old Catholic religion much like the Black Dog legend from Bungay (p192).

Staircase,
Red Mount Chapel

Red Mount Chapel, early c19 illustration, Rev'd Edward Edwards

The most direct route for any tunnel to Little Walsingham would have struck out in a south westerly direction but the mound where the music stopped is a mile and a half north west on the road to Wells. Clearly a slight detour was nothing to those who channelled pathways of the paranormal and the reason for this can be found by a glance at the map. Fiddler's Hill is an isolated round barrow and conspicuous feature in the landscape that has become both a crossing point and a place where several parishes converge. Like other ancient burial mounds it has acquired magical associations and falls into the folklore category known as 'Path from grave to lower world.'

Pilgrims were only too thankful to take the high road to Walsingham, borne along by their Christian faith, but the low road was the fairy way, the path travelled by those lured down into the world of the supernatural. Unearthly forces were abroad both below and above ground and it is tempting to see the Binham Fiddler as the poor relation of the Pied Piper. Entranced by the piper's playing the children of Hamlyn are spirited away to a cave deep in the bowels of the earth. Thomas Hardy drew on the intoxicating effect of folk music in his short story *The Fiddler of the Reels* but in the 'The Binham Fiddler' Jimmy Griggs is emboldened by the sound of his own music to venture underground where, entombed in the tunnel, he meets his death.

One intriguing coda to this tale is the discovery, made in 1933 by roadmen working at Fiddler's Hill, who cut into one side of the burial mound and unearthed the remains of two young Saxon adults and the skull of either a dog or a goat. Excited by the finds a local reporter on the *Norfolk Mercury* was moved to ask whether they proved the truth of the legend; a rare case where the evidence appears to corroborate, or at least coincide with, a long-held belief. To confuse matters the display panel at Fiddler's Hill claims that the tunnel ran from Binham to Blakeney, a claim prompted by belief in the existence of yet another tunnel, said to run inland from the vaulted undercroft of a medieval warehouse near Blakeney quay to the Carmelite priory that stood opposite the church. It was here that another blind fiddler was last seen, intent on playing his way to the other end.

Fiddler's Hill barrow

SPECTRAL SHAPES

BLACK DOGS

Tales of this ubiquitous bogey beast have been collected by folklorists from across the country with notable concentrations in Devon, reflecting the work of Theo Brown, and in Lincolnshire where Ethel Rudkin was active in the 1930s. Reports of black dog sightings have otherwise come largely from the north west and East Anglia where the folklore of the region is rich in tales of Shuck, 'a demon dog, as big as a fair sized calf, that pads along noiselessly under the shadow of hedgerows, tracking the steps of lonely wayfarers and terrifying them with the wicked glare of his yellow eyes.'[1] These are among the essential characteristics described by those who have seen the beast, but reports of this shape shifting apparition vary considerably across Norfolk in name and nature – each locality has its own version of Shuck.

At Sheringham, a traditional stronghold for coastal sightings, he is known as Shock, a headless animal with a 'white handkercher' tied over his neck. A little further along the cliffs at Northrepps he is a two-headed dog while inland at Coltishall a headless beast crosses the bridge over the Bure at midnight, and in Salhouse Shuck has one blazing eye in the centre of his forehead. The lanes around Hethersett are haunted not by a black dog but by the Faines, calf sized animals with saucer eyes, and at Geldeston in the Waveney valley Shuck was known only as The Hateful Thing, a hell hound or churchyard beast with fiery eyes and foaming jaws. According to Morley Adams writing in 1916 the 'wraithe of a donkey, which … rattles chains and breaths forth fire'[2] and who also haunts the glebe is probably another manifestation of Old Shuck. Reports of a sulphurous smell, of a sudden gust of wind that blows a man off his feet and of an approaching storm at sea all add to a sense of unease and, more ominously, to the shape of a diabolical creature rising out of the mist. The very name Shuck is derived from the Anglo Saxon *scucca* meaning devil although there are other dialect variations. In the central Norfolk parish of Garvestone he is Skeff, and 'Owd Rugman' in parts of the Wensum valley, names that, like Old Scarfe in Yarmouth, probably refer to the dog's rough shaggy coat.

Beeston Regis Priory ruins, J S Cotman, early 19c

Setting aside the sensational accounts by Marlowe (p190) and Adams (p191) apparitions do not physically attack, although they often induce fear and, on occasions, are regarded as portents of death. More recently black dogs encountered from within the oral tradition, while large and fiercesome to behold, are more likely to be preoccupied in pursuit of something in another dimension, than entirely evil. Typically a cyclist coming home late at night along a country lane, from work or a dart's match in the next village, is confronted by Shuck padding silently behind or dashing in front of the bicycle. If ignored the beast is likely to vanish just as quickly through some solid object – a hedge or brick wall. Any attempt to strike a blow is futile; a stick will pass right through it and, as one man in Neatishead found out, the force of a well aimed kick went right through the spectre and left him sprawled on the ground.

A heady mix of traditional tales and recent sightings has kept alive a belief in the hound that roams the Norfolk coast. While the particular stretch of clifftop path may vary the legend of a black dog running ashore from a shipwreck in search of his master's grave is a familiar theme. In one version he has two masters buried at Hunstanton and Yarmouth respectively and haunts the whole length of coast between the two churchyards, a benign presence and faithful companion that is more Old Shep than Old Shuck. According to another version he pads along the coast road between the priories at Beeston Regis and Bacton (Bromholm) where sailors from the wreck are buried, suggesting a possible pre-Reformation origin for the tale. By the late 19th century Shuck had already acquired a far more sinister reputation, one that inspired lurid tales in the popular literature of the day. Northrepps has its own Shuck Lane haunted by a two-headed beast with eyes like saucers and anyone unfortunate enough to see him will be dead within the year. In the 1820s an altercation in the lane between smugglers and revenue officers left two dead and stories of the fiercesome hound were probably spread abroad to deter prying eyes when the 'gentlemen' rode by. At nearby Overstrand he passes under the churchyard wall and onto the cliffs where, if the exact spot is examined soon after his disappearance, the ground will be scorched and smell of brimstone, clear evidence of his diabolical nature. It was tales like this of Black Shuck that stirred Conan Doyle's imagination while staying at the Royal Links Hotel in Cromer. During a golfing holiday with his friend Fletcher Watson the plot of *The Hound of the Baskervilles* took shape. Published the following year (1902) and set on Dartmoor, the description of ivy-clad Baskerville Hall matches exactly the Gothic turrets and crenellated parapets of Cromer Hall.

Cromer Hall, c1900

The success of Conan Doyle's thriller and the prospect of coming face to face with Shuck on the desolate marsh at Stiffkey persuaded the travel writer Christopher Marlowe to tempt fate. The result, described in lurid prose, is included in his *People and Places in Marshland* (1927). Having arranged to stay the night in a nearby cottage, Marlowe crouches down in a hollow on the edge of the marsh to wait, and as the moon rose:

> …there settled down a grim stillness which seemed pregnant with menace and I clasped my stick the tighter as I realised my absolute loneliness… The eerie silence was rent by the most appauling howl to which I have ever listened – it froze the blood in my veins and caused my hair to stand right on end and the shadow was coming nearer…
>
> With a yell of terror I jumped from the hollow and fled. Not once did I look behind, but I felt that the creature was in pursuit. Never have I run as I ran that night. Stumbling, cursing, breathing heavily, I tore up the lane and at last gained the threshold of the cottage…
>
> And as the bolt was undone and the key turned I glanced around to see a pair of ferocious eyes fixed upon me and to feel on my neck a scorching breath. The hound was actually about to spring as the door opened and I fell fainting into the arms of my host….[3]

Determined to prove the veracity of the Shuck legend it is no surprise that Marlowe 'encountered', or perhaps perceived the apparition – he was after all a writer and one, it would appear, with a vivid imagination.

Edwardian view of Burgh Castle

At Yarmouth a huge, ferocious dog with fiery eyes known as 'Old Scarfe' was heard dragging his chain along Southtown Road until, 'with solemn rites', he was eventually imprisoned in the cellars of the Duke's Head Inn by Catholic priests 'for so long a time as the waters flow beneath Yarmouth bridge'. In a variation on this candles were thrown over the bridge and Old Scarfe was doomed never to reappear until the candles had burnt out. At other times this shape-shifting animal appeared on the quayside more like a large goat with big luminous eyes and horns – Old Scarfe was the devil in disguise. The name, another dialect word like Shuck, is also said to be derived from one Baron Rudolf Scarfe, a 13th century German mercenary from the Hartz mountains who, after much wickedness, was excommunicated and fled to Burgh Castle where he continued a life of depravity. When finally slain, the Devil turned him into a huge dog and sent him back to earth to create further havoc. This is how Percy de Lisle, writing in the *Yarmouth Independent* in January 1893, interpreted the Old Scarfe legend.

The most remarkable account of Shuck appeared in 1916 in Morley Adams' *In the Footsteps of Borrow and Fitzgerald*, an early exercise in the 'Literary Pilgrimage' genre of travel writing. Reminding his readers 'that there are no more superstitious folk than those who dwell in these strange little seaside towns'[4] he claims to have been told the eerie tale by 'beach folk' without being more specific, other than to say that the huge black dog 'seems to haunt the coast from Felixstowe to Hunstanton.' In recent years folklorists have, without additional information, attempted to place the story – Porter (1974) around Lowestoft, Haining (1992) near Cromer and Westwood and Simpson (2005) in Felixstowe which, even in 1914 was hardly the sort of place where 'A strange gentleman of particularly swarthy complexion suddenly appeared in a small seaside hamlet.'[5]

He was 'evidently an Italian, but could speak English quite well. Where he came from ... nobody knew, though a great many cared.'[6] He befriended a local fisherboy and tried to persuade him to go abroad with him but when the lad refused asked him to take care of a large black dog while he was away. 'Now, strange to relate, the dog had often been seen about the village, but dog and master had never been seen together'.[7]

It was the custom of the fisherboy to go to swim in the sea, and at such times the dog invariably accompanied him. One fateful day, however, the lad swam far out to sea, and when he turned round to come back to the shore, he was horrified to find that the dog would not allow him to do so, but with horrible growlings and snapping at his legs and neck compelled him to go farther out to sea, the dog keeping close behind him. The plight of the poor lad was terrible in the extreme, and a fearful death confronted him. On, on he swam, and ever behind swam the much-dreaded Black Shuck. So frightened was he that he dared not turn his head to look at the beast, but at length he heard the panting and growling of the dog by his side, and turning his head, he was horrified to see, not the shaggy head of the dog but the head and saturnine face of the Italian. He bestowed upon the lad a hellish and triumphant grin, and then instantly resumed the form of the dog and again 'flew' at his neck with a savage snarl. Just as the boy felt that he must sink, a sailing-ship passed within hearing distance and he was hauled aboard, his neck being fearfully lacerated by the dog's teeth. The animal dived like a whale and was seen no more.[8]

The picture that emerges from these jingoistic tales is of an evil foreigner – a swarthy Italian, a debauched German aristocrat – who arrives mysteriously on these shores in the shape of a black dog. As metaphors for the threat of attack from continental Europe these tales are part of a distinct literary genre popular in the late 19th century – Invasion Literature. Among the principal exponents Conan Doyle, H G Wells, Robert Louis Stevenson and Rider Haggard who lived near Bungay and knew the black dog legend well, wrote stories in which fantastic creatures threaten the British Empire. This archetypal beast, that in other tales along the Norfolk coast emerges from the sea as the sole survivor of a shipwreck, has echoes of something equally sinister just up the coast at Whitby, the arrival of Count Dracula.

Published in 1897 Bram Stoker's Gothic horror story plots Dracula's flight from Transylvania to England in search of fresh blood. To replenish his strength he sends fifty boxes of newly dug earth aboard a Russian vessel that comes ashore in Whitby harbour during a terrible storm with the captain's lifeless body strapped to the helm. As soon as the boat runs aground an 'immense dog' is seen to leap ashore and run up the cliff face to the ruins of Whitby Abbey. The dog is not seen again but the coal merchant's large mastiff is found with its throat torn away and its belly slit open 'as if with a savage claw'. Stoker knew the seaport town well from summer holidays and had spent years researching European folklore including time in the local library. A sizeable fishing fleet operated out of Whitby harbour and followed the shoals of herring down the coast stopping off at Lynn and Yarmouth on the way. Tales of wrecks and large black dogs patrolling the cliffs travelled between these coastal communities, embellished with every retelling until, perhaps, they reached the ears of the Irish novelist who, like Conan Doyle, incorporated them into his most enduring work of fiction.

St Mary's, Bungay

THE BLACK DOG OF BUNGAY

Throughout the 16th and 17th centuries storms, floods and other extreme weather conditions were regarded as the work of the Devil inflicted on a sinful congregation as divine retribution. In the folklore of the region the Devil is most frequently portrayed as a black dog emerging like some deep sea monster to terrorise communities along the coast. Even at Blickling, which is well inland, he leaps from the mouth of a great fish in the lake. In his most celebrated incarnation, however, he arrives in Bungay not from the tidal waters of the river Waveney but out of the heavens in a ball of fire. The handsome late 15th century tower of St Mary's church, rising high above the market place, was struck by lightning during morning service on August 4th, 1577, killing two parishioners in the belfry. The record of this tragic event in the churchwarden's account book however, one which was destined to become memorable in the history of the town, makes no mention of a black dog:

> Md. A great terryble and ferfull tempest at the tyme of
> Procession upon the Sondaye such darknes, Rayne, hayle,
> Thunder & lightning as was never seen the lyke.

'The Blacke Dogg of Newgate', pamphlet, 1634

In 1577 a compendium of British history known as *Holinshed's Chronicle* reported the event in much the same way, adding only that the lightning strike 'scorched an other which hardlie escaped.' Again there is no reference to a supernatural creature. One of the chief contributors to this edition of the *Chronicle* was the Rev'd Abraham Fleming, a prolific London author and Puritan preacher. Seizing the opportunity for moral condemnation he produced his own account of that fateful day in a pamphlet entitled 'A Straunge and Terrible Wunder….' that introduced 'a horrible shaped thing' for the first time. The language is polemical, typical of sermons delivered at the time, even though Fleming asserts that his information was obtained from local people who:

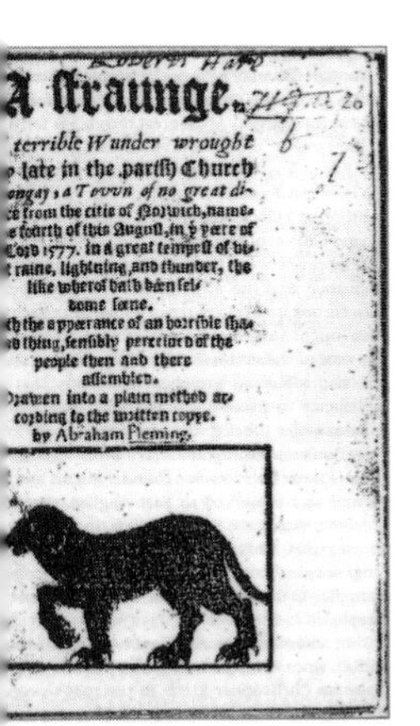

ontispiece to Abraham Fleming's tract, 1577

> were witnesses of the straungenes, the rarenesse and sodenesse of the storm, consisting of raine violently falling, fearful flashes of lightning, and terrible cracks of thunder…the Church did as it were quake and stagger ... Immediately hereupon, there appeared in a most horrible similitude and likenesse … a dog as they might discerne it, of a black colour… or the divil in such a likenesse running all along down the body of the church with great swiftnesse… passed between two persons… occupied in prayer as it seemed, wrung the necks of them bothe at one instant clene backward … passing another man … gave him such a gripe on the back that there with all he was presently drawen togither and shrunk up, as it were a peece of lether scorched in a hot fire…

The violence of the storm is not in doubt but the two people killed are no longer in the tower rather in the congregation and the black dog bursting in through the door leaves his claw marks in the woodwork. Such is the terror wrought by the tempest that those present 'thought doomes day was already come' and the message was clearly a warning to repent. Whether Fleming's pamphlet had any lasting influence on religious thinking at the time is questionable but at a stroke the Puritan cleric's unwitting contribution to the region's folklore was immense. Feeding on an undercurrent of superstition in a time of religious upheaval his embodiment of evil in the guise of a black dog was readily absorbed by the people of Bungay; overnight a folk legend was born out of a piece of religious propaganda.

Black dog weathervane, Bungay

Just over a century later another disaster, the Great Fire of Bungay (1688), swept through the town, but on this occasion there was no suggestion of divine intervention and no Fleming to exploit it. Bungay already had its 'folk' tale and the recent claim that all memory of the black dog died in the flames seems unlikely. The fire may have reduced most of the town to ashes but oral tradition is more resilient and would have kept the story alive until a new edition of 'A Straunge and Terrible Wunder', published in 1825, renewed interest in the legend and in part gave rise to the proverb that a hardened sinner 'could no more blush than the Black Dog of Bungay'. By the early 20th century he had even become a symbol of civic pride, celebrated as a weathervane on a lamp standard near the Butter Cross in 1933 and incorporated in the town's coat of arms twenty years later. In 1977, four hundred years after the black dog first made his dramatic entry St Mary's church was made redundant, leading to the suggestion that the devil may have triumphed after all.

THE BLACK DOG OF BLICKLING

Blickling is most readily associated with Sir Thomas Boleyn, driven in a phantom coach about the Bure valley drawn by four headless horses; and with his daughter, Anne (p170) beheaded by Henry VIII, who is said to haunt the hall. It is also the scene of a less well known but suitably macabre black dog legend recalled in the

19th century when Lord Lothian removed some partitions in a morning room. This seemingly innocent act caused concern in the village that it would release the dog that had once emerged from the mouth of an enormous fish taken from the lake. Once loose the dog had kept running round in circles in the hall until the arrival of a wise man from London. By opposing the straight lines of the partitions to the lines of the circles he managed to quieten the animal.

Blickling Hall from the lake

A far more colourful version comes from the pen of F J Meyrick in *Round About Norfolk and Suffolk* (1926) whose father had been rector of Blickling for some 40 years in the late 19th century. The 'wicked gentleman' at the centre of the story is thought to have been Sir Henry Hobart, late 17th century owner of the hall and a man heavily in debt. Fond of persecuting his neighbours he was killed in a duel with Oliver Le Neve in 1698. After his funeral a dog came whining to the feet of the sexton, and later that day Hobart's corpse was found torn from the ground and its lead coffin. There was another attempt to bury the body in a wood in the park but 'the common ground spat it out' and it was finally weighted with stones and lowered into the lake. Soon after the gamekeeper fished out a 'monstrous eel' which, although evil looking, he took home to be stewed. While writhing in the pan the eel vanished and 'a black dog with the dead man's eyes'[9] appeared in its place that no one could tame. 'A curse hung over the whole estate. The nobleman's young son caught small-pox, the keeper killed himself, the cook went mad, the milk turned sour and the crops were blighted.'[10] At last a famous London 'wizard' was sent for and 'at his seventh whistle the dog fawned at his feet'[11] and was led away up to the south east turret whereupon peace returned to Blickling, the curse was lifted and 'evil remained locked in the tower.'[12]

ir Henry Hobart, 1624

This of course was not the end of the story. Until now it reads very much like a piece of fireside entertainment dreamt up by Meyrick to be read aloud after dinner but his father's presence in the hall prior to his induction in the 1860s 'authenticates' the last chapter in this gruesome tale. One evening while in the drawing room a sister of Lord Lothian was convinced she had seen a black dog run across the room and disappear behind a tapestry. Next morning Lord Lothian, who knew nothing of this incident, remarked that the old turret had just been opened up, the one bricked over all those years before. Nothing more was seen or heard of the black dog until a moonlit winter's night in WWII when a young airman was walking back from Aylsham to his base at Oulton. Just beyond Blickling Hall he saw a large black dog in the middle of the road, its mouth open, but making no sound. As he advanced towards it he experienced a 'nervous tingling sensation' and then, after regarding him for a few seconds, the dog simply vanished. In the autumn of 2003 a strangely similar but quite unconnected incident, this time in broad daylight, was reported a mile south of here on the Blickling estate at Abel Heath where several lanes converge. The same eerie sensation was experienced by the witness and, from these two encounters, it would appear that the hound unwittingly released by Lord Lothian is still at large. In an intriguing shape-shifting coda to the tale there have, in recent years, been several sitings in north Norfolk, not of black dogs but large black cats. Among them is the black panther recently disturbed in a garden at Itteringham on the Blickling estate.

The black dog of legend is a versatile beast and one with no obvious pedigree. The demon dog looms large in the mythology of those ancient cultures that have settled in East Anglia and there are echoes of Hecate's pack of hell-hounds in Diana, the Roman huntress, and the Wild Hunt riding across the night sky that have fed through into local lore. In 1127, according to the *Anglo Saxon Chronicle*, the Wild Hunt was seen after the arrival of a wicked abbot at Peterborough: 'The hunters were black and big and loathsome, and their hounds all black and wide-eyed and loathsome, and they rode on black horses and black goats.' These tales, mingled with those of Odin the Norse god and the Wild Huntsman, whose black dog was left behind on earth, could well be a prototype for Shuck, though tales of the spectral hound have taken root in parts of Britain far beyond the reach of Scandinavian settlement. Lurking behind these possible influences is an ill-defined image deep in the collective subconscious echoing some mythological creature of great antiquity. Drawing on a common oral tradition, Victorian vampire literature and popular travel books appealed to the dark forces ranged against us. Whether it resides 'abroad' or deep within the human psyche Black Shuck is never far away.

THE SOUTHERY WOLF-HOUND

Set in the early middle ages when the village of Southery was still an island out in the Fens this tale, popular in local pubs at the turn of the last century, first appeared in W H Barrett's *Tales from the Fens* in 1963. It tells how monks from Ely arrived across the marshes to try and build the first Christian church on the island but were met by 'a wild, rough crowd living in turf-walled, reed-thatched huts and earning their living by catching eels and fish and robbing the boats sailing to Ely and Cambridge.'[13] After several monks working on the new church had ended up with their throats cut the abbot sent armed men to hunt down the murderers but they too suffered a similar fate and he was forced to approach the Baron of Northwold, whose land included Southery, for assistance. The Baron too had lost many men in the area so he sent a pack of wolf-hounds instead to protect the monks.

Wolf-hound, late 19c book illustration

On arrival the hounds soon began feasting on the bodies of all the dead monks and soldiers that had been left lying about but once they had chewed their way through the lot they turned on the living. The remaining monks fled back to Ely vowing never to return, while the villagers abandoned Southery to live deep in the Fen. With no fresh meat left the hounds set upon each other until 'only the fiercest and most cunning of the pack was left, a young bitch, as big as a full-grown ass.'[14] At last, weak from hunger, she was rescued by one of the few remaining Fenmen, brought up by his wife and trained to hunt the baron's deer. The monks eventually returned to continue their work but the hound, although now friendly with the Southery folk, would snarl and growl whenever the men of God were near. One day, after she had been missing for a week or more, the bitch returned with her pads all torn and bleeding as though she had walked miles out of the Fens. She was pregnant and as there were no wolves for miles around the monks knew it must be the Devil's work. When the pup arrived it looked like a cross between a dog and a wolf and when its mother died it grew to be as big as an ox and soon took on the work of getting fresh meat for the Southery folk.

outhery ruined church

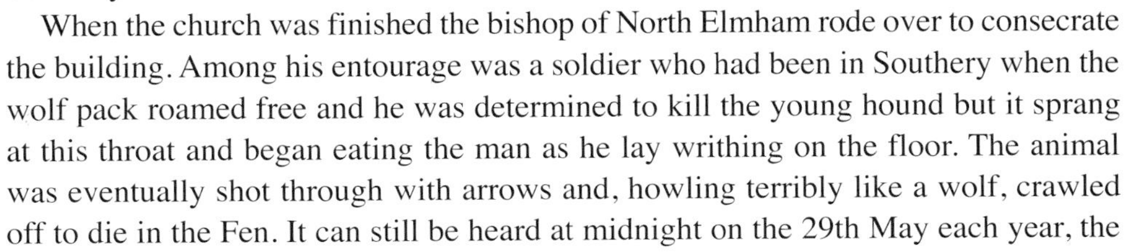

When the church was finished the bishop of North Elmham rode over to consecrate the building. Among his entourage was a soldier who had been in Southery when the wolf pack roamed free and he was determined to kill the young hound but it sprang at this throat and began eating the man as he lay writhing on the floor. The animal was eventually shot through with arrows and, howling terribly like a wolf, crawled off to die in the Fen. It can still be heard at midnight on the 29th May each year, the day when the Southery Feast was held and anyone who hears it will be dead within the year. The church that the monks built lies in ruins, replaced in 1858 by a brand new structure, but if you look closely at the corner stones of the old charnel house you will see the teeth marks made each year by the wolf-hound trying to get at the bones inside. And any Southery man, drunk or sober, will go a long way round to avoid the old church when the clock on the new one strikes twelve on the night of Southery Feast.

HYTER SPRITES

These are one of the least well known of that general category of supernatural beings called Fairies that 'have continued to live, albeit tenuously, in the memories of older Norfolk residents'.[15] They warrant a mention in Katherine Briggs' *An Encyclopaedia of Fairies* (1976) but her description of their appearance, 'small and sandy-coloured with green eyes.... They assume the bird form of sandmartins',[16] is more like those Suffolk Feriers from the Stowmarket area. There are no surviving tales of hyter sprites or encounters with them but impressions have varied from 'a bat-like figure, man-size and hovering silently in the twilight' to 'little people who lived in the woods in the Topcroft and Hempnall area.'[17] The earliest mention of them, by Walter Rye in 1873, however, describes them as beneficent with reference to their home on Blow Hill, Great Melton, but a few years later in 1885 John Varden was of the opinion that they were a more malevolent force to be shunned after dark along with other supernatural beings that haunted Cold Blow Hill (p170). Naughty children were warned 'If yew ain't quiet I'll hull [hurl] yew to the hyter sprites.'[18]

Cold Blow Hill, Great Melton

'Hyter' would appear to be a dialect word with no obvious etymological root and many variations, from 'Highty' in the Broads to 'Hyker' in north Norfolk and 'Hikey' in East Dereham. While there is no simple derivation the word may come from Old English *hedan* meaning 'to heed or guard'. Hyter or heeder sprites were often invoked as a nursery bogey, imagined rather than supernatural, to ensure the safety of children or to scare them away from potential danger, 'Hurry up home, the hyter sprites will get you' being a mild but common admonition. In general they were thought to be mischievous rather than malevolent and, like other fairies, were often blamed if things went wrong or got lost in the home.

Despite Briggs' assertion that they are an East Anglian phenomenon there is little or no evidence for Hyter sprites outside Norfolk and within the county they are more familiar on the coast and in the Broads although the evidence is sometimes patchy. At the turn of last century these two areas were still covered by a network of creeks, dykes and extensive tracks of debatable ground and it is here that the hyter sprite begins to merge with that other spectral shape that haunts the marshes, the Lantern Man. One account from north Norfolk describes how people were dissuaded from being abroad at night by a system of decoy lights so that smugglers could go about their business undisturbed:

Watchers would be placed in holes along the marshway and they would have a shaded lantern. Should any intruder happen along, their job was to run off along pre-planned routes, through difficult terrain .... After a distance, the lantern would be dowsed and any follower would be lost .... The light would be called by those in the know a Hyker Sprike! It was said to be a spindly-legged light-footed blood sucker.... [19]

LANTERN MEN

Known as 'Shiners' in those Breckland villages bordering the Fens and as 'Syleham Lights' in the Waveney valley near Harleston, tales of the Lantern Man circulated most widely in the Broads. This will o' the wisp figure took shape from the gas that, before the marshes were drained, rose to the surface and burst into flames; an *ignis fatuus* or 'foolish fire', it became a dancing, bewildering light that lead people astray. An old innkeeper heard tell of a ball of flame which was seen to float across the marshes and cling for a while to the mast of a passing wherry. Well known in East Anglia the Lantern Man's reputation as a malignant spirit has a celebrated pedigree conjured up in Milton's *Paradise Lost*:

> A wand'ring fire ....
> Which oft, they say, some Evil Spirit attends,
> Hovering and blazing with delusive Light,
> Misleads th'amaz'd Night-Wandr'er from his way
> To bogs and mires, and oft through Pond or Pool,
> There swallowed up and lost ....

Wherries on the Yare at Cantley

The Lantern Man's fiercesome reputation was based not simply on his ability to deceive those unfortunate enough to be out after dark but on his aggressive nature. There are several reports of farmers knocked from their horses and of the lanterns carried by marshmen on their way home being dashed to pieces. If he came up behind you the best advice was to lay flat on your face and hold your breath for fear of inhaling the marsh gas. Inevitably the Lantern Man was often associated with death by drowning as implied by Mrs Lubbock's recollection from Irstead:

> Before the Irstead Enclosure in 1810, Jack O'Lantern was frequently seen here on a roky [misty] night, and almost always at a place called Heard's Holde, in Alder Carr Fen Broad, ... Where a man of that name, who was guilty of some unmentionable crimes, was drowned. I have often seen it there, rising up and falling, and twistering about, and then up again. It looked exactly like a candle in a lantern.[20]

The old White Horse In
Thurlton, 1969
Line drawing, R P Garr

In Thurlton churchyard on the edge of the Broads the headstone of Joseph Bexfield, carved with a Norfolk wherry – a craft used extensively on the inland waterways – has prompted the tale of the Wherryman's Grave. Thurlton Staithe on the river Yare, halfway between Norwich and Yarmouth, was a convenient place to tie up for the night and from here a long track across the marsh led to the turnpike and the White Horse Inn. Here the wherrymen would meet for a meal and a few drinks. One evening, Bexfield, who lived locally, remembered he had left something at the staithe that his wife had asked him to get in Norwich. Despite warnings from his fellow boatmen that the Lantern Men were about that night 'popping off in hundreds',[21] Bexfield, downing another 'double hot rum', said he 'knew the old marsh too well to be led astray'[22] and bid them goodnight. Days later his body was found floating downstream between Reedham and Breydon and ever since, when the whirling sea mists from Breydon Water enshroud the marshes, a 'shadow figure' of the wherryman can be seen wandering over the marsh behind the lantern man. Bexfield's headstone records that he was drowned on August 1st 1809.

The wherryman's grave, Thurlton

RITES OF PASSAGE

Hogarth's illustration from 'Hudibras' of a Skimmington

LOVE DIVINATION

Setting aside the 'natural longings of many village maidens', girls were regarded as a burden to large families on the breadline and were either sent into service or married off as quickly as possible. This mixture of desire and desperation to avoid becoming an old maid meant that young women were always alert to signs that might reveal their future husband. In much the same way that plum stones arranged on a plate may still invoke the chant 'tinker, tailor, soldier, sailor, rich man, poor man, beggar man, thief', to determine a spouse, divination was often no more than a childish game. The following rhyme, quoted by Walter Rye in 1885, was repeated whenever a ladybird alighted on the hand:

Bishop, bishop, Barnabee
Tell me when my wedding be!
If it be tomorrow day
Take your wings and fly away
Fly to the east, fly to the west
And fly to him that I love best

The first line is probably a misreading of the Norfolk dialect term for the insect, bishee Barnybee. If the ladybird merely fluttered its wings then the desired wedding date was postponed indefinitely.

For those who put their faith in various forms of love divination – often impressionable young girls – it was essential they were carried out exactly as prescribed by tradition and at certain times of the year. Valentine's Day, Midsummer's Eve and New Year were all regarded as auspicious but St Mark's Eve was by far the most popular time to foretell one's lover. There is nothing in the life of the saint to suggest such an association but the timing of his feast day, 25th April, was a convenient springtime prelude to the much anticipated May Day festivities.

First it was necessary to predict a girl's marital state and this was done by placing a blindfold over her eyes and then arranging three bowls in front of her. The girl then discovers her fate by dipping her fingers in one of the bowls. If she chooses the empty bowl she will be a spinster, if the dirty water bowl then a widow and the bowl with clear water means she will be a bride. Alternatively the occupation of the future husband could be determined by two maidens washing the hearth and then placing two pewter pots bottom upwards on the clean surface. Then, retiring to bed, they climb the stairs backwards and in complete silence. The following morning they would rush down to see what was under each pot, an arrangement that relied on the secret co-operation of some other member of the household. A little earth signified the husband would be a labourer, a sliver of wood a carpenter, and so on.

Love divination took many forms in an attempt to reveal a girl's sweetheart, either in person or in a dream. Writing in 1830 the Rev'd Forby recalled how at midnight on St Mark's Eve young women in East Anglia would go out in the garden each with a handful of hemp seeds and recite the following lines, whereupon the future spouse was supposed to appear with his scythe.

Hemp seed I sow,
Hemp seed grow,
He that is my true love
Come after me and mow.

In another version, which took place indoors on St Martin's Eve (November 11th), hemp seed was scattered round the kitchen table and when the proposed lover appeared the sower had to be sure to escape his scythe, like an animal trapped in the standing corn, or some accident would be sure to follow. The choice of hemp seed to conjour up this imaginary figure, in this case more grim reaper than gallant suitor, may have been determined by its stupefying or hallucinatory properties. Wayside plants, perhaps because of their medicinal properties, were also often used in love divination. The number of puffs required to blow all the seeds off the head of a dandelion would determine the number of years a person must wait to be married. Girls believed the old saying that she who puts a two leaf clover in her right shoe will have the first young man she sees 'Or one of his name', and a girl who tickles her nostrils with a leaf of yarrow, or yarroway as it was known in Norfolk, must repeat the following verse:

Yarroway, yarroway, bear a white blow;
If my love loves me, my nose will bleed now.

Yarrow

The use of fasting, observing silence and/or reciting verse were all at times employed to heighten perception much like those forms of devotion practiced in a medieval monastery. They were even present in the custom described by John Glyde in 1872 of baking a 'dumb cake'. Prepared by unmarried women using an eggshell full of salt, a similar measure of wheat meal and another of barley meal, the desired effect was induced not by the ingredients but the way in which the baking was carried out. The cook must be alone and silent and to have abstained from eating that day. Just before midnight the cake would be baked before the fire and the main door left open. At the stroke of twelve the sweetheart, probably by prior arrangement if he was willing, would enter and turn the cake. In another version the cake, known as a 'dreaming cake', is divided into three portions; one is placed under the pillow and the other two eaten by girls who must then climb the stairs and into bed backwards, all in complete silence and on the stroke of midnight. Those hoping to marry might see a vision of their future husband while those destined to remain as spinsters would see nothing.

Such was the importance attached to discovering the identity of a future husband that all manner of rituals were performed on St Mark's Eve, one old custom encapsulated in the rhyme:

I pin my garters to the wall,
I hope to hear my true love call;
Whether awake or whether asleep,
I hope to hear my true love speak.

Alternatively if a girl was to sit before her looking glass at midnight with a single candle alight in a far corner of the bedroom while repeating these lines –

Come lover, come lad,
And make my heart glad,
For husband I'll have you
For good or for bad.

– she will presently see the shadowy form of her intended spouse appear in the room. On other occasions desperate remedies were employed by 'over anxious maidens' to force a lover to reveal himself. In one instance a blade bone of mutton would be taken from its hiding place and a slit made across the surface on each of three successive Friday evenings. By the principle of sympathetic magic it was firmly believed that the chosen one would cut his finger and come to have it bound up. A Norfolk woman, a woman of above average intelligence, attempted to force her would-be lover to present himself by thrusting a penknife into the post at the foot of the bed, a measure of her frustration, while reciting this rhyme.

It's not the post alone I stick,
But Will Marshall's heart I mean to prick,

Whether he be asleep or awake
I'll have him come to me and speak.

Writing in the correspondence section of *Folk-Lore* the Norfolk folklorist W B Gerish contributed the following churchyard charm given by a Chedgrave wise woman to a girl in Loddon. Part of the charm's power resides in the obscurity of its instructions but, enacted over a grave, the price of a husband is spelt out quite clearly at the end:

To gain a husband, name known or unknown,
Make your choice on a graveyard stone
Quarter-day's night if there fare a moon,
Pass thro' the church gate right alone;
Twist three crosses from graveyard bits,
Place them straight in your finger slits,
Over the grave hold a steady hand,
And learn the way the side crosses stand:
One is yourself and your husband one,
And the middle one need be named of none.
If they both on the middle cross have crossed,
His name you win, and a year you've lost;
For he who lies in the namesake mould
His soul has sold – or he would have sold,
And you give a year which the dead may use,
Your last year of earth-life that you lose.

COURTSHIP

Instead of a more forthright declaration of amorous intent, village lads in the Fens when Jack Barrett was young preferred to signal affection by means of a love token. This consisted of three ears of corn tied in a lover's knot and worn as a buttonhole. The wearer would then give a second love knot to his sweetheart who in turn showed it to her parents seeking their approval of the relationship. A week later the would-be suitor arrived at the girl's house. If, on opening the door, the girl was wearing the token over her heart then he knew his advance had been sanctioned and the tokens would then be worn throughout their courtship. If the knot was pinned on the other side of her dress then the lover must look elsewhere. A simpler version of this ritual involved a sprig of southernwood, or Lad's Love, worn in the buttonhole by youths who took to strolling the lanes in their spare time. Having contrived to pass his girl with her friends a lad would offer her his buttonhole as a form of proposal. If she was so inclined she would accept by inhaling its scent and would then announce their courtship by taking his arm.

Southernwood

A girl might also identify the object of her affection by pinning a bunch of yarrow to her dress. She would then use every opportunity to get near her beloved. If he ignored her approach she would resort to a form of divination which involved walking barefoot through a patch of yarrow at midnight when the moon was full. She then picked a bunch with her eyes closed and put it under her pillow or in a draw. If there was still dew on the flowers in the morning this was a sure sign her chosen one would come courting but if they were dry then she must try again at the next full moon. Yarrow flowers gathered on St Swithin's Day and put in a pillow would bring happiness to the couple who slept on it. In an attempt to attract a young man girls would obtain a love potion from the village wise woman, a mixture of rose, verbena and other fragrant flowers. Tea with a pinch of Dragon's Blood, or red powder made from the fruit *Calamus draco*, would also be drunk to improve the complexion.

Fenland courtship token

A courtship custom peculiar to the Fens, and one Jack Barrett heard from his grandmother, involved the making of a fur tippet, a Victorian neck warmer. It was sewn together by the courting couple using stoat or ferret pelts and padded with sheep's wool. Before completion a small silk sachet would be placed at either end of the tippet, one with cuttings from the woman's pubic hair and the other with pubic hair from her future husband. When worn the ends of the tippet would meet over the young woman's heart. This would ensure a long and productive union. The ritual object was often kept indefinitely, or at least all the while the marriage lasted, and 'Granny' Barrett's tippet was buried with her.

Another tradition, one that may have been practiced more widely, went by the name of 'bundling' in the Fens. It was a custom that the storyteller Chafer Legge thought had been introduced by migrant labourers from Ireland and, despite it being denounced from the pulpit, bundling was an accepted way to find a husband for an unmarried daughter. Through the winter muddy tracks deep in the fens were often impassable for months at a time. Young women seldom left their isolated cottages except for chapel on a Sunday and any courting had to be conducted indoors. This appears to have been actively encouraged by the girl's parents who would leave their daughter and her young man alone downstairs with a large bag of oat chaff and a few blankets piled in the corner of the room for their use. There was less necessity for this arrangement in the larger farmhouses but it often went on without parental consent when, after dark, the young suitor would climb up to his sweetheart's room with the aid of a ladder conveniently left nearby. Either way bundling often had the same desired effect and arrangements would then be hastily made for the couple to be married before the girl's pregnancy became too apparent.

PREGNANCY and BIRTH

The village midwife or handywoman was usually present at a birth but before that her services were in great demand both to encourage pregnancy and induce abortions. From the middle ages onwards, those travelling to the healing wells at Walsingham, Bawburgh or Dereham included women hoping to bear children and mandrake tea made from the root of white bryony was administered to infertile women for the same reason. Its efficacy was based on the shape of the root which often resembled a male or female figure and the aphrodisiac properties associated with the plant were absorbed by those women who drunk the concoction. Another example of this belief-by-association at work was the eating of tansy salad by those desperate to start a family. Rabbits were often observed to be plentiful where tansy grew and rabbits were renowned for producing large families. Conversely unwanted pregnancies among young girls 'married before they had been parsoned' might be terminated by severe vomiting induced by chewing hemp leaves or by taking pills prepared by the local wise woman from a mixture of hemlock, rue and pennyroyal. A miscarriage might also be brought about by eating either horseradish or parsley three times a day. In the absence of effective contraception any break in the yearly round of child rearing was a blessed relief in large, poverty-stricken households. Among the more extreme measures, a woman was advised to hold the hand of a dead man for two minutes – the male/female contact appears to have been important – and, when done, she would be spared childbirth for the next two years. To sleep with 'corpse money' under her pillow (p219) would also ensure a woman had no more children.

Tansey,
Brunfels, 1532

The importance attached to childbirth is evident from the many rites and customs associated with the event. In poor communities knowing the sex of a forthcoming child was of great concern to the parents because a boy was more likely to contribute to the family purse from a young age. This might be determined by strips of horse-radish placed under the pillows of both husband and wife. If the husband's strip turned black first then the child would be a boy, if the wife's, then a girl. Where herbs, especially parsley, sage and rosemary used in cooking, flourished in a garden this was a sign that the wife was the dominant influence and her child would be a girl. To alleviate the pain of childbirth the local midwife would make a painkilling cake. The recipe, used by Jack Barrett's mother, included hemp seed, the crushed roots of dandelion and rhubarb mixed with flour, egg yolk and gin. A slice was fed not just to the mother at the first onset of labour pains but also to the husband in attendance who would suffer sympathetic pains much like those experienced in some tribal societies. These very real pains may have occurred throughout his wife's pregnancy as a result of some psychosomatic illness like gastritis, neuralgia or, more often, toothache, known in Norfolk as 'the love pain'.

The exact time and the circumstances of a birth were closely scrutinised for signs that might indicate the baby's health and general wellbeing in later life. A child conceived during a thunderstorm would grow up to be strong and healthy and one born at midnight or during the other chime hours (three, six or nine o'clock) was blessed with the gift of second sight and could foretell the future. In deference to orthodox religious belief Sunday was the most propitious day to give birth and Friday the least favourable, but for some reason it was thought unlucky for a child to arrive on May 1st in the Fens. The midwife would use any number of ploys to prevent this, urging a pregnant woman near her full term to exercise strenuously and so induce an early delivery or to drink a strong infusion of horehound and rue followed by a mixture of gin and poppy juice to sedate her for a day. A child born with a caul on its head (p154) was a lucky child and would never drown and a bunch of yarrow hung on the cradle would produce a contented child.

To ensure a child would prosper and go up in the world this was achieved, quite literally, by first carrying the newborn upstairs. If the mother's room was at the top of the house then, carrying her baby carefully in her arms, she would climb on a chair placed near the door before going downstairs. The few weeks after a birth were always of great concern to the mother who kept a close watch on the health of her baby. Not only would a child not prosper until it had been baptised but it was in danger of being spirited away by fairies who would leave a changeling in its place. A mother could not, in all conscience, go out visiting before she had been 'churched', an act of purification once performed by the priest; and the first outing with her baby was to have it christened. If the baby cried when blessed with baptismal water it was a welcome sign that the Devil had been vanquished. The midwife performed a similar role by blowing down the baby's throat before laying it face down on her lap, placing a sixpence provided by the mother on its bottom, and saying 'Devil away!' The baby then wriggled, the coin, which would roll onto the floor, was then swiftly pocketed by the midwife who explained that it had been taken by the Devil in payment for the child's sins in a way reminiscent of 'sin eating' (p219).

Hemlock,
Conium Maculatum

MARRIAGE

Compared to the many courtship rituals and methods employed to secure a spouse, once a date had been set the marriage ceremony itself was a simple service that, because of its religious nature, has attracted little in the way of associated folklore. Bridal parties in Norfolk, especially among the families of agricultural labourers, were usually small and, according to John Varden, writing in 1885, were rarely attended by the parents of the bride and groom. There were times when the ceremony had to be conducted without a ring or with one borrowed for the occasion. It was the best man's job to arrange for the village chimney sweep to be waiting outside the church door in his soot-covered working clothes ready to kiss the bride. This would bring the couple good luck and, it was believed, would ensure she kept a clean house. Girls would strew the church path with flowers and fern leaves while the young men rang handbells and fired pistols. This, at least, was the custom peculiar to coastal villages and in the Broads while in Aylsham gunpowder fired on the blacksmith's forge was originally intended to drive away evil spirits. If, however, the marriage was disapproved of for some reason then the couple were greeted in a less friendly manner, one that might easily become an occasion for 'rough music', a form of ridicule more often reserved for extra-marital affairs.

ROUGH MUSIC

This loud and raucous noise, usually directed at those who had contravened accepted social norms, was achieved on a selection of improvised percussive utensils – pots, kettles and saucepans as well as tongs, marrow-bones, horns and whistles accompanied by chanting, jeers and laughter. Any decision to perform rough music was usually made in the local pub, either by a self-appointed group of regulars or by the more forceful individuals who would decide whether a particular transgression merited ridicule or public humiliation. This might range from the good natured teasing of newly weds or the more recent trick of fixing tin cans to the wedding car, or sustained bursts of rough music in more serious cases of domestic abuse.

A West Country Skimmington, Montague House panel, Somerset

At Walpole St Peter in the Fens married couples were greeted by children playing loudly on combs and paper, mouth organs or beating spoons on trays and pans until their demands for pennies were granted. Playful extortion of this kind was a traditional part of wedding celebrations but couples were often subject to more bawdy forms of ridicule, especially when there was a marked difference in age or some obvious physical or mental deficiency. A case in point was reported in the *Norfolk Chronicle* (August 29th, 1829) when Thomas Hubbard, aged 79, was married in Fakenham for the third time, on this occasion to Martha Frary, aged 21. Hubbard was a well known character and had supplied the town with matches and watercress for many years. Outside the church the crowd was entertained by 'Hubbard limping along with a bridesmaid…'[1] aged at least 80 and followed by 'an unfortunate cripple driving his curricle of dogs…'[2] After the ceremony 'the bridegroom was torn from his fainting partner and thrown into an open carriage decorated with ram's horns, and drawn through the principal streets of the town, amidst the firing of guns and the shouts and ridicule of the people.'[3] A scene almost as disorderly occurred on March 14th, 1832, in Thetford when a 29 year old schoolmaster named Bussey married a Mrs Judith Millon aged 78. 'A party of heroines … Attended the happy couple and performed their melodious chorus upon saucepans and kettles, and to complete the band a watchman's rattle was added.'[4]

The King's Arms, Fleggburgh

A quarrelsome couple or scold may get off lightly but wife-beating, infidelity or child cruelty would provoke a more hostile response. In extreme cases this might take a form of street theatre-cum-ritual known in Northern England as 'Riding the Stang' or a skimmington in the West Country, which included an effigy of the accused tied to a pole or astride a donkey. It would be paraded outside the victim's house, accompanied by rough music, on successive nights in an attempt to 'drum' him or her out of the neighbourhood. The effigy would then be burnt, a symbolic death reminiscent of the fate of heretics in the 17th century and those convicted of witchcraft (p137). The most famous skimmington is described by Hardy in *The Mayor of Casterbridge* (1886). Planned in the tap room of Peter's Finger among the slums of Mixen Lane, effigies of Henchard and Lucetta are paraded through the streets to the door of the guilty lovers with disastrous consequences.

While there is little evidence for such an elaborate ritual in Norfolk, examples of rough music in the Fens, where it went by the name of 'tinging', may represent a simplified version of this archaic practice. In 1904, while a young boy, Jack Barrett took part in the last known instance of tinging in Brandon Creek prompted by a persistent case of wife-beating. One night fifty or so men and boys with an ingenious selection of tin utensils set off for the culprit's cottage. The leader carried a bugle and, at intervals, a blast on the instrument would silence the assembled crowd who would then cry out, 'Clear out! Clear out!' Two hours of loud, rough 'music' and shouting was enough to persuade the husband, a well known drunkard and outsider, to catch the first train back to London.

The use of rough music might also be prompted by some perceived injustice, by an employer to his workers, or for minor crimes or misdemeanours within the community. The case brought at Rollesby Petty Sessions in February 1868 illustrates the many aspects of a skimmington. Six young men up before the court had left the King's Arms in Fleggburgh and had walked the mile or so to Clippesby singing and shouting as they went and carrying aloft an effigy seated in a chair. The procession had gone to settle a score with John Mundford, a fellow labourer, but one who had been witness in a recent case against two of the six men found guilty of poaching. When Mundford appeared at his cottage door there were cries of 'Here he comes!' and as the singing and groaning grew louder more people came out into the street to observe the spectacle. The effigy was held aloft for all to see, dressed 'in tan trousers, a white slop and a black wideawake [hat]'[5], clothes similar to those worn by Mundford, and with a placard around its neck which read 'No friend to poor man!' In the evening the effigy was taken down to the marshes and burnt amidst much merriment.

The chairman of the magistrates, Rev'd Charles Lucas, accepted that 'something viscerally connected with rural life had been played out on Clippsby marshes that day'[6], the day in question being Valentine's Day when, like other feast days in the calendar, such levity was permitted. Had Mundford attempted to placate the procession with money – the two convicted of poaching had been fined – the crowd may well have dispersed but the opportunity provided by the day had been used to exact a symbolic form of rough justice. Because of this and the nature of the disturbance – a dispute between members of the lower classes – the court handed down a lenient sentence and the defendants were bound over to keep the peace for three months.

From its use to express public disapproval it was a short step to the deployment of rough music by the mob in acts of civil disobedience that became increasingly common in rural Norfolk throughout the 19th century. One of many sources of grievance was the 1834 Poor Law Act that transferred responsibility for 'relieving' the poor from the parish to the new union workhouses in an attempt to prevent fraudulent claims. Against this background a meeting of the guardians of Freebridge Lynn Union held in Grimston schoolroom on February 5th, 1836, was cut short by the deafening sound of rough music from outside the windows. Three men from Massingham, later jailed for their part in the disorder, stepped forward to voice the demands of the mob; that the substitution of money doles for flour and bread should stop or future meetings would be disrupted in the same way.

The enclosure of common land and the extinguishment of ancient rights to gather fuel and graze livestock was another source of hostility in the countryside when rough music often accompanied direct action. At Marham a meeting in 1859 to discuss proposals to enclose and drain the fen that threatened traditional rights to cut peat, was interrupted by rough music. Another case, reported in *Norfolk News* the following year, involved attempts by the Holkham estate to enclose and embank land in Wighton used ' from time immemorial' to graze ponies and geese. Police deployed to guard the work were soon sent on their way by men from the village, accompanied by women banging pots, pans and kettles, who set about levelling the embankment. In all these cases rough music was an effective part of direct action, or 'mob violence' as it was called, against harsh injustices suffered by the rural poor in 19th century Norfolk.

Grimston school house

WIFE SELLING

Wife selling,
early c19 illustration

The most famous example of this degrading spectacle occurs again in Hardy's *The Mayor of Casterbridge* but the impulsive sale of Susan Henchard to a passing stranger by her drunk husband is not typical of the practice once widespread in the early 19th century. The treatment of his wife by Michael Henchard as disposable chattel was, however, typical of the prevailing attitude towards women. More often the transaction took place in public and involved an element of street theatre as this case from Thetford demonstrates. An account of the auction, held in the market place on Saturday 17th September 1839, was carried by a broadsheet on sale soon after:

> ... a man about forty years of age, in a shabby-genteel dress, leading a smart-looking woman, with a handkerchief round her neck and shouting with a loud voice, 'who'll buy a wife?' After arriving at the centre of the market, he mounted a chair, and offered her for sale ... A young man of plausible appearance offered 10s for her, but he was immediately opposed by an old gentleman bidding 5s more. Afterwards the young man became the purchaser for

£5. The money was paid down and the husband, on handing over the handkerchief to the purchaser, began to dance and sing, declaring he had got rid of a troublesome noisy wife, which caused much merriment in the crowd. The young woman turned sharply round and said, you know you old rascal you are jealous – you are no man, and have no need of a young wife, and that is the reason you sold me, you useless old dog ... the women began to clap their hands to him. He then said she was a gormandizing woman, and would eat any man's substance up; and declared if he had kept her another year she would have eaten him out of house and harbour ... [7]

The use of a halter, in this case a handkerchief, but more often a length of rope, the exchange of insults and payment of the agreed sum, all witnessed by the crowd, were essential elements in this ritualised drama sufficient to legitimise the transaction. In this instance the seller, John Simpson of Bra[n]denham, had lodged with the purchaser and the sale had probably already been agreed.

A FULL ACCOUNT of the EXTRAORDINARY CIRCUMSTANCE OF

A MAN

SELLING HIS WIFE

In the Market-place, Thetford,

Early c19 broadsheet

In another case, this time recounted by Mr Crawford of Wiggenhall St Germans, it appears that the tacit agreement of all three parties had been arrived at in advance. Just downstream on the Great Ouse at Upwell the local postman had been sentenced to five years in prison for stealing money while on his round. On his release he found his wife had been associating with another man. When asked she made it clear she wished to continue with the relationship, at which point her husband said she must go. He then made a halter, placed it round her neck and led her onto New Bridge. Here he sold her for a quart of beer to the man she had been living with. It appears to have been an accepted way to regularise extra-marital relations but at the time – 1875 – much of the public spectacle on display years earlier in Thetford had gone and soon after the shameful custom disappeared altogether, or took place in a tavern, and became formalised with a paper contract signed in front of witnesses.

FOLK MEDICINE

Cunning men and wise women were well versed in the medicinal properties of wayside plants, a knowledge, often jealously guarded, that forms the basis of today's herbal remedies. Ailments affecting both humans and animals (p.149) were treated in this way, either by applying the leaves of a plant directly to the area infected or by drinking an extract. More extreme measures involved transference of the disease to an inanimate object and a belief in the efficacy of the accompanying ritual. The huge variety of remedies available is best illustrated with reference to the most common complaints.

Until better drainage reduced the mosquito population that spread the disease, malaria, ague, or Bailiff of the Marshes as it was known, had been endemic in both the Fens and the Broads for centuries. The dyke diggers, reed cutters and peat diggers who laboured in the wet for much of the year could ill-afford to be off sick and came to rely on a variety of remedies to dull the effects of high temperatures and aching limbs. Horehound tea brought a measure of relief and an infusion of willow bark was believed to be efficacious on the principle that because the tree grew with its feet in water it must be good for ailments caused by dampness. The panacea for pain relief and the reduction of fever was however opium, or the Fenman's Friend. Readily available in pill form on market stalls or as the tincture laudanum from chemists it was the Victorians' drug of choice. For those unable to afford it over the counter poppy tea made from the seeds of the white opium poppy was an effective substitute – 'Poppy Tea and Opium Pill/Are the Fen cure for many an ill.' The flower, according to Enid Porter, was grown in every garden in the Fens – it is commemorated in the name Poppylot Farm in Methwold Fen – and its consumption throughout the winter months was said to explain the Fen dwellers' reputation for being 'stunted in growth and slow of wit.'

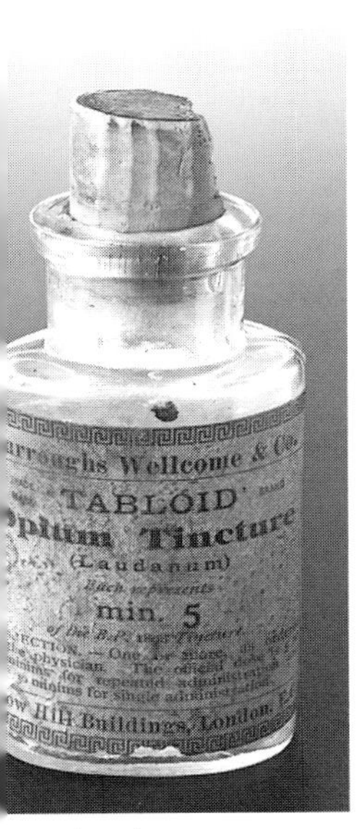

Laudanum

The range of magical charms and folk cures illustrate the lengths people were prepared to go to rid themselves of this debilitating disease, together with those muscular complaints, lumbago and rheumatism, that were the price of back-breaking toil. Garters made from eel-skin or plaited hair from the tail of a cow were often worn round a trembling limb, or a bag filled with grated horseradish round the neck. A small bag made of mouse skins filled with the dust of a puff ball along with a hardened potato, a nutmeg, the forefoot of a mole or a dried rat's tail were among the unsavoury items carried around in the pocket. Ingestive cures of the more nauseous kind involved a live spider rolled in dough and swallowed as a pill and Sir Thomas Browne's recommendation of goose dung stewed in warm beer.

One elaborate remedy similar to the cure for warts required a piece of raw beef which, for reasons best known to the charmer, must have been stolen, together with a lock of the patient's hair and nail parings, to be placed in a new earthen pan and covered with black silk. This was then buried in a wood or ground that had never been dug and as the meat decayed so the ague abated. The writer Agnes Strickland who was brought up at Reydon Hall near Southwold, provided the following elaborate ritual in *Old Friends and New Acquaintances* (1860). How often it was practised is not clear but the successful completion of each stage was necessary to its success:

Opium poppy

> Go to the four crossways tonight all alone, and just as the clock strikes twelve turn yourself about three times, and then drive a tenpenny nail into the ground up to the head and walk away from the place backwards before the clock is done striking, and you'll miss the ague; but the next person who passes over the nail will take it in your stead.

When this and all other remedies failed, a good fright was said to be effective. It certainly worked for one old lady whose husband told her the pig was dead. Horrified at the news she rushed outside to find to her great relief the pig was alive and well but as a result of the shock the fever left her and never returned.

Warts were a commonplace and unsightly skin infection at a time when soap was expensive and dirty hands were thought to contribute to the spread of the complaint. There are more folk remedies for curing warts than any other ailment and almost every village, both in Norfolk and across the country, had its own wart charmer whose services were offered freely and often in silence. Allowing for numerous local variations cures ranged from the purely medicinal to the quasi magical. The first simply involved rubbing the affected area with the milky juice of a plant – dandelion, milkwort or greater celandine – the inner skin of a broad bean pod or a sliced potato. A green sloe was sometimes used but, and here an element of superstition is required, when used it must then be thrown over the left shoulder. In each case the success of the remedy relied almost entirely on the healing properties of the plants chosen.

The second category involved a combination of traditional medicine and sympathetic magic. It had been common practice since the middle ages to rub a wart with a piece of raw meat that had been stolen, and then bury it in the ground – some said at midnight at the crossroads. As the meat rotted away so the warts would disappear. In another version, one referred to in *I Walked by Night* (1935) edited by Lilias Rider Haggard, a snail was pierced with a thorn and the ensuing slime rubbed on the warts. It was then either buried or impaled on a whitethorn bush and as it wasted away so did the warts. In each version strict secrecy was required. The simplest method available to the wart charmer was to count the number of warts in complete silence. It often worked and two weeks later the growths would be gone. Others achieved the same result by making the sign of the cross over each wart with a pin before throwing it away. A more elaborate variant involved cutting a notch, one for each wart, in the bark of an ash tree bearing its keys or seeds, together with the person's initials. As the bark regrew so the warts would heal and disappear; a case of imitative magic much like the meat or the snail rotted away.

One remedy that seems to have been a Norfolk speciality was the use of dragonflies. Held by its wings and with its mouth applied to the wart the insect would gradually pinch it off with its mandibles. At the turn of the last century the parish clerk at Edingthorpe told the vicar how, when he was a boy 'we made the writs (warts) bleed and then these things [dragonflies] would suck 'em like a leech.'[8] Enid Porter recalled a similar case from Cambridgeshire where, in the 1930s, a man was told to get a grasshopper and put it on his wart. In this instance it was the liquid left by the insect that shrunk the wart straight away. Because of its warty appearance, to hold a toad was thought to cause warts to spread and in the Norfolk Fens some cows were believed to only have three full-sized teats and one little one. This was for the fairies to take milk and if the cowman was foolish enough to use it his hand would become covered in warts.

Before the availability of a suitable vaccine the persistence of whooping cough, known as the 100 day cough, and its frequent recurrence, provided the wise woman with ample opportunities to practice her skills. The illness proved to be such a terrible distraction that the mothers of young children would try almost anything to effect a cure. The range of remedies was a measure of their increasing desperation. As with warts they often relied on the practice of transference whereby the sickness was conveyed to an animal or object and as it wasted away so the infection was believed to disappear.

The more bizarre examples of this folk 'logic' included placing a dab or some other flat fish on a child's bare chest. It was kept there by some means until the fish had died, by which time the cough too would have dried up. Along the coast sufferers were taken to the shore at ebb-tide so that the outgoing sea would bear the cough away. Snails passed through the hands of a sufferer, or the head of a live frog held in a child's mouth, were believed to have the same effect once the creature had been hung inside the chimney and had rotted away. Despite evidence to the contrary feeding a cooked mouse to a patient was widely thought to be effective. Alternatively a hair taken from a sick child and placed between pieces of bread would then be given to a dog. If the dog coughed while swallowing the hair the disease would have been successfully transferred to the animal. At other times the cure might take the form of a symbolic burial in an attempt to lay the illness to rest. The child would be laid face down in a meadow, the turf cut round it in the shape of a coffin and, once the child had been removed, the turf was inverted. As the grass withered away so the cough too would die. In a drastic variation of this remedy the child was placed head first in a freshly dug hole and the turf laid on top until he coughed, trapping the affliction in the ground. A sufferer passed through a split ash sapling would be restored to health once the tree had been bound up and had begun to heal, and a child dragged three times under a bramble with both ends rooted in the ground might expect to recover.

The other main group of remedies relied more on the effect of contact with some purifying agent and in this respect they may have been of some medicinal benefit – lifting a child to inhale the breath of a stallion, running with a flock of sheep, tying a length of tarred string round the child's neck or placing a pot of tar under its bed. Taking the patient to breathe the fumes at the local gas works was once a common treatment for whooping cough and various respiratory ailments.

DEATH DIVINATION

Long before the discovery of penicillin, antibiotics and a whole range of medical advances that we take for granted, disease and malnutrition were rife among the poor. Infant mortality was high and, among the adult population, life expectancy was painfully short. In large, extended families and tight knit communities death was never far away and on the walls of most medieval churches there were graphic depictions of the fate that awaits us all. The Three Living and Three Dead was among the most popular of allegorical themes and impressive fragments remain on view at

Wickhampton and Heydon. At Sparham two gruesome rood screen panels riddled with worm depict the Dance of Death; grinning cadavers in fashionable late 15th century dress framed by a quote from Job: 'Man that is born of woman is a few days and full of trouble. He cometh forth like a flower and is cut down.' Memorable too is the grim reaper carving at Little Barningham, complete with scythe and hourglass, perched on one corner of a Jacobean box pew like a bird of prey while outside in the churchyard the skull and cross bones motif adorns many an early headstone.

Dance of Death, 15c panel, Sparham

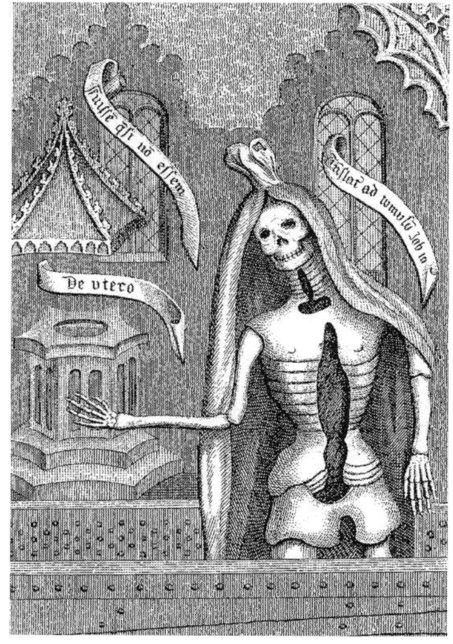

Skeleton rising from tomb, Sparham

Faced with such disturbing images of death it is no surprise that the medieval mind was preoccupied with omens plucked from the natural world – the croaking of a raven, the hoot of an owl or a robin flown indoors – omens that remained just as potent in the folklore of 19th century Norfolk together with a colourful array of additional beliefs acquired along the way. Having just buried three people in quick succession the Victorian rector of West Tofts, Augustus Sutton, was informed that the first two corpses had still been limp at the time of committal, a sure sign that there would be another death in the family within the year. Others were fond of quoting the old saying 'if you open a grave for one you will open it for two'. Hawthorn brought into the house or any Christmas festive decoration not removed from church by Candlemas Day (the Purification, February 2nd) were said to presage death before the year was out. In the same way a housewife would examine newly laundered sheets for oval creases or 'coffin folds' and the wax shapes known as 'winding sheets' formed by a guttering candle. Omens like these were most often observed in and around the home but the Rev'd Taylor of Martham recalled that when seed was still broadcast, a 'bowl' or bare patch of earth meant not just a death in the family but an accident or the death of livestock on the farm. The belief continued with the advent of the seed drill. If it went the length of the field with a clogged pipe then death would come calling before the sowing had been reaped.

Bees have long been held in high regard for their wax, used to make church candles, for the purity and nutritious quality of their honey – the nectar of the gods – and for their hives as a model of the perfect society. The behaviour of bees was closely observed and if a swarm alighted on a dead branch a death would soon follow. Conversely bees would desert a hive if they had not been informed of their owner's death. This was done by tapping the hive three times with the house key. Bees were to be treated with respect at all times and, following a bereavement, a length of black crepe would be fixed to each hive to allow their occupants time to mourn. In some villages they were also left a share of the funeral cake.

St Mark's Eve (24th April) was traditionally a time for divination when those who were to die within the year were revealed to anyone who maintained a vigil in the church porch at midnight. At the appointed hour the wraiths of those fated to die would pass into the church and remain there while those destined to recover from illness would re-emerge at length according to the period of their infirmity. Those watching did so at risk of seeing themselves or of falling asleep during the vigil, either way the consequences were dire. The Rev'd Forby, writing from west Norfolk in the 1820s, thought the practice had died out but in 1845 the Rev'd Gunn at Irstead in the Broads referred to the custom at Stalham. Here Robert Staff, formerly publican of the Maid's Head opposite the church, kept watch with two other men on St Mark's Eve. Those who were to die that same year went in singly and did not return while those who would be married went in as couples and came out together.

DEATH CUSTOMS

In May 1929 a paper on Norfolk folklore read at a meeting of the Folk-Lore Society included an astonishing reference to the practice of euthanasia known as 'Drawing the Pillow'. Not surprisingly perhaps there is no indication of where in the county this took place or whether it was once widespread but the speaker, Mark Taylor, had been alerted to the custom by a local doctor. According to the GP the death of a person 'too slow in dying' was brought about by the sudden removal of the pillow; in this way the sick person's head would fall back constricting the windpipe. When challenged, the old[9] woman responsible replied 'its not murder, its what we call "drawing the pillow"'. Naming the deed appeared to have given it legitimacy within the community whereas death by suffocation may have been deemed a more deliberate and controversial form of mercy killing.

In the 1950s, while in conversation with Enid Porter, Jack Barrett provided a more revealing account of the practice referred to on the Norfolk/Cambridgeshire border as 'snatching the pillow.' He in turn had heard of it in 1910 from an old man whose wife had been the village nurse. When a family could no longer afford to care for an elderly bed-ridden relative the nurse would be sent for to fetch the pillow; one which had been handed on in the village from one practitioner to her successor. It was said to have been covered in black lace made by a nun from Ely, as if this somehow absolved the 'executioner' or implied that the use for which the pillow was intended had received the church's blessing. When the day came the pillow would be carried through the village by the nurse; a sign for people to go indoors and draw their blinds for they would soon hear the passing bell and know for whom it tolled.

> Arriv[ing] at the house where her services were required, the nurse would be given a glass of fortifying gin. Then, crushing two opium pills, she would mix these with a strong dose of gin and spoon the mixture into the patient's mouth. Soon he would relapse into a coma. Then he was propped up in bed, the pillow behind his neck. In a short while the pillow was snatched away and his head would fall back with a jerk.[10]

According to Barrett the last woman to perform the task was the unfortunately named Mrs Feltwell. After her own death in 1902 her son, to the relief of elderly residents, threw the pillow on a bonfire, so bringing to an end this grim ritual.

Before the advent of the funeral parlour and the Chapel of Rest it was common practice for the dead to be laid out at home by the women of the family under the guidance of the village nurse. Balanced on trestles in the main room the coffin would be left open for several days before the funeral to allow friends and relatives to pay their last respects, visits which in the Norfolk Fens were known as 'viewings'. The wearing of dead men's clothes was considered unlucky and was likely to bring about one's own premature death but there were exceptions for his most valuable possessions and the viewing provided an opportunity to enquire whether the deceased's tools and much prized leather waders could be purchased.

Tomb of Sir Edward Bark[...] d.1632, South Acre, charnel house detail

It was also a time for several more gruesome funeral customs including 'Touching the Corpse'. The shock of this traumatic experience was thought, in extreme circumstances, to effect a change in the constitution of the participant and in the Fens was believed to cure cancerous growths. In Thomas Hardy's short story 'The Withered Arm' the sick woman is urged by Conjuror Trendle to place her arm on the neck of a hanged man while the body is still warm. This macabre fictional account was almost certainly based on the kind of superstitions Hardy learnt from his mother, beliefs by no means confined to Dorset. The case of Mrs Brock who 'had a puffed neck in her youth'[11] was reported from the remote Breckland parish of Stanford in 1857. Her mother had taken her the short distance to Great Cressingham having heard of a recent death in the village. Here her daughter's neck was rubbed with the hand of the dead man, whereupon 'the swelling immediately died away. It was considered to be an infallible remedy.'[12] Twenty years earlier another Norfolk girl had been taken to a viewing and rubbed all over with a dead man's hand to prevent her from dreaming about the corpse, a practice both cruel and almost certainly counter-productive – the girl was 'nearly killed with fright'. In the more remote Fens and among some of the poorest families children were sometimes made to kiss a dead relative's face in the hope that they were so traumatised by the experience it would put them off their food for the next few days.

It was deemed necessary to absolve the deceased of sins committed in this life in order for his or her soul to enter heaven and various funeral customs were employed to achieve this, customs carried out not by the village priest but by the village nurse. The simplest involved a florin (a two shilling piece) placed on the forehead of the corpse by the nurse immediately after death as payment for the transgressions of the deceased. This corpse money, as it was known in the Fens, would remain in place until just before the coffin lid was nailed down, when it was retrieved by the nurse and sold to any woman tired of childbirth. In another example of associating the end of life with the prevention of new life, the woman need only sleep with the coin under her pillow. If however it was discovered by her husband he was, by tradition, entitled to extra beer in the pub if he bought drinks with corpse money.

Memento mori, Bedingfield tomb, Oxborough

Those who attended a viewing would often find the coffin lit by candles to ward off evil spirits. The custom of burning candles or 'corpse lights' may well have had its origin in the old religion and was recalled in the saying 'You got to hold a candle to the devil …' It was also common practice to place bread and a plate of salt on the corpse. The salt, like the candles, was used as a magical protection against the forces of darkness and on a more practical level it was thought to prevent the corpse from rising or swelling.

Mourners were invited to share cakes and ale around the coffin, another custom rooted in medieval requiems, and in this way the sins of the deceased were transferred to those who had partaken of the food and drink provided. This process was a communal version of the custom, once widespread, known as Sin Eating. According to John Aubrey, writing in the late 17th century, it was common in Wales and the Welsh borders, and appears to have survived in the Fens until the late 19th century. The more elaborate versions in East Anglia involved an appointed sin eater, 'some unsuspecting person, usually a tramp' and for this reason travellers either avoided a house or refused a meal in a house where someone had recently died. Enid Porter provides an altogether more graphic account of this archaic ritual, written down by a retired schoolmistress from Little Ouse in the Norfolk Fens who died in 1906. This is the story of the sin eater that she in turn had heard from an elderly woman in the village:

> We were all sitting round the hearth; the coffin with the corpse in it was supported on two chairs; a half round of bread with a heap of salt on it was resting on the shroud covering the departed. The flickering fire light seemed to throw ghostly shadows on the walls of the darkened room, and all of us sitting there were feeling nervous. To keep us cheerful, mugs of hot tea with gin in it were handed round. One of the oldest women, who had had more than her share of gin, was in a rambling mood and began to inform us of the office of sin eater and how it was acquired by the visitor we were waiting for. This person, she told us, spoke to no one and she in turn was avoided by all. To qualify for the duty she was coming to undertake she had, in the beginning, drunk herself stupid with poppy tea until her neighbour, getting anxious, sent for the parson. He, on seeing her and after consulting with the one who had sent for him, came to the conclusion that she was past all human aid, so he did his duty by reading the church's prayers for the dying and giving her absolution. Then he left, ordering that two rushlights be placed, one at her head and one at her feet.
>
> Slowly the fumes of the poppy passed off and, as the rushlights burned themselves out, she sat up and her neighbour informed her that so far as the church was concerned she was dead and gone. All her past sins had been wiped away and, as she did not exist any more in the eyes of the church, she could not commit any more. Henceforth she could earn her living as a Sin Eater.
>
> The old woman had hardly finished speaking when a dog barking across the fen let us know that someone was coming along the drove. Then the latch of the door was lifted and a dirty old woman in a long black cape came into the room, reached for the bread and salt and ate it mouthful by mouthful. After making sure she had dropped no crumbs she held out a skinny hand and thirty pennies, which had been dipped in whitewash to make them look like silver, were handed to her on the ash shovel. One by one she picked them up and then, as silently as she had come in she departed. All of us sitting round the corpse stood up and one of us told the daughter that her mother was now in Heaven because, having no sin, she was freely admitted. We had more tea and gin as we waited for day to break – we were much too afraid to go home in the dark.[13]

Among the many points of interest in this remarkable tale is that the sin eater is not just someone like the tramp, shunned by society, but an untouchable, paid with coins passed over on the end of a shovel; someone absolved of all sin and uniquely qualified for the task she was about to undertake. The thirty pennies 'dipped in whitewash to make them look like silver' is an obvious reference to Judas, the most infamous of outcasts in the eyes of the church.

THE CIRCLING YEAR

The country maypole

PLOUGH MONDAY

Traditionally the first Monday after Twelfth Night (January 6th), Plough Monday signalled the start of the agricultural year when farm labourers returned to the fields after the Christmas break to begin preparing the ground. Celebrations, which may have evolved from rites to ensure the fertility of the soil, involved blessing the common plough housed in the church. In the middle ages it was used communally to cultivate strips in the open fields, hence the word 'ploughshare'. The plough was then decorated and paraded around the parish and the money raised was put towards maintaining the 'plough lights' in the church. These were candles kept alight throughout the year to ensure God's blessing on the land, a practice abolished at the Reformation. The ceremony was already such an important part of the festive calendar that it was soon revived, but in the absence of a religious element the money went towards the cost of food and drink for the participants.

Enid Porter was of the opinion that Plough Monday was once celebrated in most East Anglian villages but the examples she cites are mostly from Cambridgeshire. Here men and boys with blackened faces dragged a plough through the streets, threatening to plough up the pathway or grass verge of anyone who refused to donate money. By about 1900, according to Jack Barrett, the festivities were in decline at Brandon Creek but 50 years earlier Plough Monday was still an occasion for much frivolity. Molly dancers decked out with belts and garters of straw or dressed as women with girdles of horse chestnuts and acorn garters, dragged the plough around to the sound of 'music' made by the banging of buckets and old zinc baths. A meal in the Ship Inn might consist of Plough Pudding, a boiled suet pudding containing meat and onions traditionally eaten on the day. The men would then move on to the village shop where they would purchase a selection of womens' drawers and stuff them with provisions. These would then be distributed to old women in the village with much singing and dancing; a form of charity received with a mixture of gratitude and embarrassment before the revellers returned to the pub.

Mepal Molly Men, Plough Monday, Little Downham

At Brandon Creek and at Littleport in the adjoining parish morris dancers were led by a man with a long feather in his cap, a fiddler and a sweep with a broom; celebrations that may have been derived from the plough play, a pantomime or mumming play performed by the rural poor in the East Midlands. Like the neighbouring county of Cambridgeshire, Norfolk was largely arable, even in the 19th century, and the reasons for the dearth of evidence for Plough Monday celebrations are not obvious. It may simply be that Norfolk had no resident folklorist as diligent as Enid Porter. It may also be that the Puritan movement, especially strong in the county, suppressed its revival for there is evidence that, as part of the religious calendar, the ceremony was once commonplace in the middle ages.

There are references in Blomefield to the maintenance of plough lights in at least three north Norfolk churches; at Aylmerton, Binham and Holme-next-the-Sea, and the plough light was the subject of pious benefactors in Dereham – in October 1516,

Pub sign,
Beeston-with-Bittering

Gilbert Perymont left a bushel of barley 'to iche ploughlede' and in April 1542, Thomas Hawne made a bequest to the 'Ploughe Lyght of Etlying strete'. In the remote and beautiful mid Norfolk church of Beeston-with-Bittering the boss carved as a ploughshare in the north aisle roof was a reminder to medieval tenants to pay their share to the lord of the manor for using the common plough – the village pub was called The Ploughshare. At Cawston the ringers' gallery at the foot of the tower was maintained by the Plough Guild and the rare 15th century inscription along the rood beam is in the form of a prayer to ensure the success of the harvest and the barley crop in particular, so essential to the brewing of ale. It also includes a pun on the name Wat Goodale, possibly a churchwarden at the time:

> God spede the plow
> And send us ale corne enow
> Our purpose for to mak
> At crow of cok of ye plowlete of Sygate
> Be mery and glade
> Wat good ale yis work mad

The guild, an important feature of medieval Cawston, met in the Plough Inn (formerly the Guildhall) at Sygate (South gate) and when the pub closed in 1950 the brewery gave the inn sign to the church where it is on display in the nave near a plough once used at Church Farm. Beerhouse and Malthouse Farms in the parish are further reminders of the central role of brewing to the local economy.

Horse drawn plough, Salle church

The following quotation, taken from a mid 18th century source, suggests that the Plough Monday custom of molly dancing was not entirely confined to the Fens but was also celebrated in and around Norwich.

> In Christmas time, and especially on plough Monday, several Men dresse themselves in Womens Close and goes from House to House a Dancing along with fiddles where they beg for Money. These are called Kitwitches.[1]

The origin of the word is unclear – later in the same document Kitwitch is defined as 'buffoon' – but in Great Yarmouth where it took hold the word may be derived from the Dutch *kitwijk*. Traders from the Low Countries attended the Yarmouth Herring Fair regularly in the 18th century and the pejorative term *kitwijk* – a house of ill repute – may well account for both the Kitty Witches pub and Kittywitch Row (No. 95) that were once a feature of Yarmouth's notorious slum district. W C Hazlitt's *Dictionary of Faiths and Folklore* (1895) makes it clear that in Yarmouth it is women, probably from the fishing community, who dressed as men. The blood-smeared faces suggest the custom may have its roots in the distant past.

In Norfolk, and perhaps elsewhere, a female attired in some grotesque and frightful manner is called a kitch-witch, of which the etymology is not clear. Formerly the streets of Yarmouth were occasionally infested by troops of these creatures, who made a sort of house to house visitation and wore men's shirts over their own dresses and had their faces smeared with blood. [2]

Plough Monday celebrations

The tradition of molly dancing was revived in the 1980s by the Norwich Kitwitches who, for the first few years, performed as the Shitwitches due to the ambiguous nature of the original 18th century text where K and Sh appear interchangeable. In a nimble-footed article on the molly dancing group Jonathan Hooton refers back to the Plough Monday celebrations at Brandon Creek in the early 1900s when a young novice was initiated into the Plough team. Seized by members of the team the horse's tail would be lifted and the boy's nose rubbed against the vent in a memorable example of horse-play. Although it is not clear what, if any evidence, exists for the celebration of Plough Monday in Northwold on the edge of the Fens, it was 'revived' here in the 1980s and has become a popular event in the village calendar. The procession leaves the Crown P H in the evening and comes to a halt outside the lychgate to the churchyard where the plough is blessed and the crowd is entertained by Morris dancing and mummers before all return to the pub and, after an evening of celebration, the plough is stored away for another year.

VALENTINE'S DAY

The tradition of choosing a sweetheart on February 14th, the date when birds were supposed to start mating, has its origins in the court circles of medieval England and France. Chaucer and Lydgate were both moved to write poems for the day and, in Norfolk, Margery Brewes made her brief entry on the historical stage with her letter, written at Topcroft Hall, to her 'right well belovyd Voluntyn', John Paston. The custom of sending expensive lace or satin embroidered cards first became popular in the mid 19th century but in Norfolk among the rural poor who could not afford such luxuries, Valentine's Day was an eagerly awaited opportunity to solicit gifts rather than an expression of affection. Children would often gather early in the morning and go round to each of the larger houses in the village singing or reciting verses in return for money, cakes or sweets, much like carol singers on Christmas Eve. In Mundham they began by chanting:

> Old Father Valentine, draw up your window blind,
> If you wish to hear us sing, come down and let us in.

Variants were recorded in Northrepps and Great Ryburgh but the cry noted by Peter and Iona Opie c1950 that went round Ingoldisthorpe, was typical:

> Good Mother Valentine, God bless the baker
> Who'll be the giver? I'll be the taker.
> The roads are very dirty, my boots are very clean,
> And I've got a pocket to put a penny in.

In the market towns Valentine's Day was anticipated with as much excitement as Christmas Day and the shops would be stocked with all manner of gifts for weeks in advance. In Swaffham and elsewhere Valentines were delivered in person on the evening of February 13th. The front door would be opened just wide enough for the card to be thrown in attached to an apple or an orange. This would be followed by a loud rap on the door before the visitor took to his heels. The custom, enacted with great enthusiasm in Norwich until quite recently, seems to have been peculiar to the county. Presents would be left on the doorstep by Jack Valentine, usually one or other parent. He or she would then vanish mysteriously, the children having been warned that should Jack Valentine be seen he would come no more. Sometimes when a child went to pick up the present it would be whisked away on the end of a piece of string, a prank known as 'snatch Valentine', or a child might be tricked into thinking that a white envelope chalked on the doorstep was the real thing, to the evident amusement of those hiding nearby. On occasions this kind of teasing would take on a more spiteful tone when those unlucky in love received a mock present, a large box filled with nothing but paper, or, in Yarmouth and Lowestoft, a bloated herring left outside the door.

SISTERS OF RISING

As a rotten borough Castle Rising continued to send two MPs to parliament until the Reform Bill of 1838 and an air of feudal authority lingers here in the shadow of its Norman castle. The village of pretty carstone cottages is still owned by the Howards, in residence at the Old Rectory, and can trace their ancestry back to William d'Albini who raised the mighty earthworks in the early 12th century. Across from St Lawrence's church and set down from the road in suitably deferential manner is Trinity Hospital, founded in 1614 by Henry Howard, Earl of Northampton, who also endowed almshouses in Greenwich and at Clun in Shropshire.

The Sisters of Rising outside Trinity Hospital

Arranged around a central quadrangle and with its own chapel, the hospital provided accommodation for twelve spinsters and widows facing destitution. They must, however, by the constitution 'be of honest life and conversation, religious, grave and discreet ... No common beggar, harlot, scold, drunkard, haunter of taverns, inns or alehouses.' A governess kept a watchful eye on the residents to ensure the terms of the constitution were complied with. In return for sparsely furnished rooms, a small allowance and a yearly 'chaldron of coal' the elderly occupants were required to attend chapel each day and church every Sunday to pray for the founder. As a mark of their status and unfailing gratitude the sisters were also obliged to don black, cone-shaped hats and long scarlet gowns emblazoned with the badge of the Howard family, a lion *passant*, when attending service. Little has changed in the last 400 years, although the accommodation has been updated and the eligibility criteria relaxed. The hospital is still the setting each year for a genuine piece of English pageantry when, on Founder's Day in late February, the Trinity sisters in full regalia solemnly rise up and file across to the church to be met by the Bishop of Lynn and the Baron of Rising, Lord Greville Howard. The service is followed by a meal of roast turkey and cake.

GOOD FRIDAY

According to Mrs Lubbock, the Rev'd Gunn's informant at Irstead, any work done on this most holy day in the Christian calendar would have to be done again. In country districts it was considered unlucky to do laundry on Good Friday and anything hung out to dry on that sacred day would be spotted with blood. One exception, however, was baking, justified by some because Jesus, on the road to Calvary, blessed a woman who gave him bread. The death of Jesus has been commemorated, at least since the 18th century, by the baking of Good Friday buns, each marked with a cross as a reminder of His crucifixion and spiced with cinnamon to signify the spices used to embalm His body. In villages and market towns the buns were usually baked at night on Maunday Thursday and sold in the streets early on Good Friday morning by boys shouting:

> Hot Cross Buns! Hot Cross Buns!
> Give them to your daughters, give them to your sons!
> One a penny, two a penny, Hot Cross Buns!

The eating of spiced buns marked the end of Lent but loaves of bread baked on Good Friday were equally symbolic, a relic of the ancient Catholic practice known as the 'Reservation of the Sacrament.' At Brandon Creek on the Norfolk-Cambridgeshire border Jack Barrett recalled how, around 1900, his grandmother would cut a cross on one of her Good Friday loaves. It was then baked in a slow oven until it had dried out completely, then kept in a tin or hung from the ceiling in a muslin bag for a year to ensure the family did not go hungry. The slow baking ensured that the bread never went mouldy and it was sometimes grated and used to treat stomach disorders. At the end of the year it was replaced and, having been moistened, was rebaked on Easter Monday and eaten at teatime. The two end pieces of loaf not marked by the cross were then thrown in the Ouse river as a way of protecting the neighbourhood from flooding during the coming year.

ST GEORGE'S DAY

Known at one time as 'Old Rusty Guts' among the city children, Snap the Dragon is one of the most popular and colourful exhibits in the keep at Norwich Castle Museum. Brightly painted, with flapping wings and a swishing tail, the name of this rare survival is derived from its moveable lower jaw which snapped shut when chasing children during the mayor's procession. The Snap on display probably dates from the late 18th century; the last in a long line of effigies it required replacement every few years as a result of rough treatment at the hands of a boisterous crowd. The Norwich dragon was once the main attraction in an annual spectacle that had evolved from a medieval pageant in honour of St George into a great civic occasion on Guild Day which culminated in the swearing in of the new mayor. Following the Reformation the figure of St George disappeared from the festivities and Snap, once the symbol of evil in the eyes of the church, was transformed into a much loved emblem of civic pride.

As the nation's patron saint, George was a popular dedication for churches and guilds throughout England and in Norfolk, one of the most prosperous counties in the middle ages, his cult was well established. In King's Lynn the town's handsome early 15th century guildhall is dedicated to St George and in Norwich there are St George churches in Tombland and Colegate and a large mural of the saint on horse-back slaying the dragon in St Gregory's church – another, once clearly visible in St John Maddermarket, has gone. Such was the increasingly ambivalent attitude towards this mythical beast that it was used as a largely decorative device on several prominent secular buildings, notably the spandrel carving in the late medieval merchant's house in King Street now known as Dragon Hall.

Dragon spandrel, Dragon Hall, Norwich

Founded in 1385, the St George's Guild rose to become the most wealthy and powerful guild in Norwich. It initially met at St George's Inn on what is now Black-friar's Bridge (formerly St George's Bridge) where, in 1408, it agreed to 'furnish priests with capes, and the George shall go in procession and make conflict with the dragon.' On April 23rd, the saint's feast day, the guild procession was led by St George clad in armour of beaten silver and mounted on a horse bedecked with ribbons and red velvet. In keeping with the legend the saint rescued the king's daughter and pierced the dragon with his lance but by the early 16th century St Margaret had assumed the female role. She was once swallowed by a dragon only to burst from its belly and her cult was already popular in medieval Norfolk with no less than 57 churches in her name – on a benchend in St Helen's church at the Great Hospital in Norwich St Margaret rises triumphant from her dragon. She rode alongside her saviour at the head of the procession followed by the torch bearers, the mayor and aldermen in ceremonial robes, the waits or official musicians and the cantors (chanting clerics) from the cathedral. The colour of the spectacle and the sound of bells ringing out from most of the City's 35 medieval churches made for a memorable occasion. The day ended with mass at

St George,
rood screen, Ranworth

the cathedral in honour of St George but the dragon, reviled by the Catholic church, was refused entry and obliged to remain outside, seated on the dragon stone.

By the mid 15th century the medieval guild and the city corporation were increasingly locked in a power struggle. The guild, now in a handsome new guildhall on the Market Place, tightened its grip on civic authority to the extent that it survived Edward VI's attempt to abolish guilds in 1547. But by then the Reformation had already dealt a blow to its role as a religious-based institution – the figures of St George and St Margaret disappeared from the annual guild procession that was led now by Snap the Dragon. Assisted by Dick Fool and four whifflers in Tudor costume juggling swords or 'whiffles' of gleaming steel, Snap cleared a route through the crowd. At the cathedral the standard bearer would knock nine times (three by three) on the gates, much like Black Rod at the state opening of parliament, to acknowledge that the mayor and corporation had no jurisdiction over the ecclesiastical authorities. After the service the procession returned to the guildhall for the investiture of the new mayor before the assembled company retired to St Andrew's Hall for a grand feast and the mayor's ball.

St Margaret benchend, Great Hospital, Norwich

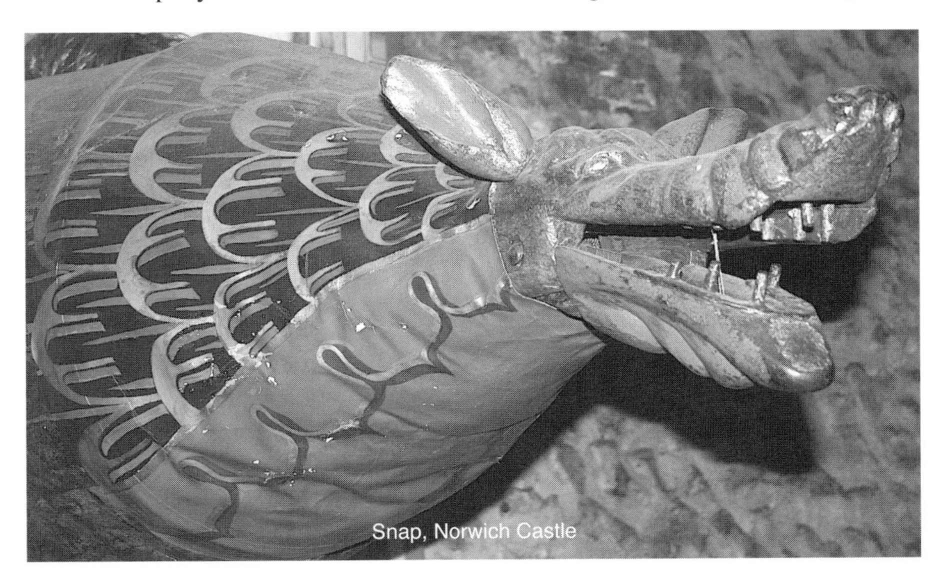

Snap, Norwich Castle

The guild eventually became St George's Company and in 1751 it was obliged to relinquish its medieval charter, and its role, by then entirely ceremonial, was indistinguishable from the mayor's civic authority. Despite this the guild day celebrations continued much as before until the Municipal Reform Act of 1835 swept away all such excess. Snap, however, refused to die and this much loved figure appeared in the city each year until 1850. Although he is now safe in his castle lair, the spirit of the dragon as a beneficent force has been revived in recent years with a dragon festival in 2014, the appearance of a large crouching dragon mural on the wall of a building in Red Lion Street and celebrations of the Chinese New Year in late January by the city's Chinese commumity. The dragon, its long sinuous tail held aloft and manipulated on wooden poles, is both a fearsome sight and benevolent symbol.

MAY DAY

The name of the month is derived from the Greek goddess Maia, a manifestation of the White Goddess, and May Day was sacred to her. At all other times of the year it was considered unlucky to bring hawthorn blossom indoors because of its smell (p62), the one exception being May Day itself. On this day, according to George Ewart Evans, the taboo was broken during this pagan festival when houses and the maypole were both decked with boughs of whitethorn in full bloom. The idea of May Day festivities as a remnant of pre-Christian fertility rights has long been dismissed by folklorists for lack of evidence but there is still a lingering suspicion that crowning the May Queen with garlands of whitethorn blossom is a re-enactment of that ancient ritual, an act of purification before her ritual sacrifice. Whitethorn heralds the onset of summer but why has a shrub that blooms most often in the middle of the month become emblematic of May Day festivities? The reason is simple; until a revision of the Gregorian calendar in 1752 resulted in the loss of eleven days May Day had occurred on May 12th, the Celtic festival of Beltane. As Richard Mabey and others have argued, the old country adage 'cast ne'er a clout ere May is out' probably refers to the bloom rather than the end of the month.

The country maypole, *The Every-Day Book*, 1827

In medieval love allegory hawthorn was emblematic 'of carnal love, as opposed to spiritual love',[3] a claim strengthened by the habit of that other 'symbol of erotic infatuation',[4] the nightingale, to sing from a whitethorn thicket at dusk. Here 'as the bird poured forth the sobbing notes, it pressed its breast against a bare thorn to intensify the bitter-sweet sound of unrequited affection'.[5] The hawthorn was sometimes used in a form of love divination whereby a girl would hang a flowering branch at a crossroads on May Eve, returning next morning to see in which direction it had been blown by the wind. From this direction her future husband would arrive. Not surprisingly the whitethorn became the lovers' tree and a trysting place for secret assignations arranged by one or other party.

The election of a mock mayor, a custom widespread in English towns in the 18th century, was a much anticipated parody of civic pomp and ceremony. Popular among the poor the 'election' often took place to coincide with the official event at a time when most people were deprived of the right to vote. The centrepiece of this raucous display of contempt for authority was the mayor himself robed in grotesque costume and carried aloft through the streets on his chair of office. In his inaugural speech, full of impossible promises, ludicrous favours were handed out and new regulations pronounced. The whole affair was conducted amid noisy celebrations that often degenerated into drunken disorder and led to the eventual suppression of such events by the very authority that was being lampooned. Public ridicule of this kind is reminiscent of the part once played by the Lord of Misrule who presided over midwinter revelries when the normal structures of society were overturned. The mock mayor was in some ways similar to the position of boy bishop elected from among cathedral choristers in the middle ages to 'rule' over the Christmas period, although in this case it was a custom sanctioned by the Catholic church.

Just north of the river Wensum is the district of Norwich once known as Pockthorpe (the Barrack Street area). From the Latin *pauca* meaning 'small' Pockthorpe was a separate medieval hamlet that grew up just outside the city wall. Proud of its own identity and aware of its peripheral status, the Pockthorpe Guild of this working class parish, founded in 1778, elected its own mock mayor each year. The mayor was sworn in with due ceremony and addressed the crowd on the green at Patterson's cellar house. Here his pledge to remove the duty off tea and sugar was received with much cheering and ribald heckling. The evening celebrations concluded with sports and fairground entertainment and the appearance of the Pockthorpe Snap who ran among the crowd grabbing hats and chasing the children. The more adventurous youths would run beneath his snapping jaws crying 'Snap, Snap steal a boy's cap, give him a penny and he'll give it back.' By the mid 19th century, as the official city guild procession declined, the Pockthorpe 'Guild' infiltrated the city and even performed in the Market Place right up until WW1. The Pockthorpe Snap now resides in the Castle Museum but in 1970 another dragon in a dilapidated state was discovered in what was then Back's Bar in the Haymarket. It may also have come from Pockthorpe where there were probably two rival Snaps in the late 19th century, one kept at the Sportsman P H and the other at the General Windham in Cowgate Street where it was displayed in the skittle alley and later sold to Back's Bar.

The Costessey Gylde, 1887

Just upstream from Norwich on the banks of the river Wensum members of the Costessey Gylde elected their own mock mayor each year. Whereas the mock mayor of Pockthorpe was little more than a caricature of civic pomp, the Costessey tradition appears to have been a more ancient mixture of May Day celebrations and manorial institutions – there is a reference in the late medieval *Paston Letters* to the mayor or bailiff of Costessey. The focal point of the ceremony, revived and elaborated in the 18th century, was the office of mayor appointed by the Gylde on May 1st and presented to the village by the recorder. Following a long speech to the assembled crowd he was charged with swearing in the newly elected mayor who was then carried on a chair decorated with leafy branches along the village street. Stopping at the houses of the principal landowners the mayor elect would rise, deliver the following greeting and request their approval:

> With mirth and joy we greet returning Spring,
> The winter's past and all it's trials o'er;
> We hear the wild birds' song, and see the flowers that bring
> Pleasure to all alike, both rich and poor.

This proved to be little more than a dress rehearsal for the main event which took place several weeks later on Whit Tuesday. After breakfast at the Falcon Inn a more elaborate procession set out for Costessey Hall along the main street decked with bunting. At its head were the banner bearers followed by a boy shepherd on a pony carrying a garlanded crook and a mounted shepherdess, both in white costumes. This pastoral tableau was not unlike today's May or Carnival Queen. In sequence behind them came the mayor in official costume with cocked hat and scarlet robe, the ex mayor, the recorder in wig and gown, and the mace bearers with hats like beadles who attempted to control the crowd much like the whifflers in the St George's Day procession in Norwich. Behind them were members of the Gylde Corporation, sword bearers wearing antique hats, musicians and, bringing up the rear, Dick Fool on a hobby horse. Favourite among this band of local worthies and springtide revellers was Costessey's own Snap the dragon who, with menacing jaws and long, twisted tail, ran about snapping his jaws and teasing pennies from the children to the delight of the crowd.

Costessey Hall

Once inside the park to Costessey Hall the procession came to a halt while the shepherd and shepherdess each recited poems extolling the virtues of the occasion, greeting 'smiling faces in dear old Cossey Street' and wishing all 'health, happiness and prosperity'. Included in this staged display of general goodwill were those servants and labourers who worked for the big house and whose grounds they now briefly occupied. The occasion concluded with the 'official' swearing in of the mayor-elect by the recorder and yet another long, pompous recitation before the participants were rewarded by the Jerningham family at the hall who 'contributed liberally to the expenses of the day, and hospitably regaled the mayor and corporation from the strong beer cellar.' With spirits revived and bellies full the assembled company headed back through the village calling at each of the five public houses before rounding off the day back at the Falcon Inn with an evening of feasting and dancing.

Whatever the origins of this Whit Tuesday custom, its revival was probably due in part to the Jerningham family and their love of ceremony. This staunchly Catholic family had helped ensure the succession of 'Bloody' Mary in 1558 and were rewarded for their loyalty with the gift of Costessey Park. In the early 19th century the original

Tudor hall was replaced by a huge neo-Gothic extravaganza, a fitting backdrop to the mayoral ceremony where the feudal lord of Costessey received felicitations from the village. The custom of electing Costessey's mock mayor eventually died out in the 1890s, mirroring the decline of the Jermingham dynasty that became extinct shortly after the hall was engulfed in flames in 1925.

There is evidence to suggest that a simplified version of the Costessey mock mayor custom formed part of the spring celebrations in other Norfolk villages. While there is no specific reference to a mock mayor, the Whit Monday festivities in Necton were organised in 1817 by the lord of the manor, Col. Mason, in an attempt to ensure that the events of the day maintained some semblance of order. Entertainment began with a parade of 'worthies, officials and performers' followed by time-honoured addresses, maypole dancing and sports. Without the presiding influence of a Col. Mason, celebrations of the Rockland 'Guile' near Attleborough held on May 16th each year were little more than an excuse for drunken revelry. Recalling the 1859 Guile the Rev'd Hemsworth was of the opinion that it represented a 'degenerative relic of the medieval guild of St John Baptist'[6] once held in St Peter's church. By the mid 19th century it centred on the re-election of a mayor 'usually some half-witted fellow or sot. Having been made drunk, he is clothed fantastically, chaired and carried through the parish'.[7] The largesse collected during the mayor's perambulation of his domain was later spent on ale. The inhabitants of several houses in the village street known as 'bough houses' were allowed to hang oak branches above their front doors and draw home-brewed beer for sale on the day of the 'Guile' fair without fear of prosecution.

Ox and ram's horns on the Hockham Stone,
Great Hockham

The village of Great Hockham was granted a charter by Henry III in 1272 to hold a week long fair each year on May Day. It became known as the Hockham Horn Fair, a reference perhaps to the time when the annual gathering was a livestock market, and to the pair of ox horns used in the custom of 'doshing'. From the brief description provided by Michael Home in *Spring Sowing* (1946) it appears that before the fair opened newcomers or outsiders would be subject to the custom before being admitted.

Hockham Horn Fair celebrations

The 'doshing' (a dialect word for dashing) required each stranger to butt the horns with his forehead and in this way acknowledge the authority of the fair and its charter. The horns, which have acquired an additional pair of ram's horns, were kept in the Red Lion overlooking the green until its closure in 1971, and now reside in the village hall. The fair, complete with maypole dancing and morris dancing by the Hockham Clodhoppers, has been revived in recent years and the doshing takes place on the Hockham Stone (p41).

WHIT MONDAY

In the middle ages Norwich was well known for the number of religious festivals and pageants that took place throughout the year. The dramatic climax occurred in late May or early June on Whit Monday when mystery plays were staged on waggons that processed through the city centre. Although there is some uncertainty about the origin of the word 'mystery' its possible derivation from the Latin *ministerium*, meaning

The Fall, nave roof boss, Norwich Cathedral

'craft', would explain the performance of mystery plays by craft guilds. The task of organising these fell to the senior guild in the city, the Guild of St Luke, patron saint of pewters, glaziers, plumbers and bell-founders, but the cost of this annual event almost ruined the guild and it eventually petitioned the mayor and corporation for help. As a result it was decided that each trade guild should stage its own pageant and by the early 16th century no less than 64 guilds were contributing to the Corpus Christi procession, a moveable feast held somewhere between May 21st and June 24th.

The plays, which each took a well known story from the bible, began in chronological order with 'The Creation of the World' by the guild of mercers, drapers and haberdashers, followed by 'Paradise' (grocers and chandlers) through to 'The Resurrection' (fishmongers and watermen). Among the most popular subjects was 'Noyse Shipp' (bakers and brewers etc) consisting largely of disputes between Noah and his wife. Equally popular was the 'Helle Carte', performed by rustics from the glaziers and carpenters guild as lewd dancing devils with a monstrous hell's mouth that opened and shut, a precursor of Snap the Dragon. The only play to have survived is the Grocers' Guild version of Adam and Eve and the accounts show that the actors, probably guild members, were paid for their efforts but, individually, less than the cost of hiring a horse to pull the pageant waggon. The last recorded performance was in 1565; soon after all guilds, except that of St George's Company, were abolished by royal statute, and the Grocers' cart, with its painted stage and gilded griffin emblem, was broken up.

Sealing of the Tomb, cloister roof boss, Norwich Cathedral

There was, in addition to the guild procession, a cycle of 42 late 15th century mystery plays known as the N-Town plays that were toured from place to place and performed in the open air, in Tombland and on Market Hill. The N stood for *nomen*, latin for 'name', which allowed for the name of the town to be inserted where the troupe was performing. The biblical themes were not unlike those incorporated in the northern mystery play cycles from York, Chester and Wakefield but the language of the original 1468 manuscript suggests an East Anglian origin. King's Lynn, Bury St Edmunds and Thetford have all been suggested and the scribe has even been located as living south of Norwich. The document was more likely a commonplace book that individual places or religious guilds could adopt and adapt as required.

The trades represented by St Luke's Guild were most closely associated with church building and repair in Norwich, notably at the cathedral where a chapel off the ambulatory was dedicated to the saint in 1422. Apart from the Grocers' Guild play, manuscripts of the other mystery plays have not survived but some of the most memorable scenes are etched in stone, part of the remarkable legacy of medieval sculpture high in the roof of the cathedral nave and its cloisters. The roof bosses along

David and Goliath, nave roof boss, Norwich Cathedral

the east range of the cloisters are a leafy bower of gilded foliage and green men (p56) but towards the north end these folkloric images are joined by a tumbler, a man grappling a dragon and a thief caught stealing washing that appears to have been taken straight from a morality play. Around the corner in the north range are scenes from the N-Town plays, notably the Sealing of the Tomb and the three Marys gazing at the Empty Tomb. Written into the same cycle is the killing of Cain by the blind archer, Lamech, a subject depicted dramatically in a nave boss sculpture that appears nowhere else in English mystery plays. In the west range of the cloisters the serpent tempts Adam and Eve, a scene from the Grocer's play re-enacted more emphatically on another central nave boss. The conflict of David and Goliath, another theme unique in medieval drama and one allotted to the Smiths' Guild, is graphically portrayed on several other bosses in both nave and cloisters. Together these bosses and the many others depicting biblical themes are 'a glorious record that is not only analogous to the drama of the time, especially the mystery plays, but a work of art which was quite possibly carved and painted by the craftsmen who participated in that drama ...'[8]

ST JAMES' DAY

In the Middle Ages, when pilgrimages to holy shrines were encouraged by the Catholic faith, those who had perhaps been to Walsingham and Canterbury and could afford to travel abroad might board a merchant ship at Yarmouth or some other east coast port bound for Bilbao. From there pilgrims would travel on foot to one of the greatest shrines in Christendom, the shrine of St James at Santiago de Compostela. On the saint's feast day, 25th July, shrines were erected in Yarmouth so that those unable to travel to Spain could offer up prayers to him. In his *Perlustration of Great Yarmouth* (1875) C J Palmer drew attention to the custom of assembling shell grottoes on August 5th, a date which equates to 25th July in the Old Calender, altered in 1752. On the 5th the narrow alleys (rows) of the town would echo to the cry of 'Pray remember the grotto.' The structures were traditionally made by local boys from oyster shells piled up to form a flat-topped mound lit from a small opening by a votive candle. The more elaborate structures had a decorative border of shells and pebbles interlaced with seaweed and those who stopped to admire the work were invited to donate a penny. These grottoes were descended from the original medieval shrines and the oyster shells were a substitute for the scallop shells, emblem of St James, that were brought back by pilgrims on their return from Compostela. The custom described by Palmer, pertains to Yarmouth and appears to have been a debased form of 'worship' unique to the town.

HARVEST CUSTOMS

The exact timing of this climax to the rural year was entirely dependent on the weather. In largely arable districts like East Anglia the whole undertaking was conducted according to a series of time-honoured customs celebrated in his poem 'The Horkey' (1802) by Robert Bloomfield who was brought up at Honnington near Thetford. Harvest was also the only time of the year when farm labourers were in a strong bargaining position and at the outset the men would elect one from their company, usually the foreman, as their Lord of the Harvest. It was his task to negotiate with the farmer the rates of pay for piecework together with food and drink allowances. A good deal struck meant that, during the month it normally took to gather in the harvest, the men could earn twice their normal daily rate. Where it had been included in the paperwork, the phrase 'twenty four fine days' ensured no time was lost through bad weather. Once terms had been agreed there was often a frolic to celebrate the start of the contract period. The Lord, followed by his deputy, the Lady of the Harvest, would then lead his line of reapers into the first field, dictate the pace and call the breaks – elevenses and fourses. The reapers also reserved the right to claim largesse in the form of a fine, usually a shilling, that went towards the main harvest supper and provided another, occasional, opportunity to down tools. This ancient custom, known as Hollaing Largesse, took place whenever a stranger wandered into the field or passed by in the lane while harvest was in full swing:

> ... the reapers would stop work, gather in a ring and join hands, one man standing in the centre, or just outside the circle, blowing a horn and shouting three times: Holla Lar! Holla Lar! Holla Lar – jees! Those in the circle, with heads bent, then called out 'o-o-o' on a low note before throwing back their heads and changing their chant to 'ah-ah-ah' prolonging it until they were out of breath...[9]

'In the Barley Harvest', P H Emerson, 1888

Latterly, with the introduction of the mechanical reaper and the threshing machine, the custom died out in the fields but continued to be performed outside large houses in the village and before tradesmen in the area who did business with the farmer. Hollaing Largesse was undoubtedly an ancient East Anglian custom, mentioned by the Suffolk agriculturalist Thomas Tusser in his *Five Hundred Points of Good Husbandry* (1557).

> Grant harvest lord more by a penie or twoo
> To call on his fellowes the better to doo.
> Give gloves to the reapers a larges to crie,
> And dailie to loiterers have a good eie,

When the corn had been safely gathered in, the last harvest waggon, known as the Horkey Load, would leave the fields stacked high with sheaves and topped off with the Lord, the reapers and a flower-crowned Queen. Decked with green boughs and a straw figure made from the last wheat sheaf, the load was drawn through the village by a handsome Suffolk Punch where the load might be douched with pails of water by the spectators. This was to ensure rain during the next growing season and, for the same reason, the straw figure, once believed to embody the spirit of the corn, was kept until the following year to ensure a good harvest. W G Clarke drew attention to the following custom, possibly manorial, that took place in Wretham, a Breckland parish where sheep grazing was an important part of the local economy. 'When the harvest work was finished by the tenants, they were to have half an acre of barley, and a ram let loose in the midst of them, and if they catched him he was their own to make merry with; but if he escaped from them he was the lord's.'[10] As a general rule, once the sheaves had been stacked in the rickyard or taken straight into the threshing barn, the celebrations could begin.

Harvest waggon, c1930, Harpley

The much anticipated Horkey Supper was provided as part of the agreement by the farmer for all those who had helped with the harvest including the women who tied and stacked the sheaves. Long trestle tables were laid out either in an empty cartshed, outside the Lord's cottage or, more often, in the farmhouse kitchen where the company sat down to a generous helping of roast beef and vegetables followed by plum pudding, all washed down with a liberal supply of strong beer. The roast beef was a particular luxury at a time when, for most labourers the only meat throughout the rest of the year was a little belly pork and the occasional rabbit pie. The meal was concluded with a number of toasts, to the good health of the farmer and the Lord of the Harvest, and a number of drinking songs rendered with great gusto as the evening wore on. One old favourite was the 'Duke of Norfolk' which saw the first singer crowned with a cushion on his head and a staff in his hand. After a series of calls and responses the 'Duke' drank another glass, the harvest horn was sounded and the crown passed to the next man and so the toast went round the table. This was followed in turn by other traditional songs like 'The Barley Mow', 'John Barleycorn' and the mysterious 'I'll sing the one O' which in response to 'What means the one O? the reply is 'When the One is left alone/No more it can be seen, O!' Depending on the weather the supper would be followed by music and dancing in the long room of the inn or on the village green.

Bell-shaped corn dolly, William Blake, Barton Turf, early c20

Harvest Festival, 1950s

The village of Paston in north east Norfolk is blessed with a huge threshing barn, the perfect place for a Horkey supper. A long table would be laid lengthwise down the middle of the barn, the company effectively divided by a great central tie beam. At the end of the meal the first song was greeted with the cry 'Well done, our side of the baulk', an invitation for the other side to respond. George Ewart Evans' assertion that the phrase was still common in that part of the county in the 1960s was confirmed by the singer Walter Pardon (p255) who lived in the next village of Knapton.

In time the Horkey Supper was replaced by the Harvest Festival service to give thanks for all the crops safely gathered in and to counter the wilder excesses of the much older supper. The church would be piled high with produce, with stooks of corn and platted loaves arranged among the garden vegetables and bunches of flowers. Among the displays were intricately woven corn dollies shaped like bells, horseshoes and carter's whips, a form of folk art that grew out of the decidedly pagan straw figures that once adorned the harvest waggons.

At the end of harvest women and children were allowed into the fields to collect up the remaining ears of corn. This customary right, the right of gleaning, made an important contribution to the cottage economy through the winter months and was both jealously guarded and strictly controlled to ensure all got their fair share. Order was achieved by appointing a Queen of the Gleaners who, much like the Lord of the Harvest, called the breaks by use of a handbell. In some villages the beginning and end of the working day was marked by the tolling of the church bell, the 'gleaning' bell.

Harvest Festival thankgiving display, c1909, Norfolk

In Yarmouth the beach community elected a Seaside Mayor each year to settle trivial disputes during the fishing season. Following his election the new 'mayor' was carried around town in a boat dressed as Neptune. The assembled company then retired to one or more of the many ale houses along the quayside to continue the celebrations. The custom gradually fell into disuse when herrings were no longer landed on the beach. It is not clear exactly when the election took place, presumably at the beginning of the herring season, but on Michaelmas Day (29th September) it had been the custom to place two stuffed figures on the canopy above the entrance to the Tolhouse Hall. The figures, seated beneath a bower, were said to represent John and Betty Joblett who, in the early 18th century, preceded the town's newly elected mayor from church, strewing flowers in his path. The Tolhouse tableau was completed with stuffed children who in number represented the 'olive branches' of the new mayor. Crowds flocked each year to see the display and 'charity children' who attended were rewarded with a bun and a penny, but, like many civic customs, it fell victim to the Municipal Corporation Reform Act. The folklorist W B Gerish was of the opinion that funds were once raised from boat builders, fish curers and all those with an interest in the fish trade for the purpose of holding a rough carnival at the end of the season when fishing crews had been paid off. At least one boat owner gave a harvest supper and dance in one of the curing houses for his men and their families.

Great Yarmouth Tolhouse

MICHAELMAS

The feast of St Michael on September 29th, was traditionally one of the quarter days in the year for settling rents and the occasion was marked by landlords entertaining their tenants with Michaelmas goose in much the same way as turkey is the traditional Christmas bird. The celebration gave rise to the 18th century proverb. 'He who eats goose on Michaelmas day, shan't money lack his debts to pay.' A version of this was the goose dinner held for inmates of the Great Hospital in Norwich, a custom established by the will of Alderman Partridge who died in 1818. One bird was sufficient for four people and, according to Enid Porter, the implement for quartering the birds is preserved in the hospital. For those Norwich residents unable to afford a goose, pastries known as 'Taffy on a Goose' were sold in bakers' shops in the city made from two pieces of sweetmeat. One resembled a man with currant eyes and buttons, much like a gingerbread man, skewered to a second sweetmeat in the shape of a goose.

Michaelmas also signalled the start of the annual Herring Fair in Yarmouth. It lasted until Martinmas (11th November) and was regulated on behalf of the king by the Cinque Ports Confederation. As part of the opening ceremony it was customary to send the first herrings caught to Norwich where twenty-four herring pies were baked on behalf of the Corporation and sent to the king, either at court where they were received with great ceremony, or wherever the sovereign happened to be. The pies were to contain in total the 'great hundred' – 120 herrings or five per pie, well seasoned with ½ oz of grains of paradilly in good standing pastry. However Thomas Browne in his *History of Norwich* refers to a letter from the Secretary of State to the Mayor in 1629 complaining about the quality of the pies. They were not well baked, there were not five herrings per pie and many had been broken in carriage. The king was much displeased, there was consternation among the city aldermen but the fate of the pastry maker went unrecorded. For all His Majesty's displeasure the custom probably survived until the Municipal Reform Act of 1835.

BOXING DAY

The custom of Hunting the Wren is traditionally associated with St Stephen's Day (Boxing Day) when groups of young men would dress up and go about the lanes beating the thickets and hedgerows to kill this 'king' of the birds. It was then nailed to a pole or placed in a cage decked with boughs and paraded from door to door in return for food and drink while the wren boys sang:

> The wren, the wren, the king of all birds,
> St Stephen's Day was caught in the furze;
> Although he is little, his family's great,
> I pray you, good landlady, give us a treat.

By virtue of its shrill song the wren was said to have betrayed St Stephen to his persecutors and so the bird is ritually stoned to death, a form of martyrdom suffered by the saint himself. This rather savage custom, at least by today's standards, was part of a more general orgy of hunting through the woods on St Stephen's Day with the squirrel and the fox first among the huntsman's quarry. It was believed, especially in northern England, that the game laws were suspended on this day and the hunt may have been a remnant of a more ancient custom enacted to preserve common rights. Once widespread in the Celtic realms of Ireland, Wales and the Isle of Man, there is evidence to suggest the custom was also practiced in England and may have been introduced to parts of East Anglia by Irish immigrants. The Rev'd Oakley Hill in his *History of the Broadland Parish of Upton* (1891) provides a rare glimpse of the custom with reference to a case of brawling at the parish church on Christmas Day 1622. It was heard before the Archdeacon's Court in April the following year when William Enderton, known as Wicked Will, and Symon Bullock, of Acle:

> did profanely and disorderlie behave themselves ... With a great whalebone upon their shoulders and with ys birds, a robin redbreast and a wrenne, tied by a thrid hanging upon the said bone, the said Willm making a great and a roaring noyse all waie of his coming, and they went staggering and reeling too and fro in the midd allie in a scoffing and a wild profane manner, by the minister's seate (the sayd minister being reading devine service) they fell downe as thoughe they were hevely or grievously loaden.[11]

The only punishment meted out to Wicked Will, the chief offender, was being ordered to acknowledge his fault 'in the face of the church.' Walter Rye, who wrote an introduction to Hill's work, regarded the incident as an example of how early customs could be accidentally preserved. The Rev'd Hill was of the opinion that the whalebone was probably preserved in the church, citing the 5 feet 4 inch long bone formerly kept in the belfry which was later removed to the rectory. This may have been a precautionary measure to ensure the 'profane' custom was not repeated, a memento of the occasion or perhaps an arrangement whereby the church could exercise a measure of control over this pagan ceremony on the eve of St Stephen. The antlers used in the annual Horn Dance at Abbots Bromley in Staffordshire were probably first kept in the church between performances for much the same reasons.

Upton church

Although Hunting the Wren was a time for merriment and celebration it was at heart a more ancient ritual. The antics in Upton church were not some drunken revelry aimed at a new Puritan dogma; Will Enderton and Symon Bullock were labouring under the burden of tradition in which:

> The robin redbreast and the wren
> Are God Almighty's cock and hen

This may help to explain the choice of a rib bone from the largest of mammals to bear the weight of these tiny creatures when the branch of a tree would have been just as effective. For its industry, vitality and loud, piercing song the wren has long been celebrated in popular culture; in songs like 'The Cutty Wren'. Here the bird is portrayed ironically as huge and difficult to kill but the hunters are rewarded by the amount of meat on the carcass. This celebration of the bird reflects its symbolic significance for early anthropologists like Sir James Frazer, author of *The Golden Bough* (1890). For them the wren had been a token bird sacred to ancient Bronze Age settlers, echoed in the saying 'kill a robin or a wren/Never prosper boy or man.' The one exception was in winter, on what became St Stephen's Day, when the wren was ritually killed – 'the king is dead, long live the king' – to ensure new life. Today there is little support for the argument that the custom has its origins in a pre-Christian past. Folklorists are keen to stress the lack of evidence for it much before the late 17th century but this may simply reflect a paucity of documentation before this time. Unless they fell foul of the law customs of this kind would have gone unrecorded and any suggestion of pagan ritual would have been suppressed by the church which makes the Upton example all the more remarkable.

According to W G Clarke the Boxing Day revelry known as Hummy Dancing took place regularly in the streets of Thetford until the late 19th century. The following account, taken from Clarke's *In Breckland Wilds*, appears to be the only reference:

> Bands of young men dressed in absurd costumes and with blacked faces, paraded the streets and at intervals gave a performance. Some of each party wore female costumes and these were chased round and round by their partners, who struck their padded backs with wooden ladles. These resounding thwacks were accompanied by the yells of both strikers and stricken. The band usually consisted of a man who played on fire-irons, another on a frying-pan, sometimes a performer on a concertina, and generally two or three with home-made stringed instruments from which a humming sound was evoked, possibly the origin of the term 'Hummy-dancers.' As the price of this travesty of the drama, offerings were solicited from passers-by, and from the residents in the vicinity of the various 'stands,' and by the end of the day most of the performers had imbibed their share of the proceeds.[12]

Clarke was of the opinion that the 'absurd performance' was probably 'a degenerate mystery play' not unlike 'St George and the Dragon'; and was of some antiquity. For many years the Thetford musicians and actors were of high repute. Both Evelyn and Pepys mentioned the Thetford fiddlers, and Shadwell in his play 'Bury Fair' referred to the 'Thetford Musick.' In terms of the blacking up, the cross dressing, the 'musical' accompaniment and the collection of money Hummy Dancing had much in common with both Hunting the Wren, and the celebrations that took place early in the New Year on Plough Monday.

The wren, *Troglodytes, Troglodytes*

SONG and DANCE MEN

Joe Anderson, James 'Duggie' Carter and Rev'd Huddle

VAUGHAN WILLIAMS

Ralph Vaughan Williams, 1902

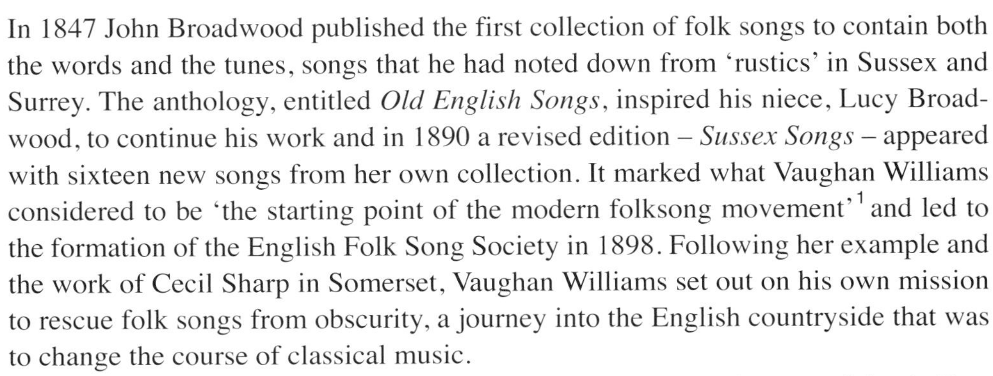

In 1847 John Broadwood published the first collection of folk songs to contain both the words and the tunes, songs that he had noted down from 'rustics' in Sussex and Surrey. The anthology, entitled *Old English Songs*, inspired his niece, Lucy Broadwood, to continue his work and in 1890 a revised edition – *Sussex Songs* – appeared with sixteen new songs from her own collection. It marked what Vaughan Williams considered to be 'the starting point of the modern folksong movement'[1] and led to the formation of the English Folk Song Society in 1898. Following her example and the work of Cecil Sharp in Somerset, Vaughan Williams set out on his own mission to rescue folk songs from obscurity, a journey into the English countryside that was to change the course of classical music.

From his Chelsea home the composer made his first collecting expedition in East Anglia to south Essex in 1903 and the village of Ingrave where Charles Potiphar sang him 'Bushes and Briars'. For Vaughan Williams this was soul music; the song was, he felt, 'something he had known all his life'[2] and the experience has passed into the folklore of English music. A year or so later, travelling deeper into East Anglia, he made the first of several visits to Norfolk where he discovered a rich bounty of songs that fed into his own orchestral work. Quite why he chose Norfolk, a county he had never been to before, is unclear, but on October 4th, 1904, just three months before boarding a train for King's Lynn, he placed a letter in the *Morning Post*. It took the form of an open invitation: 'If anyone knows of traditional songs but does not feel able to note them down correctly, I myself should be happy, wherever possible, to come and note down the songs from the mouths of the singers.'

15.—THE CAPTAIN'S APPRENTICE.

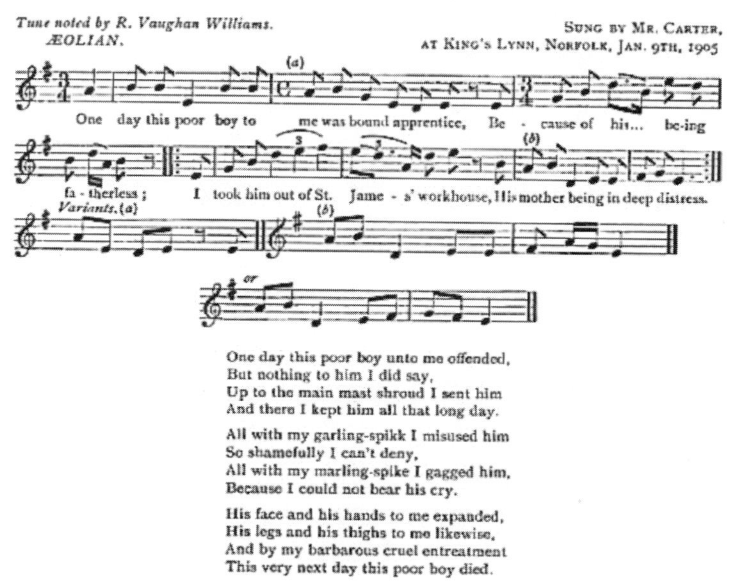
Tune noted by R. Vaughan Williams.
ÆOLIAN.

SUNG BY MR. CARTER,
AT KING'S LYNN, NORFOLK, JAN. 9TH, 1905

One day this poor boy unto me offended,
But nothing to him I did say,
Up to the main mast shroud I sent him
And there I kept him all that long day.

All with my garling-spikk I misused him
So shamefully I can't deny,
All with my marling-spike I gagged him,
Because I could not bear his cry.

His face and his hands to me expanded,
His legs and his thighs to me likewise,
And by my barbarous cruel entreatment
This very next day this poor boy died.

'The Captain's Apprentice' as it first appeared in the Journal of the Folk Song Society

Arriving in King's Lynn on January 7th, 1905, he appears to have changed trains and headed out into the Fens and the village of Tilney All Saints, as if by prior arrangement. It is possible that, as a result of his request in the national press, he had recieved an invitation from the vicar, the Rev'd Newnum, to stay at the rectory. While there Vaughan Williams took down several songs, most already known to him, from the gardener and sexton, Mr Whitby. He also noted four tunes in the neighbouring parish of Tilney St Lawrence from the fiddle player Stephen Poll. Considering the wealth of material he had managed to gather at Ingrave and at Horsham in Sussex, the results of his Fenland excursion must have been disappointing. A reporter for the *King's Lynn Advertiser* wrote '... he was about to leave the district in despair, when a curate at King's Lynn asked him if he would like to see the fishing people in the North Town.' The clergyman was the Rev'd Huddle, curate of St Nicholas' chapel that served the tight knit community of North End and Vaughan Williams spent the next week collecting a 'rich harvest' of songs, many like 'The Loss of the Ramillies', 'Just as the Tide was Flowing' and 'Captain Markee' with a nautical flavour.

St Nicholas' chapel, a large medieval church in all but name, had been built on the profits of mercantile trade but, over the years, those men who sailed out of Fisher Fleet and risked their lives on the high seas saw nothing of the prosperity they helped generate. In the 19th century North End was a series of yards off Pilot Street and North Street reeking of fish and crammed together in the shadow of the chapel. It was in this working class enclave that the Rev'd Huddle introduced Vaughan Williams to two members of his choir, retired fisherman James 'Duggie' Carter and Joe Anderson. Among the 'rich harvest' was 'The Captain's Apprentice' or, as Carter called it, 'The Prentice Boy', a song that fired the collector's imagination. In this ballad

True's yard,
North End, King's Lynn

he felt he had found 'the expression of the soul of a nation'[3] and the tune went straight into his *Norfolk Rhapsody, No.1*, first performed in August 1906, along with 'On Board a Ninety Eight' and 'A Bold Young Sailor'. 'The Captain's Apprentice', a song already popular along the east coast, is the tragic tale of a young boy who dies on board ship at the hands of a sadistic captain. With its reference to St James' Infirmary it was especially relevant to the North End community and appears to have been adapted to reflect an event still fresh in the memory of local people. In 1857 the *Lynn Advertiser* had reported the death of young Robert Eastick, late of the workhouse, who died in mysterious circumstances on board a ship named after its owner, John Sugars, of King's Lynn.

The dozen songs sung by Joe Anderson are, arguably, of more direct importance to Vaughan Williams' work. In addition to 'A Bold Young Sailor', the tune of 'Young Henry the Poacher' was used in *The English Hymnal* (1906) and 'Bold Robber' resurfaced in *Norfolk Rhapsody No.2*, first performed a year later. *Rhapsody No.3*, now lost, contained the tunes of another four songs from Lynn. Vaughan Williams also managed to collect several songs from Betty Howard and 'Lol' Benefer at a time when it was unusual for North End women to sing nautical songs, but it was several visits to the Union workhouse that proved most rewarding. Here he noted down another fine clutch of songs from old sailors like Robert Leatherday, Charles Crisp and George Elmer; in total about half the 78 songs he collected in Lynn. In most cases, unless a song was new to him, he only noted down the tune, with any melodic variations and the first verse, aware that the full text probably already existed in the form of a broadsheet. For Roy Palmer 'on the whole Vaughan Williams was more interested in the song than the singer, in the melody than the message.'[4]

'Lol' Benefer, North End, King's Lynn

For some reason, midway through his stay in Lynn, Vaughan Williams decided to take the train to Sheringham. He may have recalled an article by Kate Lee in the first (1899) *Journal* of the Folk Song Society in which, during her own collecting trip to north Norfolk, she was advised by fishermen in Wells she would likely have more luck in Sheringham or Cromer. With no local contact his journey was unproductive, just two songs including one from the level-crossing keeper. The following day he was back in more familiar territory at North End where, among the tunes he took down from William Harper in Watson's Yard was 'Edward Jagen', a song new to him. From there he went round the corner to Begley's Yard and sail maker Thomas Donger who sang him several more, notably 'Banks of Claudy', another song he had not heard before. Vaughan Williams paid one last brief visit the following year, on September 1st, while on a collecting expedition in Cambridgeshire. He took down a few last tunes and said goodbye to the fishermen whose songs of the sea had had such a profound effect on him and his music. The first version of his orchestral tone poem, *In the Fen Country,* drew on impressions of this flat landscape, formed, in part, while an undergraduate in Cambridge. The piece was finished in April 1904, but the melodic language reminiscent of English folk music in the final version owes much to the two subsequent revisions he made, especially in 1905, and the rich haul of songs he netted in King's Lynn.

Former workhouse, Depwade Union, Pulham Market

Vaughan Williams returned to Norfolk in 1908, this time a less well documented excursion to the Broads, although, from his notes, it is clear he travelled to South Walsham, Ranworth and Hickling. At Acle he noted down 'Lovely Joan' from Christopher Jay in the Bridge Inn and was so taken with the tune that he used it as an interlude in his *Fantasia on 'Greensleeves'*. A second visit to the Broads in 1910, this time to Filby and Rollesby on the 'Isle' of Flegg, was followed a year later by one last collecting trip to Norfolk. On this occasion he chose the area around Diss and the company of a fellow collector, the young composer George Butterworth, who was to meet his death at the Somme in 1916. Arriving by train in December 1911 they spent three days in the area, making straight for the Depwade Union workhouse, an austere red brick structure with radiating wings, on the main Norwich road at Pulham Market. Here, with no Rev'd Huddle to provide the introductions, they came away with a meagre selection, just seven songs. Relying more on word of mouth they set out the following day for Tibenham Long Row where, according to Vaughan Williams' widow Ursula, they appear to have followed an established routine. 'Notebooks and bicycles were the basic equipment … and a capacity to get on easy terms with the older people whose knowledge of songs and pleasure in them was still lively, as well as a cheerful capacity to drink beer in the pubs where many of the singers could still be found.' [5] At Long Row the two headed for the Three Horseshoes where

George Butterworth, 1885-1916

they noted down songs from the publican, Harry Last, and the brothers Noah and James 'Blue' Fisher who worked at Waterloo Farm. Isaac Ephraim lived at the far (west) end of Long Row near the Boot Inn, little more than a beer house, and this is most likely where Vaughan Williams recorded 'The Yorkshire Bite'. William Tufts and his son were farmers and, as Katie Howson had suggested, were unlikely to have mixed with their labourers in the pub. Their contribution of five songs was probably recorded in the farmhouse kitchen.

Although this proved to be Vaughan Williams' last field trip to Norfolk he maintained a close relationship with the county. On his return from the Great War he and his wife Adeline went to live in Sheringham with her sick brother until his death in 1921. He appeared on three occasions between the wars at the Norwich Music Festival and gave a lecture on East Anglian folk songs at the King's Lynn Festival in 1952. Here he heard a performance of his *Fifth Symphony* in St Nicholas' chapel, the place where his Norfolk journey had begun almost fifty years before.

The old Boot Inn, Tibenham Long Row

GEORGE CHAMBERS

Three years later Vaughan Williams wrote a preface to *Folksong-Plainsong* by the Norfolk clergyman Father George Chambers. Published in 1956, the year Chambers left the parish of Carbrooke where he had been vicar for thirty years, the book is dedicated to Cecil Sharp. The ideas set out in this scholarly discourse on musical origins first took shape when he began collecting folksongs in Essex during his time as assistant to the influential vicar of Thaxted, Conrad Noel. As a member of the Christian Socialist League and leading figure in the folk revival, Chambers brought his ideas to rural Norfolk where, between the wars, he reawakened the tradition of folk dancing, wrote plays performed by local children and organised WEA classes in the village school. There were summer camps for children on the coast at Eccles with music and dancing, Agricultural Workers' rallies at the vicarage and a well publicised crucifix in the church incorporating hammer and sickle iconography.

Rev'd George Chambers 1881-1969

'raise Him in the cymbals and dances', 1930s, Carbrooke church

It seems likely that Chambers continued to collect folksongs in Carbrooke; the White Hart and the Crown were both nearby and he may also have known singers as members of the choir. If so then nothing has survived except fond memories of country children singing 'with Norfolk intonation the Kyrie, Sanctus and Agnus in English plain chant.' WWII saw a great influx of American servicemen stationed at Watton airfield including men from the Appalachian mountains where Cecil Sharp had gone in search of folksongs during the Great War with his collaborator Maud Karpeles. Among the servicemen were black Americans invited by Chambers to sing spirituals in Carbrooke Church. As he recalled 'our high pitched hammerbeam roof and graceful columns made acoustics perfect for the beautiful natural harmonies of the Negro singers.'[6] In his time at Carbrooke Chambers left a lasting impression on all aspects of village life while artist friends left a fascinating legacy of Socialist folk art in the church including a colourful altar cloth with hammer and sickle hanging, like exotic fruit, from the Tree of Life, a rustic plaque of Elizabeth Chambers and a brightly painted tableau, 'Praise Him in the cymbals and dances.'

Altar cloth, Carbrooke church

JACK MOERAN and HARRY COX

It was another composer, Jack Moeran (1894-1950), who continued the collecting work begun by Vaughan Williams some twenty years earlier. Moeran's mother was from King's Lynn and his grandfather was already installed as vicar of Bacton when the family decided to settle in Norfolk. His Irish father had also entered the priesthood and accepted the joint benefice of Salhouse with Wroxham in 1905, but it was while staying with his grandfather in 1913 that Moeran noted down his first folk songs, including 'The Dark Eyed Sailor', from William Mayes, a member of Bacton church choir. Badly wounded in the Great War Moeran returned to Norfolk and embarked on his own mission to rescue the art of folk singing while it still flourished in a corner of Norfolk he knew well. The result was a sustained burst of collecting between 1921 and '24 together with another bout of fieldwork in 1926-7 that altogether produced some 150 songs. As his friend, the music critic Peter Warlock, observed in 1923 'his familiarity with the neighbourhood gave him facilities which are often denied to the stranger… he collects these songs from no antiquarian or historical motives, but because he loves them and the people who sing them.'[7]

The tradition of 'Saturday night frolics' was still a highlight of many Broadland pubs when Moeran, prompted by a suggestion he should get over to the Windmill Inn at Sutton, spent the evening jotting down 'a splendid batch of songs' from Bob 'Jolt' Miller. The singer proved invaluable not just for his own repertoire but for introducing Moeran to Harry Cox, a traditional singer with a growing reputation who impressed the composer greatly with the quality of his voice and the huge back catalogue of songs that had been handed down through his family. Here in the Windmill Moeran was convinced he had discovered a rich vein of folk singing that, writing in 1936, he felt was in danger of dying out.

Jack Moeran, 1894-1950

> It seems likely that the spontaneous singing of old songs … no longer exists, save in districts where…. those who have followed the herring. It has been customary to sing at sea, and one can visit many an inn within easy reach of Great Yarmouth where, even now, it is sometimes possible to while away a winter's evening with an impromptu concert of traditional songs. Travel further along the coast, and you will hear little of the kind. It used to be the boast of the late Bob Cox, Harry's father, that he would do a herring fishing season, sing two songs every night and never repeat himself.[8]

The old Windmill Inn, Sutton

Born in Barton Turf in 1885 Harry Cox was soon off with his father on a Saturday evening to the White Horse where Bob 'Battler' Cox was a singer and fiddler player in great demand. It was from his father that Harry learnt both the fiddle and his many seafaring songs. Like many traditional singers, he was also an accomplished musician who could knock out a tune like the 'Yarmouth Hornpipe' on the melodeon just as easily as he could a jig on his whistle. In turn Harry became a regular performer in the local pubs, not just the Windmill where Moeran first heard him, but in Potter Heigham, Ludham and Catfield. Steeped in the musical tradition of these Broadland villages he was, however, equally happy playing and singing at home for his own enjoyment.

While Moeran's second round of collecting in the late '20s proved to be his last, he arranged for Harry to travel to London in 1936, quite an undertaking for a farm labourer who had never ventured outside his native county. There, at Decca studios, he recorded 'The Bold Fisherman' and 'The Pretty Ploughboy' that were released on a 78rpm disc. Moeran's return to East Anglia in 1947 with a team of BBC engineers resulted in the very first sound recording of folk songs in the region from the Eel's Foot pub at Eastbridge in Suffolk and the Windmill at Sutton. Moeran was delighted to be re-acquainted with many old friends from the 1920s who were still singing, notably Harry Cox. The programme *East Anglia Sings*, broadcast on November 19th, 1947, on the Third programme, included four of the nine songs from the Windmill by Cox. Moeran, often regarded as a somewhat neglected figure in the history of 20th century English music, wrote several orchestral pieces – *Rhapsody No. 2*, *Stalham River* (1921), his own arrangement *Six Norfolk Songs* (1924) and *Lonely Waters* (1931) – inspired by his love of the Norfolk countryside and the songs he collected. Among lovers of traditional music his greatest contribution will always be the discovery and recording of 'that prince of singers', Harry Cox.

Harry Cox,
1885-1971

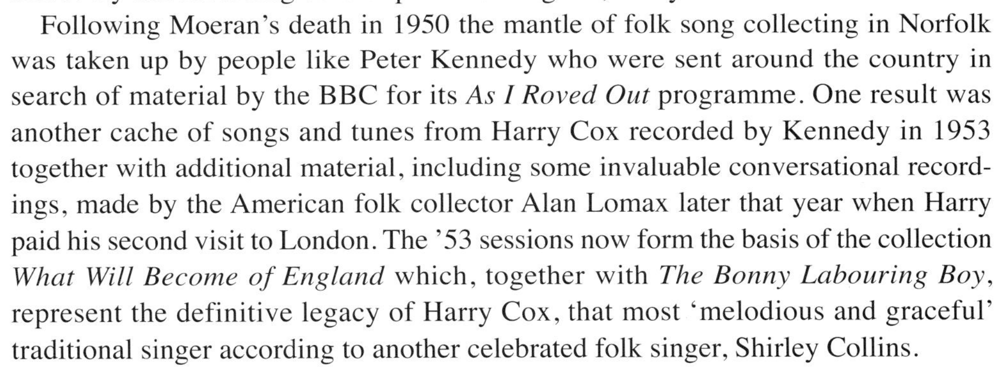

Following Moeran's death in 1950 the mantle of folk song collecting in Norfolk was taken up by people like Peter Kennedy who were sent around the country in search of material by the BBC for its *As I Roved Out* programme. One result was another cache of songs and tunes from Harry Cox recorded by Kennedy in 1953 together with additional material, including some invaluable conversational recordings, made by the American folk collector Alan Lomax later that year when Harry paid his second visit to London. The '53 sessions now form the basis of the collection *What Will Become of England* which, together with *The Bonny Labouring Boy*, represent the definitive legacy of Harry Cox, that most 'melodious and graceful' traditional singer according to another celebrated folk singer, Shirley Collins.

WALTER PARDON

The folk song revival of the 1950s that embraced Harry Cox was completely unaware of another gifted Norfolk singer called Walter Pardon who lived a few miles nearer the coast at Knapton. He was not discovered until the 1970s and the reason for his apparent neglect was simple; remarkably for a traditional singer with such an impressive repertoire he rarely sang in public. Walter lived all his life in the 19th century brick farm worker's cottage where he was born and although he came from a long line of agricultural labourers he became apprenticed to a carpenter in the neighbouring village of Paston at the age of 14, a trade that kept him busy all his working life. When it came to singing, Walter, who was blessed with an extraordinary memory, absorbed most of his uncle Billy's repertoire of songs. In the late 19th century Knapton was a 'dry' village and Uncle Billy would cycle into North Walsham where the Mitre Tavern had a proper singing room. Billy had, in turn, learnt many of his songs from his father who had learnt to read music from playing clarinet in the west gallery church band and could 'take the music of these broadsheets' that were circulating at the time.

Although, unlike his uncle, Walter was not a pub singer, there were numerous opportunities at church suppers, harvest frolics and family gatherings, when someone would shout 'Our side of the baulk'. This reference to the main ceiling beam that divided the room was a signal to where the next song should come from. Each individual had their own signature song that no-one else dared sing – for Uncle Bob it was 'Jones's Ale', Tom Gee always sang 'The Bonny Bunch of Roses' and Walter had what nobody else wanted, 'The Dark Eyed Sailor'. But in time the old songs were ridiculed by the younger generation, pub singing had died out and Walter was the last in his family to keep the musical tradition alive. He did this by singing in the privacy of his cottage for his own pleasure, often accompanying himself on the melodeon until, when he was 59, his nephew, a school teacher called Roger Dixon, gave him a tape recorder and asked him to record a few songs. This simple request proved transformative, unlocking a phenomenal treasure trove of some 180 parlour ballads, country songs and music hall 'tear jerkers' including at least 70 that Cecil Sharp would have considered folk songs.

Walter Pardon, 1914-1996

Walter's songs would have died with him but for the 'demo' tape Dixon passed on to the Norfolk folk revival singer Peter Bellamy who recognised the unique quality of Walter's voice. A copy of the tape soon reached Bill Leader who recorded the first two of five seminal albums on his own label – *A Proper Sort* in 1975 and *Our Side of the Baulk* two years later. Walter began performing at folk clubs and festivals around the country, culminating in an invitation from A L Lloyd to join a group of English folk singers at the American Bicentennial celebrations in Washington D C. For Lloyd, Walter 'had a fine feeling for the sense of the words and deep musicality' and Roy Palmer, writing in the *Dictionary of National Biography,* reflected:

> As a singer Pardon was quiet, even slightly introspective. He would begin a song in a gentle, thoughtful way, and drew in listeners, almost as if by enchantment. He allied sure musical instinct with excellent diction and first-class memory. A quiet, modest and intelligent man, he read avidly – Dickens and Hardy for preference.

Indeed the circumstances of his burial in 1996 might have been taken from a Hardy short story or one of the ballads – 'Barbara Allen' perhaps, or 'Lord Lovel' – that he sang so movingly. Mike Yates, who spent time with Walter in Knapton while recording many of his songs, was surprised to learn that he wished to be buried in the neighbouring parish, in the lonely churchyard of St Nicholas, Swafield. When a young man Walter had fallen in love with a local girl, a love that was not reciprocated and he never married. Years later she was buried at Swafield and it was his wish that they might be united in death. Months after his wish had been granted a memorial concert was held in London to raise money towards the cost of a headstone.

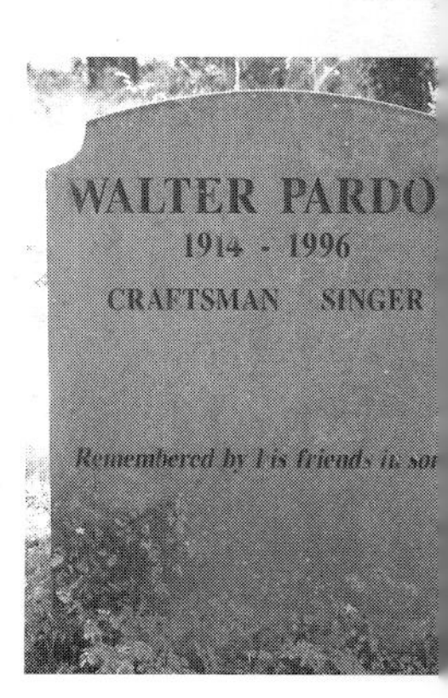

Headstone in Swafield churchyard

SAM LARNER

During the last few years of his life a retired Winterton fisherman called Sam Larner enjoyed success as part of the folk revival that had also discovered Harry Cox. Philip Donnellan, a BBC radio producer, first heard Sam singing in a pub and recorded a clutch of traditional songs for two radio programmes, *Coast and Country: The Wash,* broadcast in 1957, and *Down to the Sea* in 1959. Donnellan soon alerted Ewan MacColl and Peggy Seager who, with Charles Parker, were working on their series *Radio Ballads*. They travelled to Winterton and as MacColl recalled, recorded 'almost thirty hours of magnificent talk and three hours of songs, ballads and miscellaneous rhymes ... what a wonderful person he was! Short, compact, grizzled, wall-eyed and slightly deaf, but still full of the wonder of life. His one good eye still sparkled at the sight of a pretty girl!'[9] The result was the first of two landmark recordings, the acclaimed Radio Ballad *Singing The Fishing* that went out in August 1960, followed by the album *Now is the Time for Fishing* released the following year, a mixture of songs and anecdotes of Sam's life as a fisherman. It was, according to folk music historian, Chris Holderness, the first full length LP of a traditional singer. Charles Parker managed to bring together Harry Cox and Sam Larner for *The Singer and the Song,* broadcast on BBC Midlands in 1964, but Sam's fame as an exuberant performer was short-lived – he died the following year aged 86.

The Fisherman's Return, Winterton

The Three Mariners, Winterton, c1900

Winterton, when Sam was a lad, was a tight knit fishing village inhabited by generations of Nelsons, Gudgeons, Gaffins, Larners and Rudds who now lie in Holy Trinity churchyard. When the novelist Sylvia Townsend Warner stayed there in 1931 the place was still 'a closed community, violent and feuding, where everyone was related, and known by a nickname, like characters in the Icelandic sagas.'[10] Almost everyone earnt their living from the sea; the men in drifters out of Yarmouth followed the shoals of herring on their annual migration along the east coast while the women 'beatsters' worked at home mending nets or in the smokehouses. Like most young boys Sam first went to sea at the age of eight and four years later had signed on as a 'peggy' or cabin boy. Often away for weeks at a time the life was hard but as Sam said 'Why for me and my brothers that was either sea or gaol.' Singing was in their blood and Sam learnt quickly, mostly from his father George 'Bredler' Larner, and his uncle Jimmy Sutton, and first performed in public at the age of nine when he sung for pennies to summer coach parties. He was always in demand when his boat called in at ports along the eastern seaboard right up to Shetland where he won a singing competition in Lerwick town hall in 1909 with his version of 'Old Bob Ridley-O'. Coming home from a fishing trip was always a time for celebration and Sam usually had a few new songs he had picked up along the way. The crew would go down to either the aptly named Fisherman's Return or the Three Mariners which stood almost opposite. 'We used to get in the old pub, have a pint or two around … a drink, a song and a four-handed reel. Round we'd go and up we'd go, and we used to have a rare old, good old time.'[11] Sam's nephew, Dick Green, recalled the respect shown to singers when there was a session down the pub. Dick, his brother Bob and the trawler skipper Jack 'Starchy' George, were all singers but Sam was the pick of the bunch, a natural entertainer and a good step-dancer too.

Sam Larner,
1878-1965

A year after Sam's death the Suffolk folk collector Neil Lanham went over to Winterton and, while there, met retired fisherman Walter 'Tuddy' Rudd who got together a few singing mates, including Bob Green, for Lanham to record. Tuddy told Lanham he learnt 'An Old Man Came Courting Me' from a fish hawker called Lame Jimma'. By then The Three Mariners was closed and the fishing industry was in terminal decline. The Fisherman's Return is still open but the singing sessions that were one such a joyous expression of this seafaring community, died with it. In recognition of his outstanding achievement as a singer, a blue plaque now adorns the flint cottage in Bulwer Lane where Sam Larner lived all his life, latterly with his wife Dorcas. Martin Carthy, among his many admirers, recalled 'his impact was immediate and electrifying … I knew I had been … in the presence of genuine greatness.'[12]

Commemorative plaqu
Bulwer Lane, Winterto

STEP DANCING

Harry Cox and Sam Larner are rightly regarded as the most accomplished singers to emerge from the 1950s folk revival but it soon became apparent to the BBC producers responsible for the recording sessions that these two were part of a musical tradition still alive in communities all along the Norfolk coast. In Cromer, where music and dance went hand in hand, traditional entertainment revolved around the Davies family; crab fishermen, revered members of the town's lifeboat crew and gifted step dancers. First among equals was Henry 'Shrimp' Davies (1914-2002), coxswain of the lifeboat for 29 years, who learnt his dance steps from father Billy and from his uncle, the famous lifeboat coxswain Henry Blogg. Life at sea was hard and hazardous as Philip Donnellan discovered when he arrived in Cromer with his tape recorder in 1954. Shortly after the session he recorded one evening in The Albion pub, two of the big dancing fishermen that had taken part were drowned when their boat was hit by a freak wave. In the mid 1970s when Peter Clifton and Ann-Marie Hulme visited Cromer as part of their research into step dancing they found the fishermen danced a style based on clog dancing that Shrimp's father and uncle had picked up from a Lancashire coastguard working in the town c1905. According to Clifton and Hulme it was an example of 'an extrinsic style (absorbed) into the local tradition' compared with the 'intrinsic and deep rooted style' of Norfolk Stepping by people like Dick Hewitt, Norfolk's best known step dancer. They also identified a third style, Traveller Stepping.

As Donnellan recalled 'Two of the men that night in The Albion were not fishermen but countrymen: Percy Brown who played the melodeon and concertina like an angel, and Dick Hewitt, a slim, straight young man who danced like a demon.'[13] From a large travelling family, originally from Ireland, Hewitt was living in Southrepps when he was recorded by Seamus Ennis in the Vernon Arms, accompanied by Harry Baxter on fiddle. Ennis, who had succeeded Peter Kennedy at the BBC, was continuing to collect material for the *As I Roved Out* series of traditional music from around Britain. Himself a fine singer and musician, Ennis detected similarities with the folk music of his native Ireland and thought this had much to do with the livestock trade into Norfolk. His Southrepps recordings formed part of the *Music From Norfolk* programme that went out in January 1955. As a result Dick Hewitt was invited to perform at Cecil Sharp House and the Albert Hall but he was soon back home in pubs like the Barge at Antingham where he met up again with Percy Brown who lived near the pub. Percy, one of the country's finest melodeon players, was a woodman by trade and when Cromer fishermen came down to cut hazel sticks from a nearby plantation for their crab pots they always called on Percy before all going off to the Barge. In 1972 he was recorded for the Topic Records album *English Country Music from East Anglia*.

Percy Brown and Jimmy 'coconut' Martin,
the Black Boys, Aldborough

By 1965 Dick Hewitt had moved to Briston where, for the next ten years, he was landlord of the Three Horseshoes. It soon became a lively music venue with locals and travellers like the West family who came for the annual livestock fair and cattle auction. Held originally on the village green the fair, too, was a great musical occasion with local singing competitions in which each local village would enter its best performer. When it came to pub games the friendly rivalry at darts tournaments or quoits matches was often concluded with music and dancing and, in anticipation of this, the best musician would usually travel with his team. In Briston it was the versatile musician and dulcimer player Herbert Remmington who went with the quoits team while Walter Jeary, another fine dulcimer player and step dancer whose father kept the Cross Keys at Gunthorpe, travelled with the pub's darts team.

By the time Clifton and Hulme arrived at the Horseshoes in Briston to film Dick Hewitt in 1979 he was the only one still dancing in the Norfolk Stepping style but in Hindringham they found a place rich in music and dance, a tradition of self-made entertainment kept alive in the two village pubs by the Allisons. This step dancing family were unusual in that several performers were women, notably Angelina Allison, at a time when the pub was still largely a male domain. Along with the jigs and polkas the Broomstick Dance was occasionally performed to 'Cock o'the North' at harvest frolics. It involved holding a besom while jumping with one leg and then the other over the broom, a dance which, according to Fenman Arthur Randell, was more often part of the Horkey supper celebrations in the Wiggenhalls and elsewhere.

The Broomstick Dance performed by Arther Randell

Step dancers often wore steel tipped shoes or clogs for best effect on brick pamment floors, or on square boards that people like Dick Hewitt carried around with them, while the flamboyant Jacky Jordan was more inclined to dance on the bar of The

Railway in Wells. Musicians like George 'Gidjee' Craske from Sustead would cycle to pubs in order to play for step dancing. He was a regular at venues in and around Aylsham with his 'out-and-homer' as the one-row melodeon was called. One tune, 'The Keel Row', was reserved for the Poker Dance when, to demonstrate their skill and dexterity, performers would dance over a poker laid on the floor. Whereas Cromer had a long tradition of stepping, Sheringham, its near rival as a fishing town had a strong Methodist connection to the Salvation Army. As a result there were fewer pubs and less dancing but, as Chris Holderness has pointed out, the town has given its name to one of the most popular step dancing tunes, 'The Sheringham Breakdown'.

Percy West
Gypsy Stepping

COUNTRY DANCING

There would appear to have been no distinctive style of folk dancing in Norfolk to compare with the Sword Dance found across much of northern England or the form of Morris dancing encountered by Cecil Sharp in the Cotswolds at the turn of the last century. Although step dancing could be found in most pubs, at least in north Norfolk, it was by no means confined to the county, and Molly dancing performed at Brandon Creek on Plough Monday (p222), was a customary dance tradition more often associated with the Cambridgeshire Fens. There was however a huge appetite for country dancing in one form or another. Unlike stepping which was for solo performers, country dancing was more inclusive and the moves could be picked up more easily. Favourite among the dancers was the Heel and Toe Polka and the Norfolk Long Dance, first recorded at Sidestrand in 1929, again in Upper Sheringham and inland at Gresham and Wickmere. There were always musicians on hand to play at dances held in a room at the back of the pub or in the village hall and in some places there was even a village band for hire at family gatherings and seasonal festivities. Whit Monday celebrations, harvest frolics and the end of the herring season provided plenty of opportunities for dancing alongside local events like Wells regatta, the horse fairs at Briston and Aldborough and Fakenham races.

The post war folk revival may have rescued traditional music and brought it to the attention of a new, mainly middle class, audience, but as a form of entertainment once popular among farm labourers and fishermen its decline can be traced to the early 1960s and the advent of rock 'n roll. For the young, seduced by Elvis and the Beatles, the traditional ballads sung by their parents' generation were decidedly old fashioned and, as singers like Walter Pardon had found out, were increasingly held up to ridicule. Among the many social and economic forces eroding the viability of rural communities the greatest single blow was the wholesale closure of village pubs. Large brewery chains like Watney Mann bought up a number of local breweries in Norfolk – Steward and Patteson and Bullards among them – and promptly closed a lot of the less profitable outlets. At a stroke the heart of village life was ripped out and with it went much of the music, the games, the songs and the dancing. What remains are the buildings, often altered out of all recognition, the occasional wrought iron bracket where the sign once hung, and a litany of names: the Tuttington Ship, the Cross Keys at Gunthorpe, the Barge Inn at Antingham, the Sutton Windmill, the Three Mariners at Winterton, the Dukes Head in Hindringham, the Eight Ringers in Wells and so many more.

Billy Bennington playing the dulcimer with beaters

FOLK TALES

THE GREEN DOOR

In 1896 'The Green Lady', a tale from Hertfordshire, appeared in the journal *Folk-Lore,* one that the contributor, Alice Gomme, had learnt as a child from her nursemaid. It is followed by a shorter variant collected by the Norfolk folklorist W B Gerish from an elderly woman who had died earlier that same year aged 96. She in turn had heard it 'a score o' times' in her youth. In the Gerish version it is not the lady but her cottage door that is green and so the tale has been renamed. The implications of the colour are however the same; green is the fairies' colour and one associated with the Green Children of Woolpit in Suffolk who come from the underworld. Of the two, the girl survives and, according to one version, eventually marries a man from King's Lynn. Unlike the Woolpit place legend 'The Green Lady' is a celebrated international story, a timeless wonder tale popular in Northern Europe. Gerish later moved to Bishop Stortford, but his *Folklore of Hertfordshire* (1911) makes no reference to 'The Green Lady'. His Norfolk version is however one of the very few fairy tales to have been recorded from the county:

Once upon a time there was a poor old man who had three daughters, and the eldest said: 'Father, give me a cake and a bottle of water that I may go to seek my fortune.' Her father gave her a cake and bottle of water; and when she had gone a little way she met a little old man who asked her where she was going. She replied: 'To seek service.' 'Oh,' said he, 'give me your cake and bottle of water, and go and knock at the house with the green door, and there you'll find your fortune.' So she knocked at the door and a lady opened it, and asked her what she wanted. She told her, and the lady asked her what she could do. She made a dob (curtsey) and said: 'I can bake, and I can brew, and I can make an Irish stew.' So the lady said she would take her, but she must never look up the chimney or into the clock. The next morning the lady's daughter rode downstairs on a black cat and asked her to cut some bread and butter. The girl said she would as soon as she had finished washing the hearth. Whereupon the young lady ran up in a rage, and her mother came down, cut off the girl's head, stuck it up the chimney and put her body in the clock.

The second daughter then started to seek her fortune, and met with precisely the same adventures.

The third daughter followed in her sisters' footsteps until the young lady asked for bread and butter, when she jumped up and cut it for her immediately, whereupon they were extremely pleased. In the afternoon they went for a ride on the black cats, leaving the maid alone in the house. She immediately looked up the chimney, and in the clock, and discovered her sisters' heads and bodies. She took them in her arms and ran away with them as fast as ever she could, calling on the gooseberry bushes to cover her flight. When the lady and her daughter returned they were very angry at the loss of the maid and the bodies, so they took choppers in their hands, and, still riding the black cats, went into the garden. They asked all the bushes which way the girl had gone, but they would not answer, so they chopped them down. When they came to the gooseberry bushes the first one said: 'This way, that way, and I don't know which way.' But the other said: 'She went straight on across the river.' So they rode on into the river and were drowned.

THE DAUNTLESS GIRL

The story first appeared in print in Walter Rye's *The Recreations of a Norfolk Antiquary* (1920) under the heading 'Some New Norfolk Ghost Stories', although the author gives no indication of how it came to his attention. Like a similar tale from Cambridgeshire that Enid Porter heard in 1970, 'The Dauntless Girl' is presumably from an oral source. It appears to be set near the Suffolk border and is laced with dialect words and phrases but only in the version contained in Geoffrey Dixon's *Folk-tales and Legends of Suffolk* (1982) is the tale given a specific location – Long Melford. Again it is not clear whether this is the author's own invention.

The Dauntless Girl lived first with a farmer, and he and his friend were a-drinking one night and they ran out of liquor. So the farmer he up and say, 'Never you mind, my girl, you will go down to the public and bring us up another bottle.' But the night was very dark, so his friends, they say 'Surelie she'll be afeared to go out such a dark night by herself all alone.' But he say, 'No she won't, for she's afeared of nothing that's alive nor dead.' So she went and she brought 'em back their licker, and his friends they say it was a very funny she shewd be so bold. But the farmer he say, 'That's nuthin at all, for she'd go anywhere day or night for she ain't afeared of nothing that's alive or dead.' And he offered to bet a golden guinea that none of 'em could name a thing she would not dew. So one of 'em agreed to take the bet and they were to meet the same day as it might be next week and he was to set her her task. Meanwhile he goes to the old parson and he borrows the key to the church and then he goes to the old sexton and right-sided it with him for half a guinea to go into the church and hide himself in the dead house so that he was to frighten the Dauntless Girl when she came.

So when they all met together at the farmer's he say, '*This* is what the Dauntless Girl *won't* dew – she won't go into the church alone at midnight and go into the dead house and bring back a skull bone.' But she made no trouble about it and went down to the church all alone of herself and she opened the door to the dead house and she picked up a skull bone.

Then the old sexton behind the door he muffled out, 'Let that be, that's my mother's skull bone.' So she put it down and picked up another. Then the old sexton he muffled out again, 'Let that be, that's my father's skull bone.' So she put that down tew, and took up still another and she sang out loud, for she'd lost her temper, 'Father or mother, sister or brother, I *must* have a skull bone and that's my last word,' so she up and walked out with it, and she locked the door of the dead house behind her and she come home, and she put the skull bone on the table and she say, 'There's your skull bone, master,' and she was for going back to her work.

But him as made the bet he up and say, 'Didn't yew hear nothing, Mary?' 'Yes', she say, 'some fule of a ghost called out to me "let be, that's my father's skull bone, and let be, that's my mother's skull bone", but I told him straight that father or mother, sister or brother, I *must* hev a skull bone, so I tuk it and there't be, and then as I was goin' away arter I had locked the door I heard the old ghost a-hallering and shrieking like mad.'

Then him as had made the bet was rarely upset, for he guessed it was old sexton a-hollerin' about for fear of being locked up all alone in the dead house. And so it was, for when they ran down to let him out they found him lying stone dead on his face a dead-o-fright.

And it sarved him right to try and terrify a poor mawther. But her master gave her the golden guinea he had won.

A little while after down in Suffolk there was a squire and his mother, a very old lady and she died and was buried. But she would *not* rest and kept on coming into the house 'especially at meals.' Sometimes you could see all of her, sometimes not at all, but you'd see a knife and fork get up off the table, and play about where her hands should be. Now this upset the servants so much that they would *not* stop, and the Squire was sadly put to, to know what to do. One day he heard of the Dauntless Girl, three villages off, who was afeard at nowt. So he rode over, and told her all about it, and asked her if she would come as servant, and she said she paid no regard to ghosts so she would come, but that it ought to be considered in her wages. And so it was and she went back with the Squire. First thing she did was to *allus* lay a place regular for the ghost at meals, and took great care not to put the knife and fork criss-cross ways. And she used to hand her the vegetable and the rest just as if she were real. And would say 'Peppaw, mum' or 'Salt, mum', as it might be. This fared to please the old ghost, but nothing came of it, till Squire had to go up to London on some law business.

Next day, the Dauntless Girl was down on her knees a-cleaning the parlour grate when she noticed a thing push in through the door, which was just ajar and open out wide when it got into the room, till she turned out to be the old ghost.

Then the ghost she up and spoke for the first time and she say, 'Mary, are you afeared of me?' and the girl say, 'No, mum, I've no call to be afeared of yew, for *yew* are dead and *I'm* alive,' which fairly flummoxed the old ghost, but she went on and say, 'Mary, will yew come down into the cellar along o' me – yew musent bring a light but I'll shine enow to light you.' So they went down the cellar steps, and she shone like an old lanteen, and when they got down she pointed out to some loose tiles and said, 'Pick yew up those tiles.' So she did, and there were tew bags of gold, one a big 'un and one a little 'un, and she said, 'Mary, that big bag's for your master, and that little bag's for yew, for you are a dauntless girl and deserve it.' Then off went the old ghost and never was seen no more and the Dauntless Girl she had a main o'trouble to find her way up in the dark out of the cellar.

Then in three days' time, back came the squire and he said, 'Morning, Mary, hae yew seen anything of my mother since I've been away? and she said, 'Iss, sir, that I hev, and if yew ain't afraid of coming down into the cellar along o' me, I'll show you something.' And he larfed, and said *he* worn't afraid if *she* worn't, for the Dauntless Girl wor a very pretty girl.

So they lit a candle and went down, and she opened up the tiles and she say, 'There are the tew bags of gold, the *little* one is for yew, and the big un is for *me*.' And he say, 'Lor!' for he thought his mother might have given him the big one (and so she had), but he took what he could. And the Dauntless Girl she allus afterwards crossed the knives and forks to keep the ghost from telling what she had done. But after a while the Squire thort it all over, and he married the Dauntless Girl so arter all he got both bags of gold, and he used to stick-lick her whensoever he got drunk. And I think she deserved it, for deceiving the old ghost.

As the title suggests, the heroine is both bold and knowing and is, it appears, able to silence the ghost. At times, notably during her visit to the charnel house, the tale reads like a feminist reworking that would not be out of place in a collection of Angela Carter fairy tales. Only at the end does it take on a more traditional tone when the girl's husband reverts to 'stick-licking' his new wife. This is not punishment meted out because of her single act of deceit – the husband is unaware of this – but 'whensoever he got drunk'; an act of cruelty condoned by the narrator, but which in the real world would probably have been shamed by a display of 'rough music'.

Charnel house detail, tomb of Thomas Marsham, 1638, Stratton Strawless

THE PLOUGHMAN AND THE FAIRIES

This tale, which appeared in the journal *Folk-lore* in 1896, had been collected by P H Emerson from a Mrs Goodall who had it from her grandmother, a Mrs Brown of Winterton. Mrs Brown had died the previous year aged 102. Emerson was not only a pioneering photographer of Broadland life and landscape but his interest in East Anglian peasantry resulted in books like *English Idylls* (1889), his selection of stories from the Broads, and *East Coast Yarns* (1891) taken 'from the lips of natives'. Unlike Babes in the Wood or Tom Hickathrift the story Emerson chose to submit to *Folk-lore*, although from a local source, has no local setting but the timeless quality of a folk tale – his *Welsh Fairy Tales* had been published in 1894.

There was once a poor labourer who had a large family to support, and at that time food was dear. One day he remarked to his wife, 'I wish a nice kind of fairy would think of us. My master says I must go and plough the eleven-acre field on Monday morning; that will bring in something, anyhow.' On the Monday following he started ploughing and found a bright new shilling at the foot of the plough. He put it into his pocket and prayed for more. The second morning when he got to the field he found two bright new shillings lying on the freshly-turned furrows of the day before. These he pocketed too. On the third morning there were three new shillings. Delighted, he pocketed them and prayed for more. On his return home he said to his wife, 'I don't know when I shall finish this field, but I sha'n't hurry over it. The longer I am about it the better for me.' To that she replied, 'All right, Joe!' On the fourth morning there were four new shillings. So it went on, a fresh shilling being added each day, until he had collected quite a pile of brand new shillings. Then he thought to himself, 'I cannot keep this money from my wife any longer, as the poor children are in want.' So he gave his wife ten new shillings. She looked at them and asked immediately: 'Joe, where ever did you get all these shillings, and new too?' 'Never you mind as long as you've got it,' replied the labourer. She took the money and went to the village to shop, buying bread, butter, tea and sugar, and some other things. Joe kept given her more shillings, until one day she asked suspiciously: 'Has your master paid you your week's wages yet?' 'No, no,' he said, 'he hasn't got no change, but I can give you some more shillings.' And he did. She looked at them doubtfully and said, 'Well, Joe! all bright shillings again. They look as if they had only just been made. Where did you get them?' 'Never you mind where I got them. I sha'n't tell you,' replied her husband.

So off she went to the mill to buy flour; but when she then put down her new shillings to pay for the flour the miller asked: 'Where did you get them?' 'I dunno; my old man give them to me.' 'You must take them back to him and tell him I sha'n't take them, until he says where he got them. I have heard talk that this new money is going about from shop to shop, and I insist on knowing where he gets it from.' She returned home, and said to her husband: 'Joe, you really must tell where you get this money, for there's everybody against us now; and I expect the next thing your master will pay you off.' Whilst she was talking the miller himself entered the cottage and said: 'Good morning, Mr Hobble. I am very sorry I had to turn your wife away without flour, but I really could not take your new money unless I knew you came by it honestly – though I know you never had the character for dishonesty.' 'I don't care what you or anybody else say. I sha'n't tell you where I got that. You may keep your flour,' retorted Joe. 'Now it's no use talking like that Joe. Don't be stubborn. Do you want us all to starve?' asked his wife. Joe replied: 'I've not stolen that, and I'll starve afore I tell you all. If they won't take this money go you to my master and ax him for my week's wages.' 'That I will,' says the wife. But Joe's master said when she named her errand: 'I can't pay you. I must see your husband.' Joe's wife returned fuming to the house and upbraided her husband, saying: 'I don't know what that all means, but you had better go and see your master.' Joe jumped up and went to his master, who said: 'I've heard so much about you having so much new money – I should like to know where you get it. Has anybody left you a fortune?' 'Sir,' replied Joe, 'I sha'n't tell you.' 'No – that's it. I hear you won't tell anybody, therefore I shall give you no wages and no more work.' Joe thanked his master and walked home, and told his wife all that had happened. Being at her wit's end, she tried to pass some of the shillings at a new shop – but they had heard of it and would not accept it.

Then the gentry in the village got wind of it, and came to Joe and threatened to send him to prison if he did not say where he got his new shillings. Joe held his peace for some days, and at last was so hard pressed that he said: 'For my wife and children's sake I must tell you. I have found it every morning at the foot of the plough on the fresh mould, and now I have told you I sha'n't find no more.' Nor did he. And after the tale spread about the village many would have given much never to have interfered; but it was all in vain, for never another shilling did Joe find at the foot of his plough.

The moral of the tale is clear enough – be careful what you wish for and steer clear of the little folk. Apart from fairy loaves, the sea urchin fossils placed on cottage mantelpieces in East Anglia to ensure a regular supply of bread, fairies seldom appear in Norfolk folklore. The story itself is unlikely to have originated in Winterton, a community engaged almost entirely in the fishing trade, although the storyteller may have been among the women, mainly from the Scottish coast, who followed the shoals of herring south to Yarmouth and who may have married local men.

Fairy loaf,
sea urchin fossil

THE UNDERSEA BELLS

In her *Forgotten Folktales of the English Counties* (1970) the Somerset folklorist, Ruth Tongue, included three short stories from Norfolk, although exactly where and when they were collected is not always clear. Her source for 'The Mermaid and the Trawlermen' may have been 'a demobbed sailor' in the 1940s but the tale is set in the stormy seas off the Scottish coast. While the second tale, 'The Shuck', taken down from a Yarmouth sailor c1955, features a spectral hound peculiar to East Anglia, it reads like reworked fragments of local lore. Of the three 'The Undersea Bells' has the ring of authenticity if only because Tongue claimed it was collected by her uncle in 1905 from a Norfolk fisherman while rector of Mundesley, but as Simpson and Round have concluded Tongue 'should be regarded as a creative singer and storyteller ... not as a reliable collector.'[1]

In the old days there were many little fishing hamlets along the coast and in one village there was a church that had bells which rang out over the fog and storms to warn ships off the deadly quick-sands.

The sea gods grew angry – they hated to lose their victims. Bit by bit they broke down the coast and crept inland, until there was only the hated church standing on a crumbling cliff. The people had all fled to higher land, and only the priest went to ring God's bells to serve God's souls on stormy nights.

Clifftop tower ruin,
late c19, Sidestrand

He was old and feeble, and he knew the sea would drown him, but still he struggled to save as many souls as he could in the time left to him. He came to the church crawling at last, for the wind would not let him stand upright and the path was crumbling as he crawled, but he knew there was a ship out in the darkness that needed the warning of the church bells. The church began to crumble about him but with his last strength he grasped the bell ropes and pulled. As the bells clanged the whole tower fell in on him, and the cliff and the church slid down into the boiling sea.

In the morning the sun came out and the ship was lying safe away from the shore. The captain stared in vain at the coast.

'There's no church along the coastline but we all heard the bells last night giving us warning to keep off shore,' he said. 'I can still hear them!'

They all listened and heard them.

Then a sailor cried out in terror, 'They are still ringing *down below the sea*! Someone is warning us still!'

And they made all haste to obey.

Along that coast the fisherfolk say on bad, foggy nights the faithful old priest still rings his life-saving bells under the North Sea.

WIGGENHALL TALES

In 1939, while gathering material for his article 'Folklore from West Norfolk',[2] the author E G Bales collected a number of tales from a Mr Crawford in Wiggenhall St Germans on the banks of the Great Ouse. In the hands of a more accomplished storyteller like Jack Barrett, upstream at Brandon Creek, they might have been fleshed out but, even in the form remembered by Mr Crawford, they have the strange familiarity of folk tales. The first of these, which I have called 'Sunday Lunch', Crawford had heard from his father and was, as far as he knew, a purely local tale which explains the Norfolk dialect. The remaining tales, 'told as true', are not in dialect although the events in 'The Apple and the Stranger' are said to have occurred near King's Lynn. Stripped of any particular time and place, the arrival of a stranger disguised as a woman and the gruesome ending give the tale a universal quality. So too the dream recurring for three nights that foretells death in 'The Two Maids', although the appearance of a policeman at the end suggests a more realistic but equally macabre murder story. As an antidote 'The Leaping Horse' is the kind of humorous tale most likely to have circulated among lightermen up and down the Great Ouse between Cambridge and King's Lynn.

SUNDAY LUNCH

A woman went to church an' left her li'ul bor at hum to look ahter the dinner wot was cookin' in the boiler. There was a sheep's head an' some taters an' an apple dumplin'. Durin' the service the bor went runnin' to the church an' he called out: 'Mother, mother, come home quick.' The woman went 'sh sh' for him to be quiet. 'Sh sh be dammed,' he say, 'the sheep's head has ett all the taters an' the apple dumpling has took off his jacket to fight it.'" (Which means: all the stew was boiled together. The sheep's jaws had opened, the potatoes had gone into its mouth and the dough had boiled over the cloth.)

THE APPLE AND THE STRANGER

The master and mistress of a house went out and left the servant girl behind to look after the house. She heard a knock at the door; the girl opened it and found a woman there who asked to come in. It was pouring with rain. The girl said she could not let her in as her master and mistress were out. However, she did eventually let her in. The stranger went and sat in a chair near the fire, and soon the girl noticed that this stranger was a man. She thought she would find out. To do so, she offered 'her' an apple, but instead of giving her it she copped [threw] it to her. The stranger brought his legs together quickly. The girl's suspicions were now confirmed, as she knew that if the stranger had been a woman she would unconsciously have opened her legs as if to catch the apple in her lap. After some time the stranger fell asleep with his mouth open. The girl was cooking a joint for her master and mistress when they came home. Seeing the stranger had fallen asleep, she poured boiling fat down his throat and killed him. When the master learned what had happened, he rewarded the girl by keeping her without her being obliged to work.

THE TWO MAIDS

There were two maids at a farm, and every night the yardman used to bring up the milk, set it just inside the dairy, shut the door and go home. One night when he brought the milk up he put it in the dairy and shut the door, but he stopped in the house unbeknown to the girls. For three nights these girls had dreamed that they would be murdered in bed. They told the gardener, and he said he would sit up and watch. The yardman hid under the bed in the girls' room. The girls went upstairs to bed and the gardener stayed downstairs to watch with a double-barrelled gun. After some time he saw the door open, and without waiting to see who was there he shot and killed the yardman. The gardener locked the door and went to inform the police. On the way be met the yardman's wife and he asked her where she was going. She replied: 'You haven't shot my husband, have you?' 'There's enough done for tonight,' he said, and sent her home.

When the policeman and the gardener returned to the house they found both girls with their throats cut.

THE LEAPING HORSE

One of the horses that used to draw lighters up the river was blind and had been taught to jump over the stiles whenever the driver shouted: 'Over.' As a result of this, the horse would jump whenever anyone shouted 'Over!' to it. Some lightermen were one day waiting at a public house at Downham when a man rode up on a hunter, famous as a jumper. The lighterman said he had a horse which was a better jumper than this hunter. An argument sprang up between the lighterman and the owner of the hunter, and a wager was made. Both men took their horses into the road. The lighterman laid a piece of straw down, led his horse up to it, and shouted: 'Over!' The horse jumped as though to clear a stile. The hunter was then led up to the straw and the rider tried to make it jump, but all to no purpose, since the hunter could see no obstacle.

KEY REFERENCES

Barrett, W H *Tales from the Fens*, ed. Enid Porter, Routledge and Kegan Paul, 1963

More Tales from the Fens, ed. Enid Porter, Routledge and Kegan Paul, 1964

Burgess, Mike *Hidden East Anglia*, www.hiddenea.com

Castre, William de *Norfolk Folklore Collections,* 6 vols, 1920, Norfolk Record Office

Champion, Matthew *Medieval Graffiti: The Lost Voices of England's Churches*, Ebury Press, 2015

Evans, George Ewart *The Pattern Under The Plough*, Faber, 1966

Heslop, T A, Mellings, E, Thofner M, eds. *Art, Faith and Place in East Anglia*, Boydell Press, 2012

Knightly, Charles *Folk Heroes of Britain*, Thames and Hudson, 1982

Merrifield, Ralph *The Archaeology of Ritual and Magic*, Batsford, 1987

Norfolk and Norwich Notes and Queries (N&NN&Q) 1896-1905

Porter, Enid *Cambridgeshire Customs and Folklore*, Routledge and Kegan Paul, 1969

The Folklore of East Anglia, Batsford, 1974

Simpson, Jacqueline and Round, Stephen *A Dictionary of English Folklore*, OUP, 2000

Thomas, Keith *Religion and the Decline of Magic*, Penguin, 1973

Thompson, E P *Customs in Common*, Merlin Press, 1991

Westwood, Jennifer and Simpson, Jacqueline *The Lore of the Land*, Penguin, 2005

BIBLIOGRAPHY

Adams, Morley *In the Footsteps of Borrow and Fitzgerald*, Jarrold, 1916

Armstrong, Edward A *The Folklore of Birds*, Dover, 1970

Bales, E G, 'Folklore from West Norfolk' *Folklore*, Vol.50, 1939

Barnes, G and Williamson, T *Ancient Trees in the Landscape: Norfolk's Arboreal Heritage*, Windgather Press, 2011

Barrett, W H *A Fenman's Story*, Routledge and Kegan Paul, 1965

Barrett, W H and Garrod, R P *East Anglian Folklore and other tales*, Routledge and Kegan Paul, 1976

'Beeston Loke' 'Fiddler's Hill', *East Anglian Handbook*, 1892

Binney, E 'The` Legend of the Mistletoe Bough' *Word-lore*, Vol.2, 1927

Blomefield, Francis *History of Norfolk*, Fersfield and King's Lynn, 5 vols. 1739-75

Bowman, Marion 'Jennifer Westwood (1940-2008)', *Folklore,* Vol.119, 2008

Briggs, K M 'Historical Traditions in English Folk Tales', *Folklore*, Vol.75, 1964

An Encyclopedia of Fairies, Random House, 1976

Brown, Theo 'The Black Dog', *Folklore*, Vol.64, 1958

Browne, Thomas *Urn Burial*, London, 1658

Bulwer, Rev'd James 'Hassett's House, Pockthorpe', *Norfolk Archaeology*, Vol.7, 1872

Butcher, David *The Driftermen*, Tops'l Books, 1979

Fishing Talk, Poppyland Publishing, 2014

Carter, Michael 'A late c15 Processional Cross from Norfolk', *Norfolk Archaeology* Vol.45, 2009

Carthy, Martin 'Sam Larner', Personal Portraits No.7, *East Anglian Tradirtional Music Trust (EATMT)*

Centerwall, Brandon, S 'The Name of the Green Man', *Folklore*, Vol.108, 1997

Chambers, George *Folksong-Plainsong*, London, 1956

Champion, Matthew 'Late Medieval Painted Decoration at St Edmund's Church, Acle', *Norfolk Archaeology,* Vol.46, 2013

'Ill Wishing on the Walls: The Medieval Graffiti Curses of Norwich Cathedral, *Norfolk Archaeology,* Vol. 47, 2014

Cheetham, Francis W 'A Medieval English Alabaster Figure of St Paul', *Norfolk Archaeology*, Vol. 35, 1970

Clarke, W G 'Thetford Castle Hill', *Norfolk Archaeology*, Vol.16, 1907

In Breckland Wilds, revised R Rainbird Clarke, Heffers, 1937

Cocker, Mark and Mabey, Richard *Birds Britannica*, London, 2005

Coulton, G G 'A Medieval Inscription in Acle Church', *Norfolk Archaeology*, Vol.20, 1921
Cranworth, Emily Frances 'East Anglian Superstitions', *Eastern Counties Magazine*, 1900-01
Crossley-Holland, Kevin *The Dead Moon*, Faber, 1986
Davidson, Hilda R Ellis 'The Hill of the Dragon', *Folklore*, Vol.61, 1950
'Thor's Hammer', *Folklore*, Vol.76, 1965
Davies, John 'Romano-British cult objects from Norfolk – Some Recent Finds', *Norfolk Archaeology*, Vol.42, 1996
The Land of Boudica: Prehistoric and Roman Norfolk, Oxbow Books, 2008
Davies, John and Pestell, Tim *A History of Norfolk in 100 Objects*, The History Press, 2015
Davison, Caroline 'A "Surprising Reptile": Some thoughts on the iconography of St Benet's Abbey Gatehouse', 2014, Unpublished
Davison, Caroline and Pestell, Ronnie *Wild Waxham*, Norfolk Historic Buildings Trust
Dawson, Warren R 'A Norfolk Vicar's Charm Against Ague', *Norfolk Archaeology*, Vol. 24, 1932
Ditchfield, P H *Old English Customs: Extant at the Present Time*, 1896
Dorson, Richard *The British Folklorists: A History*, Routledge and Kegan Paul, 1968
Drury, Susan M 'English Love Divinations Using Plants: An Aspect', *Folklore*, Vol.97 1986
Dutt, William *The Norfolk Broads*, Methuen, 1903
Highways and Byways in East Anglia, Macmillan, 1901
The Ancient Mark-Stones of East Anglia, Flood and Son, 1926
Eberly, Susan S 'A Thorn Among the Lilies: The Hawthorn in Medieval Love Allegory', *Folklore*, Vol.100, 1989
Egidius 'Magic in Norfolk', *East Anglian Magazine*, Vol.1, 1935-6
Evans, George Ewart *The Horse in the Furrow*, Faber, 1960
Horse Power and Magic, Faber, 1979
Spoken History, Faber, 1987
Evans, George Ewart and Thomson, David *The Leaping Hare*, Faber, 1972
Forby, Rev'd Robert *The Vocabulary of East Anglia*, Vols I and II, 1830
Forman, Joan *Haunted East Anglia*, Jarrold, 1974
Gaule, Rev'd John *Select Cases of Conscience Touching Witches and Witchcraft*, 1646
Glyde, John Junr. *Folklore and Customs of Norfolk*, E P Publishing, 1973
Grigor, James *The Eastern Arboretum*, 1847, Nabu Press reprint, 2011
Grigson, Geoffrey *The Englishman's Flora*, Phoenix House, 1987
Grinsell, L V 'Barrow Treasure, in Fact, Tradition and Legislation', *Folklore*, Vol.78, 1967
Gunn, Rev'd John 'Proverbs, Adages and Popular Superstitions in the Parish of Irstead', *Norfolk Archaeology*, Vol. 2, 1849
Halliday, Robert 'Wayside Graves and Crossroads Burials', *Norfolk Archaeology*, Vol.42, 1994
'St Walstan of Bawburgh', *Norfolk Archaeology*, Vol.44, 2003
Hart, Rev'd. Richard 'The Shrines and Pilgrimages of the County of Norfolk', *Norfolk Archaeology*, Vol.6, 1864
Harris, Mary Corbett 'Whitsuntide Revels in Old Norfolk', *East Anglian Magazine*, Vol.25, 1965-6
Hastings, Geoffrey 'The Devil and the West Walton Tower', *East Anglian Magazine*, Vol.26, 1966-7
Hayman, Richard *The Green Man*, Shire Publications, 2015
Heaney, Seamus *Beowulf*, Faber, 1999
Heath-Coleman, Phil 'Harry Cox: Norfolk Fiddler Extraordinaire', *Musical Traditions*, 2013
Helsdon, Alan 'Ralph Vaughan Williams in Norfolk', CD-Rom, 2014
Higgins, David *The Winterton Story*, Phoenix Publications, 2009
Hines, J 'An Inscribed Lead Plaque from Holm St Benet's, Norfolk', Nytt om Runer, 19, 2006
Hoggard, Brian 'The Archaeology of Counter-Witchcraft and Popular Magic' in *Beyond the Witch Trials*,
Davies, O and de Blécourt, W Manchester UP, 2004
Gazetteer of Protective Magic Finds (Norfolk), unpublished

Holderness, Chris 'Percy Brown: Aylsham Melodeon Player', *Musical Traditions*, 2007
'E J Moeran', *Musical Traditions*, 2009
'Dick Hewitt: A True Norfolk Man', *Musical Traditions*, 2009
'Southrepps', *Musical Traditions*, 2009
'Sam Larner', *Musical Traditions*, 2013
'Hindringham': *Musical Traditions*, 2013
'The Dancing Davies: Step Dancing Fishermen of Cromer, *Musical Traditions*, 2014
Hooton, Jon 'The Norwich Kitwitches: A History', www.kitwitches.co.uk
Howes, H W 'St Walstan, Norfolk Popular Saint', *Folklore,* Vol. 37, 1926
Howson, Katie 'North End Voices', *EATMT*, 2014
'Ralph Vaughan Williams in South Norfolk', *EATMT*, 2016
James, M R 'Lives of St Walstan', *Norfolk Archaeology*, Vol.17, 1917
Suffolk and Norfolk, London, 1930
Jessopp, Augustus *Random Roaming*, Fisher Unwin, 1893
Frivola, Fisher Unwin, 1896
Johns, C and Potter T *The Thetford Treasure*, British Museum Press, 1983
Kent, Rev'd Charles *The Land of the 'Babes in the Wood'*, Jarrold, 1910
Kingsley, Charles *Hereward The Wake: 'Last of the English',* Blackie, 1913
Lane, Richard *Snap the Norwich Dragon*, Trend-Litho, 1976
Leach, Maria and Leach, J F *The Standard Dictionary of Folklore*, New York, 1972
Lee, Robert *Unquiet Country: Voices of the Rural Poor*, Windgather Press, 2005
Lee-Warner, Rev'd. H J 'The Walsingham "Wishing Wells"', *Norfolk Archaeology*, Vol.8, 1879
Linnell, Rev'd. C L S 'The Commonplace Book of Robert Reynys of Acle', *Norfolk Archaeology*, Vol.32, 1961
Lupton, Hugh *Norfolk Folk Tales*, The History Press, 2013
Luxford, Julian M 'A Further Reference to St Margaret of Holm', *Norfolk Archaeology*, Vol.45, 2008
Mabey, Richard *Flora Britannica*, Chatto and Windus, 1997
MacColl, Ewan *Journeyman: An Autobiography*, Sidgwick and Jackson, 1990
Marlowe, Christopher *People and Places in Marshland*, Cecil Palmer, 1927
Marsh, Barry 'E J Moeran in Norfolk', The Worldwide Moeran Database, 2011
Mason, Joseph 'St Edmund's Norfolk: A Study in Historical Geography', digital copy
'The Origin and Growth of the Cult of St Edmund 865-1066', NAHRG, 2010
Menefee, Samuel Pyeatt 'Circling as an Entrance to the Underworld', *Folklore,* Vol.96, 1985
Merrifield, Ralph 'Witch Bottles and Magical Jugs', *Folklore,* Vol.66, 1955
Meyrick, F J *Round About Norfolk and Suffolk*, Jarrold, 1926
Moore, Andrew and Thofner, Margit, eds. *The Art of Faith: 3500 years of Art and Belief in Norfolk*, Philip Wilson, 2010
Mortlock, D P and Roberts, C V *A Popular Guide to Norfolk Churches*, 3 Vols., Acorn Editions, 1981-5
Newman, L F 'Some Notes on Folk Medicine in the Eastern Counties', *Folklore*, 1944-5
'Some Notes on the History and Practice of Witchcraft in the Eastern Counties', *Folklore*, Vol.57, 1946
Norfolk Heritage Explorer for Bawburgh and Fordham, www.heritage.norfolk.gov.uk
Opie, Iona and Tatem, Moira *A Dictionary of Superstitions*, Oxford, 1989
Palmer, C J *The Perlustration of Great Yarmouth*, 3 Vols. G Nall, 1872-75
Palmer, Roy *Folksongs Collected by Ralph Vaughan Williams*, London, 1983
Pennick, Nigel *Folklore of East Anglia, and Adjoining Counties*, Spiritual Arts and Crafts publishing, 2006
Pevsner, Nikolaus and Wilson, Bill *Norfolk 1: Norwich and North East*, The Buildings of England, Yale, 1997
Norfolk 2: North West and South, The Buildings of England, Yale, 1999

Pinner, Rebecca *The Cult of St Edmund in Medieval East Anglia*, Boydell Press, 2015
Porter, Enid 'Some Folk Beliefs in the Fens', *Folklore,* Vol.69, 1958
'Folk Life and Traditions of the Fens', *Folklore,* Vol.72, 1961
Rabuzzi, Daniel Allen 'In Pursuit of Norfolk's Hyter Sprites', *Folklore*, Vol.95, 1984
Rayson, George 'East Anglian Folklore', *The East Anglian*, 1865-70
Reeve, Christopher *Straunge and Terrible Wunder: The Story of the Black Dog of Bungay*, Morrow and Co., 1988
Ridyard, Susan J *The Royal Saints of Anglo Saxon England: A Study of West Saxon and East Anglian Cults*, CUP, 1988
Rose, Martial *The Misericords of Norwich Cathedral*, Larks Press, 1994
and Hedgecoe, Julia *Stories in Stone: The Medieval Roof Carvings of Norwich Cathedral*, Herbert Press, 1997
Ross, Anne *Pagan Celtic Britain*, Cardinal, 1974
Ross, Ryan *Ralph Vaughan Williams: A Research and Information Guide*, London, 2008
Ryan, J S 'Othin in England', *Folklore,* Vol.74, 1963
Rye, James *A Popular Guide to Norfolk Place-Names*, Larks Press, 1991
Rye, Walter *The Norfolk Antiquarian Miscellany*, 1873-7
The Recreations of a Norfolk Antiquary, Norwich, 1920
Scarfe, Norman *Suffolk: A Shell Guide*, Faber, 1976
Stradling, Rod and Yates, Mike 'Walter Pardon', *Musical Traditions*, 2000
Suffling, Ernest R *History and Legends of the Broad District*, Jarrold, 1891
Swanton Morley Church 'Circling the Church to see the Devil', swantonmorleychurch.co.uk
Taylor, Mark R 'Norfolk Folklore', *Folklore*, Vol.40, 1929
Thompson, E P 'Rough Music Reconsidered', *Folklore,* Vol.103, 1992
Tolhurst, Marilyn 'Treasure Hunting in Forncett 1465', Norfolk Research Committee Bulletin, 1985
Tolhurst, Peter *Norfolk Parish Treasures: North and West Norfolk*, Black Dog Books, 2014
Norfolk Parish Treasures: Breckland and South Norfolk, Black Dog Books, 2015
Norfolk Parish Treasures: Mid Norfolk and the Broads, Black Dog Books, 2016
Tongue, Ruth L *Forgotten Folk Tales of the English Counties*, Routledge and Kegan Paul, 1970
Turner, Dawson *Norfolk Archaeology,* Vol.1, 1847
Twinch, Carol *In Search of Saint Walstan*, Media Associates, 1995
Varden, John T 'Traditions, Superstitions and Folklore: Chiefly relating to the Counties of Norfolk and Suffolk', *East Anglian Handbook,* 1885
Vaughan Williams, Ralph *National Music*, 1934
Vaughan Williams, Ursula *Ralph Vaughan Williams*, Oxford, 1964
Walcott, Mackenzie *The East Coast of England*, 1861
Walker, John 'A Witch Bottle from Hellington', *Norfolk Archaeology*, Vol.40, 1954
Warner, Sylvia Townsend and Ackland, Valentine *I'll Stand By You*, ed. Susanna Pinney, Pimlico, 1998
Wentworth Day, James 'The Lantern Men of Death', *East Anglian Magazine*, March, 1980
Westwood, Jennifer *Gothick Norfolk*, Shire Publications, 1989
Westwood, Jennifer and Simpson, Jacqueline *The Penguin Book of Ghosts*, 2005
Whitwell, Eric *Fact or Legend: Withburga of Dereham*, Dereham Baptist Chapel, 2003
Whyte, Nicola 'Smithdon Hill, Snettisham: The Possible Meeting Place of Smethdon Hundred', *Norfolk Archaeology*, Vol.44, 2004
Inhabiting the Landscape: Place, Custom and Memory, 1500-1800, Windgather Press, 2009
W J C 'The Fairies in East Anglia', *Word-lore*, Vol.2, 1927
Yates, Mike 'Harry Cox', *EATMT*, 2000

NOTES

THE FOLKLORISTS

1 Dorson, p.4
2 Ibid., p.7
3 Stukeley's Correspondence, Surtees Society, 1882
4 Gunn, p.292
5 Ibid., p.308
6 Glyde, p.xi
7 Cranworth, 1900, pp.117-8
8 Jessopp, 1896, p.189
9 R W Pfaff, *Montague Rhodes James*, London, 1980
10 Westwood and Simpson, p.496
11 Porter, 1976, p.16
12 Bowman, pp.346-8

SACRED SPRINGS

1 James, 1930, pp.13-14
2 Pevsner and Wilson, 1999, p.286
3 Mortlock and Roberts, Vol.2, 1985, p.36
4 Forby, Vol.2, p.401
5 Pevsner and Wilson, Vol.1, p.595

MAGIC STONES

1 Evans, 1987, p.20
2 Clarke, 1937, p.146
3 Burgess, Gorleston, www.hiddenea.com
4 *East Anglian Magazine*, April 1947, p.427
5 Whyte in *Art, Faith and Place in East Anglia*, p.171

THE GREENWOOD TREE

1 Centerwall, p.28
2 Bates, H E, *Through The Woods*, Dorset, 2011, p.45
3 Mabey, p.215
4 Plath, Sylvia, 'Whitsun', 1960
5 Leach and Leach, p.486
6 Goody, Jack, *The Culture of Flowers,* 1993
7 Grigor, p.336
8 Marlowe, p.237
9 Grigor, p.348

FIELDS OF GOLD

1 Heaney, p.XVII
2 Ashwin in *Art, Faith and Place in East Anglia,* p.290
3 Browne, Chapt. V
4 Turner, p.58
5 Jessopp, 1893, p.107

CHURCH LORE

1 Dutt, 1901, p.148
2 *N&NN&Q*, 1904, p.66
3 Mortlock and Roberts, Vol.3, 1985, p.123
4 Notes and Queries, Vol.12, 1855, pp.486-7

FOLK HEROES

1 Ridyard, p.227
2 Ibid., p.73
3 Scarfe, p.91
4/5 Barrett, 1964, p.XI
6/8 Kingsley, pp.266-9
9 Rye, *Norfolk Families*, 1913
10 Davison and Pestell, p.35
11 Rye, 1920, p.28
12 *Eastern Daily Press*, May 12th, 2016

THE EVIL EYE

1 Thomas, p.627
2 Gaule, pp.78-9
3 Adams, pp.44-6
4 Dutt, 1903, p.99
5 Thomas, p.561
6 Ibid., p.549
7 Ibid., p.559
8/9 *The East Anglian, New Series*, 1889-90, p.182
10/11 *N&NN&Q*, 1901, p.256
12/13 Kent, p.87
14 Ibid., p.84
15 Barrett, 1964, p.119
16/17 Porter, 1969, p.167
18 Kent, p.80
19/20 Taylor, p.126
21 *N&NN&Q*, 1904, p.73
22 Kent, p.82
23 *News Chronicle*, 6th January, 1947
24 Evans, 1979, p.128
25 Thelwell, M, *Eastern Counties Magazine*, 1901, pp.292-6
26/27 Evans, 1987, pp.47-8

PROTECTIVE MAGIC

1 Hines, p.15
2 Champion, 2015, p.96
3 *N&NN&Q*, 1902, p.363
4 *N&NN&Q*, 1904, p.10
5 Linnell, p.112
6 Thomas, p.212
7 Dawson, p.236
8 Vanke, in *Art, Faith and Place in East Anglia,* p.200
9 Bales, p.68
10 Simpson and Round, 2000
11 Champion, 2015, p.44

RESTLESS SPIRITS

1 Cranworth, p.118
2 Walcott, pp.109-10
3 Marryat, Florence, *There is no Death,* 1891, p.4
4 Westwood and Simpson, p.513

5 Binney, p.130
6 Rye, 1873, p.290
7 W J C, pp.40-41
8 Westwood and Simpson, p.688
9 Adams, p.194
10 Evans and Thomson, pp.167-8
11/12 E S T, *N&NN&Q*, 1850, p.468
13 Walcott, p.94
14/15 Palmer, ed., Manship's *History of Yarmouth*, 1854, p.207
16/17 Clarke, 1937, p.147
18 Westwood and Simpson, p.518
19 Varden, p.77
20 Jessopp, 1896, p.189
21 Ibid., p.147
22/23 Ibid., pp.197-8
24 Clarke, 1937, p.155
25 Dutt, 1903, pp.332-3
26 Bulwer, p.80
27 'Beeston Loke', pp.222-4

SPECTRAL SHAPES

1 Dutt, 1903, p.331
2 Adams, p.195
3 Marlowe, pp.201-03
4/8 Adams, pp.126-8
9/12 Meyrick, pp.61-5
13 Barrett, 1963, p.136
14 Ibid., p.137
15 Rabuzzi, p.74
16 Briggs, 1976, p.230
17 Rabuzzi, p.82
18 Varden, p.98
19 Rabuzzi, p.83
20 Gunn, p.299
21/22 Barrett and Garrod, p.61

RITES OF PASSAGE

1/4 *N&NN&Q*, 1897, p.216
5 Lee, p.141
6 Ibid., p.3
7 Thompson, plate XXX
8 *N&NN&Q*, 1902, p.313
9 Taylor, p.124
10 Porter, 1958, p.119
11/12 *N&NN&Q*, 1900, p.149
13 Porter, 1969, pp.26-7

THE CIRCLING YEAR

1/2 Arderon Papers quoted by Hooton
3 Eberly, p.41
4 Ibid., p.47
5 Cocker and Mabey, p.342
6/7 Ditchfield, p.134
8 Rose and Hedgecoe, p.138
9 Porter, 1974, p.66
10 Clarke, 1937, p.148
11 *N&NN&Q*, 1900, p.96
12 Clarke, 1937, p.148

SONG and DANCE MEN

1 Ross, p.258
2 Vaughan Williams, Ursula, p.66
3 Vaughan Williams, Ralph, p.123
4 Palmer, 1983
5 Vaughan Williams, Ursula, quoted in 'Ralph Vaughan Williams in the East', *EATMT*
6 Chambers, p.94
7 Marsh, 2011
8 Holderness, 'Moeran', 2009
9 MacColl, 1990
10 Warner and Ackland, p.93
11 quoted by Holderness in 'Larner', 2013
12 Carthy, *EATMT*
13 Donnellan in Holderness, 2014

FOLKTALES

1 Simpson and Round, 2000
2 Bales, pp.73-5

INDEX